THE ENVIRONMENTAL POLITICS AND POLICY
OF WESTERN PUBLIC LANDS

T0344989

THE ENVIRONMENTAL POLITICS AND POLICY OF WESTERN PUBLIC LANDS

Edited by
Erika Allen Wolters and Brent S. Steel

Oregon State University Press   Corvallis

Cover photos, left to right: "Renewable Energy, Wyoming Foot Creek" by the Bureau of Land Management Wyoming is licensed under CC BY 2.0 (https://creativecommons.org/licenses/by/2.0/); "Gordon Creek, OR" by the Bureau of Land Management Oregon is licensed under CC BY 2.0 (https://creativecommons.org/licenses/by/2.0/); "Calcutta Pile Burn December 2017" by the Bureau of Land Management California is licensed under Public Domain Mark 1.0 (https://creativecommons.org/publicdomain/mark/1.0/); "#mypubliclandsroadtrip 2016: Something Different, Zane Grey Cabin on the Rogue River" by Bob Wick/BLM is licensed under CC BY 2.0 (https://creativecommons.org/licenses/by/2.0/); "Nine Mile Canyon Area of Critical Environmental Concern, Utah" by the Bureau of Land Management is licensed under CC BY 2.0 (https://creativecommons.org/licenses/by/2.0/); "A herd of cattle cows with their calves . . . in eastern Oregon" by Bob Pool, Shutterstock.

Library of Congress Cataloging-in-Publication Data

Names: Wolters, Erika Allen, editor. | Steel, Brent, editor.
Title: The environmental politics and policy of western public lands / Edited by Erika Allen Wolters and Brent S. Steel.
Description: Corvallis : Oregon State University Press, 2020. | Includes bibliographical references and index.
Identifiers: LCCN 2020027015 | ISBN 9780870710223 (trade paperback)
Subjects: LCSH: Environmental policy—West (U.S.) | Land use—Government policy—West (U.S.) | Public lands—Government policy—West (U.S.)
Classification: LCC GE185.W47 E62 2020 | DDC 333.730978—dc23
LC record available at https://lccn.loc.gov/2020027015

Oregon State University
OSU Press

Oregon State University Press
121 The Valley Library
Corvallis OR 97331-4501
541-737-3166 • fax 541-737-3170
www.osupress.oregonstate.edu

Contents

Foreword

Growing up in a Cleveland suburb, the only public land I knew was a city block of lawn with a cannon in the center, left over from the War of 1812. Other than that, the land was taken up with housing developments, tomato farms, and other private property—no trespassing. When my husband and I moved to Colorado, the very idea of public land astonished us—land owned by everyone, shared by everyone—and so did the expanse of it, with miles and miles of grasslands and prairie lakes, range after range of snow-capped mountains. A friend explained the difference between a national park and a national forest, and we hit the trails, thrilled by the most spectacular country we had ever seen. In our eyes, public land was a great gift from the past to the future, a model of foresight and restraint.

When we moved to Oregon, we were again astonished at the great expanse of public land, open to everybody. You could start walking on public land and, a month later, you would still be walking on public land, there was that much of it. But we quickly learned that the land was not so much shared as it was contested. "Multiple use" meant "multiple battles," and an innocent owl perched bleakly against destruction. "National wildlife refuge" could mean "place to kill ducks," "national forest" could mean "national stumps," and sometimes "Native subsistence rights" meant nothing at all.

Now we live much of the year in Alaska, which has far more public land than private. In 2019, we arrived at our little coastal cabin on a day when Anchorage was hotter than Miami and 132 wildfires burned throughout the state, many of them in tundra, which used to be the soggiest land on Earth. Our place is right in the middle of the Tongass National Forest, a huge roadless area of giant forests and misty, bear-graced bays. Or, I should say, at the moment it's a roadless area, but one of Alaska's own senators is doing her best to transfer public lands to private hands, which will truck the ancient timber down new gravel roads to Asia-bound freighters.

It's all terribly confusing and impossibly arcane. Our movement across the country in a little Datsun was our own small retracing of the march of manifest destiny. From east to west, from closed to open, from private to public, from small to vast, from settled to wild, from mine to ours, from used up to open for business, from realtors to squatters with guns—in 3,336 miles, an inconceivable shift from one kind of place to another. It is no wonder that we are confused by the politics of public land. From all outward appearances, public land is a push-me, pull-you contest that plays out with political power and cold, hard cash; well-meaning and whiplashed government employees and oil-tainted politicians; Native activists on horseback and troopers in riot gear; fleets of white pickup trucks and a sage grouse with a ridiculous dance; and some of the most glorious land on the planet, maybe in the universe.

I would not have thought that anyone could make any sense of the values and politics of public land. So many agencies, so many competing interests, and two warring worldviews—at the extremes, one seeing land as a storehouse of resources to be exploited for the personal gain of the exploiters and the economic growth of the nation, the other seeing land as fecund, life-sustaining ecosystems that are beautiful manifestations of the creative urgency of the planet, to be protected and honored.

But in this volume, Erika Allen Wolters and Brent Steel have brought together the experts who can explain the evolution of public lands policies and politics in all their complexities. While their subject is complex, their prose is clear, and while their subject is torn by some of the most viciously self-interested, deceitful arguments in politics today, their prose is calm, factual, and evenhanded. No one should underestimate what a rare and valuable gift this is.

It is essential to understand without prejudice how decisions are and will be made about America's public lands, because the fate of public lands is essential to America, in at least two ways. On one hand, these playas and mountains are settings for battles over what use will be made of what pieces of land, and to whose benefit and at what cost to others. These decisions will have significant, long-range, tangible consequences. How much atmospheric and oceanic warming will flare from the fracking fields on public lands, and what suffering will it cause over how many millennia? How many and which species will survive the sixth extinction? What will be the long-range health consequences of mining practices? What terrible feedback loops will swirl from what wildfires? What lands will be open for the refugees from climate chaos and the billionaire trout fishermen?

On the other hand is the fate of the *idea* of public lands in America. In 1983, novelist Wallace Stegner wrote that "national parks are the best idea we ever had. Absolutely American, absolutely democratic, they reflect us at our best rather than our worst." What is true of national parks is true even more of public lands in general. It's a great idea to hold huge chunks of the nation's land in common, a heritage owned by everybody and nobody, protected in trust for the people and the ecosystems, for the future—not grabbed off, not fenced off, not sold off, but shared for all time. Surely it's an *American* idea, as American as the public library, an idea oriented to the future, to the improvement of all, through careful stewardship and sharing of the gifts God has given. Surely it's a *democratic* idea, that everyone has an equal claim to the land, not based on inherited wealth, not based on aristocratic standing or political patronage or private gain, but on ideals of equality and justice.

But just as surely, the idea of public lands reflects us at our best *and* at our worst. We can work together to save the sage grouse and the ranch, the spotted owl and the logging community, the salmon and the irrigated fields; humans are able to renounce narrow self-interest and work for the common good. We have shown that we can do this; in kindergarten, we learn how to share. Sharing the land offers a kind of salvation if we can pull it off.

But sometimes it seems that we can't. Men with guns or four-wheelers will take what they want or believe they deserve, politicians will pander to oil executives with a hankering for dust and money, and bureaucrats will shave the narrow edges of the law. So America's best idea is in great danger. But even if the reality is dusty and beetle gnawed and corrupted, the idea endures. And at this moment, this pivotal moment in the history of the planet, public lands may be our last best chance for a huge national thought experiment about an ethic of the common good.

Kathleen Dean Moore, Chichagof Island, Alaska

Preface

This book follows in the tradition of Charles "Chuck" Davis's *Western Public Lands and Environmental Politics*, which many teachers and professors have used over the years in their environmental politics and policy courses. The second edition of Chuck's book was published in 2001, and we were unsuccessful in persuading him to write a new edition. But we were able to have him write a contribution to this volume, for which we are very appreciative.

Chuck has been a wonderful mentor, friend, and colleague to both Erika Allen Wolters and me, and we hope this book meets his approval. Chuck's opening statement in the preface of the second edition of his book is still relevant as we look back to the summers of 2018 and 2019: "We are in the latter part of an unusually hot and dry summer the year 2000, and wildfires are burning out of control on large tracts of western lands" (2001, p. xi). Unfortunately, the increasing impacts of climate change on western public lands and the West as a whole have led to unprecedented catastrophic wildfires and loss of life, disappearing glaciers in western mountains, drought, and many western ecosystems teetering on the edge. In addition, a recent US Geological Survey study estimates that approximately one-fourth of all carbon dioxide emissions in the United States are from fossil fuel extraction and combustion from public lands (Merrill et al. 2018). We anticipate that climate change effects will exacerbate conflict over western public lands management and have therefore asked each contributor to include a discussion of climate change where appropriate.

Over the past several decades, the management and use of public lands in the western United States have become subjects of national as well as regional debate as public concern for wildlife, fish species, wilderness preservation, recreational access, and other values associated with these lands has increased substantially. These environmentally centered policies have clashed with the traditional extraction-orientated policies that have dominated the use of these lands for more than a century, resulting in often acrimonious public controversy, frequent litigation, and even violence in the case of the Malheur National Wildlife Refuge occupation in 2016 (see chap. 16). At the heart of this debate are differing philosophical and normative views about the natural environment and appropriate human relationships to that environment. These views, in turn, are connected to different conceptions of how the proper management of natural resources ought to be organized and carried out. To a substantial degree, philosophical orientations and public values concerning the environment set parameters for public policy, both for policies protecting ecosystems and for programs aimed at maintaining the economic and cultural vitality of natural resource-dependent communities.

This book is intended to provide an *interdisciplinary* perspective on assessing public values regarding the environment and public lands in the West. For the purposes of this book, we define the West according to the US Census of the eleven westernmost states in the contiguous United States: Arizona, California, Colorado, Idaho, Montana, Nevada, New Mexico, Oregon, Utah, Washington, and Wyoming (although Alaska and Hawaii are considered the West, they are somewhat outliers in discussions of western public lands because each has its own geographic, political, and ecological conditions that are unique).

Contributors to the volume represent the academic disciplines of anthropology, forest and rangeland resources, wildlife ecology, environmental policy, law, political science, public policy, and sociology. Most of the authors have extensive experience working with federal natural resource agencies, and most have published scholarly articles and books concerning issues of public lands management in the West.

This book is organized into multiple parts. In part I, Donna Lybecker provides an introduction and general overview of the various economic, social, and political factors leading to changing natural resource management paradigms in the West. John Ruple then reviews the evolving management landscape for western public lands, while Mark Brunson's chapter provides an overview of rangeland policy and management in the West. Part II of the book includes a chapter by Tom Koontz and Christean Jenkins that covers the history of national forest policy followed by a chapter on wildfire policy and climate change in the West by Eric Toman. Doug Kenney's chapter covers western water issues by examining the case of the Colorado River. In part III, John Ruple has a chapter that discusses the politics and policy of wilderness and national monuments in the West, while Robert Keiter's chapter covers the politics and policy of western national parks. Part III also contains two chapters on wildlife management and policy in the West. Lauren Anderson's chapter provides a general overview of relevant legislation to wildlife management issues, while the chapter by Hilty, Jacob, Trotter, Hilty, and Young examines endangered species and wildlife corridors within the context of climate change. Finally, part IV contains three chapters concerning energy development on public lands in the West. Anna Karmazina's chapter examines the siting of renewable energy technologies on public lands. Chuck Davis's chapter provides a general overview of oil and gas development on western public lands under Presidents Bush, Obama, and Trump. P. Casey Giordano's chapter examines the politics and policy of mining on federal lands. The final two chapters of part IV are by Shane Day, who discusses the management and politics of Native American lands, and by Simon, Wolters, and Steel, who provide a historical overview of the wise use movement and includes several case studies concerning conflict over the management of western public lands.

References

Davis, Charles, ed. 2001. *Western Public Lands and Environmental Politics.* 2nd ed. Boulder, CO: Westview Press.

Merrill, M. D., B. M. Sleeter, P. A. Freeman, J. Liu, P. D. Warwick, and B. C. Reed. 2018. *Federal Lands Greenhouse Emissions and Sequestration in the United States—Estimates for 2005–14.* Scientific Investigations Report 2018-5131, 31 pp. Reston, VA: US Geological Survey. https://doi.org/10.3133/sir20185131.

Part I

THE CHANGING WEST

Chapter 1
The Old West, the New West, and the Next West

DONNA L. LYBECKER

> Out where the handclasp's a little stronger,
> Out where the smile dwells a little longer,
> That's where the West begins;
> Out where the sun is a little brighter,
> Where the snows that fall are a trifle whiter,
> Where the bonds of home are a wee bit tighter,
> That's where the West begins.
> —Arthur Chapman, "Out Where the West Begins"

INTRODUCTION

The western United States was and is a place of stories and of reality. It includes descriptions of the open frontier, rugged individualism, and space to take one's own path, as well as wilderness and the struggles to overcome this wilderness. As Vice President Lyndon Johnson noted in a 1963 speech, "the West of yesterday is glamorized in our fiction, the future of the American West now is both fabulous and factual."

The West of the past—the "Old West"—was characterized by legendary heroes such as Jesse James, who stole from the rich but helped the poor, and Horace Tabor, who made a fortune in silver mines. Yet the Old West also included the less glamorous struggles of drought, poverty (Tabor's wife, Elizabeth "Baby Does," died poor), and death (Jesse James's robberies were brutal and at times deadly). Likewise, the current-day "New West" is a place where individuals experience beauty and grandeur in Rocky

Mountain, Yellowstone, and Yosemite National Parks, but it is also where growing numbers of people experience homelessness in the urban corridors. Understanding the western United States, particularly what the future "Next West" is likely to encompass, necessitates looking at the big picture of both mythological perceptions and realities of the Old West and the New West.

Change is a constant in the western United States. From manifest destiny to the Sagebrush Rebellion, from ranching to fracking, from boom to bust to boom again, the reality and the image of the western United States are redefined and remade. Despite this persistent change over time, however, much of the land and many of the core characteristics and values of this region remained the same. Thus the contradictions of change and consistency, the layering of the traditional and the modern, the mixing of an identity shaped through narrative and through on-the-ground change are what defines the western United States.

The sheer extent of western public lands is a major factor in both the change and the consistency of the West. Public lands support the social and economic connections to resources provided by the large, open landscapes. But with continued growing populations, related demographic and economic change, and resulting physical change, it appears the western United States is facing its largest transformation yet. The West appears set to experience change that will shift the region not only from sparse populations to fast-growing urban centers and from resource extraction to recreation, but from charted weather patterns to environments affected by extreme weather and alterations in climate. These more extensive shifts will surely affect the environment, including public lands, of the region, transforming its characteristics and the policies that shape its management. What was once a region of tentative balance between the Old West and the New West will likely need to reinvent itself into the Next West. In particular, changes to environmental policies, which affect the public lands of the region, will need to reflect the reality of this transformation while simultaneously working with the Old West and New West narratives and identities.

NARRATIVES: STORIES OF THE OLD WEST AND THE NEW WEST

As lovers of stories, people often think in narrative form (Sarbin 1986) and ascribe meanings via narrative (Mishler 1995; White 1980). Thus it is not surprising that narrative also shapes collective human behavior (Shenhav 2004) and forms a base for political discourse (Shenhav 2006). Narrative forms of political expression are based on stringing together events in an attempt to shape the present while maintaining and drawing from the past (Shenhav 2006). Thus narrative is the product of a given perspective; it does not include full reality but reveals major themes or ideas that exist. Understanding the narratives presented of a region such as the western United States helps reveal dominant perspectives and the images that people ascribe to the region. In these stories are elements of truth, desire, and foreshadowing. The ideas of the Old West and the New West are narratives. They describe truth—for example, the economic changes occurring within the region—but they also describe a constructed "reality," elements of what the storyteller desires for the region. Understanding the narratives of the Old West and the New West gives insight into where the region has been, where it is, and where it is heading. Given the importance of public lands within the western United States (according to Vincent et al. 2017, public lands comprise 47% of the eleven western states in the Lower 48), public lands comprise a fundamental aspect of these narratives. Furthermore, these narratives, along with the reality of the region, affected the development of and continue to affect the modifications to public land management and policies. Thus understanding the western United States and the changes the region will likely face requires not only recognizing the demographic, economic, and physical shifts occurring to the region, but also acknowledging its old and new narratives.

The Old West

The Old West (Bennett and McBeth 1998; Shumway and Otterstrom 2001) inspires images of cattle drives, open expanses, and the old-style frontier. This narrative describes "winning the West" or "taming" the vast, open landscape and all that is a part of that landscape. It includes iconic cowboys living off the land, hardy souls digging for gold and other valuable minerals, and small groups of individuals harvesting what the rugged landscape can provide. The narrative of the Old West is one of self-made pioneers and rural and small communities closely linked to industries dependent on resource extraction and commodity production, such as forestry, ranching, mining, and fisheries.

With this narrative as its base, the image of today's Old West focuses on the still-romanticized idea of hard-working, largely ethnically European, men (and to some degree women) whose tough individualism carries them through boom and bust cycles of the land. The people of the Old West understand the western landscape and apply this knowledge to survive economically; they appreciate the landscape for what it provides and recognize there are limits to the amount of resources that can be taken and the number of individuals who can survive on the western lands.

The New West

Although the narrative of the Old West is still evident today, a secondary narrative for the western United States also exists—that of a New West. This New West narrative links elements of the Old West to the reality of the changes pushed forward by a growing population and consequential shifts in society and technology. It recognizes the region's multifaceted evolution, acknowledging the past and present and different groups and ethnicities, and pushes toward a more heterogeneous notion of the West. But the New West also still recognizes the significant connection to the wide-open landscape and environment that define much of the West as a region. The narrative of the New West is a portrait of a mix of rural and cosmopolitan; of prized outdoor recreation with blue-ribbon trout streams, world-renowned skiing, and miles of hiking and biking trails; of rapid urbanization and growth; of technology and simplicity of living "off the land."

The New West narrative highlights environmentalism and diversity, setting up a contrast to the Old West, but it also shares the Old West's reverence of wide-open landscapes and opportunities and resources offered by the environment, along with the image of tough individualism (albeit often via extreme sports rather than long days working the land).

OLD WEST AND NEW WEST, BUT NEXT WEST?

The shifting landscape and expansion of the New West have pushed individuals of the Old West to suggest the last half century has created upheaval, bringing in outsiders who change traditional values and expose the region to modern dilemmas. Highlighting the tensions surrounding these changes, this Old West–New West conflict can be seen in recent confrontations such as the occupation of the Malheur National Wildlife Refuge in Oregon (management of public lands), the battle in the state supreme court over water rights and releases from Idaho's Lucky Peak dam (water rights), and the controversial wolf management and greater sage grouse listing across the western plains and sagebrush ecosystems (endangered species).

Furthermore, westerners are being forced to recognize the negative aspects of both the Old West and the New West. The Old West often ignores human causalities and environmental costs of the Old West's management of the western landscape and its people (Aron 2016). The New West ignores the negative aspects of amenities desired by the New Westerners—like increasing consumption of goods, a desire for extensive choices in restaurants and shopping, and easy access to the wide-open spaces—all of which have led to increased pollution, skyrocketing land prices, and pocketed poverty contrasted with extreme wealth.

Continued change through growth and the resulting social, economic, and physical changes will push both the Old West and New West to address the question, What is the Next West? Population expansion is changing the landscape that both the Old and New Wests value and utilize. Subsequently, management practices and policies affecting public lands are and must continue to change. For a region with two identities, the Old West and the New West, how will a Next West fit into the equation? Understanding the transformation from the Old to the New and looking toward what is Next can shed light on how the western United States will change and how the environmental policies, particularly those focused on public lands, may absorb these shifts.

THE BASIS FOR CHANGE: POPULATION

Population growth in the West has risen steadily since the inclusion of the region into the United States. The push by manifest destiny and the promise for space to call one's own intensified with the end of World War II and has continued. The US population in the West grew faster than any other US region in every decade of the twentieth century (Hobbs and Stoops 2002). Most recently, between 2016 and 2017, all western states grew by more than 1% except New Mexico (which grew by 0.1%) and Wyoming, which was the only western state to lose population (−1.0%) (US Census Bureau 2017).

Looking at the states with the greatest percentage population change from 2016 to 2017, seven of the top ten are in the West (see table 1.1).

This trend is also evident when looking at city growth. The urban makeup of the western United States (defined by the US Census Bureau as places with 2,500 or more residents) shifted from majority rural to majority urban in the 1910s. Since that time, this trend has intensified, with cities in the western United States experiencing substantial growth (see fig. 1.1).

Data from 2010 to 2017 reveal that cities with the top growth in population are located almost exclusively in the southern and the western United

Table 1.1. Population Change in the United States, 2016-2017

State	Percentage of Population Change
Idaho	2.2%
Nevada	2.0%
Utah	1.9%
Washington	1.7%
Arizona and Florida	1.6%
Colorado, Oregon, and Texas	1.4%
South Carolina	1.3%

Source: US Census Bureau (2017)

States (US Census Bureau 2018), and the West has the largest percentage of total population, of any region, living in urban areas (Cox 2016). This stands in contrast to the percentage of land that is urban in the West. The Northeast still maintains the highest urban land percentages, with the West having the lowest (Cox 2016). This reveals the complexity and duality of the West and shows the Old West narrative confronting the New West narrative: wide-open spaces, including public lands, that are sparsely populated and that have been and are valued for their resources exist alongside large urban centers wielding burgeoning populations.

CHANGING DEMOGRAPHICS

	1900	1910	1920	1930	1940	1950
Northeast	66.10%	71.80%	75.50%	77.60%	76.60%	79.50%
Midwest	38.60%	45.10%	52.30%	57.90%	58.40%	64.10%
South	18.30%	25.50%	28.10%	34.10%	36.70%	48.60%
West	39.90%	47.90%	51.80%	58.40%	58.50%	69.50%

	1960	1970	1980	1990	2000	2010
Northeast	80.20%	80.50%	79.20%	84.00%	84.40%	85.00%
Midwest	68.70%	71.60%	70.50%	73.90%	74.70%	75.90%
South	58.50%	64.80%	66.90%	71.50%	72.80%	75.80%
West	77.70%	83.00%	83.90%	87.60%	88.60%	89.80%

Source: US Census Bureau (2012)

Figure 1.1. Western urban population as a percentage of the total population.

Much of the population growth in the western United States is in the urban centers. This fact is important for a number of reasons, including the fact that increased migration into urban areas will result in an increased belief in the New West narrative as rural communities (subscribing to an Old West narrative) are seeing populations that are far outpaced by urban populations. The urban residents of the West fit the American Community Survey's description of urban residents (US Census Bureau 2016a, 2016b): they are younger, are more likely to be single, and have more education than those who live in rural areas. Urban residents within the United States and the West are less likely to live in the state of their birth (48.3% compared to 65.4%), own their own home (59.8% compared to 81.1%), and serve in the military (7.8% compared to 10.4%) (US Census Bureau 2016a). They are more likely to be racially and ethnically diverse; minorities comprise a larger percentage of urban populations than rural populations (although the percentage of minorities living in the rural United States is also on the rise), as more than half of all minority groups live in large metro areas or their suburbs (Frey 2011).

　　Given these facts, it is not surprising that the western United States, with a large and growing percentage of urban dwellers, increasingly has an image that supports the New West narrative. There is greater diversity in race and ethnicity and a larger shift from the traditional US conservative ideology. Examining race and ethnicity, the percentage of racial and ethnic minorities is expanding. US Census Bureau data support this fact: the second half of the twentieth century saw rapid growth of races other than white in the West, and by 1990, the West was the region with the highest percentage of races other than white (Hobbs and Stoops 2002, p. 84). Looking at political ideology for 2017, in the West, 32% of adults identified as conservative, while 30% identified as liberal (Saad 2018a). This is a slight contrast to the United States as a whole, where 35% of adults identified as conservative, and only 26% identified as liberal (Saad 2018a). Additionally, it is a marked contrast to the traditional West, where historically the conservative ideology label substantially outpaced the liberal label. Considering diversity and ideology together, the shifts seem logical. Older, ethnically white, less educated adults tend to identify as conservative, while younger, racially and ethnically not white, more highly educated people tend to identify as liberal. Thus the increase in urban-dwelling, young, ethnically diverse residents is shifting the political ideology of the region. Data show this playing out, with states that are not experiencing the intense population growth, such as Wyoming and Montana (refer to table

1.1), seeing virtually no change in ideology from 2008, while states with substantial population growth, such as Oregon and California, are seeing some of the largest decreases in the conservative label (Saad 2018b).

DEMOGRAPHICS SHIFTS AND PUBLIC LANDS

The demographic rural-urban shift is affecting public lands, especially their politics and policies. This is in large part due to the shifting preferences of the people who now call themselves westerners. The changing makeup of the people who live in the western United States has generated a new majority vision of the western landscape. Simply stated, the number of residents who lobby and vote for changes in public land uses is increasing, and there is a greater emphasis on the New West narrative.

The general characteristics of past decades' New West residents include individuals whose jobs are in a metropolitan areas but who focus nonwork time on outdoor recreation. These western migrants moved for quality of life and access to natural amenities (Krannich et al. 2011), are generally part of the postindustrial middle class, and present a profound challenge to the Old West ideas of public lands (Tracey and Sizek 2017). This group pushes the recreational values of public lands rather than resource extraction.

But there is also a second group of migrants moving to the West. These residents also often support the New West narrative, although they are less obvious supporters of this narrative. This group is composed of those who do not regularly visit public lands but who appreciate the aesthetic value of the landscape (Krannich et al. 2011). This group is varied and includes a growing number of minorities who tend to visit and use public lands at a much lower percentage than do the ethnically white. According to 2018 US Forest Service data (Flores 2018), African Americans accounted for 1.2% and Latinos or Hispanics accounted for 5.7% of visits to national forests, while ethnic whites accounted for 94.6% of national forest visits (Flores 2018). Likewise, studies focused on national parks have found similar trends, with minorities making up only 22% of national park visits (Taylor et al. 2011). Despite lack of visitation, public lands—particularly their aesthetic value—are still important to minorities (Burns et al. 2006). This group is also composed of those who moved to the western United States mainly for employment opportunities rather than for the western lifestyle. Employment opportunities in service, industry, and technology—areas not directly linked to public lands—are expanding in the region (Hogan 2016); of the top ten states for job placement, seven are within the western United States (Cohn 2018). Again, these individuals lack that direct connection to the public lands themselves but often appreciate the lands for the aesthetic value and the tourism associated with them that creates service and industry jobs. Overall, the common characteristic of the individuals that comprise this second group of migrants is a desire to consume an aesthetically and economically gentrified landscape; thus an appeal to minimize resource extraction on public land may minimize these elements.

The complexity of growing diverse populations and expanding urban centers is modifying the pressure on those who manage and develop the policies for public lands. The shifting number reveals that a greater percentage of the western population views the public lands as useful for recreational and aesthetic purposes, and the economics related to supporting those purposes, rather than the traditional natural resource extraction for economic benefit. What resources the landscape provides and the economics associated with these lands has become more complex as New West narratives and communities push again Old West narratives and economic necessities.

ECONOMIC DEVELOPMENT OF THE OLD WEST AND THE NEW WEST

With changes in population and demographics comes a change in economics. Within the western United States, this shift has a direct impact on the politics and policy of public lands. At first glance, the economy of the western United States appears to be booming. From 1970 to 2014, real personal income in the West rose substantially faster than in the other regions of the United States (Headwater Economics 2016). Likewise, employment outpaced the other regions nearly two to one (Headwater Economics 2016). Although true, this growth is not evenly distributed and in many ways delineates two western economies: that of the Old West's rural communities and that of the New West's urban centers.

ECONOMY OF THE OLD WEST

The traditional Old West economy includes dependency on natural resource-based commodity production for many small, rural communities with symbiotic relationships to the adjacent unsettled and public lands. The narrative, and much of the reality, of the Old West economy is focused on natural resource-dependent, labor-intensive jobs (farming, ranching, mining, fishing, logging), neighbors helping neighbors, and isolation from population centers and much government "meddling." These characteristics created an economy that was visually apparent—drawing economic benefit from the natural resources provided in the surrounding landscape. Old West extraction affects the landscape; grazing, mining, logging all leave visible marks of the use of the lands. As the Old West narrative suggests, however, these individuals provide for many of us (beef from grazing cattle, energy from mining coal); we all use the resources, we all hold some responsibility. According to the Old West narrative, it is the Old Westerners who understand land stewardship and how to minimize its impact so that future generations may also economically survive. Furthermore, efforts of the Old West have and continue to protect open spaces and public access. These Old West economic characteristics still exist in many rural communities and still shape much of the region's cultural mind-set.

ECONOMY OF THE NEW WEST

Over the last few decades, new forms of economic development expanded or evolved in the western United States. These included tourism, recreation, and associated service industries, along with technology. The economy of the New West generally does not directly connect people to the hands-on work within the western landscape, as does mining or ranching, but does utilize the resources provided by the landscape through tourism and associated services. Thus the New West economy is linked with public land resources, but through a reinterpretation of the resources. The New West economy provides experiences within the landscape (guide services and tourism) and the services supporting those experiences (restaurants, breweries, outdoor gear retail). The New West economy also provides jobs that have less connection to the lands but that support those individuals, the postindustrial middle class, who want access to experiences and thus live in the West. This accounts for much of the technological boom in the West; well-educated employees want the work-life balance and natural amenities that the West provides (Whitney 2015). Overall, the narrative of the New West economy focuses on the natural amenity values—scenic quality and recreational opportunities associated with undeveloped, topographically varied landscapes and ready access to open spaces.

THE ECONOMIC CHANGES AND PUBLIC LANDS

Traditionally, public lands in the West were associated with the Old West commodity production, as they were logged for timber, mined for minerals, and grazed by cattle and sheep. Subsequently, the people of the West supported resource extraction on public lands, as it financially benefitted many of them. The more recently evolving economy—built on natural amenities, renewable nature services, and the existence of minimally developed areas and clean environments—also brings supporters of public lands, but ones who do not want the visible marks of resource extraction. The West's shift away from agriculture and resource industries to a New West economy with a greater focus on recreation, technology, and service industries tipped in the 1980s. Thus, particularly since the 1980s, resource management of western public lands has made clear shifts to support the New West narrative (Krannich and Jennings 2011). This shifting management perspective emphasizes recreational uses and protection of ecologically sensitive areas and creates greater restrictions or even prohibits extractive activities (Carlton 2018; Winkler et al. 2007). This move supports the New West narrative, that of greater "conservation" of the public lands, which allows the development of trails but minimizes grazing.

It is the New West narrative supported by in-migrants to the West that has shifted public land management practices to give conservation greater priority, as new residents to the West favor more conservation. But an unintentional consequence of this change has been that the resulting policies helped attract even greater numbers of in-migrants and, more recently, seasonal residents. This expansion of in-migrants, particularly the seasonal residents who want easy access to public lands, is driving greater change—both to public land management and policy, dealing with increasing numbers visiting the public lands, and to the physical condition of the public lands themselves.

PHYSICAL CHANGE IN THE WEST

Human activities have always affected the physical setting of the West. With increasing populations in all areas of the region, there are increasing numbers of human impacts. Expansion of the Old West, such as increased mineral development, agriculture, and forestry, is occurring, but these losses are relatively small compared to urban sprawl (Center for American Progress 2018).

Urban sprawl drives expanding boundaries of cities and towns, and development of formerly natural areas. Between 2001 and 2011, the footprint of western cities and towns grew by nearly 17% (Center for American Progress 2018), and this trend continues. The sprawl of housing and commercial building accounts for half of the West's loss of natural areas (Center for American Progress 2018). This loss has occurred mainly on private land (such as ranchland sold to developers), but development associated with this building has direct impacts on public lands. For example, increasing numbers of roads and transmission lines, to both physically connect new development and to accommodate greater numbers of people visiting public lands, has affected public lands (Maffly 2018).

A second physical change involves water. As the population grows, the arid West's limited water supply is stretched thin. Add to this the droughts that have plagued the region in recent years, and there is the potential for great conflict between the Old West and the New West. The increasing usage in urban areas, including demands for green lawns and golf courses, confronts agriculture, which still uses more than 90% of consumptive water in many western states (US Department of Agriculture 2018). The politics and policies of western water directly involve public lands; western water comes from snowmelt on public lands and flows across public lands. Thus, when water shortages present, it is not only the people of the West who feel the effects, but also the physical landscape itself. Among other issues, public lands have been affected by engineering projects designed to move or store water, changing locations of water and often stressing aquifers (King 2018).

Finally, the future of the West will continue to effect physical changes, not only because of growth and water usage, but also due to climate change. The West has experienced and will continue to experience higher temperatures, lower snowpack, and the associated effects of dryer landscapes (Mote et al. 2018; Union of Concerned Scientists 2018). The West is expected to see increases in extreme weather, including the prevalence and duration of drought, particularly "mega-droughts" that last for more than two decades (Cook et al. 2015). Each of these traits will affect public lands—the ability to support cattle or sheep, the variety and size of trees, the vegetation and associated aesthetics, the temperature of water in blue-ribbon trout streams—thus affecting both the Old West and the New West narratives and forcing change to what comes next, the Next West.

NEXT WEST

Over the past decade (or so) we have seen hints as to where the Next West is heading. The Next West is maintaining narrative elements of both the Old West—independent residents living in wide-open spaces—and the New West—modernity in an environmentally clean expanse—but it is also bringing forward new issues and challenges.

Population and Demographics

If trends hold, the Next West will continue to see rapidly expanding populations, particularly in urban centers. This will also necessitate further expansion, however, intruding into some of the traditionally rural Old West areas. Thus regions of the Next West will be connected to the New West urban centers—by the transportation corridors and technology—yet they may be located in somewhat "rural" Old West settings (Headwater Economics 2015). Also, the Next West will likely be composed of growing numbers of people drawn to aspects of the quality of life of the western region but whose presence and lifestyle are changing the places and characteristics they desired. The increasing population, many of whom value the healthy lifestyle, abundant wildlife, and wide-open spaces, will physically move into and thus take over the open spaces, displacing wildlife and the natural processes for maintaining clean air and clean water.

Economics

Economically, the Next West likely includes continued expansion of consumer service industries, tourism, telecommunication, and employees working remotely. This economy will likely push the Next West toward greater development of the connection areas—increasing wildland-urban interface and moving the contrasting New West lifestyle closer to the Old West, where much of the open space and many of the public lands exist. Greater numbers of individuals residing in formerly small towns, the changing work landscape (where residents no longer help neighbors corral cattle or provide economic assistance when mineral prices are down and thus fewer miners are employed), and seasonal residents buying second homes will affect both the Old West economy and the connection within communities. Furthermore, the telecommuting, service-oriented economy will likely further the divide western residents, creating a contrast between how public land resources are viewed and who can afford to live in the region given the recreational economy's profound influence on property values.

The economy of the Next West will in part create a situation where those moving to the West for amenities are themselves destroying the amenities. This is already occurring with the displacing of ranchers and others whose lifestyles have helped maintain the open spaces, and overpopulating public lands, thus forcing development of tourist-based amenities within the "undeveloped" areas. The Next West economy just may become a rapidly growing postindustrial high-tech society that still encompasses resource extraction but slowly destroys elements of the beautiful and fragile landscape that supports western ideals.

Physical Changes

Adding to the population and economically based physical changes, the Next West will also be forced to address physical changes due to climate change. Signs of climate change in the western United States include rising temperatures, lower and earlier melting snowpack, and dryer forests, suggesting a future with increasing water scarcity in already dry regions. This will further reduce water availability for the competing needs of urban areas, recreational activities, agriculture, and mining. Furthermore, precipitation is predicted to decline 20% to 25% in the West by 2100 (Kaufman 2018), increasing pressure on groundwater supplies, driving longer and more damaging wildfire seasons, intensifying forest death, and resulting in worsening air and water quality (Union of Concerned Scientists 2018). Finally, climate change also suggests a trend of more extreme weather, meaning the possibility of floods interspersed with drought, and more extreme cold and hot weather. Each of these characteristics will affect public lands and the ability to utilize the diverse resources contained within the public lands: those utilized by the Old West and those utilized by the New West. The management and policies of these changing scenarios are of vital importance to the West. They will either find a way to help maintain the open spaces of the public lands for use by many stakeholders, or they will dictate where the West will head and who will utilize the public's public lands. The West will need to adapt, and in doing so will have to choose to either inclusively draw from the strengths of the Old West communities and the New West's diversity or exclusively focus on who can financially maintain in a rapidly changing region.

CONCLUSIONS: THE NEXT WEST AND PUBLIC LANDS

Future effects of the Next West on public lands will be substantial. More people will visit the fragile lands, causing physical change and pushing for different ideas of what the western lands should provide. There will be greater numbers supporting the New West narrative of recreational uses, modern lifestyle, and clean environment. But there will also be a need for the resources produced from the extractive industries of the Old West and a romanticization of the independent western lifestyle. And there will be the reality that none of these can exist with the force of change that the West faces. The environmental politics and policies of the western public lands will need to address all of these elements.

A shift from the Old West to the New West occurred over the past century. As change continues, the question to ask is, What is next? What is the Next West? To understand where the West is going, it is necessary to understand the reality of the region and the stories or narratives told about the region, both powerful in determining future trends and the policies that affect the West and its iconic public lands. Overall, rather than all-out change, the western United States has and is likely to continue experiencing a layering—a keeping of the old while adding the new—that now extends to the Next West. With the layering comes a more complex and diverse society, economy, and culture, a move beyond believing this region is one-dimensional to accepting a reality of multiple Wests: the rural, the urban, and the connector, all of which define themselves in part with the existence of public lands and the changing politics and policies that manage those public lands.

References

Aron, Stephen. 2016. "The History of the American West Gets a Much-Needed Rewrite." *Smithsonian Magazine*, August 16, 2016. https://www.smithsonianmag.com/history/history-american-west-gets-much-needed-rewrite-180960149/.

Bennett, Keith, and Mark K. McBeth. 1998. "Contemporary Western Rural USA Economic Composition: Potential Implications for Environmental Policy Research." *Environmental Management* 22: 371-381.

Burns, Robert, Alan Graefe, and Libby Covelli. 2006. *Racial/Ethnic Minority Focus Group Interview: Oregon SCORP*. Salem: Oregon Parks and Recreation Department, December 2006. https://www.oregon.gov/oprd/PLANS/docs/scorp/2008-2012_SCORP/OregonSCORPMinorityFocusGroupReport.pdf.

Carlton, Jim. 2018. "In the Battle for the American West, the Cowboys Are Losing." *Wall Street Journal*, March 30, 2018. https://www.wsj.com/articles/in-the-battle-for-the-american-west-the-cowboys-are-losing-1522425557.

Center for American Progress. 2018. "The Disappearing West." Accessed November 11, 2019. https://disappearingwest.org/land.html.

Chapman, Arthur. 1917. "Out Where the West Begins." In *Out Where the West Begins and Other Western Verses*. Boston, MA: Houghton Mifflin.

Cohn, Scott. 2018. "The Top 10 States in America Where You Are Most Likely to Land Your Dream Job." CNBC, July 10, 2018. https://www.cnbc.com/2018/06/29/top-10-states-to-find-a-job-in-america-in-2018.html.

Cook, Benjamin I., Toby R. Ault, and Jason E. Smerdon. 2015. "Unprecedented 21st Century Drought Risk in the American Southwest and Central Plains." *Science Advances* 1(1): http://advances.sciencemag.org/content/1/1/e1400082.

Cox, Wendell. 2016. "America's Most Urban States." Newgeography, March 8, 2016. http://www.newgeography.com/content/005187-america-s-most-urban-states.

Flores, David. 2018. *Recreating in Color: Promoting Racial and Ethnic Diversity in Public Land Use*. Washington, DC: US Forest Service, US Department of Agriculture. https://www.fs.fed.us/rmrs/science-spotlights/recreating-color-promoting-racial-and-ethnic-diversity-public-land-use.

Frey, William H. 2011. "Melting Pot Cities and Suburbs: Racial and Ethnic Change in Metro America in the 2000s." In *State of Metropolitan America*. Washington, DC: Metropolitan Policy Program at Brookings. https://www.brookings.edu/wpcontent/uploads/2016/06/0504_census_ethnicity_frey.pdf.

Headwater Economics. 2015. "Three Wests: Access to Markets Affects Performance." October 15, 2015. https://headwaterseconomics.org/economic-development/trends-performance/three-wests-explained/.

Headwater Economics. 2016. "West's Economy Outperforming Rest of United States." March 16, 2016. https://headwaterseconomics.org/economic-development/trends-performance/west-wide-summary/.

Hobbs, Frank, and Nicole Stoops. 2002. *Demographic Trends in the 20th Century: Census 2000 Special Reports*. CENSR-4. Washington, DC: US Government Printing Office. https://www.census.gov/prod/2002pubs/censr-4.pdf.

Hogan, Dwayne. 2016. "Why Americans Are Moving to Southern and Western States." Move.org, updated April 14, 2016. https://www.move.org/why-americans-are-moving-to-southern-and-western-states/.

Johnson, L. B. 1963. "Remarks, Dinner for Gale McGee." July 13, 1963. Speech Collection, Lyndon Baines Johnson Presidential Library, Austin, TX.

Kaufman, Rachel. 2018. "Water Crisis in the West: Can the Region Overcome Worsening Drought?" *CQ Researcher* 28(18): 417-440. http://library.cqpress.com/cqresearcher/document.php?id=cqresrre2018051100.

King, Anna. 2018. "Deepening Drought in Western U.S. Costs Ranchers Money and Heartache." NPR, July 8, 2018. https://www.npr.org/sections/thesalt/2018/07/08/619229814/deepening-drought-in-western-u-s-costs-ranchers-money-and-heartache.

Krannich, Richard S., and Brian Jennings. 2011. "New West and Old West: Attitudes and Behaviors Regarding Natural Resource Uses and Management." In *People, Places and Landscapes: Social Change in High Amenity Rural Areas*, edited by R. S. Krannich, A. E. Luloff, and D. R. Field, 81-108. New York: Sprinter Science + Business Media.

Krannich, Richard S., A. E. Luloff, and Donald R. Field. 2011. "Putting Rural Community Change in Perspective." In *People, Places and Landscapes: Social Change in High Amenity Rural Areas*, edited by R. S. Krannich, A. E. Luloff, and D. R. Field, 9-25. New York: Sprinter Science + Business Media.

Maffly, Brian. 2018. "Utah's Remote Roads to Get More Maintenance Money, but Critics Fear the Move Will Scar Public Lands." *Salt Lake Tribune*, July 25, 2018. https://www.sltrib.com/news/environment/2018/07/25/utahs-remote-roads-get/.

Mishler, Elliot G. 1995. "Models of Narrative Analysis: A Typology." *Journal of Narrative and Life History* 5(2): 87-123.

Mote, Philip W., Sihan Le, Dennis P. Lettenmaier, Mu Xiao, and Ruth Engel. 2018. "Dramatic Declines in Snowpack in the Western US." *Climate and Atmospheric Science* 1(2): https://www.nature.com/articles/s41612-018-0012-1.

Saad, Lydia. 2018a. "Conservative Lead in U.S. Ideology Is Down to Single Digits." Gallup, January 11, 2018. https://news.gallup.com/poll/225074/conservative-lead-ideology-down-single-digits.aspx.

Saad, Lydia. 2018b. "Conservative-Leaning States Drop from 44 to 39." Gallup, February 6, 2018. https://news.gallup.com/poll/226730/conservative-leaning-states-drop.aspx.

Sarbin, T. R. 1986. "The Narrative as a Root Metaphor for Psychology." In *Narrative Psychology*, edited by T. R. Sarbin, 3-21. New York: Praeger.

Shenhav, Shaul R. 2004. "Once upon a Time There Was a Nation: Narrative Conceptualization Analysis, the Concept of 'Nation' in the Discourse of Israeli Likud Party Leaders." *Discourse and Society* 15(1): 81-104.

Shenhav, Shaul R. 2006. "Political Narratives and Political Reality." *International Political Science Review* 27(3): 245-262.

Shumway, J. Matthew, and Samuel M. Otterstrom. 2001. "Spatial Patterns of Migration and Income Change in the Mountain West: The Dominance of Service-Based, Amenity-Rich Counties." *Professional Geographer* 53: 492-501.

Taylor, Patricia A., Bruke D. Grandjean, and James H. Gramann. 2011. *National Park Service Comprehensive Survey of the American Public 2008-2009: Racial and Ethnic Diversity of the National Park System Visitors and Non-Visitors.* Natural Resource Report NPS/NRSS/SSD/NRR–2011/432. http://npshistory.com/publications/social-science/comprehensive-survey/nrr-2011-431.pdf.

Tracey, Caroline, and Julia Sizek. 2017. "The New West: Why Republicans Blocked Public Land Management." *The Guardian,* July 2, 2017. https://www.theguardian.com/environment/2017/jul/02/public-lands-new-west-republican-park-management.

Union of Concerned Scientists. 2018. "Global Warming in the Western United States." Updated June 25, 2018. https://www.ucsusa.org/global_warming/regional_information/ca-and-western-states.html#.W4HRuM5KiUk.

US Census Bureau. 2012. *United States Summary: 2010. 2010 Census of Population and Housing.* CPH-2-1. Washington, DC: US Government Printing Office. https://www.census.gov/prod/cen2010/cph-2-1.pdf.

US Census Bureau. 2016a. "New Census Data Show Differences between Urban and Rural Populations." Release Number CB16-210. December 8, 2016. https://www.census.gov/newsroom/press-releases/2016/cb16-210.html.

US Census Bureau. 2016b. "Measuring America: Our Changing Landscape." December 8, 2016. https://www.census.gov/library/visualizations/2016/comm/acs-rural-urban.html.

US Census Bureau. 2017. *Estimates of Resident Population Change for the United States, Regions, States, and Puerto Rico and Region and State Rankings: July 1, 2016 to July 1, 2017.* NST-EST2017-03. Washington, DC: US Census Bureau.

US Census Bureau. 2018. "Census Bureau Reveals Fastest-Growing Large Cities." Release Number CB18-78. May 24, 2018. https://www.census.gov/newsroom/press-releases/2018/estimates-cities.html.

US Department of Agriculture. 2018. "Irrigation and Water Use." Accessed January 26, 2020. https://www.ers.usda.gov/topics/farm-practices-management/irrigation-water-use.aspx.

Vincent, Carol Hardy, Laura A. Hanson, and Carla N. Argueta. 2017. *Federal Land Ownership: Overview and Data.* CRS Report R42346. Washington, DC: Congressional Research Service. https://fas.org/sgp/crs/misc/R42346.pdf.

White, H. 1980. "The Value of Narrativity in the Representation of Reality." *Critical Inquiry* 7(1): 5-27.

Whitney, Eric. 2015. "Tired of the Big City? Consider Telecommuting from Montana." NPR, July 28, 2015. https://www.npr.org/2015/07/28/426858376/tired-of-the-big-city-consider-telecommuting-from-montana.

Winkler, Richelle, Donald R. Field, A. E. Luloff, Richard S. Krannich, and Tracy Williams. 2007. "Social Landscapes of the Inter-Mountain West: A Comparison of 'Old West' and 'New West' Communities." *Rural Sociology* 72(3): 478-501.

Chapter 2
Western Public Land Law and the Evolving Management Landscape

JOHN RUPLE

The histories of our nation and of the lands that we inhabit are inextricably intertwined. Ranchers, miners, loggers, and intrepid homesteaders of the Old West embody the ideals of the manifest destiny era that set the United States on a trajectory that continues to shape the choices we make today. Laws enacted to speed westward expansion and resolve land ownership indelibly marked the western landscape, where the vast majority of public lands are found today.

The US government acquired the western frontier with federal blood and treasure, and then enacted laws conveying much of that landscape to states, railroads, and the indomitable men and women who personified Old West ideals. The laws that transferred millions of acres of land out of federal ownership and that retained other lands as part of our nation's treasured landscapes also created property rights and expectations that provide important sideboards on our transition to a New West. Some of those laws remain in force, supplemented by new laws protecting wildlife, wild places, and the public's voice in public land management. Public land mangers face a difficult task in finding the balance required by a complex legal framework, and communities that grew up around Old West imperatives sometimes struggle to adapt to New West values.

Understanding the role public lands have played in American history helps explain who we are today. This understanding illuminates the tensions underpinning disputes like the takeover of the Malheur National Wildlife Refuge and state efforts to wrest control of public lands from the federal government. Lurking behind these battles are long-simmering questions over the values we seek from our public lands. As past is prelude, we must understand where we came from as we chart a course defining a Next West.

PUBLIC LAND ACQUISITION

The original thirteen states secured title to land from the Atlantic Ocean to the Mississippi River with their victory in the Revolutionary War. The thirteen states possessed complete sovereignty over that land until forming a central government and ceding title to 237 million acres of land to the newly formed federal government (Bureau of Land Management 2018). Land cession was critical to the initial survival of the United States. Landlocked states like Delaware, New Hampshire, and Rhode Island feared that states like Virginia and Georgia, which claimed title to vast tracts of the western frontier, would have disproportionate political and economic power in our emerging nation. State claims to the western frontier also overlapped and invited conflicts between both settlers and the several states. The resulting cloud on land titles made orderly settlement more difficult. Ceding land title to the federal government equalized power between the fledgling states, resolved competing state claims of title to the western frontier, and paved the way for western settlement (Gates 1968).

Farther west, the federal government obtained title to 1.6 billion acres of land not from the states but from foreign powers. This land, most of which was acquired from France in 1803 through the Louisiana Purchase, stretched from the Mississippi River to the Pacific Ocean and today is included in portions of fifteen states between the Mississippi River and the Rocky Mountains.[1] The Republic of Texas was annexed into the United States in 1845.[2] The Pacific Northwest came into the Union a year later via the Oregon Compromise with Great Britain.[3] Much of the Southwest was obtained from Mexico in 1848 in the Treaty of Guadalupe Hidalgo, which also ended the Mexican-American War.[4] The final major land acquisition occurred in 1867 when the United States purchased 365 million acres—what would become Alaska—from Russia.[5] Along the way, the United States dispatched Native Americans' claims to the land, either through treaties or at the point of a gun.

PUBLIC LAND DISPOSAL

Once the federal government had secured title to the western frontier, Congress created federal territories and set forth the manner in which those territories would be governed. When the population within a federal territory reached a critical mass and the territory's citizens agreed to the requirements for statehood, Congress then passed laws creating new states out of federal territories.[6] Title to land within newly minted states, however, remained in

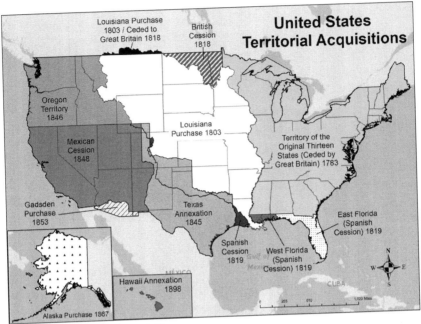

Figure 2.1. US territorial acquisitions.

federal hands until those lands were disposed of by the federal government—and the federal government disposed of lots of land.

Millions of acres passed out of federal ownership, building the country's economic foundation, opening the West to settlement, and uniting vast expanses of land into a unified nation. To support nascent western state governments, the federal government granted 224 million acres of land to those states (Gates 1968, p. 804). States were then free to sell or develop that land in order to fund infrastructure development, pay for public schools and universities, build state capitals, and construct hospitals and other public buildings. States like Nevada quickly sold off most of the land that had been granted to them. States like New Mexico retained the majority of the land they received and continue to manage those lands to generate revenue for public institutions. Most of the granted lands were conveyed to the states in scattered one-square-mile blocks, incentivizing states to develop all regions within their borders. These scattered state sections, however, can cause management conflicts when the federal and state governments pursue different management objectives across the same checkerboarded landscape. These challenges will only increase as we move from the Old West, to the New West, and into the Next West.

To pay war debts and encourage westward expansion, the federal government also sold or granted vast tracts of public lands to veterans, miners, homesteaders, towns, and railroads. The most desirable lands, such as those in fertile river valleys and lands rich with timber, were acquired first. Other lands that were more difficult to homestead and less profitable to develop remained in federal ownership (Gates 1968, chap. XV).

The scale of federal land disposal is striking. In total, almost 1.3 billion acres of public lands, an area larger than all of Spain, were transferred out of federal ownership (Bureau of Land Management 2018, p. 5). These disposal efforts, while successful in encouraging western expansion, resulted in what Coggins and Glickman (2010, §2:9) describe as a "crazy quilt" of land ownership that continues to generate a plethora of disputes over access and permissible land uses.

RATIONALIZING A FRAGMENTED LANDSCAPE

The federal government has a long history of trading developable federal lands for nonfederal lands that lie within sensitive landscapes. Such exchanges can rationalize a fragmented landscape, improve access, and address management challenges. But conflicting management objectives and ownership fragmentation remain serious challenges in much of the West. While land exchanges can be difficult to negotiate, they represent a concrete way of addressing a pervasive problem. They may also reflect a rare opportunity for a win-win solution in the increasingly polarized debate over the future of public lands.

The 1998 Utah School and Land Exchange Act is a compelling example of how rationalizing a landscape can benefit all involved. The act implemented an agreement conveying to the federal government 379,739 acres of state trust land (an area approximately the size of the island of Oʻahu), including 176,699 acres within the Grand Staircase-Escalante National Monument, 80,000 acres of inholdings within lands managed by the National Park Service, 47,480 acres within Indian reservations, 70,000 within national forests, and 2,560 acres in Kane County coal fields. In exchange, the federal government conveyed to the state 138,647 acres of federal land plus valuable mineral rights, all of which were in areas deemed suitable for development. Additionally, the state received $50 million in cash and the right to $13 million in potential future royalties from mineral development that occurred on federal lands. The lands conveyed to the state were also consolidated into more manageable blocks, thereby minimizing management conflicts while lowering costs for the state.[7]

The exchange, in sum, eliminated the threat of development from national parks and monuments, national forests, and Indian reservations while affording the state the opportunity to responsibly generate revenue that was dedicated to supporting public schools and institutions. While the exchange was far larger than most land trades, it demonstrates the mutual benefits that can be realized through cooperation and hard work.

MANAGING OUR PUBLIC LANDS

Just over 643 million acres (slightly more than the combined area of Alaska, California, and Texas) remain under federal control, and most of this land is located in the eleven contiguous western states and Alaska. "Public lands" are the dominant subset of these lands, and they include lands managed by the Bureau of Land Management (BLM), the US Forest Service (USFS), the National Park Service (NPS), and the US Fish and Wildlife Service (FWS). The BLM, NPS, and FWS are all part of the Department of the Interior. The USFS is part of the Department of Agriculture. Indian reservations and Department of Defense lands also dot the landscape, but access to these lands is generally limited. Such lands are therefore not considered public lands in the common sense of the term.

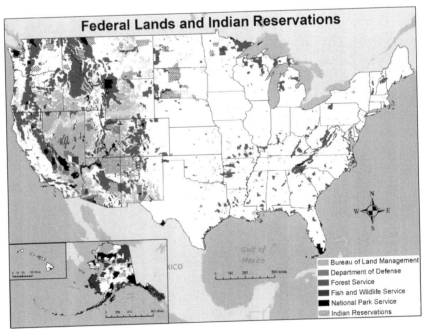

Figure 2.2. Federal lands and Indian reservations.

Each of the four major public land management agencies has a slightly different management focus, though all are required to balance competing uses. The USFS is the oldest of the four federal land management agencies, and today the USFS administers 154 national forests and 20 grasslands that total 192.9 million acres of land. Congress first authorized the president to set aside public lands as forest reserves in 1891.[8] Forest reserves were renamed national forests when the USFS was founded in 1905. National Forest System lands, like all of our nation's public lands, are predominantly in the West.

National forests were initially created to "improve and protect the forest within their boundaries, or for the purpose of securing favorable conditions for water flows, and to furnish a continuous supply of timber for the use and necessities of the citizens of the United States."[9] Congress revised the USFS's mission in 1960 by passing the Multiple-Use Sustained-Yield Act,[10] and again in 1976 when it passed the National Forest Management Act.[11] Together, these acts expanded the USFS's mandate to include recreation, livestock grazing, and wildlife and fish habitat conservation. Gifford Pinchot, the first chief of the Forest Service, presciently summed up the mission of the Forest Service well before the passage of these two acts: "to provide the greatest amount of good for the greatest amount of people in the long run" (US Forest Service 2019).

Today, as Gifford Pinchot foretold, National Forest System lands are managed in a manner that requires balancing competing commercial uses and almost 150 million visitors annually "in the combination that will best meet the needs of the American people."[12] That is no small task, particularly in light of competing opinions regarding what constitutes an appropriate balance. Striking that balance will only become more difficult as we adapt to the twin challenges of climate change and rapid demographic transitions. Much depends on how we, as a society, define the New West values that we choose to pursue.

While the USFS was the first public land management agency, the BLM is our nation's largest landlord. Today, the BLM administers more federal lands than any other agency, 248.3 million acres (Bureau of Land Management 2018, p. 7). The BLM manages a diverse landscape, most of which involves rangeland and high desert in the eleven contiguous western states as well as vast stretches of land in Alaska. The BLM also administers subsurface minerals on approximately 700 million acres that are owned by the federal government (Bureau of Land Management 2018, p. 7). The BLM was formed in 1946 by merging the General Land Office and the Grazing Service. The General Land Office had been created in 1812 to oversee disposal of the federal lands, while the Grazing Service had been established in 1934 to administer grazing on public rangelands.

Prior to 1934 and passage of the Taylor Grazing Act,[13] the federal government made little effort to manage livestock grazing on public lands. The Taylor Grazing Act reversed that trend, responding to widespread overgrazing, drought, and the expanding dust bowl. The act marked a profound change in public land management philosophy, moving the federal government in general, and the BLM in particular, toward more active stewardship of public lands. The act creates grazing districts that included portions of the public domain deemed "chiefly valuable for grazing and raising forage crops."[14] For the first time, those grazing livestock on public lands were required to obtain permits from the federal government. Ranchers were also required to pay at least nominal fees for the use of federal land and forage. Of at least equal importance, proposed grazing districts were withdrawn from all forms of homestead entry or settlement, marking the beginning of the end of the public land disposal era.

The second major shift involving the BLM came in 1976 with enactment of the Federal Land Policy and Management Act (FLPMA).[15] FLPMA, which was the product of a multiyear public land law reform effort and a blue-ribbon commission, repealed a host of statutes facilitating disposal of federal public lands. FLPMA replaced these disposal laws with a commitment to retain most public lands in federal ownership unless disposal was deemed in the national interest. FLPMA further recognized numerous non-commodity values, pivoting the BLM toward multiple-use, sustained-yield management. The pivot away from disposal and toward multiple-use management marked a major organizational shift, requiring a balancing of recreation, mining, oil and natural gas development, grazing, logging, watershed protection, wildlife and fish habitat management, cultural resource stewardship, and resource protection. This pivot, while embraced as long overdue by many, was seen by others as an assault on the manifest destiny-era values and hard work that settled the West. The rewriting of public land policy and shift in management priorities proved to be a critical moment in the emergence of the Sagebrush Rebellion.

Where the BLM is the leader in domestic livestock grazing management, the FWS focuses on wildlife and management of the National Wildlife Refuge System. The earliest effort to set aside federally owned lands for wildlife preservation occurred in 1868 when President Ulysses S. Grant protected the Pribilof Islands in Alaska as a reserve for the northern fur seal (US Fish and Wildlife Service 2019). President Grant's actions were confirmed by Congress the following year. Congress and presidents have expanded the National Wildlife Refuge System many times over the years that followed.

The FWS was formed in 1940 by combining the Bureau of Biological Survey with the Bureau of Fisheries. Today, the FWS administers 89.1 million acres of federal land, 86% of which is located in Alaska. The FWS, which is directed to conserve plants and animals, has a more focused mission than either the BLM or the USFS. Species and habitat protection as well as wildlife-related activities like bird-watching and hiking are given preference over consumptive uses such as logging, grazing, and mineral extraction. Such consumptive uses are permitted provided that these activities are compatible with the species' needs.[16]

The NPS was created in 1916 to manage the national park units established by Congress and national monuments proclaimed by the president, unless a president directs another agency to manage the monument. The NPS has a dual mission: to preserve unimpaired natural and cultural resources and values, and to provide for public enjoyment of park system lands.[17] The National Park System has grown to 408 units with 79.8 million acres of federal land, approximately two-thirds of which is located in Alaska. Park units include spectacular natural areas like Yellowstone and the Grand Canyon as well as important places in American history like Gettysburg National Military Park and the Statue of Liberty National Monument. National Park System units also include unique historic and prehistoric sites like Mesa Verde National Park and Dinosaur National Monument. With gems such as these, it is not surprising that NPS-managed units receive 330 million visits annually, necessitating a careful balance between facilitating enjoyment and preserving unique and often sensitive resources.

STATUTORY OVERLAYS

These four federal agencies each seek to balance a host of competing land uses within the unique statutory mandates that apply to the resources within their charge. In addition to the substantive direction each agency receives, Congress has also enacted both substantive and procedural statutes that apply across all four agencies. Three of the most important overlays are the Wilderness Act of 1964[18] (discussed more fully in chap. 7 of this volume, "Wild Places and

Irreplaceable Resources: Protecting Wilderness and National Monuments"), the Endangered Species Act of 1973,[19] and the National Environmental Policy Act of 1969.[20]

The Wilderness Act of 1964 was passed to protect lands that remain wild and untrammeled by man. Wilderness, under the act, is defined as "an area of undeveloped Federal land retaining its primeval character and influence, without permanent improvements of human habitation, which is protected and managed so as to preserve its natural conditions."[21] Mechanized access and infrastructure development are generally prohibited within wilderness areas.

The Wilderness Act initially designated 54 wilderness areas containing 9.1 million acres of National Forest System lands. Congress also required a review of other National Forest System lands as well as National Park System units and national wildlife refuges for the existence of wilderness character. Suitable units were then recommended for inclusion in the Wilderness Preservation System. While the Wilderness Act made no mention of BLM-managed lands, Congress imposed similar wilderness review requirements in 1976 with passage of FLPMA.[22]

Since passage of the Wilderness Act, Congress has enacted more than a hundred bills designating additional wilderness areas. Today, the Wilderness Preservation System consists of over 765 units encompassing 110 million acres of public land, or an area about 10 million acres larger than the entire state of California. There are also millions of acres of BLM wilderness study areas as well as USFS roadless areas that are managed to avoid impairing their wilderness character until Congress decides whether to include these lands in the Wilderness Preservation System. The protections afforded by wilderness designations include some of the most restrictive requirements applicable to public lands and are seen by many as preserving a priceless gift to future generations. Others, however, see commodity production and economic development opportunities foregone, and bitterly oppose additional wilderness designations.

The Endangered Species Act (ESA) serves as another critically important statutory overlay that can directly affect public land management and use. Passed in 1973 to provide a means to conserve imperiled species and the ecosystems upon which they depend, the ESA prohibits any "act which actually kills or injures wildlife. Such an act may include significant habitat modification or degradation where it actually kills or injures wildlife by significantly impairing essential behavioral patterns, including breeding, feeding, or sheltering."[23]

Under the ESA, actions on federal land as well as those requiring federal authorization or that receive federal funding require consultation between the FWS and the federal agency undertaking the action. National Oceanic and Atmospheric Administration Fisheries is charged with implementing the ESA for marine and anadromous species, and it takes on consultation obligation when those species are involved. Consultation with these agencies is intended to "ensure that any action authorized, funded, or carried out by such agency . . . is not likely to jeopardize the continued existence of any endangered species or threatened species or result in the destruction or adverse modification of [designated critical] habitat."[24]

Like the Wilderness Act, the ESA is either loved or loathed, depending on where one sits. The act's detractors see it as an unnecessary burden on economic development that sacrifices good-paying jobs for limited benefit. The act's fans see it as the last bulwark against species extinction and of profound moral significance.

A crystalizing example of the ESA's reach came in 1990 when the FWS protected the northern spotted owl. The owl's decline was attributed in large part to the aggressive logging of old-growth forests in the Pacific Northwest, and the lawsuits that followed the owl's ESA listing shut down old-growth logging of northern spotted owl habitat in California, Oregon, and Washington.[25] While the forest management practices that imperiled the owl left lasting scars on the landscape and deserve strong criticism, the human cost of protection cannot be ignored. Timber harvests from federal land in that region fell by 80% between 1989 and 1994, and 14,000 forest products jobs were lost.

The National Environmental Policy Act (NEPA) is at least equally polarizing. NEPA, depending on who you ask, is either the Magna Carta of environmental laws or a job killer that unnecessarily delays well-intentioned and much-needed development. NEPA requires that federal agencies identify and consider the impacts of their actions and alternative means of attaining the objectives of those actions before undertaking any "major Federal action significantly impacting the quality of the human environment."[26] Large, complex, or controversial projects may necessitate completion of an Environmental Impact Statement (EIS), though EISs represent less than 1% of all projects undergoing NEPA review. Most projects are analyzed in either an environmental assessment (EA) or categorical exclusion (CE), both of which require much less time and fewer resources to complete (US Government Accountability Office 2014, p. 7. Most federal land management plans completed by the four major land management agencies cover millions of acres and require completion of an EIS concurrent with management plan development. Project-level authorizations, which can range from campground and road repairs to some mineral development and timber harvest projects, are usually subject to review in an EA or CE.

Critically, NEPA does not require that federal agencies choose the least environmentally damaging alternative. Rather, NEPA requires that public input be considered, and that agencies take a hard look at the environmental consequences of their actions before rendering a decision.[27] Balancing competing uses required by our public land manager's management mandate and conducted under the public vetting required by NEPA can be challenging. Indeed, the kinds of actions analyzed in an EIS are often divisive front-page news, and NEPA can provide the legal vehicle to challenge those projects on procedural grounds.

THE SEARCH FOR BALANCE

Striking an acceptable balance between preservation of environmental values and accommodation of land uses and commodity development is easier said than done. While nearly everyone agrees that balance is important, what constitutes an appropriate balance is often hotly disputed. As others have suggested, our public lands are essentially political lands. Their future will be guided by the tradeoffs struck through the political process. Congress will continue to play an important role in developing the policies that are reflected in our land-use laws, and our courts will inevitably have growing influence in interpreting and enforcing laws enacted by Congress.

Attaining balance is difficult because public lands provide an incredibly broad suite of benefits to the American people—from timber, oil, natural gas, and livestock fodder to clean water, pristine vistas, wildlife habitat, and recreation getaways. Our national forests, for example, continue to be a rich source of timber, with over 2.5 billion board feet of timber harvested from National Forest System lands during 2017. That is enough timber to build roughly 160,000 new 2,500-square-foot homes every year. While significant, however, timber harvests from National Forest System lands have declined significantly from the peak harvest of 12.7 billion board feet in 1987, often with profound impacts on timber-dependent local communities and economies.

Federal lands are also a major source of oil and natural gas, with onshore federal lands producing 166 million barrels of oil and 3.2 trillion cubic feet of natural gas during 2015, and oil production from federal lands has risen each of the last ten years (Humphries 2016, pp. 3-4). While production has increased, the percentage of oil produced from federal lands (excluding off-shore federal lands) has held steady at approximately 5% of domestic production. Onshore natural gas production from federal lands currently accounts for about 11% of all national production, down from 18% in 2009. According to the Congressional Research Service, this decline "mostly reflects the dramatic growth in non-federal production rather than the decline in total federal production" (Humphries 2016, p. 4). Coal produced from federal lands has accounted for roughly 40% of total domestic coal production over the past decade (Hoover 2018, p. 15) but coal production is declining steadily as utilities transition to natural gas and renewable energy.

Revenue generated from commodity development on federal public lands is shared with the states and counties where the development occurs. The amount of revenue paid to the states and counties varies by resource and the laws directing revenue disposition, but a few key examples are useful. During 2017, the eleven contiguous western states received a total of $1.78 billion in federal funds that were tied directly to public lands. This includes roughly half of all revenue from leasable minerals such as oil and natural gas found on federal lands. It also includes BLM, USFS, and FWS revenue-sharing as well as payments intended to offset lost tax revenue because federal lands are not subject to state or local taxes (Headwaters Economics 2019).

But not all values are reflected adequately in revenue statistics. Twenty-four percent of the water supply in the contiguous United States originates on federal land, and national forests and grasslands supply 51% of the water supply in the West (US Forest Service 2014, p. 46). Our forests and public lands supply millions of homes with potable water and support vast agricultural operations that help feed our nation. Activities that occur on our public lands, whether human caused or naturally occurring, can directly affect the quantity, quality, and timing of water available to downstream users.

Non-commodity-generating uses of our public lands have also increased steadily in recent decades. According to the Bureau of Economic Analysis, the outdoor recreation economy accounted for 2% ($373.7 billion) of gross domestic product in 2016, and the outdoor recreation economy is growing much faster than the overall economy (Bureau of Economic Analysis 2018,

p. 2). According to the Outdoor Industry Association, during 2017, outdoor recreation supported 7.6 million American jobs, $65.3 billion in federal tax revenue, and $59.2 billion in state and local tax revenue (Outdoor Industry Association 2017, p. 2). This means that more than two and a half times as many Americans are directly employed by hunting and fishing (483,000) than by oil and gas extraction (180,000) (Outdoor Industry Association 2017, p. 7). The implications are clear. Our public lands are a powerful engine for economic growth, and the evolution of values associated with the shift from Old West, to New West, to Next West will have profound distributional impacts.

As these numbers also suggest, more people are visiting our public lands than ever before. Funding for public land maintenance, however, has not kept pace with agency needs. The NPS estimates that it will require $10.93 billion to address the accumulated maintenance backlog. While the NPS backlog has received significant attention, other federal land management agencies face similar maintenance challenges. The USFS estimated its fiscal year (FY) 2016 backlog at $5.49 billion, most of which was for roads and buildings. The FY2016 FWS backlog was estimated at $1.40 billion, and the BLM backlog was estimated at $0.81 billion. In total, the four agencies that manage public lands in the United States face a maintenance backlog of over $18.6 billion, in large part because of decades of congressional funding shortfalls and because most of the revenue generated from our public lands is not reinvested in their management (Vincent et al. 2017, p. 22).

EVOLUTION AND TRANSFORMATION

The story of our public lands is the story of evolution and transformation. It is also the story of struggle between differing visions for our public lands. Laws enacted during the era of manifest destiny that followed the War of 1812 were intended to foster privatization and settlement of a seemingly endless frontier, secure territory against claims of foreign nations, and fuel economic development. As a nation, we succeeded on all fronts. While some have benefited handsomely from the bounty that our public lands can provide, others have found themselves at the mercy of what Charles Wilkinson calls "the lords of yesterday"—laws enacted in a different era and under imperatives that can seem counter to New West values (Wilkinson 1992).

Sometimes these laws create powerful incentives that entrench old ways of doing business and inhibit more progressive policies. Sometimes entrenched policies, like those favoring old-growth logging and coal mining, are displaced by new social norms and economic realities like endangered species protection and renewable energy development. To some, these are the logical outgrowth of societal change. But these changes can sometimes feel more revolutionary than evolutionary to communities that have grown up around promises, whether expressed or implied, of ready access to public lands and the resources they contain. The pain associated with change can be particularly acute for communities that fail to anticipate change.

And our nation has changed dramatically since its founding in 1776. At that time there were fewer than three million people in the United States (US Census Bureau 1949, p. 25), the western frontier began with the Appalachian Mountains, and Meriwether Lewis and William Clark had yet to map a route to the Pacific Ocean. The United States is now home to almost 330 million people, and the West is growing at twice the pace of the rest of our country. Many rural communities are in decline while western cities are among the fastest-growing communities in the country (US Census Bureau 1977, table 10; 2017). During the first decade of the twenty-first century, more than two million acres of natural areas in the West were lost to human development, with Wyoming and Utah experiencing the largest percentage change in area modified by human hands (Center for American Progress 2016).

The United States is also struggling to adapt to a changing climate, which is hitting western public land states especially hard. Western states are warming faster than the Lower 48 as a whole and are projected to experience increases in temperature, declining snowpack, and reduced streamflow over the coming decades. These changes will increase competition for finite water resources. These changes will also likely result in more frequent and severe wildfires that will in turn affect the vegetative communities and the wildlife habitat that they provide. Our changing climate illuminates the important role public lands play in protecting biodiversity, facilitating wildlife migration and dispersal, and adapting to changing realities. Uncertainty regarding future climatic conditions and their impact on public lands complicates the already enormously difficult job of public land management, and that is a job that increasingly must occur at a landscape scale and across agency boundaries.

It is, in many ways, a perfect storm. Unprecedented demands are being placed on our finite public lands by a rapidly growing population with an appetite for an ever-broadening suit of values. Public land management agencies, however, lack the resources needed to meet these challenges. These changes, and environmental laws that can complicate commodity production, have left a number of westerners feeling disenfranchised, and that disenfranchisement appears to be at the heart of a recent rebirth of the Sagebrush Rebellion.

As we look to the future of our public lands, we must recognize that, as Coggins (2008, p. 489) explains, "biological sciences cannot tell us how much Wilderness is enough, and economists cannot calculate whether the money spent to save bald eagles was worth it." We are faced with trade-offs that will define us as a society and determine the future that we will leave for those that follow.

Several lessons seem clear: the value of our public lands is much more than the sum total of their economic outputs. Public lands are home for diverse communities of Native Americans whose ties to the land run to time immemorial. For many of what our neighbors to the north would aptly call First Nations, the land defines who they are. We have seen the voices of Native Americans grow stronger as they fight projects like the Keystone XL Pipeline, lobby the White House to designate the Bears Ears National Monument, and sue when the next administration does away with those protections. Native Americans are also an important voice in wildlife management issues ranging from salmon to buffalo and almost everything else in between. No matter how these battles conclude, Native Americans are likely to emerge as a stronger and more determined voice on public land management issues.

Public lands helped define us as a pioneering nation that was, and remains, rich in opportunities. Public lands held the promise of a better life that propelled generations of Americans westward. Descendants of the pioneers have deep and abiding ties to the land, ties made stronger by generations of dependence upon its bounty. The latest generation of pioneers, now clad in Polartec and Gore-Tex, are staking their own claim to our finite public lands, and tourism-based economies are booming. Our public lands are loved, but they are at risk of being loved to death.

At a time when politics are becoming increasingly acrimonious, it is more important than ever to walk the proverbial mile in the shoes (or boots) of other public land users. Discontent appears to stem as much from the belief that one's voice is unheard or ignored as it does from the different visions for the future of a landscape that we all hold dear.

Change is natural, even if the pace of change occurring on public lands seems overwhelming. Our public lands are no longer a limitless supply of natural resources. As Keiter (2018, p. 138) noted, about half of the federal estate, roughly 310 million acres, has some protective status. In the Lower 48, approximately 146 million acres, or nearly 40% of federal lands, are under some form of protection. Some traditional uses of our public lands were displaced by these designations, and other uses may decline as societal values evolve and we rebalance uses to reflect these evolutionary changes. This will be painful for some. In the past, communities have too often failed to anticipate or adapt to changes that, in hindsight, were clearly inevitable. Hopefully, we can learn from the past and help communities transition to a more sustainable relationship with our public lands. If we fail to act proactively, if we allow communities to be dislocated by foreseeable changes, we will only cement the growing divide over the future of landscapes that help define us as a nation.

Legal Citations

1 Treaty between the United States and the French Republic, Apr. 30, 1803.

2 Joint Resolution for annexing Texas to the United States, Mar. 1, 1845, 5 Stat. 797.

3 Treaty with Great Britain in Regard to the Limits Westward of the Rocky Mountains, June 15, 1946, 9 Stat. 869.

4 Treaty of Peace, Friendship, Limits, and Settlement with the Republic of Mexico, Feb. 2, 1848, 9 Stat. 922.

5 Treaty with Russia for the Purchase of Alaska, Mar. 30, 1867, 15 Stat. 539.

6 Northwest Ordinance of 1787, 1 Stat. 51.

7 Utah School and Lands Exchange Act of 1998, H.R. Rep. No. 105-598 (June 24, 1998).

8 Forest Reserve Act of 1891, Mar. 3, 1891, 26 Stat. 1103; repealed by 90 Stat. 2791 (1976).

9 An Act Making Appropriations for Sundry Civil Expenses of the Government for the Fiscal Year Ending June Thirtieth, Eighteen Hundred and Ninety-Eight, and for Other Purposes, June 4, 1897, 30 Stat. 11, 35; codified at 16 U.S.C. § 475 (2012).

10 16 U.S.C. §§ 528-31.

11 16 U.S.C. §§ 1600-14.

12 16 U.S.C. § 531(a).

13 43 U.S.C. §§ 315-315n (as amended).

14 43 U.S.C. § 315.

15 43 U.S.C. §§ 1701-84.

16 16 U.S.C. § 668dd.

17 16 U.S.C. § 1.

18 16 U.S.C. §§ 1131-34c.

19 16 U.S.C. §§ 1531-41.

20 42 U.S.C. §§ 4321-4333.

21 16 U.S.C. § 1131(c).

22 43 U.S.C. § 1782(a).

23 16 U.S.C. § 1531(b).

24 15 U.S.C. § 1536(a)(2).

25 Seattle Audubon Society v. Moseley, 798 F. Supp. 1484, 1493–94 (W.D. Wash. 1992).

26 42 U.S.C. § 4332(2)(C).

27 Robertson v. Methow Valley Citizens Council, 490 U.S. 332, 350 (1989).

References

Bureau of Economic Analysis. 2018. "News Release: Outdoor Recreation Satellite Account: Prototype Statistics for 2012-2016." Press release, September 20, 2018.

Bureau of Land Management. 2018. *Public Land Statistics 2017*. Washington, DC: Bureau of Land Management, US Department of the Interior.

Center for American Progress. 2016. "The Disappearing West." Last updated May 17, 2016. https://disappearingwest.org.

Coggins, George Cameron. 2008. " 'Devolution' in Federal Land Law: Abdication by Any Other Name." *Hastings Environmental Law Journal* 14 (2008): 485.

Coggins, George Cameron, and Robert L. Glickman. 2010. *Public Natural Resources Law*. 2nd ed., vol. 1. Ann Arbor, MI: Thomson Reuters.

Gates, Paul W. 1968. *History of Public Land Law Development*. Washington, DC: Public Land Law Review Commission.

Headwaters Economics. 2019. "Economic Profile System." Accessed November 9, 2019. https://headwaterseconomics.org/tools/economic-profile-system/about/.

Hoover, Katie. 2018. *Federal Lands and Related Resources: Overview and Selected Issues for the 115th Congress*. CRS Report R43429. Washington, DC: Congressional Research Service.

Humphries, Marc. 2016. *U.S. Crude Oil and Natural Gas Production in Federal and Nonfederal Areas*. CRS Report R42432. Washington, DC: Congressional Research Service.

Keiter, Robert B. 2018. "Toward a National Conservation Network Act: Transforming Landscape Conservation on the Public Lands into Law." *Harvard Environmental Law Review* 42 (2018): 61-138.

Outdoor Industry Association. 2017. "The Outdoor Recreation Economy." Accessed November 9, 2019. https://outdoorindustry.org/wp-content/uploads/2017/04/OIA_RecEconomy_FINAL_Single.pdf.

US Census Bureau. 1949. *Historical Statistics of the United States 1789-1945: A Supplement to the Statistical Abstract of the United States*. Washington, DC: US Census Bureau, US Department of Commerce.

US Census Bureau. 1977. *Statistical Abstract of the United States 1977*. Washington, DC: US Census Bureau, US Department of Commerce.

US Census Bureau. 2017. *Annual Estimates of the Resident Population for the United States, Regions, States, and Puerto Rico: April 1, 2010 to July 1, 2016*. Nst-Est2016-01. Washington, DC: US Census Bureau, US Department of Commerce.

US Fish and Wildlife Service. 2019. "Short History of the Refuge System." Accessed November 9, 2019. www.fws.gov/refuges/history/over/over_hist-a_fs.html.

US Forest Service. 2014. "U.S. Forest Resource Facts and Historical Trends." Accessed March 9, 2020. https://www.fia.fs.fed.us/library/brochures/docs/2012/ForestFacts_1952-2012_English.pdf.

US Forest Service. 2019. "About the Agency." Accessed November 9, 2019. www.fs.fed.us/about-agency.

US Government Accountability Office. 2014. "National Environmental Policy Act." Accessed March 9, 2020. https://www.gao.gov/assets/670/662546.pdf.

Vincent, Carol Hardy, Laura A. Hanson, and Carla N. Argueta. 2017. *Federal Land Ownership: Overview and Data*. CRS Report R42346. Washington, DC: Congressional Research Service. https://fas.org/sgp/crs/misc/R42346.pdf.

Wilkinson, Charles F. 1992. *Crossing the Next Meridian: Land, Water, and the Future of the West*. Washington, DC: Island Press.

Chapter 3
Rangeland Policy and Management in a Changing West
Political Marginalization and a Crisis of Trust

MARK W. BRUNSON

On the night of July 4, 2018, an ill-advised Independence Day celebration ignited dry grass and shrubs in Martin Creek Canyon, 50 miles northeast of Winnemucca, Nevada. Six days later, National Aeronautics and Space Administration (NASA) satellites recorded that the Martin Fire, as it was now known, had grown to cover an area 57 miles long and 31 miles wide. It was the largest wildfire in the United States at the time, with 635 firefighters assigned to contain it. By August 2, 2018, when the Bureau of Land Management (BLM) declared the fire fully contained, it had burned an estimated 435,500 acres, or a little more than 680 square miles, almost all of it public land. No one was hurt and no inhabited structures were lost, but local ranchers who held permits to use the land lost cattle as well as forage needed to sustain their surviving livestock. Rural businesses lost income owing to power outages when wildfire interrupted transmission lines and when tourists canceled planned visits because of the fire and smoke (Rothberg 2018).

Lightning-sparked wildfires have always been part of the western US landscape (Wright and Bailey 1982). But wildfires larger than 1,000 acres have increased in frequency, size, and date of occurrence across the western United States since 1984 (Dennison et al. 2014). In the region known as the Great Basin—which covers most of far northeastern California, southern Idaho, southeastern Oregon, Nevada, and western Utah—these changes pose a threat to rangeland ecosystem health and human values. Because most Great Basin rangeland is owned and managed by the federal government, addressing the challenge of wildfire has become one of the region's most pressing and vexing public land policy challenges.

On a national scale, however, this challenge remains largely invisible. In the days that the Martin Fire was the nation's largest, covering an area more than half the size of the state of Rhode Island, it drew little national attention. No news of the huge blaze appeared in nationally circulated newspapers such as the *New York Times, Washington Post,* or *USA Today.* Although rangelands occur from Alaska to Florida, covering 761 million acres, or about 31% of the total US land area (Havstad et al. 2009), rangeland issues and events rarely penetrate the national consciousness.

This relative lack of visibility is reflected in federal policies that fail to account for rangeland contexts. In late August 2018 the Federal Emergency Management Agency (FEMA) denied the state of Nevada's request for a Fire Management Assistance Grant for recovery from the Martin Fire because it "did not threaten such destruction as would constitute a major disaster" (Spillman 2018). It is difficult for rangeland wildfires to qualify for federal assistance because they rarely meet the criterion of posing threats to large numbers of homes or improved property. More than 1,600 square miles of rangeland burned across all of Nevada in 2018, yet little help was available for businesses or individuals harmed by wildfire. By federal statute, those losses were not important enough to constitute "emergencies."

The lack of attention paid to rangeland issues exemplifies what Reynolds et al. (2007) called the "Dryland Development Paradigm." Seeking to explain why global desertification is a social issue as well as an environmental problem, the authors identified a "dryland syndrome" that explains why rangelands may be especially vulnerable to environmental shocks as well as social upheaval. Arid, semiarid, and dry subhumid landscapes not only receive less precipitation than other regions, but also the precipitation they do receive is more variable and less predictable. Soil fertility is often low, and soils are easily damaged by tillage. Human populations are sparser, more remote from markets, and more distant from the centers and priorities of decision makers (Reynolds et al. 2007). Not coincidentally, dryland (i.e., rangeland) populations are said to be among the most ecologically, socially, and politically marginalized populations on Earth (Khagram et al. 2003). While residents of rangeland regions in the highly developed United States are less vulnerable than others across the globe, their concerns nonetheless can be marginalized relative to their fellow citizens elsewhere. Accordingly, rangeland issues and concerns tend to gain less political attention, and policy interventions aimed at other regions can have unintended consequences for rangeland management.

This chapter explores historical factors that underlie the current situation of federal rangelands, as well as some major challenges facing rangeland management on those lands, especially but not limited to those influenced by climate change. These include environmentally detrimental land uses such as energy production and unregulated off-highway vehicle use, nonnative species invasions and their influence on wildfires and habitat loss, and disputes over grazing rights and local control of federal lands. I argue that factors of political and social marginalization tend to exacerbate those challenges, and current environmental politics and policies are not designed to mitigate them.

RANGELANDS IN THE UNITED STATES

Geography and History

Rangeland is a name given to lands managed primarily to maintain natural conditions, where vegetation is dominated by grasses, grasslike plants, forbs, or shrubs. Because they occur in arid and semiarid climates, rangelands are characterized by limited water and nutrients and low annual biomass production (Havstad et al. 2009). This definition, while seemingly narrow in scope, nonetheless encompasses a wide variety of landscapes, including shrublands, deserts, tundra, most wetlands, and some grasslands. Despite low biological productivity, rangelands have long been occupied by humans who depended upon them to provide forage for domestic livestock, habitat for wild game, and sources of edible wild plants. More recently, rangelands have also been recognized for their value as watersheds for rural and urban uses; sources of renewable and nonrenewable energy resources and minerals; settings for recreation activities; and habitat for diverse plants, insects, and animals.

Despite their contributions to lives and livelihoods, US rangelands historically have been considered less important or valuable than other land types. After Thomas Jefferson dispatched teams of explorers to learn about his newly acquired Louisiana Purchase, expedition mapmaker Edwin James reported that the region "is almost wholly unfit for cultivation, and of course, uninhabitable by a people depending upon agriculture for their subsistence. Although tracts of fertile land considerably extensive are occasionally to be met with, yet the scarcity of wood and water, almost uniformly prevalent, will prove an insuperable obstacle in the way of settling the country" (Meinig 1993, p. 76).

Soon pioneer settlers learned how to turn what James labeled as the "Great American Desert" into cropland. Thanks to the stimulus of the various Homestead Acts passed between 1862 and 1916, 1.6 million settlers acquired ownership of more than 270 million acres of what was previously government-held land (Porterfield 2004). Most of that acreage lay west of the Mississippi River, and most of it was rangeland. A stipulation of the Homestead Act was that the land had to be "improved"—which generally meant farming it, often with the aid of irrigation—and occupied for five years. This process continued through the end of the nineteenth century, and in Alaska well into the twentieth century, with homesteading theoretically still possible until the act was repealed with passage of the Federal Land Policy and Management Act of 1976 (FLPMA) (Fischman et al. 2014).

As the homesteading era ended, much of the federal estate remained unsettled because it was too dry, too cold, too rocky, or too marshy to serve as farmland or townsites. Of the unclaimed lands, those that held special scenic, recreational, scientific, or environmental value became the jurisdiction of the National Park Service, while outstanding wildlife habitats were the domain of the US Fish and Wildlife Service. The US Forest Service (USFS) was created to reserve lands that could serve as reliable sources of timber and water. Some of what remained was ultimately turned over to the Department of Defense for military training and testing purposes; the rest fell under the jurisdiction of the Bureau of Land Management (BLM), created in 1946 to administer the land primarily for livestock grazing, minerals extraction, and land transfers (Fischman et al. 2014). With passage of FLPMA thirty years later, the BLM shares with the Forest Service a legal mandate to manage the land for multiple uses. About 167 million acres of the BLM estate and 95 million acres of national forest are considered rangeland. Today, the states with the greatest proportion of land area in federal ownership are dominated by rangeland, while the states where rangeland was largely converted to cropland have some of the smallest proportions of federal land (table 3.1).

The Societal Context of Federal Rangelands

Upon settlement of the western range, towns and cities began to arise in the most hospitable locations, typically where streams provided reliable water sources. Rangeland cities such as Albuquerque, Denver, Las Vegas, Phoenix, and Salt Lake City attracted commerce and, of course, people. Later, scenic rangeland areas became home to those who settled in smaller cities like Bend,

Table 3.1. Proportions of Rangeland-Dominated States in Federal Ownership

State	Percentage That Is Rangeland
Western States	
Arizona	38.6%
California	45.8%
Colorado	35.9%
Idaho	61.6%
Montana	29.0%
Nevada	84.9%
New Mexico	34.7%
Oregon	52.9%
Utah	64.9%
Washington	28.5%
Wyoming	48.1%
Prairie States	
Iowa	0.3%
Kansas	0.5%
Nebraska	1.1%
North Dakota	3.9%
Oklahoma	1.6%
South Dakota	5.4%
Texas	1.8%
US total	27.4%

Source: Vincent et al. (2017)

Boise, Idaho Falls, or St. George for the dry climate and access to outdoor recreation and other amenities. In recent decades the fastest-growing states have tended to be those with large expanses of federal rangeland. While the US population as a whole has grown by 31% since 1990, the population of Arizona has grown by 94%, Colorado by 73%, Idaho by 74%, Utah by 80%, and Nevada by an astounding 254% (US Census Bureau 2018).

Despite this growth, the political importance of rangeland states has not grown proportionately. Excluding California, which has extensive tracts of rangeland in the eastern half of the state, the eight states of the Lower 48 with significant proportions of federal rangeland (Arizona, Colorado, Idaho, Nevada, New Mexico, Oregon, Utah, and Wyoming) account for 49 of the

538 electoral college votes, a bit more than 9%. Students at the nation's most elite academic institutions, which supply a disproportionate number of federal policymakers (Parmar 2008), rarely come from the interior western states (3.3% of the graduating class of 2021 at Harvard, 3.7% at Yale, and 3.0% at Princeton). Accordingly, it is less likely that decision makers will understand rangeland issues, or that those issues will gain prominence in nationwide political debates. Although California may seem like an exception, political trends within that state mirror those of the nation as a whole, sparking a secession movement in rural far northern and northeastern California endorsed by officials and residents of twenty-one counties who argue that locally important issues are ignored in a state where the policy debate is dominated by urban coastal politicians and concerns (Branson-Potts 2018).

Not all rangelands are in public ownership. Because the grasslands of the Great Plains proved fertile when irrigated, millions of acres of rangeland were plowed to grow grain crops and cotton. Millions more acres in those same states are managed as private pasturelands. When large numbers of farms failed during the Dust Bowl era of the 1920s and 1930s, the government reacquired some lands in the western Great Plains that eventually were designated as national grasslands managed by the US Forest Service (Duram 1995); however, these lands remain a small component of the federal estate.

Just as conversion to farmland added value to rangelands in the nineteenth and early twentieth century, so have other land-use conversions today. As urban populations have grown, vast expanses of privately owned rangeland have been converted to residential use in the sprawling suburbs of Denver, Las Vegas, Phoenix, Salt Lake City, and the cities of California. This urbanization, combined with the sparse settlement of rural areas in those states, has meant there are more metropolitan residents in the rangeland states of Arizona (94%), Nevada (90%), Oregon (91%), Utah (87%), and Washington (89%) than in the United States as a whole (86%) (US Census Bureau 2018). Over time the interests of those metropolitan areas likewise have diverged from those of their rural neighbors, causing marginalization at the state level as well.

CHALLENGES FOR FEDERAL RANGELAND MANAGEMENT AND POLICY

Land Uses and Impacts

Grazing management. Livestock grazing has long been a predominant use of public rangelands. Prior to passage of the Taylor Grazing Act in 1934, oversight of cattle and sheep grazing was virtually nonexistent, and over-grazing was a significant source of degradation and desertification (Kassas 1995). Even after the creation of the Bureau of Land Management twelve years later, livestock grazing had such primacy that the agency was sometimes derisively referred to as the Bureau of Livestock and Mining (Bradley and Ingram 1986). Over time, a system has emerged whereby the BLM issues leases and permits to ranchers who are bound by terms and conditions that specify when forage can be used, how many animals can graze in an allot-ment, how water and fence improvements must be maintained, and how to accommodate permitted uses. Permittees are charged a fee set annually under a formula established by Congress in 1986. The fee typically ranges between $1.35 and $2.00 per animal unit month, that is, the amount of forage that can be consumed by a cow-calf pair, a horse, or five sheep or goats in a month. The actual amount of grazing that occurs in a given year may be less than what is permitted depending on factors such as wildfire, drought, or market condi-tions. Leases cover a ten-year period and are renewable subject to an environ-mental assessment conducted under the National Environmental Policy Act (NEPA). As of October 2018, the BLM administers nearly 18,000 permits, mainly for cattle or sheep grazing, on more than 21,000 allotments, while the US Forest Service administers nearly 6,000 permits on national forests and grasslands. Some units of the National Park Service and US Fish and Wildlife Service also allow grazing, either to meet resource management objectives or to accommodate "grandfathered" uses that had been in existence prior to designation of a particular refuge or park unit.

The policy challenge for public land livestock grazing is balancing local economic benefits and cultural traditions with potential environmental costs on lands held in trust for all citizens. Environmental impacts can vary greatly depending on how carefully an allotment is managed or monitored, and upon environmental conditions affected by climate as well as vegetation type. In some places the ecological cost can be significant, especially in riparian areas along rangeland streams (Armour et al. 1994; Fleischner 1994). But impacts of overgrazing on federal land have decreased thanks to scientific grazing man-agement principles drawn from a century of rangeland research (Sayre 2017). Restoration efforts increasingly are implemented on federal lands, albeit with mixed success (Pilliod et al. 2017; Pyke et al. 2015). Environmental activ-ists often argue that the only solution to degradation is to remove cattle from the public range (Donahue 1999; Molvar 2018), but on lands historically grazed by large herbivores the removal of cattle can lead to significant problems as well, including loss of biodiversity and increased wildfire intensity (Papanastasis 2009). Accordingly, federal agencies instead seek to carefully regulate stocking levels, seasons of use, and intensity of grazing by livestock.

The effects of climate change on livestock use of federal rangelands are not yet well understood. Climate projections predict warmer, drier conditions in the southern Great Plains and Southwest, warmer and wetter conditions in the northern Great Plains, and warmer winters and summers in the Northwest and Great Basin with reduced snowpack (Briske et al. 2015). Vegetation changes including loss of forage due to climate change have already been observed in southern Arizona and New Mexico (Brown et al. 1997). In the public lands-dominated Southwest (including Arizona, Southern California, Nevada, New Mexico, and Utah), animal agriculture accounts for about one-third of total agricultural revenue (USDA National Agricultural Statistics Survey data; see Havstad et al. 2018), creating great pressure to maintain such uses, yet these lands can expect longer and more severe droughts in future decades.

Wildfire and invasive species. Wildfires pose many challenges for federal rangelands. Fires are growing larger, with few years that don't see at least one rangeland fire greater than 100,000 acres in size (Scasta et al. 2016). Financial costs of wildfire management also are skyrocketing, placing ever-increasing strain on agency budgets (Hand et al. 2016). Wildland fire suppression costs for the Forest Service alone topped $2.5 billion in 2017, forcing the agency to use millions of dollars that had been allocated to other programs. Congress addressed the fire funding issue in 2018 by a creating a fire suppression account that the Forest Service can draw upon according to each year's need (US Department of Agriculture 2018), but the effects of this change are not yet known.

Exacerbating the problem is the spread of invasive annual cheatgrass (*Bromus tectorum*), which now is pervasive across the western portion of the US rangeland region. Cheatgrass expansion has been linked to major increases in fire frequency (Balch et al. 2013; Bradley et al. 2018), as well as habitat degradation for wildlife species (Pyke et al. 2015; Wisdom and Chambers 2009). Nonnative species invasions pose enormous economic and environmental costs nationwide (Pimentel et al. 2005), and public rangelands are no exception. DiTomaso (2000) estimated that more than three hundred nonnative weed species had become established on rangelands. Policy fixes have largely involved efforts to prevent weed introduction (e.g., regulations requiring backcountry horse outfitters to use certified weed-free feed) as well as supporting research and development of biological control options.

There are clear connections between the increase in large wildfires in western rangelands, spread of invasive annual grasses, and climate change. Climate scientists predict that the potential for large fires will grow throughout the West (Barbero et al. 2015). Indeed, climate change is already changing rangeland ecosystems. Since 1985 the high deserts of the Great Basin and Columbia Plateau have warmed by as much as 1.4°C, and temperatures are predicted to continue increasing, especially in winter and at night (Snyder et al. 2019). Wildfire seasons likely will come earlier in the year and last longer, likely increasing the total rangeland acreage burned annually. Data from Nevada, New Mexico, Oklahoma, and Wyoming demonstrate that the worst conditions come when a hot, dry year follows a wetter year (Scasta et al. 2016), such as was experienced in Nevada and the Great Basin in 2018.

Wild horses and burros. One of the most vexing challenges for public rangelands is the management of wild horses and burros. Horses and burros were introduced to the North American continent by Spanish explorers and missionaries beginning in the 1500s, and escapees soon established free-roaming herds on western rangelands. Responding to public concern about mistreatment and exploitation of wild horse herds, Congress passed the Wild Free-Roaming Horses and Burros Act in 1971 to protect wild equids on BLM and Forest Service land. Agencies designated horse management areas (HMAs) and set appropriate management levels (AMLs) of horses or burros that could be sustainably maintained on each HMA. As of March 1, 2018, wild horse and burro populations on BLM lands exceeded AML in nine of the ten states where they are found. Overall, the agency estimated that 81,951 horses and burros ranged on BLM land, whereas the AML was calculated at 26,690 (Bureau of Land Management 2018). Overpopulation causes considerable damage to vegetation and soils, as well as to seeps and springs important for other rangeland wildlife (Davies et al. 2014). Climate change is likely to exacerbate those impacts as droughts become more frequent and water scarcer owing to diminished winter snowpack. Because federal law prohibits lethal control of horses except where euthanization is needed for animal welfare purposes, the primary management tool is periodic roundups. Private citizens may adopt wild horses under certain conditions, but most "surplus" animals are shipped after capture to BLM-leased pastures on private lands. As of this writing, there were more than 45,000 horses and burros in BLM holding facilities, where caring for the animals costs nearly $50 million annually (Frey and Thacker 2018).

Energy development. Among potentially damaging land uses, energy development often draws public attention. US energy production is increasing, much of it coming from private rangelands. Meanwhile, oil and gas production on federal lands has increased by 60% over the past decade, and 90% of BLM land is open to oil and gas leasing and development. Between 2009 and 2016, bids were received for new leases on eight million acres of BLM land, although only about half of those acres are in production (Center for Western Priorities 2017). The highly visible footprint of energy production includes not only well pads but also roads and pipelines, which can fragment wildlife habitats (Brittingham et al. 2014). Among renewable energy sources, wind and biofuels production from rangelands is centered on private lands of the Great Plains, but US solar energy potential is greatest in Arizona, southeastern California, southern Nevada, and New Mexico, where sites on federal land have been developed or are under consideration. Most utility-scale solar installations occur on shrublands and deserts, often near protected areas, leading to land cover changes that can negatively affect the ability of those lands to support native plants and wildlife (Hernandez et al. 2015).

The climate change impacts on energy production occurring on public land are largely unknown. Unconventional fossil fuel development, especially natural gas production using hydraulic fracturing, requires large amounts of water (Kreuter et al. 2016), which could be in more limited supply owing to climate change. Knowledge is limited about how to restore rangeland energy production zones after production ceases, and the eventuality of climate change only increases that uncertainty (Winkler et al. 2018).

Motorized recreation. Another rangeland use posing challenges for federal land policy and management is off-highway vehicle recreation. Both the BLM and Forest Service have expressed concern about the increase in this use and its impacts (Cordell et al. 2005). Cordell also estimated that 18.6% of Americans age sixteen or older participated in off-highway vehicle recreation in 1999-2004. While most activity occurs on designated trails and improved gravel roads, there also is considerable overland use, with potential impacts to soils, vegetation, and wildlife (Ouren et al. 2007). Federal land managers in recent years have paid more attention to off-highway vehicle management, creating new designated-use areas while closing the most vulnerable environments. Research suggests that these efforts may be having desired effects on reducing the negative impacts of this form of recreation (Custer et al. 2017). As with energy production, climate change is more likely to affect efforts to restore landscapes degraded by off-highway vehicles, although use itself may decline owing to more frequent extreme weather events (Evans 2019) as well as potential higher expenses if climate mitigation policies are adopted that increase the cost of fuel.

Policy Disputes over Rangeland Uses

Despite a history of being largely unwanted, federal rangelands have values that increasingly are being recognized (Brunson 2014; Havstad et al. 2007). With growing recognition of rangeland values comes greater competition among stakeholders. Should livestock grazing be the predominant use of federal rangelands, as was the case in the twentieth century, or should policies shift to favor amenity uses and biodiversity protection? How should federal policy address the growing demand to use public lands for both renewable and nonrenewable energy production? How should federal land management address environmental changes due to climate change, wildfire, and nonnative invasive species? And whose interests should be best served on rangelands that are held in trust for all Americans but are most heavily enjoyed and depended upon by local residents?

For decades, federal rangeland policy was largely directed by a small circle of ranchers, agency specialists, and western members of Congress (Dana and Fairfax 1980). As attention to environmental impacts grew nationwide in the 1960s and 1970s, rangeland issues remained a low priority as activists focused on national forest timber harvest, air and water pollution, and wilderness protection. By the 1990s, however, some activists had turned their attention to public rangelands in a movement they called "Cattle Free by '93" (Starrs 1994). In the first (and thus far only) effort to determine how Americans as a whole view the management of publicly owned rangelands, Brunson and Steel (1994, 1996) conducted three parallel surveys: telephone surveys of Oregon residents and nationwide, and a mail survey of residents in seventeen Oregon counties where livestock grazing is a traditional and economically important land use. They found that attitudes generally were rooted in a limited understanding of rangelands and their management, especially among national and urban Oregon respondents. A clear dichotomy existed between attitudes of rural westerners and those of urban and suburban residents. Urban residents were more likely to support preservationist approaches to range management and less likely to support the multiple-use approach enshrined in federal law. Moreover, this dichotomy was most pronounced among respondents from urban parts of the West. Similar rural-urban differences have been found in subsequent surveys in parts of the Great Basin (Gordon et al. 2014; Shindler et al. 2011).

The urban-rural divide is exemplified in disputes about wild horses and burros. The fate of wild horses is of interest to a diverse range of stakeholders, including horse advocates and animal rights organizations on one side, and ranchers, hunters, and some environmental groups on the other. Scientific evidence suggests that horse populations are far above carrying capacity, with significant negative environmental costs as well as costs to horse health and survival (Davies et al. 2014). Yet members of the general public view the horse issue through a different lens, shaped by deep-seated and positive cultural norms regarding horses as a species, as well as distrust of land managers (Beever et al. 2018). The benefits of knowing that horses can roam free on public lands accrue mainly to these citizens, most of whom are urban residents, while the negative impacts are borne largely by rural residents as well as by the rangelands themselves.

In the absence of nationwide interest in or knowledge about rangeland issues, both among the public and by policymakers, current debates about the future of federal rangelands largely reflect the divergent concerns of urban and rural westerners. Political marginalization remains a factor even when the debate shifts from the national to regional scales. But debates over federal policy typically cannot be resolved at the regional level because they require acts of Congress. Instead, efforts to influence rangeland policy typically follow one of three paths. First, decisions may be made within federal bureaucracies. Especially in the Department of Interior, appointees to high-level positions typically are elected officials in the president's party from western states. In the absence of strong interest from Congress or presidential administrations, decisions about rangeland policy and management are often made at the cabinet department level (Davis 2001). An inevitable result is that when a new political party ascends to the White House, decisions made at the cabinet level usually reverse previous decisions by appointees of the opposing party, creating a whiplash effect that can infuriate rural westerners whose livelihoods depend on rangelands.

Second, debates can occur at the state level. In recent years, such debates have led—especially in interior western states—to increasing calls by conservative-leaning legislatures and governors for transfer of federal lands to state control (Wayland et al. 2018). State officials argue that because the Constitution does not mention public lands—indeed, the nation's founders could not have imagined the need for government administration of lands unsuited for farming or commercial development—the administration of such lands must be left to the states as stipulated in the Tenth Amendment. They also argue that because states are closer to the land itself, they are more capable of managing the land effectively. Conversely, opponents of federal-to-state land transfers argue that the federal government is in a better financial position to manage the land—especially when fire suppression can cost half of an agency's budget—and that states will be forced to sell off land to meet budgetary needs, cutting off the public's access.

Finally, citizens displeased by the policy outcomes in Washington, DC, and state capitals turn to the courts to try to block policy decisions. In conservative states such as Utah or Idaho where one party dominates legislative politics, the voices of those who oppose extractive and commodity uses of public lands are disenfranchised. Groups like the Idaho-based Western Watersheds Project have been active in initiating legal action to block decisions on rangelands they see as intended to sustain livestock grazing on public lands. Yet, unlike in the case of federal timber harvest, such efforts so far have been largely ineffective in dislodging the entrenched system of grazing permits that has existed since the mid-twentieth century (Wood 2006).

Underlying all three of these policy paths is a gradual but pervasive dissolution of trust in natural resource management institutions (Stern and Baird 2015). Trust in all manner of authoritative institutions has been declining in the early twenty-first century (Tyler 2016), but especially in institutions of the federal government (Cooper 2018). When trust in rangeland management agencies decreases, so do positive attitudes toward the policies and practices of those agencies. Gordon et al. (2014) compared beliefs about the acceptability of fuels management practices on public rangelands among Great Basin respondents surveyed in 2006 and again in 2010, finding that by far the best predictor of change in beliefs was trust in agencies' ability to safely and effectively implement the practices. Trust levels rose among urban populations while declining among rural residents, possibly owing to the political shift that occurred when the Republican administration of George W. Bush was replaced by the Democratic administration of Barack Obama.

CONCLUSIONS AND IMPLICATIONS

Reynolds et al. (2007) proposed that rangelands and their residents are marginalized within larger national contexts because rangelands tend to be less biologically and economically productive, and their human populations sparser and remote from political power centers. While the Dryland Development Paradigm was applied to developing nations, similar phenomena play out in policy disputes over federal rangelands. Resource uses often accrue benefits to persons living in urban areas far from the western range, whether those benefits are largely economic as in the case of energy development, or appreciative and symbolic as in the case of wild horse and burro management. In turn, residents of western rangeland regions can become disaffected by the perception of marginalization, leading to increasingly rancorous disputes as well as efforts to wrest control of rangelands from Washington, DC, through various means. The question remains: Can policy mechanisms reduce marginalization by empowering local interests, without sacrificing the general public's interests in land held in trust for all Americans?

The answer may lie in policies that encourage localized flexibility in solutions to rangeland challenges while maintaining federal control over the lands themselves. Proposed methods for ameliorating the challenges to federal rangeland management require the improved use of social-ecological systems frameworks (Bestelmeyer and Briske 2012; Brunson 2012; Hruska et al. 2017). Such approaches employ scientific analysis, stakeholder engagement, and agency expertise to focus on how social and political components of ecosystems interact with ecological components at multiple scales. Institutional flexibility, as opposed to rigid laws and policies applied uniformly across the nation, can promote adaptive management and foster resilience (Charnley et al. 2018). Because loss of trust underlies many disputes over federal rangelands, resilient policy mechanisms are needed that can maintain or even build trust (Stern and Baird 2015). Participatory approaches to problem solving and knowledge sharing, which build trust through frequent social interaction and mutual respect, are more likely to support sustainability and system resilience (Charnley et al. 2018).

This is especially important as rangelands are increasingly affected by climate change. Havstad et al. (2018) argue that creative livestock grazing strategies—for example, shifting to more drought-adapted breeds of cattle—may be feasible to adapt to climate change in the Southwest, but this can occur only through carefully applied adaptive management. Because impacts of climate change are likely to differ geographically, it is unlikely that national-scale policies can effectively facilitate the sort of varied adaptation strategies that can accommodate the needs and capacities of livestock operators (Briske et al.

2015). Such strategies must also consider geographically varying social contexts, such as the degree to which ranchers can find alternative forage from nonfederal sources, as well as pressure to use grazed lands for recreation and other appreciative activities. Similar approaches may be feasible for addressing disputes over other land uses. Such efforts are novel, and likely many will fail or fall short of expectations, but it is clear that traditional policies have not been able to address the growing challenges confronting the management of western public rangelands.

References

Armour, Carl, Don Duff, and Wayne Elmore. 1994. "The Effects of Livestock Grazing on Western Riparian and Stream Ecosystem." *Fisheries* 19(9): 9-12.

Balch, Jennifer K., Bethany A. Bradley, Carla M. D'Antonio, and José Gomez-Dans. 2013. "Introduced Annual Grass Increase Regional Fire Activity across the Arid Western USA (1980-2009)." *Global Change Biology* 19(1): 173-183.

Barbero, Renaud, John T. Abatzoglou, Narasimhan K. Larkin, Crystal A. Kolden, and Brian Stocks. 2015. "Climate Change Presents Increased Potential for Very Large Fires in the Contiguous United States." *International Journal of Wildland Fire* 24(7): 892-899.

Beever, Erik A., Lynn Huntsinger, and Steven L. Petersen. 2018. "Conservation Challenges Emerging from Free-Roaming Horse Management: A Vexing Social-Ecological Mismatch." *Biological Conservation* 226: 321-328.

Bestelmeyer, Brandon T., and David D. Briske. 2012. "Grand Challenges for Resilience-Based Management of Rangelands." *Rangeland Ecology and Management* 65(6): 654-663.

Bradley, Bethany A., Caroline A. Curtis, Emily J. Fusco, John T. Abatzoglou, Jennifer K. Balch, Sepideh Dadashi, and Mao-Ning Tuanmu. 2018. "Cheatgrass (*Bromus tectorum*) Distribution in the Intermountain Western United States and Its Relationship to Fire Frequency, Seasonality, and Ignitions." *Biological Invasions* 20(6): 1493-1506.

Bradley, Dorotha M., and Helen M. Ingram. 1986. "Science vs. the Grass Roots: Representation in the Bureau of Land Management." *Natural Resources Journal* 26(3): 493-518.

Branson-Potts, Hailey. 2018. "In California's Rural, Conservative North, There Are Big Dreams for Cleaving the State." *Los Angeles Times*, March 17, 2018.

Briske, David D., Linda A. Joyce, H. Wayne Polley, Joel R. Brown, Klaus Wolter, Jack A. Morgan, Bruce A. McCarl, and Derek W. Bailey. 2015. "Climate-Change Adaptation on Rangelands: Linking Regional Exposure with Diverse Adaptive Capacity." *Frontiers in Ecology and the Environment* 13(5): 249-256.

Brittingham, Margaret C., Kelly O. Maloney, Aïda M. Farag, David D. Harper, and Zachary H. Bowen. 2014. "Ecological Risks of Shale Oil and Gas Development to Wildlife, Aquatic Resources, and Their Habitats." *Environmental Science and Technology* 48(19): 11,034-11,047.

Brown, James H., Thomas J. Valone, and Charles G. Curtin. 1997. "Reorganization of an Arid Ecosystem in Response to Recent Climate Change." *Proceedings of the National Academy of Sciences* 94(18): 9729-9733.

Brunson, Mark W. 2012. "The Elusive Promise of Social-Ecological Approaches to Rangeland Management." *Rangeland Ecology and Management* 65(6): 632-637.

Brunson, Mark W. 2014. "Unwanted No More: Land Use, Ecosystem Services, and Opportunities for Resilience in Human-Influenced Shrublands." *Rangelands* 36(2): 5-11.

Brunson, Mark W., and Brent S. Steel. 1994. "Public Attitudes toward Federal Rangeland Management." *Rangelands* 16(2): 77-81.

Brunson, Mark W., and Brent S. Steel. 1996. "Sources of Variation in Attitudes and Beliefs about Federal Rangeland Management." *Journal of Range Management* 49(1): 69-75.

Bureau of Land Management. 2018. "Wild Horse and Burro Program." Accessed November 11, 2019. https://www.blm.gov/programs/wild-horse-and-burro.

Center for Western Priorities. 2017. "The Oil and Gas Leasing Process on U.S. Public Lands." Accessed November 11, 2019. http://westernpriorities.org/issues/drilling-on-public-lands/.

Charnley, Susan, Hannah Gosnell, Kendra L. Wendel, Mary M. Rowland, and Michael J. Wisdom. 2018. "Cattle Grazing and Fish Recovery on US Federal Lands: Can Social-Ecological Systems Science Help?" *Frontiers in Ecology and the Environment* 16(S1).

Cooper, Joseph. 2018. *Congress and the Decline of Public Trust.* New York: Routledge.

Cordell, H. Ken, Carter J. Betz, Gary Green, and Matt Owens. 2005. *Off-Highway Vehicle Recreation in the United States, Regions and States: A National Report from the National Survey on Recreation and the Environment (NSRE).* Asheville, NC: US Forest Service, Southern Research Station. https://www.srs.fs.usda.gov/pubs/ja/ja_cordell013.pdf.

Custer, Nathan A., Lesley A. DeFalco, Kenneth E. Nussear, and Todd C. Esque. 2017. "Drawing a Line in the Sand: Effectiveness of Off-Highway Vehicle Management in California's Sonoran Desert." *Journal of Environmental Management* 193: 448-457.

Dana, Samuel Trask, and Sally K. Fairfax. 1980. *Forest and Range Policy, Its Development in the United States.* 2nd ed. New York: McGraw-Hill.

Davies, Kirk W., Gail Collins, and Chad S. Boyd. 2014. "Effects of Feral Free-Roaming Horses on Semi-Arid Rangeland Ecosystems: An Example from the Sagebrush Steppe." *Ecosphere* 5(10): 1-14.

Davis, Charles. 2001. "Politics and Public Rangeland Policy." In *Western Public Lands and Environmental Politics*, edited by Charles Davis, 87-110. Boulder, CO: Westview Press.

Dennison, Philip E., Simon C. Brewer, James D. Arnold, and Max A. Moritz. 2014. "Large Wildfire Trends in the Western United States, 1984-2011." *Geophysical Research Letters* 41(8): 2928-2933.

DiTomaso, Joseph M. 2000. "Invasive Weeds in Rangelands: Species, Impacts, and Management." *Weed Science* 48(2): 255-265.

Donahue, Debra L. 1999. *The Western Range Revisited: Removing Livestock from Public Lands to Conserve Native Biodiversity.* Norman: University of Oklahoma Press.

Duram, Leslie A. 1995. "The National Grasslands: Past, Present and Future Land Management Issues." *Rangelands* 17(2): 35-42.

Evans, Gary W. 2019. "Projected Behavioral Impacts of Global Climate Change." *Annual Review of Psychology* 70: 449-474. https://doi.org/10.1146/annurev-psych-010418-103023.

Fischman, Robert L., George C. Coggins, Charles F. Wilkinson, and John D. Leshy. 2014. *Federal Public Land and Resources Law.* 7th ed. New York: Foundation Press.

Fleischner, Thomas L. 1994. "Ecological Costs of Livestock Grazing in Western North America." *Conservation Biology* 8(3): 629-644.

Frey, Nicki, and Eric Thacker. 2018. *Wild Horses and Burros: An Overview.* Utah State University Extension Factsheet. Logan: Utah State University, February 2018. https://digitalcommons.usu.edu/cgi/viewcontent.cgi?article=2852&context=extension_curall.

Gordon, Ryan, Mark W. Brunson, and Bruce Shindler. 2014. "Acceptance, Acceptability, and Trust for Sagebrush Restoration Options in the Great Basin: A Longitudinal Perspective." *Rangeland Ecology and Management* 67(5): 573-583.

Hand, Michael S., Matthew P. Thompson, and David E. Calkin. 2016. "Examining Heterogeneity and Wildfire Management Expenditures Using Spatially and Temporally Descriptive Data." *Journal of Forest Economics* 22: 80-102.

Havstad, Kris M., Joel R. Brown, Richard Estell, Emile Elias, Albert Rango, and Caiti Steele. 2018. "Vulnerabilities of Southwestern U.S. Rangeland-Based Animal Agriculture to Climate Change." *Climatic Change* 148(3): 371-386.

Havstad, Kris M., Debra P. C. Peters, Rhonda Skaggs, Joel Brown, Brandon Bestelmeyer, Ed Fredrickson, Jeffrey Herrick, and Jack Wright. 2007. "Ecological Services to and from Rangelands of the United States." *Ecological Economics* 64(2): 261-268.

Havstad, Kris, et al. 2009. "The Western United States Rangelands: A Major Resource." In *Grassland: Quietness and Strength for a New American Agriculture*, edited by W. F. Wedin and S. L. Fales, 75-94. Madison, WI: American Society of Agronomy.

Hernandez, Rebecca R., Madison K. Hoffacker, Michelle L. Murphy-Mariscal, Grace C. Wu, and Michael F. Allen. 2015. "Solar Energy Development Impacts on Land Cover Change and Protected Areas." *Proceedings of the National Academy of Sciences* 112(44): 13,579-13,584.

Hruska, Tracy, Lynn Huntsinger, Mark Brunson, Wenjun Li, Nadine Marshall, José L. Oviedo, and Hilary Whitcomb. 2017. "Rangelands as Social-Ecological Systems." In *Rangeland Systems: Processes, Management and Challenge*, edited by David D. Briske, 263-302. Cham, Switzerland: Springer Open.

Kassas, Mohammed. 1995. "Desertification: A General Review." *Journal of Arid Environments* 30(2): 115-128.

Khagram, Sanjeev, William Clark, and Dana Firas Reed. 2003. "From the Environment and Human Security to Sustainable Security and Development." *Journal of Human Development* 4(2): 289-313.

Kreuter, Urs P., et al. 2016. "State of Knowledge about Energy Development Impacts on North American Rangelands: An Integrative Approach." *Journal of Environmental Management* 180: 1-9.

Meinig, Donald W. 1993. *The Shaping of America: A Geographical Perspective on 500 Years of History*. Vol. 2, *Continental America, 1800-1867*. New Haven, CT: Yale University Press.

Molvar, Erik. 2018. "Livestock Grazing on Federal Public Lands Is a Privilege—Not a Right." *The Hill*, April 22, 2018. https://thehill.com/opinion/energy-environment/384270-livestock-grazing-on-federal-public-lands-is-a-privilege-not-a.

Ouren, Douglas S., et al. 2007. *Environmental Effects of Off-Highway Vehicles on Bureau of Land Management Lands: A Literature Synthesis, Annotated Bibliographies, Extensive Bibliographies, and Internet Resources*. US Geological Survey Open File Report 2007-1353. Reston, VA: US Geological Survey.

Papanastasis, Vasilios P. 2009. "Restoration of Degraded Grazing Lands through Grazing Management: Can It Work?" *Restoration Ecology* 17(4): 441-445.

Parmar, Inderjeet. 2008. "A Neo-Conservative-Dominated US Foreign Policy Establishment?" In *United States Foreign Policy and National Identity in the 21st Century*, edited by Kenneth Christie, 37-49. New York: Routledge.

Pilliod, David S., Justin L. Welty, and Gordon R. Toevs. 2017. "Seventy-Five Years of Vegetation Treatments on Public Rangelands in the Great Basin of North America." *Rangelands* 39(1): 1-9.

Pimentel, David, Rodolfo Zuniga, and Doug Morrison. 2005. "Update on the Environmental and Economic Costs Associated with Alien-Invasive Species in the United States." *Ecological Economics* 52(3): 273-288.

Porterfield, Jason. 2004. *The Homestead Act of 1862: A Primary Source History of the Settlement of the American Heartland in the Late 19th Century*. New York: Rosen.

Pyke, David A., et al. 2015. *Restoration Handbook for Sagebrush Steppe Ecosystems with Emphasis on Greater Sage-Grouse Habitat—Part 1. Concepts for Understanding and Applying Restoration*. US Geological Survey Circular 1416. Reston, VA: US Geological Survey.

Reynolds, James F., et al. 2007. "Global Desertification: Building a Science for Dryland Development." *Science* 316(5826): 847-851.

Rothberg, Daniel. 2018. "'It's Gone, It's Gone': Nation's Largest Wildfire in Nevada Devastates Ranches, Sage Grouse." *Nevada Independent,* July 12, 2018. https://thenevadaindependent.com/article/its-gone-its-gone-nations-largest-wildfire-in-nevada-devastates-ranches-sage-grouse.

Sayre, Nathan. 2017. *The Politics of Scale: A History of Rangeland Science.* Chicago: University of Chicago Press.

Scasta, John D., John R. Weir, and Michael C. Stambaugh. 2016. "Droughts and Wildfires in Western U.S. Rangelands." *Rangelands* 38(4): 197-203.

Shindler, Bruce, Ryan Gordon, Mark W. Brunson, and Christine Olsen. 2011. "Public Perceptions of Sagebrush Ecosystem Management in the Great Basin." *Rangeland Ecology and Management* 64(4): 335-343.

Snyder, Keirith A., Louisa Evers, Jeanne C. Chambers, Jason Dunham, John B. Bradford, and Michael E. Loik. 2019. "Effects of Changing Climate on the Hydrological Cycle in Cold Desert Ecosystems of the Great Basin and Columbia Plateau." *Rangeland Ecology and Management* 72(1): 1-12. https://www.sciencedirect.com/science/article/pii/S1550742418302355.

Spillman, Benjamin. 2018. "Wildfire Ravaged Remote Nevada Communities—Then FEMA Rejected Aid Request." *Reno Gazette Journal,* August 30, 2018. https://www.rgj.com/story/life/outdoors/2018/08/30/fema-rejects-nevada-fire-relief-request-heller-masto-amodei-ask-why/1145673002/.

Starrs, Paul. 1994. "'Cattle Free by '93' and the Imperatives of Environmental Radicalism." *Ubique* 14: 2-8.

Stern, Marc J., and Timothy D. Baird. 2015. "Trust Ecology and the Resilience of Natural Resource Management Institutions." *Ecology and Society* 20(2): 14.

Tyler, Tom R. 2016. "Trust in the Twenty-First Century." In *Interdisciplinary Perspectives on Trust,* edited by Ellie Shockley, Tess M. S. Neal, Lisa M. PytlikZillig, and Brian H. Bornstein, 203-215. Cham, Switzerland: Springer.

US Census Bureau. 2018. "Population and Housing Unit Estimates Database." Accessed November 12, 2019. https://www.census.gov/programs-surveys/popest/data/data-sets.html.

US Department of Agriculture. 2018. "Secretary Perdue Applauds Fire Funding Fix in Omnibus." Accessed November 11, 2019. https://www.usda.gov/media/press-releases/2018/03/23/secretary-perdue-applauds-fire-funding-fix-omnibus.

Vincent, Carol Hardy, Laura A. Hanson, and Carla N. Argueta. 2017. *Federal Land Ownership: Overview and Data.* CRS Report R42346. Washington, DC: Congressional Research Service. https://fas.org/sgp/crs/misc/R42346.pdf.

Wayland, Tyler, Lisa West, Jose Mata, and Benjamin L. Turner. 2018. "Why Are Proposed Public Land Transfers a Source of Extreme Conflict and Resistance?" *Rangelands* 40(2): 53-64.

Winkler, Daniel E., et al. 2018. "Beyond Traditional Ecological Restoration on the Colorado Plateau." *Restoration Ecology* 26(6): 1055-1060. https://doi.org/10.1111/rec.12876.

Wisdom, Michael J., and Jeanne C. Chambers. 2009. "A Landscape Approach for Ecologically Based Management of Great Basin Shrublands." *Restoration Ecology* 17(5): 740-749.

Wood, Robert S. 2006. "The Dynamics of Incrementalism: Subsystems, Politics, and Public Lands." *Policy Studies Journal* 34(1): 1-16.

Wright, Henry A., and Arthur W. Bailey. 1982. *Fire Ecology: United States and Southern Canada.* New York: Wiley-Interscience.

Part II

FOREST, WILDFIRE, AND WATER

Chapter 4

Professionalism versus Politics

The Century-Long Battle over National Forest Policy

TOM M. KOONTZ AND CHRISTEAN JENKINS

INTRODUCTION

Professionalism in government administration is the idea that government employees will apply their expert knowledge and skills neutrally in the face of competing interests. Professionalism has long had an uneasy relationship with the rough-and-tumble world of politics. The US Constitution allows the president to appoint officers to help execute the laws. This power of appointment came to be known as the spoils system ("to the victor go the spoils"), after newly elected President Andrew Jackson replaced a large number of federal agency employees with his supporters in 1829. Under the spoils system, rather than neutral application of the law, personnel serving in the executive branch support the president's political agenda.

But staffing government agencies with political supporters rather than trained professionals can make agencies less competent. This was particularly problematic as industrialization and modernization in the United States made administration tasks more specialized and required particular skill sets. By the late nineteenth century, calls for reform led to the passage of the Pendleton Civil Service Reform Act. This law created the US Civil Service Commission to establish rules for merit-based hiring and firing, and it allowed the president to decide which positions would be subject to the act. Initially, only 10% of federal agency positions were covered, but this was an important first step in creating the professional civil service we see today (Our Documents 2019).

As the Pendleton Act was starting to take hold, the US federal government was setting aside millions of acres of forested land in the West, demarcating it in forest reserves rather than transferring it to private ownership. The spoils system meant that administrative positions in the bureaucracy were filled not by professional experts based on merit, but by supporters of winning candidates based on loyalty. As McCarthy (1992, p. 187) noted, timber agents in charge of managing the forest reserves were "either spoilsmen or appointees of spoilsmen—watchmakers, bookkeepers, veterinarians, saloon operators, protegees of eastern party bosses—whose primary goal was personal gain and not forest protection."

Criticisms of the spoils system, and the power wielded by political party leaders and corporations, grew into the Progressive reform movement at the dawn of the twentieth century. Reformers championed direct democracy (including citizen initiatives and the election of US senators), breaking up corporate monopolies, and professionalization of management. These causes were epitomized in two individuals whose efforts would change the trajectory of federal forest management for the next century, Theodore Roosevelt and Gifford Pinchot. These men put in motion a long-standing tension between professionalism and politics that is visible today, even as prominent forest issues have grown from timber harvesting and fires to include environmental protection and global climate change.

To understand the tension between professionalism and politics in the context of public forest policy, we begin with the origin of public forest lands and the agency charged with managing most of them, the US Forest Service. A brief history of the agency and its management of national forests describes the creation of these forests for conservation, including the role of fire in garnering political support while promoting professional management. The Forest Service grew and evolved its professional forestry practices to address increasing demands for timber and other uses following World War II. But by the end of the twentieth century, the traditionally timber-dominant focus of national forest policy had given way, through the politics of lawmaking and litigation, to ecosystem management. More recently, fire and climate change challenges have highlighted complementarities and tensions between professionalism and politics.

CREATION OF NATIONAL FORESTS FOR CONSERVATION

Following US independence in 1776, the young nation began westward expansion through wars, treaties, and land purchases. As soon as these lands were acquired, efforts were underway to transfer them out of the public domain and into private ownership. National leaders valued the revenue that land sales could provide for the government. In addition, putting acreage into private hands promoted economic development and western settlement. Starting in 1862, several laws created programs to give or sell land to settlers who promised to inhabit, irrigate, or otherwise improve it. The most famous of these, the Homestead Act of 1862, granted 160 acres to any citizen willing to settle the land and cultivate it for at least five years. Nearly 300 million acres were transferred under this law, mostly in the eastern United States, where fertile lands made 160 acres sufficient for successful farming (Cubbage et al. 2017). Larger allocations were made in the arid West under laws such as the Desert Land Sales Act. Other laws granted land to railroad companies in exchange for building tracks across the continent. Finally, states received a portion of federal lands within their borders at statehood. Over the years, settlers and railroad companies received title to many western lands viewed as favorable for trade and settlement, yet hundreds of millions of acres remained unclaimed.

As the nineteenth century drew to a close, there was growing concern that too much land was ending up in the hands of large corporate syndicates and monopolies rather than yeoman farmers. Timber operators had practiced "cut and run" logging for decades, leaving unproductive, denuded landscapes in their wake. Writers such as George Perkins Marsh identified environmental harms, and concern grew that the country would face severe shortages of wood. Areas east of the Mississippi River saw their forest cover reduced from 70% to 20% (MacCleery 2011). The Progressive reform movement was raising awareness of this and other dangers of unbridled capitalism. In response, Congress passed the General Revision Act of 1891, authorizing the president to set apart and reserve forest land in the public domain. These forest reserves would not be sold to private owners; rather, they would be conserved in perpetuity for the benefit of all Americans.

But reserving lands as public domain does not determine how to manage them. By 1897, nearly forty million acres of forest lands had been reserved under the General Revision Act (Cubbage et al. 2017). Management direction was established with the Organic Act of 1897, which authorized the secretary of the interior to manage forest reserves for three purposes: (1) preserve and protect the lands, (2) secure favorable water flows, and (3) furnish a continuous supply of timber for the people of the United States.

As the national government began engaging in forest reserve management, President Theodore Roosevelt took office in 1901. An avid outdoorsman and hunter, Roosevelt championed the conservation of natural resources. He found a like-minded conservationist and close confidante in Gifford Pinchot, an American who studied scientific forestry in France and became a fellow member of the Boone & Crockett Club, a leading conservation organization. Pinchot served as chief of the fledgling Division of Forestry in the US Department of Interior starting in 1898, championing scientific forestry in the national interest. After battling political barriers to scientific forestry in the Department of Interior, he gained a transfer of his agency to the US Department of Agriculture (USDA) in 1905. The newly positioned agency was renamed the US Forest Service, and Pinchot was its first chief. As he built the Forest Service to manage the nation's forest reserves (now called national forests), Pinchot personally recruited like-minded foresters from the Yale School of Forestry to join the agency. With a focus on professionalism and science, the Forest Service enjoyed high morale and unity of purpose.

Outside the agency, the new Forest Service struggled to gain sufficient congressional budgets to manage millions of acres of national forests. In 1907, opponents were able to remove the president's authority through General Revision Act to designate lands as national forest, with an amendment tacked on to a spending bill. The Forest Service budget was squeezed so tight that Pinchot used his salary to meet payroll for some of his employees, and funding for maintenance and management was routinely denied (Egan 2009). By 1910, the agency faced persistent attacks from politicians and land barons who wanted to disband the agency and transfer lands to private ownership as a means to increase timber. But help was on the way, ironically, from the forest itself in the form of catastrophic wildfires.

The summer of 1910 saw drought conditions across the West, including forested areas of Idaho, Montana, and Washington. Thousands of small fires flared in the Bitterroot Mountains in August. Nearly ten thousand men from across the country were gathered to fight the fires, but windy conditions overwhelmed their efforts. A roaring inferno engulfed three million acres in two days, killing eighty-seven people and sending smoke as far east as New York (Egan 2009).

In the aftermath of these fires, Pinchot argued for greater resources and the opportunity to add national forests in the East, to better conserve them. Public sentiment was with him, and the Weeks Act of 1911 authorized the secretary of agriculture to purchase forestland from private owners in order to protect streams and headwaters in the eastern United States. Also that year,

Congress doubled the money in the Forest Service budget for roads and trails, something Pinchot had been requesting for years. It put the young agency on firm footing as a powerful steward of the nation's public forests. It also led to the agency's "10:00 a.m." policy, which was to put out any wildfire by ten o'clock the next morning (Manning 2018). While this heightened suppression reduced tree losses to wildfire in the short term, in the long run it caused large fuel buildup and set the stage for increased wildfires that we deal with today.

GROWTH AND EVOLUTION OF NATIONAL FOREST POLICY

The growing Forest Service applied scientific forestry techniques to the national forests. As Pinchot argued, the aim was to provide the "greatest good, for the greatest number, in the long run." But the balance of competing uses began to tilt heavily toward timber production, especially as timber demand skyrocketed with World War II and the postwar boom years. Soldiers returning home sparked rapid economic growth, including home construction. To meet rising timber demand, the Forest Service applied large-scale techniques such as hillside terracing, clear-cutting, and increased mechanization.

Even as timber demand rose, so did recreational use of national forests. An expanded highway system and growth of automobiles gave urbanites ready access to far-flung national forests for weekend getaways and family vacations. These additional uses occurred alongside the increasing timber cutting as well as long-standing uses by ranchers, hunters, fishermen, prospectors, and the original directive to protect watersheds from excessive erosion and flooding. The Forest Service saw its role as providing multiple uses for many different interests; it was the "can-do" organization (Dunsky and Steinke 2005).

As timber and nontimber uses increased, some forest visitors began questioning Forest Service management priorities. Why, they asked, were large swaths of forested hillsides being clear-cut? What happened to favorite patches of wildlife habitat? Such questions were met with Forest Service efforts to convince the public that the agency was the expert and knew what is was doing (Koontz 2007). As Pinchot had established decades before, the agency was confident in its decisions and determined not to be influenced by the uninformed opinions of politicians and the public (Kaufman 1960).

But the Forest Service was not independent from politics. The politics of timber positioned the agency between congressional appropriations committees, timber industry, and timber-dependent rural communities. Hoberg

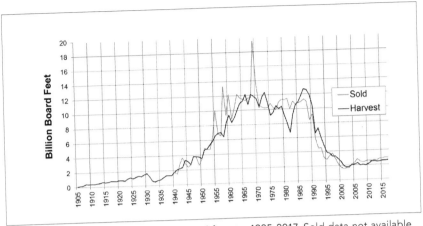

Figure 4.1. Timber harvested from national forests, 1905-2017. Sold data not available before 1940. Source: US Forest Service (2018).

(2001, p. 57) describes this as the "traditional timber regime" of mutually reinforcing preference for higher timber harvesting. Members of Congress gave the agency sufficient budget to conduct timber sales, the timber industry supported these congressmen in their reelection bids, and local communities who enjoyed steady jobs in the woods reelected these congressmen. In addition, the Twenty-Five Percent Fund Act of 1908 required the agency to share 25% of its revenue from timber sales with the state in which the forest is located, to be used to fund county roads and schools. This further boosted local support for timber harvesting. Timber harvest levels ratcheted up (see fig. 4.1). Because timber production was part of the agency employees' shared view of professionalism, they did not see tension with politics—at least not yet.

Although the timber industry and many timber-dependent communities supported the Forest Service's heavy timber emphasis, the chorus of voices calling for greater environmental protection grew louder. When the agency seemed unwilling to listen, critics turned to politics to force change. They pushed for and won a raft of environmental protection laws in the 1970s to constrain the agency's actions, including the National Environmental Policy Act, Clean Water Act, Endangered Species Act, and National Forest Management Act. These laws led the Forest Service to hire a more diverse set of personnel, with professional expertise beyond the traditional field of silviculture (timber management). For example, by 1981, silviculturalists were in the minority, joined by wildlife biologists, engineers, hydrologists, landscape architects, and planners (Tipple and Wellman 1991). The laws included procedural requirements prescribing how forest managers were to make decisions, what items must be included in planning, where clear-cutting was allowed, and which species to protect. In other words, the laws constrained the agency managers' ability to manage forests according to their professional judgment.

The Forest Service was further constrained by the need to defend its actions in court. The new laws of the 1970s became powerful tools for environmental groups to litigate Forest Service actions. The number of court cases against the agency rose sevenfold in fifteen years (Jones and Taylor 1995). The biggest litigation of all was the battle over the northern spotted owl, a rare bird inhabiting old-growth forests in the Pacific Northwest. This region accounted for a large share of the agency's timber sales, and a court ruling in 1989 halted timber harvesting over millions of acres of northern spotted owl habitat. The courts ruled that the agency had failed to follow requirements of the National Forest Management Act and Endangered Species Act.

With timber sales dramatically reduced, the Forest Service shifted toward an "ecosystem management" paradigm in the 1990s. This approach put scientific management front and center but tempered it with stakeholder collaboration. And it was a new kind of science—managers integrated scientific information across disciplines and cooperated across agency boundaries to learn about the ecosystem. Forest Service Chief Dale Robertson announced in 1992 that national forest management would be based on the ecosystem management approach. In 1997, a US Department of Agriculture committee of scientists developed a strategic plan for national forest management. This plan emphasized ecological constraints as primary and that economic and commodity uses were only to be pursued within those constraints (Hoberg 2001). By 2003, most Forest Service employees reported that the principles of ecosystem management were being successfully implemented (Butler and Koontz 2005).

Ecosystem management changed the orientation of national forest policy toward the health of the ecosystem and away from timber maximization (Honick 2015). The decline in timber sales was met with a decrease in political support for agency budget requests. Without the "traditional timber regime" (Hoberg 2001) to encourage congressional appropriations based on timber sales, the agency had to be attentive to the shifting political winds to make the case for its budgets. Once again, the biggest opportunity for the agency to gain budget resources came from the forest itself, in the form of catastrophic wildfires.

NATIONAL FOREST PRIORITIES IN THE NEW CENTURY: A FIRE-DOMINATED LANDSCAPE

In 2005, the Forest Service celebrated its one hundredth anniversary. A century after its founding by Gifford Pinchot, who placed the agency on a solid footing of professionalism and scientific forestry, the Forest Service inhabited a shifting landscape. A diverse collection of agency professionals, representing a variety of scientific and other fields, struggled to find unity of purpose. Multiple competing stakeholders, armed with laws prescribing forester actions and lawyers to back them up, pressured the agency to advance their particular visions of forest management, while the agency tried to project an image of neutral professionalism. As one forester quipped, "if everybody is mad at us, we must be doing something right" (Dunsky and Steinke 2005). But as the agency faced conflicting stakeholder demands, budget challenges, and lack of personnel unity, employee morale tumbled. By 2009, the agency ranked 206th out of 216 federal agencies in overall employee satisfaction (Brown et al. 2010).

Over the past two decades, wildfire management has become a dominant force shaping Forest Service policy. Buildup of fuels in the forests, aided by the Forest Service's long-standing emphasis on fire suppression, has fed large wildfires across the West. With more people moving to the wildland-urban interface, in harm's way of wildfires, political demands have grown to prioritize firefighting. In 2000, the National Fire Plan was developed in response to an intense fire season, along with a ten-year strategy and implementation plan to ensure "sufficient firefighting readiness" by "working with communities to reduce hazardous fuel buildups, restoring fire-affected ecosystems, and equipping communities with wildland firefighting tools for reduced fire risk" (US Forest Service 2002). In 2003, President Bush signed into law the Healthy Forests Restoration Act. This law reduced procedural requirements for the Forest Service in vegetation management of fire-prone areas, and it authorized up to $760 million per year for the agency to conduct projects related to fire safety in the wildland-urban interface (Steelman and DuMond 2009). These projects included expedited timber harvests to reduce fuel loads, a flashpoint for environmental opposition. But timber harvest volume remained at less than one-fifth of the peak harvest volumes of 1987 (see fig. 4.1 above).

The dominance of fire management can be seen in agency staffing and budgets. Staffing for fire more than doubled, from 5,700 employees in 1998 to more than 12,000 in 2015. In contrast, staff for land management fell from 18,000 to less than 11,000 in the same period (US Forest Service 2015b). The agency's annual expenditures on wildland fire management, compared to other categories, is shown in figure 4.2. Wildland fire management spending has consistently dwarfed all other categories, including all funds spent to manage the national forests. The increasing cost of fire has meant borrowing, dipping into emergency funds, and cutting funds from other budget areas such as facility maintenance, research, and fisheries and wildlife. For fiscal year 2019, $2.5 billion of the requested $4.77 billion budget is anticipated to go toward wildland fire management, and at the current pace the agency is expected to spend two-thirds of its budget on wildland fire by 2025 (US Forest Service 2015b).

Wildfire policy often pits professional expertise against politics. A growing number of Forest Service professionals call for using fire science to reduce threats, rather than focusing on extinguishing all fires. This includes the science of hazardous fuels reduction, especially prescribed burns that reduce fuel loads in a controlled setting. Forest ecologists point out the important role fire plays in some ecological communities and claim that prescribed burns can reduce occurrences of catastrophic wildfires. But use of this management tool is limited by politics. Local communities fear prescribed burns

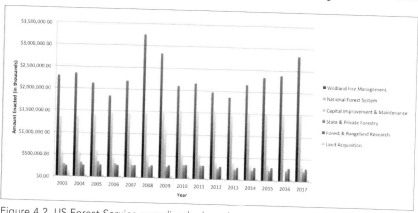

Figure 4.2. US Forest Service spending by broad category in nominal dollars, 2003–2017 (not adjusted for inflation). Source: US Forest Service (2005a, 2005b, 2006, 2007, 2008, 2009, 2010, 2011, 2012, 2013, 2014, 2015a, 2016, 2017b).

getting out of control, and they dislike the smoke (Gillis 2017). Existing laws, including the Clean Air Act and Endangered Species Act, limit prescribed burns, which worsen air quality and harm species in the short term (Graw 2017). Today, prescribed fires make up less than 10% of the acres treated for fuel reduction (Graw 2017). But efforts are underway to increase fuel reduction measures. In 2018, Vicki Christianson, interim chief of the Forest Service, stated the agency is changing its approach to wildfire management. She mentioned efforts to overcome the "cultural barriers" in the West against prescribed fire, and barriers from agency metrics that measure the percentage of fires that are quickly suppressed (Schick 2018a). At the same time, the agency is rolling out a fire risk assessment analytic tool using Geographic Information Systems, vegetation maps, and population data to better calculate where to focus their efforts (Schick 2018b). Also, Congress changed how funding is allocated for wildfires, through the Federal Land Assistance, Management, and Enhancement Act of 2009 and passed a budget in 2018 that changed funding for wildfire suppression in order to free up funds for fuel reduction, including prescribed burns (Profita and Mapes 2018). Thus professionalism and politics are converging to address the wildfire challenge, although the degree to which the public will support more prescribed burns remains to be seen.

As shown in figure 4.2 above, wildfire management accounts for the lion's share of Forest Service budget expenditures. The second-highest share is spent on the National Forest System category, which accounts for activities on the nation's 154 national forests. The breakdown of this category is shown in figure 4.3. The largest National Forest System expenditure is for forest products, including timber. This amount has risen 37% in nominal dollars between 2003 and 2018, which is on par with inflation during this time period, thus a stable amount in real dollars, even as the volume of timber sold rose over 75%. The agency argues that spending on forest products is a means to improve watershed quality, wildlife habitat, and the health of landscapes while also reducing fuel loads and providing economic opportunity to communities. Next come recreation, heritage, and wilderness. Expenditures in nominal dollars have remained relatively flat over the past fifteen years, failing to keep up with inflation or with the additional five million annual recreational visits over this time period (US Forest Service 2017a). Similarly, expenditures on vegetation and watershed management as well as wildlife and fisheries habitat management have not kept up with inflation. Finally, minerals and geology

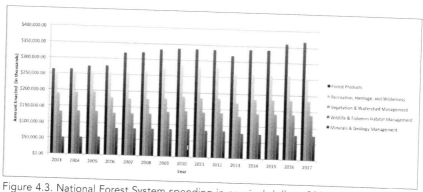

Figure 4.3. National Forest System spending in nominal dollars, 2003-2017 (not adjusted for inflation). Source: US Forest Service (2005a, 2005b, 2006, 2007, 2008, 2009, 2010, 2011, 2012, 2013, 2014, 2015a, 2016, 2017b).

management received a boost starting in 2006, reflecting efforts to develop natural resources to gain independence from the importation of goods from foreign countries as part of the ongoing War on Terror.

While figures 4.2 and 4.3 show how the Forest Service allocates funding internally, the agency's external political environment is visible in annual congressional budgets. The Forest Service is primarily funded through discretionary funds, money that comes from Congress through the annual appropriations process. The process begins with the president submitting a request to the House and the Senate. Within the House and Senate, a congressional budget is decided upon, and then appropriations committees determine how funds will be allocated among federal agencies. Other federal money comes from mandatory spending (predetermined amounts previously decided upon by Congress through legislation) and supplemental funds. If discretionary and mandatory funds are exhausted, federal agencies can request additional money from the federal government to help cover remaining costs. These additional funds are designated as supplemental funds and sometimes as emergency funds in budget reporting, which is frequently used for wildfire suppression (Hoover 2018). Another type of supplemental funding is cap funding, which is when a cap, or designated set amount, is placed on an account and additional funding is provided from a separate account to pay for costs that accrue past the set amount. Cap adjustments have been used for suppression expenses to reduce the amount of money pulled from nonfire accounts.

Over the past decade, discretionary appropriations to the agency have fluctuated between $4.5 billion and $5.7 billion (fig. 4.4), including peaks in

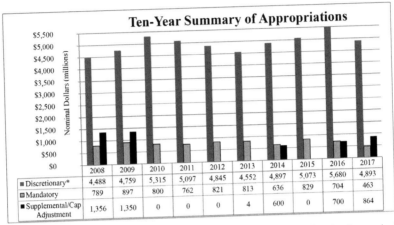

Figure 4.4. Annual congressional appropriations to the US Forest Service in nominal dollars, 2008-2017. Note that data for 2017 were not finalized at time of this figure's original publication. The actual amount for 2017, according to the agency's FY 2019 budget justification, was Discretionary $5,631, Mandatory $444, and Supplemental/Cap Adjustment $0 (in millions of dollars). Source: US Forest Service (2016).

2010 and 2016 when the agency received additional money for wildland fire management (Hoover 2017). These numbers are nominal values; adjusted for inflation, they represent a declining budget over time, with the 2017 budget less than the 2008 budget in real dollars, even as timber sold, recreational visits, and wildfire expenditures increased.

CLIMATE CHANGE POLICY IN THE FOREST SERVICE

No review of Forest Service professionalism and politics would be complete without discussing climate change. Climate change affects conditions in our national forests in many ways. Perhaps most salient is the greater frequency and intensity of drought, which makes forests more susceptible to wildfires. Many national forests are located in mountainous regions, where climate change has reduced snowpack and altered water flows. As climate changes, plant and animal species range is altered. In addition, warmer temperatures enable the spread of insects, pests, and disease that would otherwise be held in check. These damages can cause large-scale tree die-offs, which add to fuel buildup that drives wildfires. Conversely, forest management can affect greenhouse gas emissions. Trees remove carbon from the atmosphere as they grow, and management practices to promote faster tree growth, over more acreage, can help sequester carbon.

In February 2008, under the Bush administration, Forest Service Chief Gail Kimball called on agency leaders to develop a strategic framework to address climate change. This framework, drafted later that year, outlined seven goals, including reducing greenhouse gases through land management, using science to increase understanding of future implications of climate change, and integrating climate change into agency policy. To assist in implementation, recommended actions accompanied each goal. Two years later, under the Obama administration, the USDA also developed a strategic plan in line with the goals described by the Forest Service. Using these frameworks, a roadmap focusing on assessment, engagement, and management was published in 2010 to help with the implementation of the agency's climate change-related goals. In conjunction with this roadmap, administrators developed a scorecard to track implementation on all national forests and grasslands by 2015. But a 2017 Office of Inspector General's report on the roadmap and scorecard concluded that the agency lacked outcome-based performance measures, and it was unclear the degree to which the agency had met its climate change goals (US Department of Agriculture Office of Inspector General 2017).

Forest Service scientists have been researching climate change for more than twenty years. As of 2016, the agency included 150 scientists in the Research and Development Division studying many aspects of climate change. The Forest Service has built an infrastructure to support climate change management and research, including an Office of Sustainability and Climate, and a Climate Change Resource Center. Under the Trump administration, web pages for these offices are still present, but some have not been updated; for example, the Office of Sustainability and Climate website (https://www.fs.fed.us/climatechange/advisor/) accessed in August 2018 indicated it was last updated February 18, 2016, and the most recent scorecard report is for 2016.

The agency's climate change efforts are reflected in the annual budget justifications that accompany the agency's requests for funding. These requests are political documents in that they make an argument to the president and Congress about why the agency should receive its requested amounts. The annual requests are made prior to the fiscal year for which they are requesting—for example, fiscal year 2011 runs from July 1, 2010, to June 30, 2011—and the request was made February 2010. These documents are typically 300-600 pages in length. Figure 4.5 shows the number of times the terms "climate change," "global climate," and "global warming" are used in each request document over the past sixteen years. The flurry of climate planning within the agency starting in 2008 was reflected in a rise in frequency of the terms "climate change," "global climate," and "global warming" in external communications with Congress. There were two peak years of use of the terms, in early 2011 for fiscal year 2012 and in early 2016 for fiscal year 2017. At the start of the Trump administration, use of the terms fell sharply for the 2018 and 2019 budget requests.

Climate change efforts in the Forest Service suggest that professionalism has largely prevailed over politics. Agency scientists have examined climate change impacts for the past two decades, and agency administrators explicitly sought to incorporate it into management starting in 2008. These efforts continued across the Bush and Obama presidencies, and as control of Congress shifted from Democrats to Republicans. Under the Trump administration, as climate change has been openly questioned and many federal efforts to address it have been dismantled, elements of the Forest Service's climate change policy infrastructure remain. But administration web pages have been unevenly updated since 2016, and the significant drop in use of the terms "climate change," "global climate," and "global warming" in the 2018 and 2019 budget requests suggest the agency is downplaying its efforts on this front.

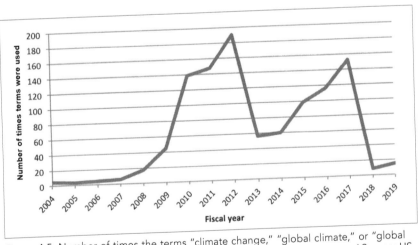

Figure 4.5. Number of times the terms "climate change," "global climate," or "global warming" appear in US Forest Service annual budget request documents. \Source: US Forest Service (2004, 2005a, 2005b, 2006, 2007, 2008, 2009, 2010, 2011, 2012, 2013, 2014, 2015a, 2016, 2017b, 2019.

CONCLUSION

The Forest Service began with a struggle between professional forestry and political influence. As Congress sought to reduce the reach of the Forest Service's control over lands, Pinchot and Roosevelt sought more men and money to manage the forests scientifically. Catastrophic wildfires of 1910 delivered support for the agency to manage more lands, and it did so under the banner of professional forestry and multiple use. The agency applied its can-do spirit to tackling fire, working to suppress all wildfires. As the "greatest good for the greatest number" came to mean heavy timber harvesting, interests of Congress and the Forest Service aligned, and tensions between professionalism and politics subsided.

But tensions resurfaced with the dawn of the environmental era, as non-timber stakeholders increasingly questioned the Forest Service's management choices. These stakeholders prevailed upon Congress in the 1970s to pass several laws protecting the environment and reducing the agency's autonomy to manage as it saw fit. The agency was forced to add a multitude of diverse voices and professions into its once-unified organization, and by the 1990s, timber harvests from national forests were reduced to a fraction of their high-water mark. Professionalism came to include not only timber production, but also ecological protection and the new paradigm of ecosystem management. It also embraced fire science and ecology, which stressed the beneficial role of fire on the landscape. Prescribed fire began to be used as a tool to reduce fuel loads, yet public opinion and politics emphasized fire suppression over prevention. Finally, climate change science began to be incorporated explicitly into Forest Service planning more than a decade ago, but such efforts appear to be less explicit in the Trump administration.

As the Forest Service embarks on its second century of managing the national forests, its cadre of professionals continues to pursue scientific management. Meanwhile, the politics of federal funding have buffeted the agency, which shoulders the weight of more demands even as its budget has not kept pace with inflation. The biggest component of its funding at present is wildfire management, a political issue that seems to be bridging the partisan divide. Under the Trump presidency, agency scientists continue to address climate change, although less explicitly—budget requests under Trump seldom refer to climate change, and public engagement through the website has diminished. Thus the balance between professionalism and politics will likely continue to evolve.

References

Brown, Greg, Trevor G. Squirrell, and Charles C. Harris. 2010. "Growing Organizational
    Challenges for the US Forest Service: Results of a Longitudinal Study in a Period of Major
    Environmental Change." *Journal of Forestry* 108(2): 77-85.
Butler, Kelly F., and Tomas M. Koontz. 2005. "Theory into Practice: Implementing Ecosystem
    Management Objectives in the USDA Forest Service." *Environmental Management* 35(2):
    138-150.
Cubbage, Frederick, Jay O'Laughlin, and M. Nils Peterson. 2017. *Natural Resource Policy.*
    Long Grove, IL: Waveland Press.
Dunsky, Steve, and Dave Steinke, dirs. 2005. *The Greatest Good: A Forest Service Centennial
    Film.* DVD. Washington, DC: US Forest Service.
Egan, Timothy. 2009. *The Big Burn: Teddy Roosevelt and the Fire That Saved America.* New
    York: First Mariner Books.
Gillis, Justin. 2017. "Let Forest Fires Burn? What the Black-Backed Woodpecker Knows." *New
    York Times,* August 6, 2017. https://www.nytimes.com/2017/08/06/science/let-forest-
    fires-burn-what-the-black-backed-woodpecker-knows.html.
Graw, Michael. 2017. "We Know How to Fight Wildfires Effectively: Why Don't We Do It?"
    Massive Science, October 10, 2017. https://massivesci.com/articles/wildfire-prevention-
    california-controlled-burn/.
Hoberg, George. 2001. "The Emerging Triumph of Ecosystem Management: The
    Transformation of Federal Forest Policy." In *Western Public Lands and Environmental
    Politics,* edited by Charles Davis, 55-85. Boulder, CO: Westview Press.
Honick, Alan. 2015. "Seeing the Forest." Vimeo video, 00:31:22. April 16, 2015. https://
    vimeo.com/125160364.
Hoover, Katie. 2017. *Forest Service Appropriations: Five-Year Data and Trends and FY2017
    Budget Request.* CRS Report R43417. Washington, DC: Congressional Research Service.
    http://nationalaglawcenter.org/wp-content/uploads/assets/crs/R43417.pdf.
Hoover, Katie. 2018. *Wildfire Management Funding: Background, Issues, and FY 2018
    Appropriations.* CRS Report R45005. Washington, DC: Congressional Research Service.
    https://fas.org/sgp/crs/homesec/R45005.pdf.
Jones, Elise, and Cameron Taylor. 1995. "Litigating Agency Change: The Impact of the Courts
    and Administrative Appeals Process on the Forest Service." *Policy Studies Journal* 23(2):
    310-336.
Kaufman, Herbert. 1960. *The Forest Ranger.* Baltimore, MD: Resources for the Future.
Koontz, Tomas M. 2007. "Federal and State Public Forest Administration in the New
    Millennium: Revisiting Herbert Kaufman's *The Forest Ranger.*" *Public Administration
    Review* 67(1): 152-164.
MacCleery, Douglas. 2011. *American Forests: A History of Resiliency and Recovery.* Durham,
    NC: Forest History Society.
Manning, Richard. 2018. "Combustion Engines." *Harper's Magazine,* August 2018. https://
    harpers.org/archive/2018/08/lolo-peak-rice-ridge-mega-fires/.
Marsh, George Perkins. 2003. *Man and Nature.* Seattle: University of Washington Press.
    [Originally published 1864.]
McCarthy, Michael. 1992. "The First Sagebrush Rebellion: Forest Reserves and States Rights
    in Colorado and the West, 1891-1907." In *The Origins of the National Forests,* edited by
    Harold Steen, 180-198. Durham, NC: Duke University Press.
Our Documents. 2019. "Pendleton Act." Accessed November 12, 2019. https://www.
    ourdocuments.gov/doc.php?flash=true&doc=48.

Profita, Cassandra, and Jeff Mapes. 2018. "Want to Prevent Megafires? Let Forest Burn." Crosscut, August 24, 2018. https://crosscut.com/2018/08/want-prevent-megafires-let-forests-burn.

Schick, Tony. 2018a. "Forest Service Chief Talks Need for New Fire Management, Fuel Treatments." EarthFix, July 30, 2018. https://www.opb.org/news/article/forest-fire-management-fuel-treatments/.

Schick, Tony. 2018b. "Can Moneyball Fix How the West Manages Wildfire?" EarthFix, July 16, 2018. https://www.opb.org/news/article/fire-wildfire-west-management-science-data-risk-moneyball/.

Steelman, Toddi A., and Melissa Elefante DuMond. 2009. "Serving the Common Interest in US Forest Policy: A Case Study of the Healthy Forests Restoration Act." Environmental Management 43(3): 396-410.

Tipple, Terence, and J. Douglas Wellman. 1991. "Herbert Kaufman's Forest Ranger Thirty Years Later: From Simplicity and Homogeneity to Complexity and Diversity." Public Administration Review 51(5): 421-428.

US Department of Agriculture Office of Inspector General. 2017. Forest Service's Plan for Addressing Climate Change. Audit Report 08601-0005-41. Washington, DC: US Department of Agriculture Office of Inspector General. https://www.usda.gov/oig/webdocs/08601-0005-41.pdf.

US Forest Service. 2002. Report of the Forest Service, FY 2001. Washington, DC: US Forest Service. https://www.fs.fed.us/sites/default/files/media/types/publication/field_pdf/report-fs-fy2001.pdf.

US Forest Service. 2004. FY 2004 Budget Justification. Washington, DC: US Forest Service. https://www.fs.fed.us/budget_2004/documents/fy2004_budget_justification.pdf.

US Forest Service. 2005a. Fiscal Year 2005 Budget Justification. Washington, DC: US Forest Service. https://www.fs.fed.us/sites/default/files/fy-2005-budget-justification-pdf.pdf.

US Forest Service. 2005b. Fiscal Year 2006 Budget Justification. Washington, DC: US Forest Service. https://www.fs.fed.us/sites/default/files/fy2006-forest-service-budget-justification.pdf.

US Forest Service. 2006. Fiscal Year 2007 Budget Justification. Washington, DC: US Forest Service. https://www.fs.fed.us/sites/default/files/fy2007-forest-service-budget-justification.pdf.

US Forest Service. 2007. Fiscal Year 2008 Budget Justification. Washington, DC: US Forest Service. https://www.fs.fed.us/sites/default/files/legacy_files/fy2008-forest-service-budget-justification.pdf.

US Forest Service. 2008. Fiscal Year 2009 Budget Justification. Washington, DC: US Forest Service. https://www.fs.fed.us/sites/default/files/legacy_files/fy2009-forest-service-budget-justification.pdf.

US Forest Service. 2009. Fiscal Year 2010 Budget Justification. Washington, DC: US Forest Service. https://www.fs.fed.us/sites/default/files/fy2010-president-budget request-justification.pdf.

US Forest Service. 2010. Fiscal Year 2011 Budget Justification. Washington, DC: US Forest Service. https://www.fs.fed.us/sites/default/files/legacy_files/fy2011-forest-service-budget-justification.pdf.

US Forest Service. 2011. Fiscal Year 2012 Budget Justification with Errata. Washington, DC: US Forest Service. https://www.fs.fed.us/sites/default/files/fy2011-budget-justification-errata-061510.pdf.

US Forest Service. 2012. Fiscal Year 2013 Budget Justification. Washington, DC: US Forest Service. https://www.fs.fed.us/sites/default/files/legacy_files/fy2013-justification.pdf.

US Forest Service. 2013. *Fiscal Year 2014 Budget Justification*. Washington, DC: US Forest Service. https://www.fs.fed.us/sites/default/files/fy2014-forestservice-budgetjustification-final.pdf.

US Forest Service. 2014. *Fiscal Year 2015 Budget Justification*. Washington, DC: US Forest Service. https://www.fs.fed.us/sites/default/files/media/2014/25/2015-BudgetJustification-030614.pdf.

US Forest Service. 2015a. *Fiscal Year 2016 Budget Justification*. Washington, DC: US Forest Service. https://www.fs.fed.us/sites/default/files/media/2015/07/fy2016-budgetjustification-update-four.pdf.

US Forest Service. 2015b. *The Rising Cost of Wildfire Operations: Effects on the Forest Service's Non-Fire Work*. Washington, DC: US Forest Service. https://www.fs.fed.us/sites/default/files/2015-Fire-Budget-Report.pdf.

US Forest Service. 2016. *Fiscal Year 2017 Budget Justification*. Washington, DC: US Forest Service. https://www.fs.fed.us/sites/default/files/fy-2017-fs-budget-justification.pdf.

US Forest Service. 2017a. *National Visitor Use Monitoring Survey Results: 2016 National Summary Report*. Washington, DC: US Forest Service. https://www.fs.fed.us/recreation/programs/nvum/pdf/5082016NationalSummaryReport062217.pdf.

US Forest Service. 2017b. *Fiscal Year 2018 Budget Justification*. Washington, DC: US Forest Service. https://www.fs.fed.us/sites/default/files/usfs-fy18-budget-justification.pdf.

US Forest Service. 2018. "FY 1905-2017 National Summary Cut and Sold Data and Graphs." April 11, 2018. https://www.fs.fed.us/forestmanagement/documents/sold-harvest/documents/1905-2017_Natl_Summary_Graph.pdf.

US Forest Service. 2019. *FY 2019 Budget Justification*. Washington, DC: US Forest Service. https://www.fs.usda.gov/sites/default/files/usfs-fy19-budget-justification.pdf.

Chapter 5

Wildland Fire Policy and Climate Change
Evolution of Fire Policy and Current Needs

ERIC TOMAN

INTRODUCTION

Wildland fires have long shaped the western United States, influencing the type, density, and arrangement of vegetation across the landscape. Since the early days of habitation in the region, humans have grappled with how to live with fire. On one hand, wildfires can lead to harmful effects to human settlements and cause near-term ecological damage. On the other hand, fire plays an important ecological role and in many cases serves to maintain the health of natural systems and the provision of key ecological services. Beginning in the early 1900s, wildland fires were primarily viewed as destructive events that posed substantial risk to the growing human population in the western United States, and efforts to suppress fires were prioritized. As time progressed, recognition of the ecological benefits of fire grew and caused some to reevaluate the emphasis on fire suppression. Moreover, as has become clearer in recent years, our success in removing most fires from the landscape has served to increase the risk of catastrophic fires, largely owing to an increase of vegetative material that acts as fuel. These increased fire risks are further amplified by the changing climate, which has contributed to developing fire-prone conditions. It is in this context that many researchers and managers have called for a new paradigm of how we think about and live with fire in the western United States (e.g., Calkin et al. 2011; Dombeck et al. 2004; Thompson et al. 2018).

Today's forests, grasslands, and other undeveloped landscapes that we think of as natural are in actuality a product of human influences. Ultimately, decisions about preservation, harvest, development, access, and use have all played a role in the development of our "natural" landscapes. Perhaps most influential are decisions that result, intentionally or not, in suppressing or amplifying ecological processes, as these decisions may lead to large-scale and long-term ecological changes. In this chapter we consider the complex and interacting effects of policy and management related to wildland fire on current and potential future conditions. We begin by considering the current state of wildland fire management and expected effects of climate change. Then we describe the evolution of wildland fire policy and how this has influenced conditions on the ground. The chapter concludes by considering policy and management actions that can contribute to increased resilience of natural and social systems given current and expected future conditions. A quick note on terminology: in this chapter we follow the phrasing used within the wildfire management community (table 5.1).

CURRENT CONTEXT: WILDLAND FIRE POLICY AND MANAGEMENT

Wildland fire management is a high-stakes endeavor and has long been viewed as central to the mission of federal natural resource management agencies (namely, the US Forest Service in the Department of Agriculture and the National Park Service, US Fish and Wildlife Service, Bureau of Land Management, and Bureau of Indian Affairs in the Department of the Interior). There is no singular statute or existing legislation that sets specific policy for

Table 5.1. Wildland Fire Terminology

Term	Definition
Prescribed fire	Any fire intentionally ignited by management actions in accordance with applicable laws, policies, and regulations to meet specific objectives.
Wildfire	An unplanned, unwanted wildland fire, including unauthorized human-caused fires, escaped wildland fire use events, escaped prescribed fire projects, and all other wildland fires where the objective is to put the fire out. (Note: this definition is currently under review.)
Wildland	An area in which development is essentially nonexistent, except for roads, railroads, powerlines, and similar transportation facilities. Structures, if any, are widely scattered.
Wildland fire	Any nonstructure fire that occurs in vegetation or natural fuels. Wildland fire includes prescribed fire and wildfire.

Definitions from National Wildfire Coordinating Group (2019)

wildland fire. But because a number of federal, state, and tribal agencies and organizations are involved in wildland fire management, a robust structure has been developed with representatives across agencies to develop and coordinate federal fire policy and management guidelines. These coordination efforts seek to provide consistency in general policy based on an agreed-upon set of guiding principles, common definitions for relevant terminology, and agreements for managing specific fire events, including the command structure for decision making, agreements regarding sharing resources, and allowing personnel to work across jurisdictional boundaries (US Department of the Interior Office of Wildland Fire 2017).

Wildland fire policy has evolved substantially since the early 1900s. Initial policy strictly emphasized the control and suppression of all fire. Although such efforts were largely successful in the near term, this emphasis on excluding fires from the landscape has actually served to increase the risk of future wildfires, a situation often referred to as the wildfire paradox, as management efforts to suppress wildfires led to a buildup of vegetation (e.g., fuel for wildfires) and increased continuity between existing fuel (allowing for fire to be carried along the surface or into the tree canopy) (Arno and Brown 1991; Calkin et al. 2015). The wildfire paradox illustrates the potential for differential outcomes of policy across scales of time and spatial extent. In many cases, the policy of fire suppression was successful at immediately extinguishing ignited fires, reducing the near-term and local risks of negative effects. Over time and at larger spatial scales, however, the success of fire suppression has actually resulted in increased vulnerability to future impacts across the landscape.

As illustrated in figure 5.1, the annual amount of acres burned by wildfires has increased over the last thirty-five years. The average number of acres burned annually increased over each of the last several decades (1980-1989, 2.98 million acres; 1990-1999, 3.32 million acres; 2000-2009, 6.93 million acres; 2010-2018, 7.09 million acres). These figures illustrate that these increases are not necessarily linear over time; rather, the average number of acres burned annually doubled between the 1990s and 2000s. Moreover, this increase has occurred despite the relative success of "initial attack" efforts, where aggressive suppression efforts that seek to extinguish wildfires immediately upon detection result in successfully extinguishing between 97% and 99% of fire starts (Calkin et al. 2005), and as record expenditures are spent on wildfire suppression with more than $2 billion in expenses in 2015 (for

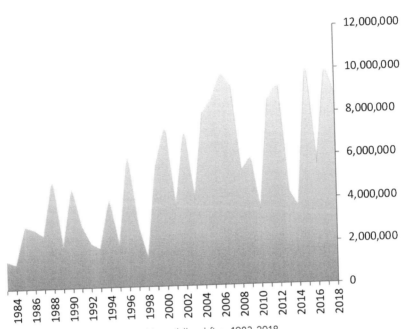

Figure 5.1. Total acres burned by wildland fire, 1983-2018.

the first time) and exceeding $3 billion in 2018 (National Interagency Fire Center 2019a).

While research has long recognized the ecological benefits of fire and wildland fire policy has long allowed for allowing some naturally ignited fires to burn to achieve resource benefits, in practice, most ignitions are still treated with aggressive initial attack efforts (Calkin et al. 2015). This begs the question: If aggressive wildfire suppression efforts are limited in their ability to prevent losses and protect communities, why are these approaches still emphasized? Surprisingly, a relatively limited number of studies have examined the wildland fire decision-making context; however, findings to date do suggest some key points. Ultimately, wildland fire management decisions are made within a complex context. From a policy perspective, wildland fire management decisions are not only subject to guidance provided by overarching fire policy, but must also comply with a suite of other relevant laws and resulting agency policy. In any given situation, fires may affect water and air quality (regulated by the Clean Water Act and Clean Air Act) or have impacts on protected or sensitive species protected by the Endangered Species Act (directly through harming individuals or through negative impacts to their habitat). Wildland fires that pose a potential threat to valuable resources substantially raise the stakes regarding their management, particularly if homes or private property are at risk. Understandably, such situations may lead to an emphasis on aggressive suppression efforts; however, Stephens et al. (2016) argue that this may lead to "tunnel vision," where fire management decisions are evaluated solely on the expected negative outcomes to specific, valued resources. Similarly, other researchers have found that wildland fire management decisions may be biased toward local and near-term impacts rather than longer-term outcomes at larger spatial scales (Thompson 2014; Wilson et al. 2011). This tendency toward discounting long-term risks compared to short-term risks is not limited to fire managers but is common in decisions including risk and uncertainty, and thus will require intentional intervention and support to overcome (e.g., Maguire and Albright 2005; Wilson et al. 2011).

Further complicating the decision-making environment, in addition to the risks posed to resources, managers must also weigh the potential for personal liability or negative impacts to their career if they decide to engage a wildland fire less aggressively (Calkin et al. 2011; Donovan et al. 2011). Aggressive fire suppression is likely to be viewed as more defensible if negative impacts occur (Ager et al. 2014). Ultimately, these cumulative influences provide substantial incentive to aggressively suppress fires and may limit the ability to consider the effects of such decisions on long-term risks to desired ecological conditions or the risks posed to communities despite the potential for such an approach to negatively influence the resilience of human and natural systems (Stephens et al. 2016).

CLIMATE CHANGE AND WILDLAND FIRE

While the wildland fire decision-making context is exceedingly complex, it is further complicated by impacts resulting from ongoing climatic changes. Climate is a key driver of wildland fire activity (Schoennagel et al. 2017). Historical reviews have illustrated a strong association between wildfire activity and climate variables—particularly temperature and drought (Marion et al. 2012; Westerling et al. 2006; Whitlock et al. 2008). Not surprisingly, one of the primary ways climate change influences wildfire is through alterations in weather patterns. These changes may result in both near- and long-term impacts. In the near term, increased temperatures, extended heat events, or decreased precipitation can increase the risk of wildland fire activity. Over the longer term, changes in temperature and precipitation can influence the suitability of growing conditions for particular species (Vose et al. 2018) and lead to increased mortality directly (e.g., vegetation dying from a lack of adequate precipitation) as well as indirectly through changes in the incidence of and susceptibility to pests and disease. In other words, a changing climate can stress the natural vegetation historically present in a given location and lead to a die-off as the current conditions no longer meet the needs of the vegetation (e.g., inadequate supply of water), while the remaining stressed vegetation may be less able to defend against pests and disease.

Some recent cases illustrate how the effects of climate change may interact with other disturbance events with the potential to result in unprecedented impacts to forested ecosystems. Vose et al. (2018) illustrate the potential interactive effects of disturbance events by reviewing recent changes in Sierra Nevada forests. Their review illustrated how five years of drought (ending in 2017) weakened trees and made more them susceptible to substantial bark beetle outbreaks. Overall, more than 129 million trees were killed across 7.7 million acres between 2010 and 2017. Impacts were particularly acute in some locations, with up to 70% mortality in a single year. The western pine beetle was the primary insect responsible for these losses. Given that the pine beetle primarily targeted ponderosa pine trees, this outbreak contributed to changing the composition of local forests by shifting from a ponderosa pine-dominated system to one dominated by incense cedar. The mortality and shifting species were expected to contribute to an increased risk of high-intensity surface fires and larger wildfire events (Stephens et al. 2018).

Similar trends are apparent across the western United States. While pine beetles and other pests are native to many western forests, their populations and their associated impacts are typically limited, at least in part, by the typical climatic conditions. In many western forests, winter temperatures were previously cold enough to reduce pine beetle populations; however, warming temperatures in recent years have resulted in increased beetle populations with a concomitant expansion in the number of acres affected by pine beetles (affecting more than 25 million acres in the western United States since 2010) (Vose et al. 2018). Increased tree mortality leads to an increased risk of wildfire as more fuel is available to burn.

As these examples illustrate, conditions in many forests throughout the western United States are changing. Reviewing the current body of research, Vose et al. (2018) concluded that the frequency and magnitude of severe ecological disturbances, including wildfire, were expected to lead to rapid and potentially long-lasting changes in forest structure (species present and their composition) and function (the ecological services they provide). These changes illustrate a need to shift how we think about fire. The current approach to fire management has been developed on the basis of historical trends, as past fire occurrence, behavior, and intensity are considered as proxies to estimate future wildfire events and likely outcomes. While there has always been substantial variability in actual wildland fire activity in any given year, conditions have occurred within a range of historic conditions. But recent years suggest that we may be entering a new era of wildfires where expectations based on historic trends no longer apply (Schoennagel et al. 2017).

As one example, the "fire season" (the annual period during which forest conditions were particularly conducive to wildfires and when most historical wildfires occurred) has grown longer in recent years owing to increased temperatures and earlier snowmelt (Gergel et al. 2017; Westerling et al. 2006. At the same time, summer drought conditions have intensified and increased wildfire risk (Dennison et al. 2014; Littell et al. 2016). Substantial research suggests fire occurrence will continue to increase in future years with specific changes depending on local conditions (e.g., Hawbaker and Zhu 2012; Litschert et al. 2012; Littell et al. 2016).

The last few fire seasons illustrate how destructive this new era of wildfire may be. Early 2017 began with above-normal precipitation west of the Rocky Mountains (National Interagency Coordination Center 2018). While the increased precipitation was welcome, particularly in California, as it came on the heels of a prolonged drought, precipitation rates exceeding 200% of normal led to challenges of its own, including threatening a near-catastrophic failure of the Oroville Dam in February 2017 (leading to the evacuation of more than 180,000 people) (National Interagency Coordination Center 2018). Moreover, this early-season precipitation contributed to the growth of substantial fine fuels (including grasses, needles and leaves) less than one-fourth of an inch in diameter, which can dry quickly and ignite rapidly, contributing to increased fire risks later in the season (National Wildfire Coordinating Group 2019). Above-average precipitation continued throughout much of the spring and summer in Northern California.

In their annual summary of the fire season, National Interagency Coordination Center (2018) described summer 2017 as "historically unique" with "an abrupt shift in the weather pattern" in early July, leading to excessive heat events, earlier melting of mountain snowpacks, and drying out the above-average amounts of fine fuels. Many parts of the country experienced above-average fire activity across the year (153% of the ten-year average in terms of acres burned). Disaster response resources were further stretched by the impacts of several hurricanes (Hurricanes Harvey, Irma, and Maria) on Florida, Louisiana, Texas, and particularly Puerto Rico and the US Virgin Islands in August and September. While autumn weather brought decreased temperatures and increased precipitation to much of the western United States, California remained drier than usual. These dry conditions combined with wind events contributed to the development of several large wildfires, including the Thomas Fire that burned 281,893 acres (at the time the largest fire in California history) and the Tubbs Fire that burned 36,807 acres and 5,643 structures and resulted in twenty-two fatalities). In California alone, 11,012 structures were lost to wildfires in 2017, far exceeding the national average of 2,836 structures lost annually. Further illustrating the interactive nature of climate, fire, and weather influences, subsequent autumn rain fell on a landscape where much of the existing vegetation had been removed. This led to substantial erosion and, in some tragic cases, mudslides and debris flows that contributed to a further twenty-one fatalities in January 2018.

Winter 2018 again saw substantial variation in precipitation rates across the West, with above-average precipitation in the eastern and northern United States (mountain snowpack 200% of normal in northern Rocky Mountains) but lower-than-average rates in the Great Basin, California, and Southwest (mountain snowpack 50% of normal) (National Interagency Coordination Center 2019). Weather patterns in the West generally followed expected trends, with the exception of the drought conditions that persisted in the coastal states through summer and autumn (National Interagency Coordination Center 2019). The wildfire season was active, with an above-average number of acres burned (8,767,492 acres; 132% of the ten-year national average). California again experienced substantial wildfire activity, including the Mendocino Complex Fire that burned 459,123 acres (the largest fire in California history). Similar to 2017, two late-season wildfire events were particularly destructive. Ignited on November 8, the Woolsey Fire burned 96,949 acres and gained national attention as it burned through expensive neighborhoods and destroyed the homes of several celebrities in Malibu, California (1,643 structures were lost while three fatalities occurred). Ignited on the same day, the Camp Fire quickly burned through the community of Paradise in Northern California, burning 153,336 acres, destroying

18,793 structures, and resulting in eighty-six fatalities (CalFire 2019). The Camp Fire exhibited extreme fire spread, moving at a rate of 80 acres per minute, leaving little time for residents to evacuate (National Interagency Coordination Center 2019). The Camp Fire was the deadliest wildfire in the past century in the United States (National Interagency Coordination Center 2019) and was the costliest worldwide natural disaster in 2018 (estimated losses of $16.5 billion) (Löw 2019).

WILDFIRE MANAGEMENT CONTEXT: THE WILDLAND-URBAN INTERFACE

As the above discussion illustrates, climate variables exhibit a strong influence on wildfire. Ongoing changes in these climatic variables have already and are expected to continue to lead to changes in wildfire activity, intensity, and impacts. Further complicating matters, the emphasis on fire suppression over the past century has modified forest conditions and in many cases has heightened the risk of future wildfires. On their own, these changes would heighten the importance of adapting current wildland fire policy to address these new conditions. As recent fire seasons in California illustrate, however, wildfire events result in severe impacts not only to forests but also to human communities.

Critical to any new approach to address our current wildfire problem in the United States is a better understanding of how to address fire in what has come to be known as the wildland-urban interface (WUI), defined as "areas where houses meet or intermingle with undeveloped wildland vegetation" (Federal Register 2001). Across the country, 9.5% of the US land area is classified as WUI, with substantially higher levels in some locations (Radeloff et al. 2018a). Recent analyses indicate that the WUI is growing. Between 1990 and 2010, land classified as WUI grew by 189,000 km^2 ("an area larger than Washington State") while adding 12.7 million houses and 25 million people (Radeloff et al. 2018b). Moreover, the rate of growth is high (33%) and exceeds the growth rate of other designated land types.

Many of the most destructive wildfires in recent years have occurred in the WUI. The impact of a wildfire cannot be fully appreciated by the number of acres burned, as even relatively "small" wild fires in WUI areas can affect thousands of residents and threaten communities even though they may have a limited spatial extent. Moreover, wildfires burning in the WUI are more complicated to manage and may result in increased risk to firefighters because they may be managed more aggressively to avoid potential loss of life and property among local residents. Not surprisingly, there is a positive correlation between proximity of WUI communities and suppression costs; suppression costs increase the closer wildfires occur to communities (Fitch et al. 2017).

POLICY AND MANAGEMENT APPROACHES TO ADDRESS CURRENT WILDFIRES

Ultimately, while wildfires are a natural disturbance in western forests, fire occurrence, behavior, and resulting impacts are influenced directly and indirectly by human factors. Today's fires burn within a human-dominated landscape, as current forest conditions represent the legacy of past management decisions as well as changing temperatures, shifting precipitation patterns, and prevalence of pests driven by ongoing climatic changes. Moreover, wildfires burning within this context are likely to have the potential for both greater ecological (owing to burning with a greater intensity than was typical) and human impacts (given the growth of the WUI and private development within natural landscapes). The interactive effects of these changes have resulted in a particularly complex reality for contemporary wildfire management. This begs the question, Does current wildfire policy provide sufficient guidance to successfully manage current wildfire challenges?

To address this question, in the following section we review the evolution of wildfire policy and management over time and consider the adequacy of current policy to address today's wildfire management realities.

HOW DID WE GET TO WHERE WE ARE TODAY? THE EVOLUTION OF WILDFIRE POLICY

Since their very establishment, land management agencies have had wildfire management as central to their missions. In the earliest days of these agencies, fire suppression was considered a key tenet of professional forestry. Indeed, Gifford Pinchot, the first chief of the US Forest Service, believed that it was a forester's responsibility to control fires (Hays 1999) to conserve forest resources that were viewed as important for future development (Pyne 1997). While agency priorities have changed over time, as we describe below, wildfire management is still viewed as central to the ability to achieve broader agency goals.

Fire Policy from 1900 to 1960: Fire Exclusion

As European settlement advanced westward across the United States, undeveloped lands were largely viewed as providing a stock of valuable resources that could fuel the nation's growth. Early natural resource management was focused on applying the most efficient methods to extract the resources of interest with little consideration of long-term impacts of this extraction. While it may be easy to find fault with such decisions now, it is important to recognize the broader context within which such decisions were made. At the time, there was limited understanding of the interrelated nature of ecological systems and how changes to one component could lead to a diverse range of future outcomes, including some that are relatively unintuitive (such as aggressive suppression of wildfires in the short term, leading to larger and more destructive wildfires in the future). Moreover, throughout much of the nineteenth and early twentieth centuries, a large portion of the US population relied directly on natural resource extraction and use for their livelihoods. The sheer vastness of the undeveloped land contributed to what has been referred to as the "myth of superabundance"—a belief that resources were so plentiful that they could never be exhausted by development (Callicott 1994).

This began to change in the late nineteenth century as impacts began to emerge from previous land management practices during the western expansion of European civilization. Forested lands in the northern lake states (portions of Michigan, Minnesota, and Wisconsin) experienced extensive and often wasteful logging (Williams 1989). The standard logging practices of the time consisted of removal of the valuable trees while leaving behind substantial woody material, including less desirable tree species as well as branches and debris from harvested trees (material known as "slash" to foresters). This slash would dry out and become a substantial fire hazard, creating the potential for catastrophic fires.

The deadliest wildfire in US history occurred under such conditions. On October 8, 1871, a wildfire burned through Peshtigo, Wisconsin, and several other small communities, resulting in more than a thousand fatalities. Although specific estimates vary, the fire is thought to have burned nearly one million acres, quickly moving through the slash left in harvested areas. While devastating to those who experienced the fire firsthand, the fire did not garner widespread popular attention—indeed, it was largely overshadowed by the Great Chicago Fire that occurred on the same day. In the end, the Peshtigo

Fire resulted in limited introspection about how common management practices of the time may have contributed to the impacts.

While several wildfires occurred in the subsequent years, the next fires recognized for their historical impact took place forty years later in several locations across the western United States. Spring 1910 saw snows melt earlier than normal, while precipitation amounts were lower than average. Several fires were ignited throughout the summer from natural (lightning) and human sources (including inadvertent fires started by homesteaders and sparks from coal-powered locomotives) (Egan 2009). By midsummer, several wildfires burned across the western United States as drought conditions continued to worsen. Estimates vary, but it is thought that between 1,700 and 3,000 wildfires were burning in early August in northern Idaho and western Montana (US Forest Service n.d.). The US Forest Service, at the time a relatively new and controversial agency established only five years earlier, in 1905, assembled several crews of rangers, miners, foresters, and military troops to combat these fires, prevent a loss of valuable timber, and protect the developing human settlements in the region, primarily timber towns developed to support the extraction, processing, and shipping of timber products. The firefighting crews were estimated at close to 10,000 strong, and they had largely been effective at containing the wildfires through much of the summer (Busenberg 2004). But things changed dramatically on August 20, as gale-force winds swept across the region, causing several fires to escape containment. Over the next two days, new wildfires started, merged with others, and burned across the landscape while the laboring crews did everything in their power to slow and direct their spread. Eighty-six people were killed as the wildfires burned an estimated three million acres. Entire towns were destroyed, and billions of board feet of valuable timber were consumed in Idaho, Montana, and Washington in two days (Egan 2009). The scale of the wildfires and the resulting impact captured national attention in a way the Peshtigo Fire had failed to do. Since its founding just five years earlier, there had been substantial debate regarding the value of the US Forest Service, with many western residents and elected representatives actively arguing for the agency to be dissolved (Egan 2009). Yet the narrative emerging from the 1910 wildfires provided a rallying point for supporters of the agency, including Chief Gifford Pinchot and his ally, US President Theodore Roosevelt. The agency emerged from this period with increased support for its mission of conserving forestlands for the long-term benefit of the nation. Wildfires were viewed as destructive events that not only threatened the life and safety of residents and those working in the forests but also wasted valuable timber needed to continue to fuel the nation's development (Pyne 2001). Congress soon passed legislation (Weeks Act of 1911) that gave the US Forest Service substantial power in shaping national wildland fire policy by creating financial incentives for states to cooperate with the agency in pursuing an aggressive approach to suppress wildfires as well as an ability to draw on an emergency budget to support fire suppression (Busenberg 2004).

Considering the impact of the 1910 wildfires, it is not difficult to understand how the dominant paradigm came to consider wildfires almost exclusively as destructive events that posed both near- and long-term threats to the nation (however, even at this early time there were some dissenting views from the Southeast and West Coast that advocated for the use of fire as a management tool; see van Wagtendonk 2007 and Smith 2017 for additional discussion). From this perspective, fire exclusion (extinguishing all fires as soon as possible after ignition) was viewed as the most rational approach to wildland fire management. Over the next several years, the US Forest Service as well as other federal and state natural resource management agencies continued to improve their efforts to prevent the ignition of fires through public education campaigns and development of equipment, infrastructure, training, and a robust command and control structure designed to suppress all wildfires as soon as possible. In 1935, the US Forest Service formalized the fire exclusion policy that had been operating in practice in what was referred to as the "10:00 a.m. policy," which directed that all fires would be extinguished by ten o'clock in the morning on the day following detection (van Wagtendonk 2007).

In the near term, these efforts proved largely successful, and the average annual acres burned declined substantially throughout the twentieth century, particularly after the new equipment and workforce developed for World War II were engaged actively suppressing wildland fires (Busenberg 2004; National Interagency Fire Center 2019b). But evidence began to emerge of unintended consequences of the fire exclusion policy. In the 1960s, scientists and managers began to associate ecological changes such as increasing tree density and limited regeneration of some desirable species, among others, with the absence of fire (Agee 1993; Bond et al. 2005). Emerging scientific research began to illustrate a more complex view of the role of fire in developing and maintaining forest systems (Agee 1997). It was increasingly recognized that fire played an important role in managing competition between vegetation, with different species gaining an advantage depending on the frequency or intensity of fire events. For some tree species, fires are required for regeneration because heat is needed to open their cones to release seed.

Evidence also began to emerge that the vegetative changes resulting from wildland fire suppression may actually serve to increase future fire risks. Specifically, fire suppression allowed for a buildup of flammable material (woody debris, dead trees, needles, etc.) as well as an increasing density of live vegetation, providing a pathway for ignited fires to extend from the forest floor to the tree canopy (Agee 1997; Dombeck et al. 2004). Thus there was increasing recognition that while fire exclusion may reduce near-term risks, the resulting vegetative changes actually made the forests more vulnerable to destructive fires and a loss of valuable timber as well as increase risk to human communities in the long term. Such outcomes were in direct opposition to the goals of fire suppression, contributing to more questions about the legitimacy of the fire exclusion policy (Busenberg 2004).

Land management priorities also expanded within the twentieth century to reflect the growing understanding of ecological systems and increasing public concern for environmental protection. Several environmental laws established in the middle of the twentieth century exemplify the broadening priorities of agency management. Some notable laws are highlighted in table 5.2 below. Although these laws do not expressly determine agency policy toward wildland fire, wildland fire management activities are expected to be compatible with and contribute to achieving the specific goals identified within these laws. Moreover, forest management plans mandated for development on a rolling basis by the National Forest Management Act also include guidance for wildfire management decisions in all national forests. Importantly, no specific federal statute establishes wildfire policy (Stephens et al. 2016); rather, wildfire policy is developed through designated interagency committees consisting of senior personnel with final review and approval granted by agency leadership (US Department of Agriculture and US Department of the Interior 2009).

Fire Policy from 1960 to 2000: Experimentation with Limited Fire Use

Although fire exclusion was the dominant paradigm of wildland fire policy and management throughout the early twentieth century, some practitioners and scientists outside this mainstream perspective advocated for alternative

Table 5.2. Subset of Key Laws Influencing Management of National Forests

Law	Year Established	Brief Summary
Multiple Use and Sustained Yield Act	1960	Specifies that national forests should be managed for multiple uses, including timber, range, water, recreation, and wildlife. Gives additional priority to nontimber uses.
Wilderness Act	1964	Provides a mechanism to designate lands for protection with limited human development, including for management activities. Natural processes given priority.
National Environmental Policy Act	1969	Requires consideration of environmental impacts of management decisions. Requires consideration of public input in planning.
Endangered Species Act	1973	Designates species at risk of extinction and requires federal agencies act to protect and recover listed species.
National Forest Management Act of 1976	1976	Requires strategic planning for national forests and grasslands. Provides direction for implementation of forest and wildfire management projects.

approaches to fire management. Early research reported that some residents were using intentionally ignited fires to manage vegetation and reduce the potential for destructive wildfires (Hough 1882). Even after the 1910 fires largely solidified belief in the destructive nature of fire within the US Forest Service, individual forest managers still experimented with intentional use of fire, then referred to as "light burning," to manage vegetation (Smith 2017). This minority voice argued for the importance of better understanding and applying light burning to protect and maintain desired forest resources and reduce the vulnerability of forest systems to more destructive fires. As recognition of the unintended consequences of fire exclusion increased more generally, this type of experimentation with limited use of fire began to increase.

The federal approach toward wildland fire began to shift on a larger scale the late 1960s. The Department of Interior created a committee to examine wildlife management issues in 1962. In their review, the committee began to apply emerging scientific information that recognized the interconnected nature of forest systems and advocated for using an ecosystem approach to management, including integration of natural disturbance processes such as wildland fire (van Wagtendonk 2007). In response to the committee's recommendations, the National Park Service modified their policy to allow for some use of fire to achieve management objectives in 1968. Individual parks were then allowed to develop plans that had a more liberal approach to using fire. Sequoia-Kings Canyon National Park was the first to implement such a plan (in 1968), and a few additional parks joined them over the next few years (Saguaro National Monument in 1971 and Yosemite National Park in 1972) (van Wagtendonk 2007). The US Forest Service had also begun to reevaluate their approach to land management following the 1964 passage of the Wilderness Act with its emphasis on preserving natural landscapes and processes. Like the National Park Service, the US Forest Service officially modified their policy to allow some use of fire in 1968 (Busenberg 2004). In 1972, the first wildland fire was allowed to burn to achieve resource objectives on Forest Service land in Montana's Selway-Bitterroot Wilderness Area. In 1978, the Forest Service officially moved away from the 10:00 a.m. fire suppression policy (van Wagtendonk 2007).

On the ground, implementation of these new policies typically included the development of wildland fire management plans that designated zones across the landscape, each with specified management alternatives ranging from suppression of all wildland fires in some areas to allowing naturally ignited fires to burn in designated areas while also allowing for management-ignited fires (typically referred to as prescribed fires) in some cases. In practice, most ignitions were still aggressively suppressed. This has led some authors to argue that the policy of fire exclusion was still largely applied, even as evidence emerged of its failure to achieve agency goals (see Busenberg 2004 for a discussion of how fire exclusion has been perpetuated as the dominant policy focus).

Over the next several years, wildland fires were managed under this hybrid approach and either immediately suppressed or, in limited cases, allowed to burn under predetermined prescriptions. Manager-ignited prescribed fires were also increasingly used as fire management programs began to develop. While some fires managed under these alternative approaches resulted in local-level impacts and caused some reconsideration of unit-level plans, there was little national attention paid to this shifting approach to wildland fire management until the 1988 fire season.

The summer of 1988 saw substantial fire activity in and around Yellowstone National Park. Given its iconic status as the world's first national park, these fires garnered media attention, and people across the nation followed the daily reports provided by the major news networks. Much of the discussion emphasized that the fires had been allowed to burn both within Yellowstone National Park and on adjacent national forestlands for more than a month before suppression activities were ramped up (van Wagtendonk 2007). In late July, dry and windy conditions led to rapidly increasing fire, resulting in fire managers deciding to actively suppress the fires. By the time the fires were contained, over 1.3 million acres had burned in the greater Yellowstone area. The public response was overwhelmingly negative with charges of irresponsible management resulting in substantial damage to such a prized area (van Wagtendonk 2007).

The Yellowstone fires prompted the Departments of Agriculture and the Interior to complete a review of the then-current national fire policy. Overall, these reviews reaffirmed support for the natural role of fire in forested eco-systems but also identified shortcomings with current fire management plans (van Wagtendonk 2007). Secretaries of both departments suspended the practice of allowing naturally ignited fires to burn until steps could be taken to strengthen interagency communication and establish clear decision criteria for management decisions (Rothman 2007). Management use of fire declined in the subsequent years before beginning to increase again as time passed, and new, more robust management plans were adopted. Over time, the successful recovery of the Yellowstone forests has been touted as a success story of ecosystem management and an illustration of the resilience of forest systems even after severe disturbance (Stephens et al. 2016).

Wildland Fire Policy in the 2000s

Wildland fire policy continued with this similar hybrid approach through the 1990s. An additional fire policy review in 1995 described fire as a "criti-cal natural process" that "must be reintroduced into the ecosystem" (US Department of Agriculture and US Department of the Interior 1995). The report also noted that managers should have the ability to choose from a spectrum of management options, from full suppression to allowing naturally ignited fires to burn. With a degree of prescience, the report also emphasized the importance of the WUI. WUI areas would prove to be highly critical to wildland fire management in the subsequent years.

Throughout the 2000s, fire received national attention nearly every year (fig. 5.1). The decade began with a prescribed fire that escaped containment in Bandelier National Monument in New Mexico (ignited May 4, 2000). The resulting fire, known as the Cerro Grande Fire, covered 48,000 acres, threatened the Los Alamos National Laboratory, and burned 255 structures, mostly in the community of Los Alamos. This wildfire prompted substantial attention to the practice and potential consequences of management-ignited prescribed fire, ultimately prompting another review of wildfire management. This review provided continued support for the dual approach to wildfire management and resulted in additional clarification regarding management use of fire. Overall, the use of prescribed fires continued at a fairly consistent rate despite concerns among fire managers regarding the risks associated with fire use (National Interagency Coordination Center 2018).

Beyond the Cerro Grande Fire, the year 2000 saw a substantial increase in wildfire activity in the United States. Overall, just under 7.4 million acres burned, a 122% increase from the ten-year average of acres burned in the 1990s and the highest annual total since the 1950s, while suppression costs exceeded $1 billion for the first time. In many ways the 2000 wildfire season appears to be an inflection point that signaled entry into a different era of wildfire activity. While there is substantial interannual variation, total acres burned by wildfire trended higher beginning in 2000 (see fig. 5.1). Moreover, the number of large-scale fires also began to increase; of the 198 wildfires larger than 100,000 acres recorded since 1997 (when consistent records are available), 189 (95%) occurred in 2000 or later (National Interagency Fire Center 2019c). The impacts of this increased fire activity were particularly felt in the WUI; more than 9,000 structures were lost to wildfires between 2002 and 2004. Perhaps not surprisingly, suppression costs have also generally increased since the turn of the century, with average annual suppression costs increasing from $453,498,600 in the 1990s to $1.3 billion in the 2000s (National Interagency Fire Center 2019a).

In response to these fire impacts, a number of federal initiatives (e.g., the National Fire Plan, Ten Year Comprehensive Strategy, and Healthy Forests Restoration Act, or HFRA) focused on fire and fuel management. Two main themes run through these initiatives. First, they emphasize the use of fuel treatments, such as prescribed fire and mechanized thinning, to reduce the likelihood of fire particularly near communities. Second, these policies recognize that the wildland fire issue is too extensive to be managed by resource agencies alone and call for an unprecedented degree of collaboration with a broad array of stakeholders, including citizens in forest communities. As part of these initiatives, an effort was also made to identify those communities near federal lands that were most at risk to wildfire as a way to prioritize those areas most in need of attention. The resulting list included 11,376 communities across the United States. At that time, 9,600 communities were found to have no ongoing efforts to reduce hazardous fuels within or adjacent to their communities. To address this challenge, the HFRA encouraged the development of Community Wildfire Protection Plans (CWPPs) with the intention of bringing together the diverse range of local-level stakeholders to identify areas with the greatest risk of fire and preferred risk-reduction strategies. Thousands of CWPPs have been developed across the western United States, contributing to increased awareness of local wildfire risk and in many cases supporting efforts to reduce the likelihood of fire near homes (by engaging residents in efforts to remove fuels and make other changes to reduce their fire risk) and targeting implementation of fuels reduction efforts on nearby public lands (largely through the use of prescribed fire and mechanized thinning to remove vegetation).

A review of the social science research related to wildfire management completed near the end of the 2000s found high levels of understanding of the threat posed by wildfire to forest communities, adoption of some efforts to reduce the risk of fire on private property, and strong support for the use of mechanical methods and manager-ignited prescribed fire to reduce fuels (Toman et al. 2013). Indeed, across studies in multiple locations, 80% of study participants indicated support for some use of these practices. Generally, participants were willing to give managers greater discretion to use thinning than prescribed fire treatments. Limited research has examined acceptance of managing naturally ignited fires to achieve desired outcomes (the approach taken with the Yellowstone fires); however, the available findings suggest lower acceptance of this practice (ranging from 33% to 60% depending on the specific scenario) likely owing to perceived risks of escaped fires and subsequent negative outcomes (Kneeshaw et al. 2004; Winter 2002).

As the 2000s came to a close, resource management agencies completed another review of federal wildfire policy. While reaffirming the dual approach to wildfire management (suppression and fire use, depending on conditions and resource management goals), the review noted that even with the emphasis on the WUI in their previous review, the challenge of managing wildfires in the WUI had proven to pose a more complex challenge than previously expected (US Department of Agriculture and US Department of the Interior 2009). In response, they called for greater coordination across federal, state, and local jurisdictions to manage conditions within the WUI.

Since 2010, wildland policy has continued with a focus on prefire efforts to reduce the risk of catastrophic fires; suppression of wildfires when they are deemed to pose a threat to life, property, or specified resource conditions; and use of fire in carefully determined conditions. Substantial effort has been undertaken to make further progress with efforts to prepare communities for fire while also developing tools to better support fire managers' ability to sort through information and make decisions aligned with their identified goals during a fire event. Despite these substantial investments, the average number of acres burned and suppression costs (topping $3 billion for the first time in fiscal year 2018) have continued to increase.

WHERE DO WE GO FROM HERE? WILDFIRE POLICY IN A CLIMATE-CHANGED WORLD

Unfortunately, there is no simple solution to today's wildland fire situation. Current conditions on the ground reflect the influence of several decisions made across multiple levels over the past century or more. While long-running efforts to suppress fires are often correctly implicated in raising current wildfire risks, several less obviously connected decisions—such as zoning and development, and our inability to meaningfully reduce greenhouse gas emissions—have also substantially contributed to current conditions and the associated wildfire risks. Thus addressing current wildfire risks will require more than the incremental steps seen over the last fifty years to slowly shift away from a strict fire suppression policy in limited situations, efforts to build awareness and support for fire and fuel reduction activities among local residents, or advances in coordination across jurisdictions involved in fuels reduction and fire suppression activities. While important, as the outcomes of recent years have indicated, efforts undertaken to date have proven insufficient to substantially address the current wildfire situation. To be clear, this is not meant as a slight against natural resource management agencies with responsibility for developing and implementing wildland fire policy (such as the US Forest Service, National Park Service, and Bureau of Land Management). Rather, the reality is that many of the factors contributing to today's wildland fire management situation are outside the jurisdiction of these agencies.

Despite the state policy shifts to allow some naturally ignited fires to burn, in practice, fire suppression has continued as the dominant management approach. Although more recent data are difficult to come by, between 1999 and 2008, an average of 0.4% of wildland fires were allowed to burn to achieve desired outcomes on 204,000 acres (just under 3% of annual average of acres burned; data from National Interagency Fire Center 2019d). This emphasis on suppression is likely influenced in part by the culture developed within the agencies over time, where suppression is viewed as the default alternative viewed as safer and less "wasteful" of valuable resources. Such inclinations are likely further encouraged by the wildland fire management decision environment, as recent research suggests that systematic factors strongly incentivize engaging in aggressive efforts to suppress fires even when such actions may not align directly with managers' stated objectives (Calkin et al. 2015).

At the local level, decisions are constrained by the need to comply with other related laws that are often more narrowly focused on a particular resource. Stephens et al. (2016) argue that such constraints may lead to "tunnel vision," with management decisions focused on particular resource issues while potentially missing other important system-level changes that may have long-standing impacts beyond the particular resource of concern. For example, restricting the use of fire to protect current habitat for an endangered species in the near term may result in unintended, negative changes to the habitat over the long term owing to changing species and potentially an increased likelihood of a catastrophic fire and resulting loss of habitat.

One particularly perverse consequence of the current situation is the effect that increased suppression costs have had on the ability of the forest agencies to accomplish other management objectives. Over the last several years, an increasing portion of the annual budget for the US Forest Service has gone toward fire suppression costs, while 16% of the agency budget went to fire in 1995; in 2017, more than half of the agency's budget was used for wildfire management activities (Kutz 2018). These increasing costs resulted in reallocating money originally slated for other purposes to cover fire suppression costs, potentially resulting in the unintended consequence of increasing the likelihood of wildfire in the future by shifting money away from projects aimed at restoring forest conditions and reducing fuel levels. Thankfully, this problem may have been alleviated through the federal budget passed by Congress in 2018 that set up an emergency fund from which the Forest Service can draw, beginning with the 2020 federal budget when suppression costs exceed their allocated fire suppression budget. The legacy of missed opportunities and backlog of uncompleted projects from past years will take several years to work through, however.

Even if the US Forest Service and other federal agencies are able to find success restoring forest conditions in a way that is amenable to fire playing a more natural role, there are several factors that influence the state of wildland fires that are outside the control of natural resource managers. From land-use development to climate change, a broad range of seemingly disparate factors, each with their own policy arena, affect the occurrence and impacts of wildland fires. Natural resource agencies have limited ability to affect all but a limited set of these factors.

With that in mind, the question remains, How can wildland fire policy be adapted to successfully navigate the challenges posed by this new era of wild-fires? Not surprisingly, given the complexity of the situation and the years it has taken to arrive at current conditions, there are no quick or easy answers to this question. That said, the first step in adapting to today's reality is to recognize that wildland fires are going to occur on the landscape, likely more frequently than they have in the past. While there has been an increasing recognition of the role of fire within forested ecosystems over the past century, there has still generally been at least an implicit expectation that fires could be controlled before causing substantial harm to forest communities. The experiences of the last few fire seasons have shattered those illusions. Ultimately, a policy of fire exclusion is simply not feasible, and attempting to pursue such an approach may contribute to a false sense of security among politicians and communities and slow down any efforts to make meaningful changes on the harder questions influencing wildfires and their resulting impacts.

Given these starting conditions, discussions of wildland fire policy should shift to consider how to adapt ecological and human systems to be more resilient in the face of wildland fires. From an ecological perspective, others have argued for the need to substantially transition management to emphasize restoration of ecological conditions and processes (e.g., Stephens et al. 2016). Ecological restoration, defined as "the process of assisting the recovery of an ecosystem that has been degraded, damaged, or destroyed" (Society for Ecological Restoration 2004), has substantial promise to provide a framework to think about wildfire within a broader context and over longer timescales than the typical approach that largely emphasizes short-term risks to a narrow set of resources (Stephens et al. 2016). Moreover, recent research suggests that using an ecological restoration framework can encourage stakeholders, who may have different preferences for forest management priorities, to focus on more abstract values where they are more likely to find common ground to overcome the conflict that has long characterized forest management decisions (Toman et al. 2019).

The concept of resilience can also provide a useful framework for considering the necessary adaptation within forest communities required by a changing climate. Beginning with resilience as the desired state, these communities can reframe the discussion from one that holds fire exclusion as the default to recognizing the reality of conditions on the ground and providing incentive to engage in proactive preparation for the occurrence of wildland fire and develop plans and mechanisms for how to shape resulting effects and recover when a fire does occur (Abrams et al. 2015). Moreover, such an approach could engender a broader conversation about the range of factors that contribute to successful communities, with benefits likely to accrue to thinking about not only wildland fire but also other adverse events. A developing body of research examining community resilience identifies the importance of recognizing the distinct character of different communities within their surrounding ecological and social context while illustrating potential pathways to develop increased resilience (Paveglio et al. 2018).

These are much more complicated questions than those typically addressed by existing wildland fire policy. While natural resource agencies have made admirable efforts to move ahead with restoration efforts and encourage community preparation efforts, the success of these efforts has been mixed across the landscape. The conditions that influence the occurrence and impacts of wildland fire exceed the jurisdiction of any one agency or organization to address. As a multijurisdictional and multiscale issue, it is unclear who is positioned to provide leadership to consider fire within the broader, complex system within which fires function. But without consideration of the multiple variables that influence whether wildland fires occur, their behavior following ignition, and the resulting impacts, we will not be able to address the full scope of the current challenge and will generally find ourselves playing catch-up and reacting as conditions on the ground change. The most common recommendations for fire policy moving forward typically involve calls for more acres treated through application of fire and mechanical means to reduce fuels that may burn in unplanned ignitions (e.g., Vose et al. 2018). While such recommendations are logical, as they address some aspects of the current problem (increasing fuel loads, particularly around communities) and generally fall within the scope of federal natural resource agencies, they will likely be inadequate to effectively address the current wildland fire dilemma. Even a more radical shift from the status quo to establish resilience as the guiding concept for resource management (as suggested by Stephens et al. 2016) will only address limited aspects of the fire dilemma. Unless these efforts include some opportunity and authority to consider relevant topics at a higher level, they will likely exclude key questions that influence future fire outcomes, including WUI development and community preparation (typically considered at local or regional level). Moreover, such an approach would still be limited to addressing issues within the purview of the agencies and would be largely silent on agreements regarding climate change mitigation (typically considered at regional to global levels with negotiating power closely held by appropriate executive officer) and thus would have modest ability to address one of the key drivers of ongoing wildfire trends.

CONCLUSION

Forested systems across the western United States have experienced substantial ecological change over the past century as a result of fire and forest management actions. Such changes are currently compounded by ongoing climate change and have resulted in a shift in wildfire activity with increasing frequency of and impacts from wildfire events. Combining these changes with increased development within the WUI has resulted in a substantial number of communities at risk to wildfire.

An effective response to this current situation requires more than the incremental approach to adapting wildland fire policy than has been evident up to this point. Such a shift requires a changed approach to considering wildland fire across multiple scales. At the national level, it seems critical to move away from treating wildland fires as unexpected disruptions occurring in isolation from other management initiatives that merit an immediate, emergency response every fire season. By focusing on the short-term impacts of fire, this approach sets up a juxtaposition where wildfire will likely be viewed as being in conflict with other ecological objectives in need of control and, ironically, may contribute to increased risk of fire in the future by shifting resources from efforts to restore ecological conditions to increase the resilience of forest systems to wildfire events. Rather, wildland fire should be viewed as a core ecological process that provides critical functions to ecological systems that will likely be increasingly linked with the success and well-being of WUI communities.

Such efforts can contribute to meaningful improvements on the ground and, hopefully, buy time for agreement to be reached at a greater level on productive actions to address climate change. The challenge is daunting. Effectively addressing climate change will require coordination from global to local levels, including governments, organizations, and citizens living in widely different circumstances, holding different perspectives, and being driven to achieve different goals (Maibach et al. 2009).

Progress on these larger issues will be slow going. In the meantime, wildland fire policy and management will be best served to emphasize resilience in the new era of wildfire.

References

Abrams, Jesse B., Melanie Knapp, Travis B. Paveglio, Autumn Ellison, Cassandra Moseley, Max Nielsen-Pincus, and Matthew S. Carroll. 2015. "Re-Envisioning Community-Wildfire Relations in the U.S. West as Adaptive Governance." *Ecology and Society* 20(3): 34. http://dx.doi.org/10.5751/ES-07848-200334.

Agee, Jim K. 1993. *Fire Ecology of Pacific Northwest Forests*. Washington, DC: Island Press.

Agee, Jim K. 1997. "Fire Management for the 21st Century." In *Creating a Forestry for the 21st Century*, edited by K. A. Kohm and J. F. Franklin, 191-202. Washington, DC: Island Press.

Ager, Alan A., Michelle A. Day, Charles W. McHugh, Karen Short, Julie Gilbertson-Day, Mark A. Finney, and David E. Calkin. 2014. "Wildfire Exposure and Fuel Management on Western US National Forests." *Journal of Environmental Management* 145: 54–70.

Arno, Stephen F., and James K. Brown. 1991. *Overcoming the Paradox in Managing Wildland Fire in Western Wildlands*, 40–46. Missoula: Montana Forest and Conservation Experiment Station, University of Montana.

Bond, William J., Ian Woodward, and Guy F. Midgley. 2005. "The Global Distribution of Ecosystems in a World without Fire." *New Phytologist* 165(2): 525–538.

Busenberg, George. 2004. "Wildfire Management in the United States: The Evolution of a Policy Failure." *Review of Policy Research* 21(1): 145-156. https://doi.org/10.1111/j.1541-1338.2004.00066.x.

CalFire. 2019. "Camp Fire." Accessed November 12, 2019. https://www.fire.ca.gov/incidents/2018/11/8/camp-fire/.

Calkin, David C., Mark A. Finney, Alan A. Ager, Matthew P. Thompson, and Krista M. Gebert. 2011. "Progress towards and Barriers to Implementation of a Risk Framework for US Federal Wildland Fire Policy and Decision Making." *Forest Policy and Economics* 13: 378–389.

Calkin, David E., Krista M. Gebert, J. Greg Jones, and Ronald P. Neilson. 2005. "Forest Service Large Fire Area Burned and Suppression Expenditure Trends, 1970–2002." *Journal of Forestry* 103(4): 179–183.

Calkin, David E., Matthew P. Thompson, and Mark A. Finney. 2015. "Negative Consequences of Positive Feedbacks in US Wildfire Management." *Forest Ecosystems* 2:9. https://doi.org/10.1186/s40663-015-0033-8.

Callicott, J. Baird. 1994. "A Brief History of American Conservation Philosophy." In *Sustainable Ecological Systems: Implementing an Ecological Approach to Land Management*, 10-14. General Technical Report RM-247. Fort Collins, CO: US Forest Service.

Dennison, Phillip E., Simon C. Brewer, James D. Arnold, and Max A. Moritz. 2014. "Large Wildfire Trends in the Western United States, 1984–2011." *Geophysical Research Letters* 41(8): 2928–2933. doi:10.1002/2014GL059576.

Dombeck, Michael P., Jack E. Williams, and Christopher A. Wood. 2004. "Wildfire Policy and Public Lands: Integrating Scientific Understanding with Social Concerns across Landscapes." *Conservation Biology* 18: 883–889.

Donovan, Geoffrey H., Jeffrey P. Prestemon, and Krista Gebert. 2011. "The Effect of Newspaper Coverage and Political Pressure on Wildfire Suppression Costs." *Society and Natural Resources* 24: 785–798.

Egan, Timothy. 2009. *The Big Burn: Teddy Roosevelt and the Fire That Saved America.* New York: Houghton Mifflin Harcourt.

Federal Register. 2001. "Urban Wildland Interface Communities within Vicinity of Federal Lands That Are at High Risk from Wildfire." *Federal Register* 66: 751-777. https://www.federalregister.gov/documents/2001/01/04/01-52/urban-wildland-interface-communities-within-the-vicinity-of-federal-lands-that-are-at-high-risk-from.

Fitch, Ryan A., Yeon S. Kim, Amy E. M. Waltz, and Joe E. Crouse. 2017. "Changes in Potential Wildland Fire Suppression Costs Due to Restoration Treatments in Northern Arizona Ponderosa Pine Forests." *Forest Policy and Economics* 87: 101-114. https://doi.org/10.1016/j.forpol.2017.11.006.

Gergel, Diana R., Bart Nijssen, John T. Abatzoglou, Dennis P. Lettenmaier, and Matt R. Stumbaugh. 2017. "Effects of Climate Change on Snowpack and Fire Potential in the Western USA." *Climatic Change* 141(2): 287–299. doi:10.1007/s10584-017-1899-y.

Hawbaker, Todd J., and Zhiliang Zhu. 2012. "Projected Future Wildland Fires and Emissions for the Western United States." In *Baseline and Projected Future Carbon Storage and Greenhouse-Gas Fluxes in Ecosystems of the Western United States*, edited by Zhiliang Zhu and Bradley C. Reed, 1-12. Reston, VA: US Geological Survey. https://pubs.usgs.gov/pp/1797/pdf/pp1797_Chapter8.pdf.

Hays, Samuel P. 1999. *Conservation and the Gospel of Efficiency: The Progressive Conservation Movement, 1890-1920.* Pittsburgh: University of Pittsburgh Press.

Hough, F. B. 1882. *Report on Forestry.* Washington, DC: Government Printing Office.

Kneeshaw, Katie, Jerry J. Vaske, Alan D. Bright, and James D. Absher. 2004. "Situational Influences of Acceptable Wildland Fire Management Actions." *Society and Natural Resources* 17(6): 477-489.

Kutz, Jessica. 2018. "Fire Funding Fix Comes with Environmental Rollbacks." High Country News, March 29, 2018. https://www.hcn.org/articles/wildfire-fire-funding-fix-includes-environmental-rollbacks.

Litschert, Sandra E., Thomas C. Brown, and David M. Theobald. 2012. "Historic and Future Extent of Wildfires in the Southern Rockies Ecoregion, USA." *Forest Ecology and Management* 269: 124–133. doi:10.1016/j.foreco.2011.12.024.

Littell, Jeremy S., David L. Peterson, Karin L. Riley, Yongqiang Liu, and Charlie H. Luce. 2016. "A Review of the Relationships between Drought and Forest Fire in the United States." *Global Change Biology* 22(7): 2353–2369. doi:10.1111/gcb.13275.

Löw, Petra. 2019. "The Natural Disasters of 2018 in Figures." Munich RE, August 1, 2019. https://www.munichre.com/topics-online/en/climate-change-and-natural-disasters/natural-disasters/the-natural-disasters-of-2018-in-figures.html.

Maguire, Lynn A., and Elizabeth A. Albright. 2005. "Can Behavioral Decision Theory Explain Risk-Averse Fire Management Decisions?" *Forest Ecology and Management* 211(1): 47–58.

Maibach, Edward, Connie Roser-Renouf, and Anthony Leiserowitz. 2009. *Global Warming's Six Americas: An Audience Segmentation Analysis.* New Haven, CT: Yale Project on Climate Change, George Mason University Center for Climate Change Communication.

Marlon, Jennifer R., et al. 2012. "Long-Term Perspective on Wildfires in the Western USA." *Proceedings of the National Academy of Sciences* 109(9): E535–E543.

National Interagency Coordination Center. 2018. *Wildland Fire Summary and Statistics Annual Report 2017*. Boise, ID: National Interagency Coordination Center.

National Interagency Coordination Center. 2019. *Wildland Fire Summary and Statistics Annual Report 2018*. Boise, ID: National Interagency Coordination Center.

National Interagency Fire Center. 2019a. "Suppression Costs (1985-2018)." Accessed November 12, 2019. https://www.nifc.gov/fireInfo/fireInfo_documents/SuppCosts.pdf.

National Interagency Fire Center. 2019b. "Total Wildland Fires and Acres (1926-2017)." Accessed November 12, 2019. https://www.nifc.gov/fireInfo/fireInfo_stats_totalFires. html.

National Interagency Fire Center. 2019c. "Wildfires Larger Than 100,000 Acres (1997-2018)." Accessed November 12, 2019. https://www.nifc.gov/fireInfo/fireInfo_stats_ lgFires.html.

National Interagency Fire Center. 2019d. "Wildland Fire Use Fires and Acres by Agency." Accessed November 12, 2019. https://www.nifc.gov/fireInfo/fireInfo_stats_fireUse.html.

National Wildlife Coordinating Group. 2019. "Glossary." Accessed November 12, 2019. https://www.nwcg.gov/glossary/a-z.

Paveglio, Travis B., Matthew S. Carroll, Amanda M. Staseiwicz, Daniel R. Williams, and Dennis R. Becker. 2018. "Incorporating Social Diversity into Wildfire Management: Proposing 'Pathways' for Fire Adaptation." *Forest Science* 64(5): 515-532.

Pyne, Stephen J. 1997. *Fire in America: A Cultural History of Wildland and Rural Fire*. Seattle: University of Washington Press.

Pyne, Stephen J. 2001. *Year of the Fires: The Story of the Great Fires of 1910*. New York: Viking Penguin.

Radeloff, Volker C., Miranda H. Mockrin, and David P. Helmers. 2018a. "Mapping Change in the Wildland Urban Interface (WUI) 1990–2010: State Summary Statistics. University of Wisconsin-Madison." http://silvis.forest.wisc.edu/data/wui_change.

Radeloff, Volker C., et al. 2018b. "Rapid Growth of the US Wildland-Urban Interface Raises Wildfire Risk." *Proceedings of the National Academy of Sciences* 115(13): 3314-3319. https://doi:10.1073/pnas.1718850115.

Rothman, Hal K. 2007. *Blazing Heritage: A History of Wildland Fire in the National Parks*. New York: Oxford University Press.

Schoennagel, Tania, et al. 2017. "Adapt to More Wildfire in Western North American Forests as Climate Changes." *Proceedings of the National Academy of Sciences* 114: 4582–4590.

Smith, Diane. M. 2017. *Sustainability and Wildland Fire: The Origins of Forest Service Wildland Fire Research*. FS-1085. Missoula, MT: US Forest Service.

Society for Ecological Restoration. 2004. *The SER International Primer on Ecological Restoration, Version 2*. Washington, DC: Society for Ecological Restoration International Science and Policy Working Group.

Stephens, Scott L., Brandon M. Collins, Eric Biber, and Peter Z. Fulé. 2016. "U.S. Federal Fire and Forest Policy: Emphasizing Resilience in Dry Forests." *Ecosphere* 7(9): 1-19.

Stephens, Scott L., Brandon M. Collins, Christopher J. Fettig, Mark A. Finney, Chad M. Hoffman, Eric E. Knapp, Malcolm P. North, Hugh Safford, and Rebecca B. Wayman. 2018. "Drought, Tree Mortality, and Wildfire in Forests Adapted to Frequent Fire." *BioScience* 68(2): 77–88. doi:10.1093/biosci/bix146.

Thompson, Matthew P. 2014. "Social, Institutional, and Psychological Factors Affecting Wildfire Incident Decision Making." *Society and Natural Resources* 27(6): 636–644.

Thompson, Matthew P., Donald G. MacGregor, Christopher J. Dunn, David E. Calkin, and John Phipps. 2018. "Rethinking the Wildland Fire Management System." *Journal of Forestry* 116(4): 382-390. doi:10.1093/jofore/fvy020.

Toman, Eric, Melanie Stidham, Sarah McCaffrey, and Bruce Shindler. 2013. *Social Science at the Wildland-Urban Interface: A Compendium of Research Results to Create Fire-Adapted*

Communities. 75 pp. General Technical Report NRS-111. Newtown Square, PA: US Forest Service, Northern Research Station. https://www.nrs.fs.fed.us/pubs/43435.

Toman, Eric, Emily H. Walpole, and Alexander Heeren. 2019. "From Conflict to Shared Visions: Science, Learning, and Developing Common Ground." In *A New Era for Collaborative Forest Management: Policy and Practice Insights from the Collaborative Forest Landscape Restoration Program*, edited by W. H. Butler and C. Schultz, 103-118. Milton Park: Routledge.

US Department of Agriculture and US Department of the Interior. 1995. *Federal Wildland Fire Management Policy and Program Review*. Final Report. Washington, DC: US Department of Agriculture and US Department of the Interior. https://www.forestsandrangelands. gov/documents/strategy/foundational/1995_fed_wildland_fire_policy_program_ report.pdf.

US Department of Agriculture and US Department of the Interior. 2009. *Guidance for Implementation of Federal Wildland Fire Management Policy*. Washington, DC: US Department of Agriculture and US Department of the Interior. https://www.nifc.gov/ policies/policies_documents/GIFWFMP.pdf.

US Department of the Interior Office of Wildland Fire. 2017. "Governance." January 18, 2017. https://www.doi.gov/sites/doi.gov/files/uploads/chapter_2_responsibilities_and_ governance.pdf.

US Forest Service. n.d. *The Great Fire of 1910*. Washington, DC: US Forest Service. https:// www.fs.usda.gov/Internet/FSE_DOCUMENTS/stelprdb5444731.pdf.

van Wagtendonk, Jan W. 2007. "The History and Evolution of Wildland Fire Use." *Fire Ecology* 3(2): 3-17.

Vose, James M., et al. 2018. "Forests." In *Impacts, Risks, and Adaptation in the United States: Fourth National Climate Assessment*. Vol. 2, edited by D. R. Reidmiller et al., 232–267. Washington, DC: US Global Change Research Program. doi:10.7930/NCA4.2018.CH6.

Westerling, Anthony L., 2016. "Increasing Western US Forest Wildfire Activity: Sensitivity to Changes in the Timing of Spring." *Philosophical Transactions of the Royal Society B: Biological Sciences* 371: 20150178. doi:10.1098/rstb.2015.0178.

Westerling, Anthony L., Hugo G. Hidalgo, Daniel R. Cayan, and Thomas W. Swetnam. 2006. "Warming and Earlier Spring Increase Western U.S. Forest Wildfire Activity." *Science* 313(5789): 940–943.

Whitlock, Cathy, Jennifer R. Marlon, Christy Briles, Andrea Brunelle, Colin J. Long, and Patrick Bartlein. 2008. "Long-Term Relations among Fire, Fuel, and Climate in the N-W US Based on Lake-Sediment Studies." *International Journal of Wildland Fire* 17(1): 72–83. https://doi.org/10.1071/WF07025.

Williams, Michael. 1989. *Americans and Their Forests: A Historical Geography*. 599 pp. Cambridge: Cambridge University Press.

Wilson, Robyn S., Patricia L. Winter, Lynn A. Maguire, and Timothy Ascher. 2011. "Managing Wildfire Events: Risk-Based Decision Making among a Group of Federal Fire Managers." *Risk Analysis* 31: 805–818.

Winter, Patricia L. 2002. "Californians' Opinions on the Management of Wildland and Wilderness Fires." In *Homeowners, Communities, and Wildfire: Science Findings from the National Fire Plan*, edited by Pamela Jakes, 84-92. Washington, DC: US Forest Service.

Chapter 6
The Changing Fate of Western Rivers
The Case of the Colorado

DOUG KENNEY

As early as the writings of John Wesley Powell in the late 1800s, residents of the West have been warned of the dangers of thinking about land and water separately (Powell 1878). This is particularly true in arid and semiarid regions, where western historian Wallace Stegner (1954) famously observed, "Water is the true wealth in a dry land." Nonetheless, the institutions for land and water management remain largely disconnected in many locales and contexts. Notable exceptions exist. One example is the creation of the National Forest System a century ago, founded largely upon the goal of protecting the integrity of watersheds responsible for fueling the region's rivers and streams. Another is the water development apparatus established by the 1902 Reclamation Act, which acknowledged that settlement of the lands of the West was impractical without large-scale water development and distribution. More recently, the proliferation of watershed groups across the region, especially the Northwest, has ushered in a new era of holistic thinking, responsive to the combined role of human activities and the hydrologic cycle in shaping the fate of both land and water resources.

Today, the connections between land and water are further highlighted by, of all things, changes in the atmosphere. Global climate change is having a pronounced impact in the West, influencing weather, land cover, extreme events, and, ultimately, the fate of the rivers that give the region its unique character and value. Even more than population growth, climate change is squeezing water supplies in basins throughout the West, escalating conflicts among cities, farms, and the environment. To the extent that there is insufficient water to go around, the results become evident not only in the streams, but also on the lands that rely on the limited water supply.

This chapter briefly summarizes the impact of a changing climate on the West's water resources, followed by a case study of one of the most hard-hit locations: the Colorado River Basin. The Colorado is the primary river basin of the arid and semiarid West, once characterized by Marc Reisner (1986, p. 125) as the "most legislated, most debated, and most litigated river in the entire world." While every basin has important contextual differences, the Colorado is especially well suited to illustrate the tight and evolving relationship between air, land, and water in the West. There, available streamflow has declined by one-fifth since the start of this century—a trend that is almost certain to continue, with profound consequences (Xiao et al. 2018).

WATER AND CLIMATE CHANGE

Since the industrial revolution of the mid-1700s, global atmospheric CO_2 concentrations have increased from roughly 280 ppm to 400 ppm—the highest level in 800,000 years (Intergovernmental Panel on Climate Change 2013). The predictable result has been warming. Much of the western United States is nearly 2°F warmer today than it was just thirty years ago (Hansen et al. 2010; Lukas et al. 2014). This warming is almost certain to continue and accelerate. Using results from thirty-seven climate models and assuming a medium- to low-emissions scenario, most places in the West are expected to warm from 2.5° to 5° by 2050 (compared to the 1971-2000 baseline). Trends in precipitation are much more difficult to predict but are expected to be modest, with research increasingly suggesting a potential for slightly more precipitation throughout much of the West, especially the Northwest.

From the standpoint of water users, the salient question is: How will these changes influence water availability? The science community has repeatedly addressed this critically important and complex question since the early 1980s (e.g., Revelle and Waggoner 1983). This research—increasingly confirmed by experience—suggests that no resource is more directly affected by climate change than water (Cayan et al. 2016). Climate change is water change, as almost every facet of the hydrologic cycle is governed, at least in part, by heat (or more precisely by energy). The impacts are evident in virtually every western watershed. The most significant influence on the hydrologic cycle is the change in evapotranspiration (ET) rates. The relationship between heat and evaporation is direct and well understood. The relationship between rising temperatures and transpiration is more complex. Most salient in many regions is the reality that rising temperatures extend the growing season, as the spring snowmelt already comes one to six weeks earlier in most western watersheds, and the first freeze of fall has been correspondingly delayed (Cayan et al. 2016). Both native plants and irrigators take advantage of this expanding window, increasing consumption and depleting stream-flows. This is most evident in the arid and semiarid basins of the West, where runoff is small in proportion to total precipitation, and even small increases in ET result in large reductions in runoff and streamflow (Woodhouse et al. 2016). This trend is expected to continue and accelerate even in places receiving gains in precipitation, as the impact of warming overwhelms any modest precipitation increases (Udall and Overpeck 2017).

Future water availability is also negatively affected by the fact that much of the region's water infrastructure was designed to mimic past hydrologic conditions. Nearly all major rivers in the West are fed primarily by snowmelt. Snowpack is, in most regions, the primary source of water storage, and the institutions and infrastructure of water management are based on this annual accumulation and melting of snow. But snow is melting earlier, and many storms that previously resulted in snowfall now result in rain. These trends are important in that they have serious implications for water storage. Where snowpacks are large and melt slowly over the course of the spring and summer, the snowpack essentially serves the purpose of seasonal reservoir storage. But if the snow melts early—or arrives as rain in the first place—then it may rush downstream before it can be used by cities and farms, possibly leaving water users high and dry later in the summer months. These impacts have been particularly noticeable in the Northwest, where the earlier snowmelt trend is most pronounced and where large water storage reservoirs have not been a staple of water management to the degree seen in more arid regions (Sproles et al. 2013).

A further complication comes from the way in which the changing climate is creating bigger and more frequent extreme events, including droughts, floods, and massive storms (Cayan et al. 2016). Extreme events are normally categorized on the basis of their recurrence interval. A one hundred-year flood, for example, is a flood of a size that typically occurs once in a hundred years, or, more precisely, has a one in one hundred chance of occurring in any given year. The design of almost all water infrastructure and management regimes is based on these recurrence intervals, calculated using historic records of climate and hydrology. In a changing climate, however, those records are increasingly irrelevant, and the assumption that the future will look like the past is increasingly flawed. This realization, termed by Milly et al. (2008) as "the death of stationarity," has huge implications for water management. What if the so-called hundred-year drought now occurs every twenty-five years? What if the maximum amount of flow expected to rush down a dam spillway is now twice the original design capacity? What if streamflows show unprecedented year-to-year swings from high to low? For many water managers, these are not hypothetical questions.

THE UNFOLDING COLORADO RIVER CRISIS

The Physical and Institutional Setting

As is typical for an arid region, the Colorado is a relatively small river in terms of flow, lying outside the top twenty US rivers. It is, however, a long river, draining a vast and diverse basin. The river originates high in the Colorado Rockies, the start of a roughly 1,500-mile journey through the semiarid and arid Southwest to the Gulf of California (also known as the Sea of Cortez). The basin covers approximately 244,000 acres in the United States and 12,000 acres in northwestern Mexico.

One of the defining features of the basin is the abundance (and variety) of public lands. Weatherford and Brown (1986, p. 2) estimated that the "federal government owns 56 percent of the basin's land area, the Indian tribes 16.5 percent, the states 8.5 percent, and private interests only 19 percent." The headwaters of the Colorado are primarily national forests; the middle third is dominated by an unprecedented concentration of national parks and monuments, as well as vast national grasslands; while the lower Colorado is home to most of the basin's Indian reservations. It is that relative sliver of private land, however, where the river is most aggressively employed.

The Colorado River is at least a partial water supply for nearly 40 million people, most living outside the hydrologic basin (Cohen 2011). Many of the West's fastest-growing states reside in the Colorado River Basin, with growth concentrated in booming cities like Denver, Las Vegas, Los Angeles, and Phoenix. The dominant water user, however, is agriculture, which accounts for roughly 70% of human consumption (Cohen et al. 2013). Nearly five million acres of land are irrigated with water from the Colorado, with the most productive lands in the Lower Basin. The basin also supports a thriving recreation-based economy, as well as heavy industry such as mineral and oil and gas development. The river is highly regulated by roughly two dozen major storage and diversion facilities (Fradkin 1981). Most notable are the nation's largest storage reservoirs bracketing the Grand Canyon: Lake Mead and Lake Powell. These reservoirs, combined with several smaller structures, allow the storage of roughly four years of average flow. This is among the highest values found anywhere in the world. By comparison, the Columbia River infrastructure can capture about four months of flow.

Many of the most significant diversion structures are found downstream along the California-Arizona border and exist mainly to sustain agricultural and municipal water users in those states (Cohen 2011; Cohen et al. 2013). Within Southern California, the All-American Canal and Colorado River Aqueduct withdraw more than one-fourth of the river's annual flow, while the Central Arizona Project taps another 10%. In both states the bulk of this water goes to some of the most productive agricultural lands in the country, lands that are virtually uninhabitable without these water imports. Much smaller, but more numerous, out-of-basin diversions occur upstream, particularly in Colorado, where twenty-nine different projects move water across (and under) the continental divide to Front Range water users. Some of these efforts were operational before the start of the twentieth century.

The institutional setting is equally varied, featuring a collection of treaties, compacts, federal law, state water laws, and other key rules collectively known as the "Law of the River" (MacDonnell et al. 1995). The centerpiece of the Law of the River is the Colorado River Compact of 1922, which allocates the majority of the river's flow between the states of the Upper Basin (Colorado, New Mexico, Utah, and Wyoming) and the Lower Basin (Arizona, California, and Nevada), with provisions for future allocations to Mexico and Native American communities. This was done using a heretofore unused tool in water management: the Compact Clause of the US Constitution (Article I, Section 10). The appeal of the interstate compact was that it reserved water for the slow-growing states upstream, while allowing federal river development to begin for the rapidly populating states downstream. This type of water reservation was not possible under the doctrine of Prior Appropriation, the state water allocation regime primarily emerging from mining communities across the West, which is based on "first in time, first in right." The system awards a permanent right to use water on a given stream segment to those who get there first, meaning, for example, that a user (perhaps a farm, city, or mine) that started using water in 1870 would always have a more senior right than one that began in 1930. If water supplies in any given year were insufficient to satisfy both rights, then the first (senior) user is entitled to use their full right before the junior user gets any. Like much of western water law, the system was designed to encourage rapid settlement—which was clearly happening in the early twentieth century in the lower reaches of the Colorado River Basin— but not upstream, where populations and growing seasons lagged far behind. The compact addressed this reality by acknowledging that river development was an immediate need downstream, but that such development needed to be done in a way that reserved some water for the eventual use of the states upstream. With that deal in place, the compact was signed in 1922.

Almost immediately after federal ratification of the interstate deal, river development began, most notably on the structure eventually named the Hoover Dam (completed in 1936). Several additional projects and agreements—including a water treaty with Mexico (1944) and dozens of tribal water settlements—soon followed, creating the core of the physical and institutional setting that exists today.

Outside the Colorado River Basin, the interstate compact tool rolled throughout the West, establishing a pattern of quantitative interstate water allocations unlike anywhere else in the world (Kenney 2014). Among the western rivers featuring interstate water allocation compacts are the Arkansas, Bear, Belle Fourche, Canadian, Klamath, Pecos, Republican, Rio Grande, South Platte, and Yellowstone Rivers. Much like the Colorado River agreement, most of these agreements divide the right to consume the river's flow among the relevant basin states, while leaving most other resources (including groundwater) and issues (such as water quality and environmental protection) unaddressed, omissions that today are driving a host of interstate conflicts. Within the western states, Prior Appropriation still prevails, establishing a "nested" water allocation framework at the interstate and intrastate scales.

The net result of this physical and institutional development has been the settlement of the West, the intended goal of Congress. The use of water development as a tool for land development is certainly not unique to the Colorado River Basin or to the American West, but few places can match the success achieved herein. More than 75 million people now reside in the West. The irony is that this effort appears to have been too successful in many regions, as human uses have overshot reliable water supplies. In this regard, the Colorado River is an extreme example, but it is likely one that will become increasingly commonplace—especially given the accelerant of climate change.

The Era of Scarcity

The Colorado River remains at the cutting edge of western water management, but in a different context. The challenge today has been described as "undevelopment," a term used to acknowledge that the most pressing need in the basin is to reform infrastructure and for institutions to encourage fewer water withdrawals and less consumption. At the heart of this challenge is the observation that consumption in recent years has exceeded natural inflows, an inherently unsustainable approach to water management made possible only by drawing down the huge storage reservoirs in the basin (see fig. 6.1).

The Law of the River significantly over-allocates the river, a problem derived by two climate-related surprises. The first happened in the negotiation of the 1922 compact, when negotiators had access to only a couple decades of streamflow measurements to estimate average flows. With the benefit of hindsight, we now know that was one of the wettest periods in the basin's history, leading the negotiators to seriously overestimate the amount of water available for allocation—a problem compounded by assigning fixed quantities rather than percentages to each basin (a problem avoided in most future interstate compacts) (Meko et al. 2007). The compact allocates the rights to 7.5 million acre-feet (maf) per year of consumption to both the Upper and Lower Basin, while the 1944 treaty reserves an additional 1.5 maf/year for Mexico. This total, 16.5 maf, far exceeds the twentieth-century average streamflow of just under 15 maf/year. This problem was only a problem on paper until actual consumption climbed past 15 maf/year, right at the turn of the twenty-first century. The new century brought the second climate-related

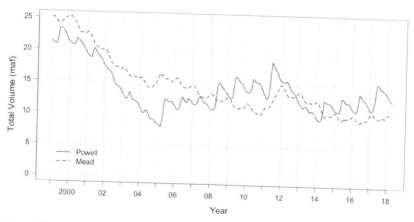

Figure 6.1. Storage in Lakes Mead and Powell, 1999–2018. Courtesy of Brad Udall.

surprise: a rash of drought years, combined with newly raised temperatures, that further sapped the flow of the river. Thus far in the twenty-first century, the flow of the Colorado is approximately 12 maf/year, 20% below the twentieth-century average (Xiao et al. 2018). While it is certainly possible that this trend will reverse, there is a rapidly growing body of science suggesting that this is likely not a drought but a persistent drying trend, described by Colorado River Research Group (2018) as "aridification."

The challenge facing the Colorado is one that is likely to become the norm in the West: How can institutions and infrastructure built on the premise of encouraging and facilitating water consumption be retooled to encourage conservation? Unlike previous water management challenges in the basin, this is not primarily an engineering challenge; those are easy. Rather, the Colorado River is awash in equity problems (Robison and Kenney 2013). For example, the Lower Basin states use more than their 7.5 maf allocation, while the Upper Basin states use less. Given that, it is hard to demand conservation from the Upper Basin users, even if the Lower Basin uses generate the majority of economic benefits in the basin. That was not the deal codified in the compact. If the Lower Basin users can succeed in efforts to scale back to 7.5 maf/year (something they are actively working on), then that presumably frees up water that Upper Basin users have every legal right to use, thereby negating the system benefits of water conservation. Is it fair to stop these new Upper Basin uses? Going further, municipal water use is much more economically valuable than irrigation uses and serves the population centers where the vast majority of basin residents reside. Does that mean that irrigators should bear the brunt of looming curtailments, even though they are growing crops that sustain those urban residents, and even though they were the first users of water in the basin? Actually, to that point, they were not the first users. The Law of the River is nearly absent in reserving water for the environment, and while the rights of Native American communities are now well established in law, many communities still lack access to water. How can these oversights be remedied if the pressing need is to accomplish net reductions in consumption?

One recent effort to better understand the challenges and potential solutions was the *Colorado River Basin Water Supply and Demand Study*, an ambitious technical investigation led primarily by the Bureau of Reclamation, US Department of the Interior (2012). The study used a variety of water demand and water supply scenarios (one of which included climate change projections) to estimate future imbalances should no significant actions be taken. Those results quantified not only the growing magnitude of the supply/demand imbalance, but also the difficultly in identifying a clear vision for what a sustainable future might look like. The study highlighted that each water user group has different levels of water security, risk thresholds, and risk management opportunities, and these shift depending on the water management behavior of other water users. This shift results from many forces, ranging from the age of the water use (and its intrastate priority), the physical location of the water use (as well as the location of infrastructure), the economic resources of the water user, and the specifics (and specific errors) in the allocation framework documents. It is a heterogeneous collection of water users. The fate of all water users may be intertwined, but we are not all in this together.

Lacking a unified vision about what management regime is truly sustainable or equitable, organizing collective action is difficult. Despite this reality, however, Colorado River management has changed dramatically in the last fifteen years. Increasingly, stakeholders are opting for cooperation and negotiation over polarization and litigation. The decision-making tent is slowly expanding to include environmental interests and, to a lesser extent, Native American tribes. Negotiations are occurring at virtually every scale—substate, interstate, basin-wide. There is some reason for optimism. Whether or not these processes can lead to solutions at a pace sufficient to avoid catastrophic shortages, however, remains in doubt. Should the water delivery system "crash," then clear winners and losers will emerge, and the opportunity for cooperative problem solving may dry up completely.

WATER, LAND, AND THE ROAD FORWARD

Notably absent from the preceding discussion of the unfolding Colorado River crisis was its link to public lands and public resources. Those links certainly exist, but with few exceptions, water management regimes are typically developed independently of public land and resource management. Rather, management is almost entirely focused on the withdrawal of water to meet human uses—uses that occur primarily on private lands. The exceptions to this rule are important. On the Colorado, the main exceptions revolve around hydropower generation and, more generally, the relationship between the big dams on the system and the functioning of the river corridors downstream (Adler 2007). Perhaps the best example on the Colorado is the Grand

Canyon, immediately downstream of Glen Canyon Dam. Since 1996, the Glen Canyon Dam Adaptive Management Program has tried to balance the largely incompatible objectives of river regulation and the environmental and recreational values associated with Glen Canyon National Park and Glen Canyon National Recreation Area (Schmidt et al. 1998). Similar, but much more pronounced, struggles have shaped water management in other regions of the West, especially the Northwest, where competing goals of power production and salmon recovery have tormented resource managers for decades (National Resource Council 1996). These long-standing conflicts between human and environmental instream uses will continue to be a feature of western water management, but looking forward, the primary battlegrounds will lie well beyond the actual stream corridors and begin only after the water has left the channel.

The nature of these conflicts is shaped by two parameters: jurisdictions and sectors. At the macroscale, most of the large western rivers have been allocated among the relevant basin states, a first step in dividing up the flow among increasingly finer jurisdictions, such as districts, municipalities, and, ultimately, individual properties and users. This is primarily what western water law is designed to accomplish. For all the benefits that this achieves, these allocation processes have undermined the integrity of western rivers—every bit as much as the concrete and steel infrastructure—as the conception of a river as a whole, intact living body is lost. Also lost, in many cases, is the sense of a river basin community, as each jurisdiction (and sub-jurisdiction) is its own entity with its own rights and own risk portfolio. In other words, if I'm in a better position than my neighbor, then I may be sympathetic, but it's ultimately not my concern.

This leads to the second parameter: sectors. Among human water users, there are two primary players: irrigators and municipal and industrial water users. The numbers vary from state to state, but generally at least 70% of human water consumption (and often much more) in the West occurs in agriculture, whereas the vast majority of people and economic activity are concentrated in cities. Again, the linkages between the two sectors are tight; farmers provide city dwellers with food and open spaces, while cities provide the revenue and services needed by rural populations. As water becomes scarcer across the West, however, the two sectors are increasingly in competition. Skillfully managing that conflict has become the front line in water management, and arguably among the biggest challenges in the West overall.

To be clear, the conflict is not between farmers and cities; rather, it is between rural areas and cities. To the extent that farmers "lose" water to cities, it is normally because they have chosen to sell their rights, often at prices that handsomely reward the farmer. These are voluntary arrangements. To the extent that there is a victim in these stories, it is the broader rural community, and specifically those individuals whose livelihoods and budgets depend on farmers buying materials and services associated with irrigated agriculture (National Research Council 1992). These are the invisible players in existing systems of water rights. As seen in places like Crowley County, Colorado, when the farmers sell their water rights, the communities literally dry up and disperse as winds scour barren fields and abandoned homes and businesses (Devine 2015). This process is known as buy-and-dry, and it is the widely feared result of the trajectory emerging in many basins, including much of the Colorado River Basin.

Is there an alternative? One alternative is urban water conservation. If a city can meet the water demands associated with population growth by conserving water, then the pressure on rural areas is avoided. There are many reasons to think this can be done. The major cities of the West—including Albuquerque, Denver, Las Vegas, Los Angeles, Phoenix, San Francisco, Seattle, and many others—use roughly the same amount (or less) of water today than they did several decades ago, despite having some of the most rapidly growing populations in the country (Colorado River Research Group 2015). That is a tremendous (and largely unknown) success story, but at least two caveats are in order. First, conservation is likely to get progressively more difficult (and expensive), as the easy opportunities have been targeted first. Second, even if total water demands are kept flat, the extremes associated with a changing climate provide a strong incentive for further expanding water systems (and water rights) to buffer expected drought conditions—including potential "megadroughts" lasting several decades (Ault et al. 2016). Conservation in the agricultural sector is another option, but one with its own complications. In many locations, such as the Colorado River Basin, farmers have been highly successful in using water more efficiently, that is, getting increasingly larger yields from an unchanged level of water consumption (Bureau of Reclamation, US Department of the Interior 2015). That is encouraging, but much like the urban success story, this is not a net reduction in use, which is ultimately what is needed in the Colorado and other western basins. In most cases, actually reducing water consumption in the agricultural sector requires taking land out of production, an outcome that is problematic to rural economies and that can also trigger the "use it or lose it" tenets of western water law, which say that a water right that is not fully used can be reduced accordingly. Many of those rules are being revised in statehouses around the West, but the fear of harming a water right—often the most valuable asset that a farmer owns—remains a serious conservation deterrent.

One potential solution is a class of evolving relationships known as alternative transfer methods, or ATMs (Colorado Water Conservation Board 2012). In a nutshell, these are deals that call upon farmers to temporarily reduce water consumption, usually by a rotational fallowing, with the conserved water going to an urban user who compensates the farmer for any lost crop yields. Some arrangements are ongoing, while others may function only in drought years or other special circumstances where city water systems are under stress. In theory, such arrangements can bolster the reliability of city water systems, while maintaining sufficient farming activities and revenues to sustain rural economies. Such arrangements are evolving across the West, particularly in Southern California, and in the case of the recent Colorado Water Plan, they have been identified as a desirable solution to looming water shortages. A host of legal, technical, and cultural obstacles have slowed widespread ATM adoption, but there are ample reasons to think that they are the right path forward.

CONCLUSION

To say that water scarcity is the defining characteristic of water management in the West is not a bold statement, and on the surface, it is not any different than the assessments readily found in reports from the region's homesteading era. But important differences exist. Unlike earlier times, the challenge today is not primarily one of applying engineering to increase supplies, that is, of harnessing and diverting rivers to serve awaiting fields and growing towns. In almost all western subbasins, that work has been done, and those opportunities are exhausted. The challenge today is to cap, or even reduce, the consumption for water. As illustrated by the Colorado River case study, limiting or reducing water consumption raises a host of legal and technical issues, as well as issues better described as socioeconomic and cultural. The world of western water management is getting more complicated in many ways, including the growing influence of climate change on rivers and water delivery systems. The traditional linear practice of using historical records to statistically describe flow regimes, and to then size and build appropriate infrastructure and institutions, is largely antiquated. While we cannot precisely say what the future will look like, it almost certainly will not look like the past or the present. This places a premium on regimes that emphasize risk management and adaptive management.

Overlying all of this is the observation that the relationship between water management and land management will also likely need to evolve. The traditional notion that water development is a necessary precursor to land development and economic expansion is not necessarily invalid, but is now much too simplistic. Today, a failure to innovate in the water sector may not merely close the door to future expansion, but it also may threaten the viability of existing economies and communities. Just maintaining the status quo is, in many cases, a formidable achievement. Additionally, there are many reasons to think that the best opportunities for economic growth may lie in industries and activities that do not require additional water, or that depend on leaving water undistributed instream. The best paths to prosperity in the New West will likely be those that emphasize water resource protection and conservation, not development and consumption. For many in the water resources community, this is new territory.

References

Adler, Robert. 2007. *Restoring Colorado River Ecosystems: A Troubled Sense of Immensity.* Washington, DC: Island Press.

Ault, Toby R., Justin S. Mankin, Benjamin I. Cook, and Jason E. Smerdon. 2016. "Relative Impacts of Mitigation, Temperature, and Precipitation on 21st-Century Megadrought Risk in the American Southwest." *Science Advances* 2(10): e1600873.

Bureau of Reclamation, US Department of the Interior. 2012. *Colorado River Basin Water Supply and Demand Study.* Washington, DC: Bureau of Reclamation, US Department of the Interior. https://www.usbr.gov/watersmart/bsp/docs/finalreport/ColoradoRiver/CRBS_Executive_Summary_FINAL.pdf.

Bureau of Reclamation, US Department of the Interior. 2015. *Colorado River Basin Stakeholders Moving Forward to Address Challenges Identified in the Colorado River Basin Water Supply and Demand Study.* Phase 1 Report: Executive Summary. Washington, DC: Bureau of Reclamation, US Department of the Interior. https://www.usbr.gov/lc/region/programs/crbstudy/MovingForward/Phase1Report/fullreport.pdf.

Cayan, Daniel R., Michael D. Dettinger, David Pierce, Tapash Das, Noah Knowles, F. Martin Ralph, and Edwin Sumargo. 2016. "Natural Variability, Anthropogenic Climate Change, and Impacts on Water Availability and Flood Extremes in the Western United States." In *Water Policy and Planning in a Variable and Changing Climate,* edited by Kathleen A. Miller et al., 17-42. Boca Raton, FL: CRC Press.

Cohen, Michael J. 2011. *Municipal Deliveries of Colorado River Basin Water.* Oakland, CA: Pacific Institute. http://pacinst.org/publication/municipal-deliveries-of-colorado-river-basin-water-new-report-examines-100-cities-and-agencies/.

Cohen, Michael J., Juliet Christian-Smith, and John Berggren. 2013. *Water to Supply the Land: Irrigated Agriculture in the Colorado River Basin.* Oakland, CA: Pacific Institute. http://pacinst.org/publication/water-to-supply-the-land-irrigated-agriculture-in-the-colorado-river-basin/.

Colorado River Research Group. 2015. "The Case for Conservation." May 2015. www.coloradoriverresearchgroup.org.

Colorado River Research Group. 2018. "When Is Drought Not a Drought? Drought, Aridification, and the 'New Normal.'" March 2018. https://www.coloradoriverresearchgroup.org/uploads/4/2/3/6/42362959/crrg_aridity_report.pdf.

Colorado Water Conservation Board. 2012. *Alternative Agricultural Water Transfer Methods Grant Program Summary and Status Update.* Technical Memorandum. Denver, CO: CDM Smith.

Devine, Brian. 2015. "The Legacy of Buy-and-Dry and the Challenge of Lease-Fallowing in Colorado's Arkansas River Basin." Master's thesis, University of Colorado, Boulder.

Fradkin, Philip L. 1981. *A River No More.* Tucson: University of Arizona Press.

Hansen, J., R. Ruedy, M. Sato, and K. Lo. 2010. "Global Surface Temperature Change." *Reviews in Geophysics* 48: RG4004, doi:101002/2010RG000345.

Intergovernmental Panel on Climate Change. 2013. *Climate Change 2013: The Physical Science Basis. Contribution of Working Group I to the Fifth Assessment Report of the Intergovernmental Panel on Climate Change,* edited by T. F. Stocker et al. Cambridge: Cambridge University Press. doi:10.1017/CBO9781107415324.

Kenney, Douglas S. 2014. "History of River Governance in the United States." In *Sustainability in River Basins,* edited by A. Dehnhardt and U. Petschow, 109-134. Munich: Oekom.

Lukas, Jeff, Joseph Barsugli, Nolan Doesken, Imtiaz Rangwala, and Klaus Wolter. 2014. *Climate Change in Colorado: A Synthesis to Support Water Resources Management and Adaptation.* Report for the Colorado Water Conservation Board. Boulder: University of Colorado.

MacDonnell, Lawrence J., David H. Getches, and William C. Hugenberg Jr. 1995. "The Law of the Colorado River: Coping with Severe Sustained Drought." *Water Resources Bulletin* 31(5): 825-836.

Meko, David M., Connie A. Woodhouse, Christopher A. Baisan, Troy Knight, Jeffrey J. Lukas, Malcolm K. Hughes, and Matthew W. Salzer. 2007. "Medieval Drought in the Upper Colorado River Basin." *Geophysical Research Letters* 34(10): 1-5. https://doi.org/10.1029/2007GL029988.

Milly, P. C. D., Julio Betancourt, Malin Falkenmark, Robert M. Hirsh, Zbigniew W. Kundzewicz, Dennis P. Lettenmaier, and Ronald J. Stouffer. 2008. "Climate Change: Stationarity Is Dead: Whither Water Management?" *Science* 319(5863): 573-574.

National Research Council. 1992. *Water Transfers in the West: Efficiency, Equity and the Environment.* Washington, DC: National Academy Press.

National Research Council. 1996. *Upstream: Salmon and Society in the Pacific Northwest.* Washington, DC: National Academy Press.

Powell, John Wesley. 1878. *Report on the Lands of the Arid Region of the United States, with a More Detailed Account of the Lands of Utah.* Washington, DC: Government Printing Office.

Reisner, Marc. 1986. *Cadillac Desert: The American West and Its Disappearing Water.* New York: Penguin.

Revelle, R. R., and P. E. Waggoner. 1983. "Effects of a Carbon Dioxide Induced Climatic Change on Water Supplies in the Western United States." In *Changing Climate,* 419-432. Washington DC: National Academy of Sciences Press.

Robison, Jason, and Douglas S. Kenney. 2013. "Equity and the Colorado River." *Environmental Law* 42(4): 1157-1209.

Schmidt, John C., Robert H. Webb, Richard A. Valdez, G. Richard Marzolf, and Lawrence E. Stevens. 1998. "Science and Values in River Restoration in the Grand Canyon." *BioScience* 48(9): 735-747.

Sproles, E. A., A. W. Nolin, K. Rittger, and T. H. Painter. 2013. "Climate Change Impacts on Maritime Mountain Snowpack in the Oregon Cascades." *Hydrology and Earth System Sciences* 17: 2581–2597. doi:10.5194/hess-17-2581-2013.

Stegner, Wallace. 1954. *Beyond the Hundredth Meridian: John Wesley Powell and the Second Opening of the West.* New York: Penguin Books.

Udall, Bradley, and Jonathan Overpeck. 2017. "The Twenty-First Century Colorado River Hot Drought and Implications for the Future." *Water Resources Research* 53: 2404-2418. https://doi.org/10.1002/2016WR019638.

Weatherford, Gary D., and F. Lee Brown, eds. 1986. *New Courses for the Colorado River.* Albuquerque: University of New Mexico Press.

Woodhouse, Connie A., Gregory T. Pederson, Kiyomi Morino, Stephanie A. McAfee, and Gregory J. McCabe. 2016. "Increasing Influence of Air Temperature on Upper Colorado River Streamflow." *Geophysical Research Letters* 43: 2174–2181. https://doi.org/10.1002/2015GL067613.

Xiao, Mu, Bradley Udall, and Dennis P. Lettenmaier. 2018. "On the Causes of Declining Colorado River Streamflows." *Water Resources Research* 54(9): 6739-6756. doi:10.1029/2018WR023153, https://agupubs.onlinelibrary.wiley.com/doi/abs/10.1029/2018WR023153.

Part III

WILDERNESS AND WILDLIFE

Chapter 7

Wild Places and Irreplaceable Resources
Protecting Wilderness and National Monuments

JOHN RUPLE

This chapter discusses wilderness both as an idea that has had an evolving meaning and as a legal construct. It also discusses national monuments on public lands, another legal construct that has been used to protect a wide range of resources, including wilderness character. These areas overlap, but that overlap is far from complete, and the objectives underpinning these two designations, while complimentary, are not identical.

WILDERNESS

There are two kinds of wilderness, at least for the purposes of this chapter. Small "w" wilderness is wilderness as we envision it when we close our eyes. It is sometimes feared and sometimes revered—it is what Roderick Nash calls "the geography of the mind" (Nash 2014). Like fine art, we know it when we see it, but we often have difficulty developing a common definition or agreeing upon its value. Big "W" Wilderness, while rooted in Nash's geography of the mind, reflects the legal constructs that we as a nation have developed to steward our wild places. Big W Wilderness is the proper noun we use to identify the protected bubbles that exist on the maps of our public lands.

In his famous book *Wilderness and the American Mind*, Nash traces the evolution of the idea of wilderness. Nash explains that wilderness is a concept steeped in history and defined as much by what it is not as by what it is. In the beginning, wilderness was the antithesis of Eden. When society expelled its undesirable members, it cast them out into the wilderness. Yet Europeans subdued much of their wilderness, converting wild lands to a managed pastoral landscape long before most European explorers ever set foot on the "New World."

To the first European settlers, the wilderness of the New World stood in stark contrast to the managed estates they left behind. America, to European settlers, was a wild, mysterious, and often dangerous place. There were no Gardens of Versailles, no rolling pastures, no neatly manicured croplands. The wilderness of the New World teemed with wild beasts not found in the Old World. This wilderness was also inhabited by Native peoples with whom European settlers often clashed. Europeans sought to build what John Winthrop called a city on the hill—a hill that both literally and metaphorically had to be cleared before that city could thrive.

With time, and as European settlers strengthened their toehold in the New World, the wilderness came to be seen less as threat and more as a frontier teaming with bounty. It became a place where manifest destiny could play out, where rugged individuals—ranchers, loggers, miners, and pioneers—could all seek their fortunes, and where the bounty was limitless. The intrepid pioneer flourished, as did railroads and mining magnates. Buffalo and passenger pigeons fell to our unbridled enthusiasm, and by 1890, the US Census Bureau had declared the frontier closed.

With time, growing economic prosperity, disenchantment with an increasingly urbanized life, and the allure of testing oneself led some back to the land. The likes of Aldo Leopold and John Muir extolled the virtues of wilderness, not just as a source of raw materials to fuel our growing nation, but also as a source of inspiration to nurture the soul. National leaders like Theodore Roosevelt and William O. Douglas championed the benefits of wilderness, while photographers from William Henry Jackson to Ansel Adams brought the beauty and grandeur home to urban-dwelling Americans. To many, wilderness became a restorative salve for the wounds of industrialization and over-civilization. Wilderness also became a treasure to be safeguarded and passed down to future generations. For still others, its transcendent worth grew from its import to nonhuman species and to its very existence, even for those who were unlikely to ever venture into the wild. Small w wilderness, in short, grew more abstract and removed from our earlier individual and immediate existence.

Evolving meanings of wilderness gave rise to desires for Wilderness protections, and in 1864, the federal government granted to the state of California what would eventually become Yosemite National Park.[1] That land was later converted into a national park, and in 1905, the park was returned to the federal government.[2] In 1872, President Ulysses S. Grant set aside lands near the headwaters of the Yellowstone River in Wyoming as the United States' first national park.[3] In 1924, the US Forest Service designated the first official wilderness area within the Gila National Forest of New Mexico (Coggins and Glicksman 2018, §25:1).

But the drumbeat of progress marched on, and epic battles between those intent on unlocking the economic riches that grow from or that reside just under the surface of our wild lands met the earnest cries of a populace growingly interested in protecting untrammeled landscapes. Developers won some battles: in 1923 the Tuolumne River was dammed, flooding the Hetch Hetchy Valley and part of Yosemite National Park. Construction of the Glen Canyon Dam began in 1956, flooding rugged and remote canyons on par with those of the Grand Canyon. But preservationists won, too, thwarting efforts to dam the Colorado River through the Grand Canyon and to dam the Green River through Dinosaur National Monument. The tension between preservation and development grew, and in 1964, passage of the Wilderness Act[4] ushered in the era of big W Wilderness.

The Wilderness Act was the culmination of decades of effort to set aside from development a significant portion of those places that remained untouched by human hands. It was, and remains, the strongest tool in the conservation arsenal for protecting the small w wilderness values that have taken on such profound importance to many Americans.

With its passage, the Wilderness Act instantly designated fifty-four wilderness areas that encompassed 9.1 million acres across thirteen states. Wilderness areas are overlay designation, and today, the four main federal land management agencies—the Bureau of Land Management (BLM), US Forest Service, National Park Service, and US Fish and Wildlife Service—manage a combined 110 million acres of Wilderness. These wilderness areas overlay national parks, national forests, national wildlife refuges, and a host of other designations.

Once designated, wilderness areas are managed to preserve the area's wilderness character and are "devoted to the public purposes of recreational, scenic, scientific, educational, conservation, and historical use."[5] Wilderness areas are now highly valued as strongholds for biodiversity and for the ecosystem services that they provide. Except as otherwise authorized by the act or by subsequent legislation creating individual wilderness areas, roads, motorized vehicles or equipment, mechanical transport, and structures or installations are all prohibited within wilderness areas. Exceptions are allowed to accommodate valid existing uses, private land inholdings, and critical agency functions like wildfire suppression.[6]

The act sets lofty goals: to "assure that an increasing population, accompanied by expanding settlement and growing mechanization, does not occupy and modify all areas within the United States and its possessions, leaving no lands designated for preservation and protection in their natural condition."[7] In defining Wilderness, the act states:

> Wilderness, in contrast with those areas where man and his works dominate the landscape, is hereby recognized as an area where the earth and its community of life are untrammeled by man, where man himself is a visitor who does not remain. An area of wilderness is . . . an area of undeveloped Federal land retaining its primeval character and influence, without permanent improvements or human habitation, which is protected and managed so as to preserve its natural conditions and which (1) generally appears to have been affected primarily by the forces of nature, with the imprint of man's work substantially unnoticeable; (2) has outstanding opportunities for solitude or a primitive and unconfined type of recreation; (3) has at least five thousand acres of land or is of sufficient size as to make practicable its preservation and use in an unimpaired condition; and (4) may also contain ecological, geological, or other features of scientific, educational, scenic, or historical value.[8]

In addition to converting all US Forest Service-managed "wilderness," "wild," and "canoe" areas into big W Wilderness, the act directed the secretary of agriculture to review all Forest Service "primitive" areas for possible inclusion in the Wilderness Preservation System. The secretary would make recommendations to the president, who would advise Congress on his recommendations for additions to the system. Congress would then act on those recommendations as it deemed appropriate because, under the act, only Congress can designate wilderness areas.[9]

The secretary of the interior was likewise charged with reviewing potential wilderness areas managed by the National Park Service and the US Fish and Wildlife Service, and to recommend to the president any such areas deemed suitable for Wilderness designation.[10] As with National Forest System lands, the president would then submit recommendation to Congress, and Congress would make the final determination regarding Wilderness designations.

Public lands managed by the Bureau of Land Management were not addressed in the Wilderness Act, though the Federal Land Policy and Management Act of 1976 directed the secretary of the interior to inventory the lands under its control and to identify lands with wilderness character-istics. The secretary would then report to the president which of these areas were suitable for inclusion in the Wilderness Preservation System, the presi-dent would forward his recommendations to Congress, and Congress would make such additions to the system as Congress deemed appropriate.[11]

Congress, of course, does not always act expeditiously on the recom-mendations brought before it, and both the Wilderness Act and the Federal Land Policy and Management Act include important interim protections for Wilderness-quality lands until Congress acts on presidential recommenda-tions. Forest Service primitive areas in existence when the Wilderness Act was passed into law are subject to regulations protecting their wilderness attributes until Congress declares otherwise.[12] Similarly, BLM-managed lands that were recommended for Wilderness designation (known as wilderness study areas, or WSAs) are subject to a statutory obligation that management not impair their suitability for future Wilderness designation until Congress acts on those recommendations.[13] Recommendations to designate millions of acres of Wilderness remain pending decades after those recommendations were first brought before Congress, and congressional inaction has created a class of lands that are effectively managed as Wilderness. These lands are called "de facto Wilderness" by their detractors.

Since 1964, the Wilderness Preservation System has grown to include 765 areas encompassing 110 million acres (171,883 square miles) across forty-four states and Puerto Rico. In 1980, the passage of the Alaska National Interest Lands Conservation Act marked the single largest addition to the system, expanding it by over 56 million acres. Overall, however, only about 5% of the United States (an area slightly larger than the state of California) is protected as Wilderness, and with over half of America's Wilderness in Alaska, only about 2.7% of the contiguous United States (an area about the size of Minnesota) is protected as Wilderness (Wilderness Connect 2017). An additional 12.6 million acres of BLM land receives interim protection as part of a wilderness study area (Bureau of Land Management 2018). The Forest Service also manages approximately 58 million acres of inventoried roadless areas that, while not part of the Wilderness Preservation System, are generally closed to road construction or timber harvesting to protect small w wilderness attributes (Hoover 2018).

Additions to the Wilderness Preservation System and interim protections for lands that are subject to Wilderness designation proposals have been controversial. In 1972, the Forest Service began conducting its Roadless Area Review and Evaluation (RARE), which identified 56 million acres of land as eligible for Wilderness designation. But RARE recommended adding only 12.3 million acres to the Wilderness Preservation System (see Coggins and Glicksman 2018, §§25:15, 25:9). The environmental community harshly criticized RARE for ignoring suitable roadless areas, and for recommending permanent protections for only a small portion of eligible lands. While legal challenges to RARE were playing out, the Forest Service began updating its roadless review, effectively mooting much of the litigation.

In 1977, the Forest Service began its second review, known as RARE II, which proposed 15 million acres of Wilderness designations plus additional study for 10.8 million acres. Litigation again ensued, and much of that litigation was resolved over the years that followed, as Congress designated millions of acres that had been inventoried as eligible under RARE II as new wilderness areas. Other RARE II lands were released from further Wilderness consideration and reopened to development.

The roadless controversy reemerged in 1999, when the secretary of agriculture imposed a temporary moratorium on road construction in inventoried roadless areas. In 2001, the Forest Service issued the Roadless Rule, which prohibited road construction and timber harvesting on approximately 58 million acres of inventoried roadless areas. Nine lawsuits followed and were eventually resolved, with most of the 2001 Roadless Rule being upheld. Roadless areas in the Tongass National Forest, however, were temporarily withdrawn from protection under the Roadless Rule pursuant to a 2003 litigation settlement agreement, and that withdrawal was made permanent in a later federal rule.

The Bush administration, never happy with the 2001 Roadless Rule, issued what became known as the 2005 Roadless Rule, which allowed state governors to propose roadless area revisions within their states. Like its predecessors, the 2005 Roadless Rule found itself mired in litigation. Court of Appeals decisions in 2009 and 2011 reinstated the 2001 Roadless Rule, and in 2012, the US Supreme Court refused to review those decisions. Roadless

WILD PLACES AND IRREPLACEABLE RESOURCES

Rule exemptions that applied to national forests in Alaska were also struck down and litigation appeared to be at an end when, in 2016, the Supreme Court again refused to take up the fight. But battles over roadless areas die hard, especially when old-growth timber in Alaska's Tongass and Chugach National Forests are involved. On August 2, 2018, the Forest Service announced that it intended to issue a new "Alaska state-specific" Roadless Rule that will presumably attempt to open more National Forest System lands to logging. If past is prologue, that rule will surely face intense scrutiny.

BLM lands that have been inventoried as containing wilderness characteristics have also been mired in controversy. While ongoing obligations to inventory wilderness-quality lands and to update management provide flexibility to respond to new information or changed conditions, these continuing obligations also create a level of uncertainty that has not always sat well in communities with economies tied closely to resource extraction. Litigation has addressed whether the BLM has an ongoing obligation to inventory lands with wilderness characteristics as well as the BLM's responsibility in managing lands that new inventories identify as possessing wilderness character.[14] Some of the most contentious litigation has involved ownership of routes and roads across public lands. The state of Utah has been particularly aggressive in pursuing these claims, in part to thwart efforts to designate additional Wilderness, and in part to control activity in wilderness (see Coggins and Glicksman 2018, §15:19, which discusses litigation over title to roads and routes on public lands).

Other attacks on wilderness have proceeded on the theory that the Wilderness Act granted Congress the exclusive power to designate wilderness areas. Land management decisions and presidential designation that resulted in protection of wilderness character, some contend, impermissibly encroached on Congress's power to designate wilderness areas. Chief among these was an unsuccessful 2004 challenge to the Grand Staircase-Escalante National Monument in Utah.[15] That challenge brings us to the Antiquities Act of 1906.

THE ANTIQUITIES ACT AND NATIONAL MONUMENTS

Congress enacted the Antiquities Act of 1906[16] largely in response to looting of Native American sites in the American Southwest (Collins and Green 1978, p. 1055; Squillace 2003, p. 477). Congress realized that they were ill equipped to identify threatened public lands and sensitive resources, or to swiftly develop the site-specific protections those lands required. In passing the Antiquities Act, Congress therefore delegated to the president the discretionary authority to

> declare by public proclamation historic landmarks, historic and prehistoric structures, and other objects of historic or scientific interest that are situated on land owned or controlled by the Federal Government to be national monuments. ... The limits of the parcels shall be confined to the smallest area compatible with the proper care and management of the objects to be protected.[17]

Congress also endowed the president with the power to withdraw national monument lands from availability for future mineral development, homesteading, and other forms of land "disposal."[18] Such withdrawals are a standard part of all modern monument proclamations.

President Roosevelt designated Devil's Tower, the iconic butte that rises dramatically from the prairie surrounding the Black Hills, as the nation's first national monument on September 24, 1906. Since 1906, sixteen presidents—Republicans and Democrats alike—have used Antiquities Act authority to designate 157 national monuments across twenty-nine states, the District of Columbia, and several US territories (National Parks Conservation Association 2017). Congress has added national monuments forty-eight times and elevated monuments to a more protective status, normally that of a national park, on thirty-eight occasions (National Parks Conservation Association 2017). The Grand Canyon in Arizona, Arches in Utah, Olympic in Washington State, Acadia in Maine, and Grand Teton in Wyoming all began as national monuments (National Parks Conservation Association 2017). Sites indelibly inked in our nation's history were also protected as national monuments—sites such as the Statue of Liberty, Pearl Harbor, Thomas Edison's home and laboratory, and Harriet Tubman Underground Railroad.

National monuments differ from national parks in several important ways. First, while national parks are established exclusively by Congress, national monuments can be established by presidential proclamation. This allows the president to sidestep the legislative process and act more expeditiously, potentially over the objections of Congress. Second, Congress has codified into law directions that apply to all national parks: park managers are directed to preserve unimpaired natural and cultural resources and values of parks, and to provide for park enjoyment by the public.[19] No such blanket management direction applies with respect to national monuments. Instead, presidents are free to impose the management direction they deem most appropriate. At the larger national monuments that are found mostly in the West, this has resulted in a trend toward management that retains a working landscape where livestock grazing continues, where hunting is allowed, and where visitor facilities are less developed.

Additional protections for national monuments come from inclusion in the National Landscape Conservation System, or NLCS. The NLCS includes national monuments, wilderness study areas, and components of the National Wilderness Preservation System that are managed by the BLM. In 2000, Secretary of the Interior Bruce Babbitt administratively created the NLCS as a way of shifting BLM culture toward protection of sensitive landscapes, coordinating management of conservation lands under a single office and emphasizing the importance of conservation as a component of the BLM's mission. In 2009, Congress codified the NLCS into law, directing the secretary of the interior to manage lands within the system "in a manner that protects the values for which the components of the system were designated."[20] Protection of national monument resources now represents the will of Congress as signed into law by the president.

While some monuments, like Grand Teton and the Grand Staircase-Escalante, were controversial at the outset, local communities generally grow to embrace the economic opportunities and amenities that national monuments provide. Indeed, monuments can be an economic engine for rural economies. But national monuments that stand to displace extractive activities like mining, logging, oil and gas development, or livestock grazing have provoked the ire of some local communities. On eight occasions, monument designations have been challenged in court, though no designation challenge has ever succeeded. In 1920, for example, the US Supreme Court upheld President Roosevelt's designation of the 808,000-acre Grand Canyon National Monument (later expanded and elevated to national park status).[21] The Supreme Court made quick work of arguments that the Grand Canyon was not an "object" within the meaning of the Antiquities Act, first affirming that the act empowered the president "to establish reserves embracing 'objects of historic or scientific interest,'"[22] and then holding that the Grand Canyon "is an object of unusual scientific interest." It is the greatest eroded canyon in the United States, if not in the world, is over a mile in depth, has attracted wide attention among explorers and scientists, affords an unexampled field for geologic study, [and] is regarded as one of the great natural wonders.[23]

Fifty-six years later, in the only other national monument challenge to reach the Supreme Court, the court again gave objects of "historic or scientific interest" a broad reading, concluding that an endemic fish and the pool it inhabited in the Death Valley National Monument in California were objects of historic or scientific interest within the meaning of the Antiquities Act and therefore appropriately protected by a national monument designation.[24]

While some recent national monument designations have been criticized as too big, and therefore as inconsistent with congressional intent to restrict monuments to the "smallest area compatible with the proper care and management of the objects to be protected,"[25] these arguments have never gained traction with the courts. At 808,000 acres (1,263 square miles), the Grand Canyon National Monument was obviously quite large, and that monument has since been expanded to over 1.2 million acres and elevated to national park status (Ruple 2019 discusses the history of national monument modifications and the multiple Grand Canyon expansions). By 1936, presidents had designated six monuments larger than 1,000 square miles without congressional objection, further solidifying the president's power to create large monuments.

But the way monuments are proclaimed has changed over the past century. Early proclamations contain little more than the most basic identification of the resources to be protected, a rudimentary boundary description, and a perfunctory withdrawal of monument lands from homesteading and land disposal laws. Modern monument proclamations invariably include a lengthy description of the objects and values to be protected, their importance to science and humanity, and language that withdraws lands within a monument from availability for land disposal or future mineral development. Modern monument proclamations also frequently specify other requirements, like limitations on construction of new roads, that protect monument resources. More specific management requirements are developed through a planning process that normally begins shortly after monument designation.

The breadth of a president's authority under the Antiquities Act creates a unique opportunity to tailor each monument proclamation to local issues and needs. For at least two decades, presidents have increasingly taken advantage of that authority. Recent monument proclamations are likely to recognize state primacy in water rights permitting and wildlife management; the ability to continue livestock grazing; and the importance of creating management plans in consultation with state, local, and tribal governments to ensure that those closest to the land have a voice in how that land is managed.[26] Recent monument proclamations also specifically address Native American use of forest products, firewood, and medicinal plants, where those issues have regional significance.[27]

Flexibility and recognition of local concerns, however, are not always enough to avoid controversy. On December 4, 2017, and at the behest of Utah politicians, President Trump carved the 1.9-million-acre Grand Staircase-Escalante National Monument in Utah into three smaller monuments.[28] Together, the three replacement monuments protect just over half of the original monument's area. On the same day, President Trump shrank the 1.3-million-acre Bears Ears National Monument, also in Utah, by approximately 85%.[29] The Grand Staircase-Escalante National Monument had been created by President Clinton twenty-one years earlier.[30] Bears Ears was but a year old, having been established at the behest of five Native American tribes shortly before President Obama left office.[31] It was the first national monument ever designated at the behest of tribal governments.

President Trump's actions reflect the two largest reductions to a national monument that have ever been made by a president, and they open lands excluded from the monuments to mineral exploration and development. The five Native American tribes that had proposed Bears Ears, as well as multiple scientific, conservation, and environmental organizations, quickly sued to invalidate President Trump's reductions to Bears Ears. Legal challenges to the reductions to the Grand Staircase-Escalante National Monument also came almost immediately, setting up a battle over the authority granted to the president in the Antiquities Act that appears destined for Supreme Court review.[32]

The monuments' defenders contend that the Property Clause of the US Constitution endows Congress with power over public lands, and with it, the power to create and revise national monuments. They then argue that in passing the Antiquities Act, Congress delegated to the president the power to create national monuments, but that Congress never bestowed the president with the power to radically reduce monuments. The lack of a grant of power to revise national monuments is not surprising, they argue, as there was no need for such delegation. While exigencies necessitated quick action to protect lands, no similar urgency demands expedited monument reduction. Had Congress intended to grant a two-way grant of power, it would have said so clearly, as it did in other statutes empowering presidents to both create and revise other designations involving the public lands. The plaintiffs also point out that in 1976 Congress enacted the Federal Land Policy and Management Act, which comprehensively rewrote federal public land law, expressly reigning in the president's implied powers over public lands. For further discussion of the legal arguments for and against monument reductions, see Ruple (2019).

Supporters of President Trump's reductions counter that in passing the Antiquities Act, Congress did not expressly deny the president the power to revise boundaries. At a minimum, the president should be able to reduce a monument to ensure that it is "confined to the smallest area compatible with the proper care and management of the objects to be protected." They also argue that, absent an express prohibition, courts should look to congressional acquiescence in twenty or so prior presidential reductions to national monuments, which gives the presumption of a president's power to revise a national monument. President Trump, in reducing the two monuments, also argued that the designations were unnecessary, as other laws provide adequate protection for monument resources (Ruple 2019).

Arguments that national monument lands and resources are adequately protected by other laws strain credulity by ignoring that two million acres that were previously closed to mineral development are now open for mining as well as oil and gas development.[33] Thousands of archaeological and paleontological sites were also excluded from the two monuments, and that exclusion directly affects legal protections (Ruple et al. 2018). Congress, in codifying the National Landscape Conservation System, which includes national monuments managed by the Bureau of Land Management, expressly directs the BLM to protect the values that led to monument designation.[34] That direction disappeared for those lands excised from the monument.

Reliance on congressional acquiescence in prior reductions, however, is more appealing. As proponents of monument reduction note correctly, presidents have revised and reduced monuments on eighteen prior occasions. But a closer look is telling: most prior reductions corrected errors in the description of the objects being protected or in describing their surrounding landscape. Other revisions excluded from a monument private land and infrastructure that predated the monument's designation. Still other reductions occurred in conjunction with concurrent additions of land to the same monument, improving protection for the objects identified in the original monument proclamations. Finally, on three occasions, reductions responded to the existential threats posed by World Wars I and II. None of these prior reductions appear to provide much justification for more recent events, which seem to be driven by a policy preference for energy development over conservation. Similarly, while congressional acquiescence in prior monument reductions may arguably have endowed the president with such powers, the passing of more than a half century since the last reduction may imply that such powers, if they existed at all, have withered on the vine. And even if that power survived, presidential powers were reined in by the Federal Land Policy and Management Act of 1976. (For a review of all prior national monument reductions authorized by US presidents, see Ruple et al. 2018.)

How the courts resolve these questions has tremendous import for our public lands. If President Trump's actions are upheld, the presumptive permanence of national monuments evaporates, and every national monument becomes subject to revision at the whim of future administrations. Congress unquestionably has the power to resolve the dispute by restoring the two monuments or by affirming their reductions. Congress also can define presidential powers under the Antiquities Act in ways that prevent the recurrence of these debates. Congress, unfortunately, appears reluctant to wade into the fray.

We are left with the tensions noted at the beginning of this chapter: those between the competing American ideals of harvesting nature's bounty for the betterment of civilization, preserving wild places for future generations, and considering nature as a source of inspiration to nurture the soul. It is a tension that is playing out across the spectrum of public land management, and it appears destined to become only more contentious as a growing population competes for finite resources.

Legal Citations

1 Stat. 325-26 (1864).
2 Joint Resolution Accepting the Recession by the State of California of the Yosemite Valley Grant and the Mariposa Big Tree Grove in the Yosemite National Park, S.J. Res. 115, 58th Cong. (enacted) reprinted at 33 Stat. 1286 (1905).
3 17 Stat. 32-33 (1872).

4 16 U.S.C. §§ 1131-36.

5 16 U.S.C. § 1133(b).

6 16 U.S.C. § 1133(c).

7 16 U.S.C. § 1131(a).

8 16 U.S.C. § 1131(c).

9 16 U.S.C. § 1132.

10 16 U.S.C. § 1132(c).

11 43 U.S.C. § 1782.

12 16 U.S.C. § 1132(b).

13 43 U.S.C. § 1782(c).

14 Oregon Natural Desert Association v. Bureau of Land Management, 625 F. Supp. 3d 1092 (9th Cir. 2010).

15 Utah Ass'n of Counties v. Bush, 316 F. Supp. 2d 1172 (D. Utah 2004).

16 54 U.S.C. §§ 320101-303.

17 54 U.S.C. §§ 320310(a) and (b).

18 54 U.S.C. §§ 320310(a) and (b).

19 16 U.S.C. § 1.

20 16 U.S.C. § 7202(c)(2).

21 Cameron v. United States, 252 U.S. 450 (1920).

22 Cameron v. United States, 252 U.S. 450 (1920).

23 Cameron v. United States, 252 U.S. 450 (1920), 456.

24 Cappaert v. United States, 426 U.S. 128, 142 (1976).

25 54 U.S.C. § 320301(b).

26 See, e.g., Proclamation No. 9297, 80 Fed. Reg. 41969 (July 10, 2015); Proclamation No. 9232, 90 Fed. Reg. 9975 (Feb. 24, 2015) (Browns Canyon National Monument, recognizing state authority over wildlife management); Proclamation No. 6920, 61 Fed. Reg. 50223 (Sept. 18, 1996) (Grand Staircase-Escalante National Monument, maintaining existing livestock grazing); Proclamation No. 9298, 80 Fed. Reg. 41975 (July 10, 2015) (Berryessa Snow Mountain National Monument, coordinated planning with state, local, and tribal governments).

27 See, e.g., Proclamation No. 9194, 79 Fed. Reg. 62303 (Oct. 10, 2014) (San Gabriel Mountains National Monument, guaranteeing monument access for "traditional cultural, spiritual, and tree and forest product-, food-, and medicine-gathering purposes"); Proclamation No. 8946, 78 Fed. Reg. 18783 (March 25, 2013) (Río Grande Del Norte National Monument, ensuring "the protection of religious and cultural sites in the monument and provide access to the sites by members of Indian tribes for traditional cultural and customary uses," and "traditional collection of firewood and piñon nuts in the monument for personal non-commercial use consistent with the purposes of this proclamation"); Proclamation No. 8868, 77 Fed. Reg. 59275 (Sept. 21, 2012) (Chimney Rock National Monument, to "protect and preserve access by tribal members for traditional cultural, spiritual, and food- and medicine-gathering purposes, consistent with the purposes of the monument, to the maximum extent permitted by law").

28 Proclamation No. 9682, 82 Fed. Reg. 58089 (Dec. 4, 2017).

29 Proclamation No. 9681, 82 Fed. Reg. 58081 (Dec. 4, 2017).

30 Proclamation No. 6920, 61 Fed. Reg. 50223 (Sept. 18, 1996).

31 Proclamation No. 9558, 82 Fed. Reg. 1139 (Dec. 28, 2016) (Bears Ears National Monument).

32 Wilderness Society v. Donald J. Trump, 1:17-cv-02578 (D. D.C.) (consolidated Grand Staircase-Escalante cases); and Hopi Tribe v. Donald J. Trump, 1:17-cv-02590 (D. D.C.) (consolidated Bears Ears cases).

33 Proclamation No. 9681, 82 Fed. Reg. 58081 (Dec. 4, 2017), at 58085; Proclamation No. 9682, 82 Fed. Reg. 58089 (Dec. 4, 2017), at 58093-94.
34 16 U.S.C. § 7202(c)(2).

References

Bureau of Land Management. 2018. *Public Land Statistics 2017*. Washington, DC: Bureau of Land Management, Department of the Interior.

Coggins, George Cameron, and Robert L. Glicksman. 2018. *3 Public Natural Resources Law*, vol. 3. 2nd ed.

Collins, Robert Bruce, and Dee F. Green. 1978. "A Proposal to Modernize the American Antiquities Act." *Science* 202 (4372): 1055-1059.

Hoover, Katie. 2018. *Federal Lands and Related Resources: Overview and Selected Issues for the 115th Congress*. CRS Report R43429. Washington, DC: Congressional Research Service.

Nash, Roderick Frazier. 2014. *Wilderness and the American Mind*. 5th ed. New Haven, CT: Yale University Press.

National Parks Conservation Association. 2017. "Antiquities Act Designations and Related Actions." Updated January 13, 2017. https://www.npca.org/resources/2658-monuments-protected-under-the-antiquities-act.

Ruple, John C. 2019. "The Trump Administration and Lessons Not Learned from Prior National Monument Modifications." *Harvard Environmental Law Review* 43: 1-76.

Ruple, John C., Michael Henderson, and Ceci Caitlin. 2018. "Up for Grabs—The State of Fossil Protection in (Recently) Unprotected National Monuments." Georgetown Environmental Law Review Online, October 5, 2018. https://www.law.georgetown.edu/environmental-law-review/blog/up-for-grabs-the-state-of-fossils-protection-in-recently-unprotected-national-monuments/.

Squillace, Mark. 2003. "The Monumental Legacy of the Antiquities Act of 1906." *Georgia Law Review* 37: 473-610.

Wilderness Connect. 2017. "About Wilderness." Last modified December 12, 2018. www.wilderness.net/NWPS/fastfacts.

Chapter 8
National Parks
Preserving America's Natural and Cultural Heritage

ROBERT B. KEITER

National parks—widely regarded as "America's best idea"—are designed to preserve the natural and cultural heritage of the United States. A unique part of federal public lands, national parks attract visitors from near and far who come to marvel at Yellowstone's astonishing geothermal features, Yosemite's soaring cliff faces, the eye-popping Grand Canyon, and other remarkable natural attractions. They come to see Yellowstone's bison and bears and to absorb the deep solitude of Canyonlands' austere backcountry. And they come for adventure—for the thrill of navigating the Grand Canyon's pulsing whitewater, to climb the soaring Grand Teton, to surf the waves at Cape Hatteras, and to paddle through Voyageurs' watery wilderness. Generations of American families have made summer pilgrimages to the national parks, establishing traditions that endure today. Though most visitors come away with long-lasting personal memories of these storied places, few are acquainted with the National Park System's rich history, the profound changes it has undergone, or the challenges it confronts today. Although seemingly well-protected natural sanctuaries, national parks are never far removed from the political, social, and economic forces that regularly buffet the nation's public lands.

In 1872, Congress enacted legislation establishing Yellowstone National Park in northwestern Wyoming as the world's first national park. The bill retained this extraordinary landscape in public ownership as a "pleasuring ground" to be maintained in its "natural condition" for present and future generations.[1] Congress soon built upon the Yellowstone idea with the designation of additional national parks to protect other stunning western settings from falling into private hands or being exploited for profit. By 1916, it was clear that these early national parks constituted an emergent system, prompting Congress to pass the National Park Service Organic Act,[2] which created the National Park Service and instructed the new agency to preserve these lands in an unimpaired condition. Since then, the National Park System has grown to more than 415 units covering 84 million acres with sites in each of the fifty states. A political creation from the beginning, the much-beloved national parks occupy a unique, preservation-oriented position on the nation's public lands.

This chapter explores the evolution of national parks as part of the nation's public land system, emphasizing the vital role parks play in promoting nature conservation. It begins by outlining the basic legal framework governing the national parks. It then explains how, within that legal framework, the national park idea has evolved over the years in response to changes in public values and advances in scientific knowledge. Next, it reviews how the National Park System has expanded over time, noting the importance of public sentiment and ecological knowledge in driving that growth. Given the dynamic nature of American society, the chapter concludes by highlighting current challenges confronting the national parks and reflecting on how these challenges are being addressed to ensure the future of this remarkable system devoted to preserving our natural world and cultural legacies.

ESTABLISHING AND MANAGING NATIONAL PARKS

Adopted in 1916, the National Park Service Organic Act has survived the test of time and continues to guide management of the ever-expanding National Park System. The Organic Act provides that the "fundamental purpose" of the national parks is "to conserve the scenery and the natural and historic objects and the wild life therein and to provide for the enjoyment of the same in such manner and by such means as will leave them unimpaired for the enjoyment of future generations."[3] The act further grants the National Park Service authority to adopt rules and regulations governing the use and management of the parks.[4] Over time, Congress has amended the act, both clarifying and expanding the Park Service's role and responsibilities. In 1970, the General Authorities Act established that the growing assortment of differently named units within the National Park System constituted a single system and should be managed as such.[5] It also instructed the Park Service to prepare general management plans for each unit to address park visitation and to ensure that park resources were adequately protected.[6] In 1978, responding to the destructive impacts caused by upstream logging outside Redwood

National Park, Congress adopted the so-called Redwood Amendment, which not only reaffirmed its commitment to the original organic mandate but also prohibited derogation of park values unless "directly and specifically provided by Congress."[7]

Other amendments to the Organic Act have expanded the Park Service's responsibilities. In 1998, Congress adopted the Omnibus National Park System Act, requiring for the first time that the Park Service "assure that management of the National Park System is enhanced by the availability and utilization of a broad program of the highest quality science and information."[8] The legislation also explicitly acknowledged that national parks were part of larger landscapes.[9] In 2016, Congress adopted the National Park Service Centennial Act, instructing the Park Service to "ensure that management of system units . . . is enhanced by the availability and use of a broad program of the highest quality interpretation and education," including programs that enable people to engage with the natural world, promote diversity, and reflect current scientific research.[10] Other Organic Act amendments have sought to clarify the Park Service's role in recommending additions to the National Park System, including the criteria to be used in evaluating the "national significance, suitability, and feasibility" of the proposed area.[11] Moreover, Congress has twice revised the Park Service's concessions policies, clarifying that park resource values take priority over visitor uses, limiting in-park visitor accommodations and services to those that are "necessary and appropriate," and promoting greater competition among concessioners.[12] Simply put, Congress has confirmed that the Park Service's first obligation is to safeguard park resources in an unimpaired condition, while gradually expanding the agency's responsibilities toward meeting this obligation.

Other important laws that extend across all public lands also apply to the national parks and have helped to shape the system and its management. The Wilderness Act of 1964—enacted in part as a reaction to the Park Service's early penchant for constructing roads, hotels, and other facilities inside the parks—prohibits any structures, other development activity, or motors inside designated wilderness areas to ensure the lands remain "untrammeled" and "primeval" in character.[13] Although the Park Service expressed early opposition to the wilderness legislation (Miles 2009), Congress has designated nearly 44 million acres of national park land as wilderness, paradoxically giving the agency the largest wilderness portfolio among the four federal land management agencies (Wilderness Connect 2019). The Endangered

Species Act extends powerful legal protection to species verging on extinction, essentially supplementing the protection that wildlife generally enjoys within the parks under the Organic Act but also requiring the Park Service to consult with the US Fish and Wildlife Service whenever its actions might affect a protected species or its habitat.[14] The National Environmental Policy Act requires federal agencies to prepare an environmental impact statement whenever their actions might significantly affect the human environment,[15] which ensures that the Park Service must carefully evaluate new construction proposals and visitor activities, such as the number of tour boats in Glacier Bay National Park.[16] Further, the Clean Air Act and Clean Water Act provide national parks with important legal protection against polluting activities occurring outside park boundaries.

Drawing upon its authority under the Organic Act, the Park Service has promulgated regulations and policies that further define its management priorities and strategies. Park Service regulations designed to protect park resources and visitors are legally enforceable; they vest park officials with the authority to close sensitive areas and to impose limits on hunting, fishing, recreational activities, firearm use, and similar activities.[17] Individual park managers are authorized to establish specific regulations for their parks through the superintendent's compendium, which can entail additional limits on vehicles, bicycles, fishing, research specimen collection, climbing, and the like. Further, the Park Service's *Management Policies* provides additional guidance on such matters as interpretation of the Organic Act, wildlife management, wilderness management, wildfire, cultural resources, and Native American uses (National Park Service 2006). Although not regarded as legally enforceable,[18] these management policies are binding on agency employees, setting useful standards for those charged with preserving park resources and values.

The judiciary has played an important role in interpreting and applying these laws in cases challenging controversial park management decisions or involving external activities perceived as threatening park resources. Several cases have posed the question of whether the agency's resource protection responsibilities take precedence over visitor enjoyment, for example, when mountain biking was negatively affecting trail conditions or when jeep access was adversely affecting stream conditions. The courts have consistently ruled that resource protection must take priority in order to meet the Organic Act's mandate to preserve the parks in an unimpaired condition for the benefit of future generations. A more difficult question arises when the threat to park resources arises outside the park in the form of an external pollution source or energy development on adjacent lands (Sax and Keiter 1987, 2006). In these cases the courts have recognized that the Park Service has an obligation to protect park resources from impairment, but the agency does not have the authority to prohibit activities that are otherwise legally permitted on nearby lands. As a result, the agency must work collaboratively with its neighbors, engaging in their planning and environmental review processes and seeking to influence decisions that might harm park resources (National Park Service 2006). One fruitful avenue for engagement has been the emergent notion of ecosystem-scale management, which enables agencies and landowners to take full account of the broader landscape through comprehensive resource management planning efforts.

THE NATIONAL PARK IDEA

Within this legal framework, the national park idea is not really one idea but rather an amalgam of ideas that have evolved over time, reflecting economic, social, scientific, and other shifts in the nation's values and priorities. Early national park policy was defined by the so-called Lane Letter, released in 1918 with Secretary of the Interior Franklin Lane's signature for the purpose of interpreting the new Organic Act and explaining the new Park Service's approach to resource management (Lane 1918). Much has transpired and changed since then, including the interstate highway system, dramatic population growth, increased leisure time and personal wealth, advances in scientific knowledge, and new outdoor recreation equipment. As these changes have taken hold and fostered increased park visitation, the national park idea has evolved, as have the Park Service's management priorities and strategies (Keiter 2013).

In the beginning, most of the early national parks were undeveloped, wilderness-like settings remote from population centers. To attract visitors and fulfill the public enjoyment dimension of its mandate, the Park Service encouraged visitation to the parks, primarily by building roads, hotels, and other visitor facilities that inevitably altered the wilderness character of the parks. The agency's ostensible goal was to enable people to see and experience these extraordinarily scenic places, which in turn would help secure public support for the new National Park System and thus needed congressional funding. The advent of the automobile in the early twentieth century soon made park visitation a reality for many Americans, especially as the country's highway system improved (Sutter 2002). The result was to transform the national parks from a wilderness setting into a tourist destination, such that today more than 320 million people visit annually, resulting in overcrowding in several parks at popular times. Along the way, to protect park scenery and ensure a favorable visitor experience, the Park Service extinguished wildfires and exterminated predators, oblivious to the ecological implications of these policies. In the words of a Park Service historian, the agency engaged in "façade management" to safeguard the scenery and enhance visitation (Sellars 1997).

To accommodate park visitors, the Park Service turned to the private sector and enlisted concessioners to oversee the necessary hotels, dining halls, stores, and other facilities. Because the Park Service had no experience providing these types of visitor services, the ensuing public-private partnership has endured for the past century, though not without conflicts over appropriate levels of development and visitor services. Concessioners focus primarily on the bottom line, which means serving more and more visitors in the parks—an incentive that can effectively turn the national park into a mere commodity. Similar incentives are at work in adjacent gateway communities that cater to park visitors. Intent on maximizing the economic returns from visitors, gateway communities have promoted activities inconsistent with the national park experience, sometimes even creating a Coney Island-type atmosphere. As these communities grow, it is often at the expense of the nearby park, with subdivision expansion displacing wildlife and overall development creating pollution problems. Such growth lends a strong commercial dimension to the national park idea. Although the Park Service can exercise control over concessioners, it has little control over gateway communities (Keiter 2013).

From early on, the national parks have been viewed as prime recreation settings. Lane (1918) described the parks as "this national playground system," asserting that "the recreational use of the national parks should be encouraged in every practicable way." It went on to endorse "all outdoor sports," giving special notice to "mountain climbing, horseback riding, walking, motoring, swimming, boating, and fishing," but not hunting, which was banned in national parks from the outset (Dilsaver 1994). This early commitment to outdoor recreation led Yosemite to bid for the 1936 Winter Olympics and prompted the construction of swimming pools, ski areas, golf courses, and the like. Concerned about the impact and appearance of these myriad recreational activities, critics charged that the Park Service was becoming a

"Super Department of Recreation" and a "Playground Commission" (Sellars 1997). Eventually, to protect against environmental degradation and to ensure an enjoyable visitor experience, the Park Service put restrictions on the types of recreational activities permitted in the parks as well as limits on the number of people allowed to engage in different activities, including back-country camping permits and Grand Canyon river-rafting limitations (Keiter 2013). The courts have consistently upheld the agency's regulatory authority and decisions, citing its responsibility to safeguard park resources from impairment.[19]

The Park Service's early commitment to scenic preservation largely ignored science as a basis for managing park resources. With the agency's workforce principally composed of landscape architects, the goal was to maintain a beautiful—albeit static—scene that appealed to visitors. That changed, however, in the mid-1960s in response to the Leopold Report (Leopold et al. 1994), which examined the Park Service's wildlife management policies and concluded that the agency was wrongly disregarding science and thus imperiling park ecosystems. The report was clear about how the Park Service should proceed: "As a primary goal, we recommend that the biotic associations within each park be maintained or where necessary recreated, as nearly as possible in the condition that prevailed when the area was first visited by white man. A national park should represent a vignette of primitive America" (Leopold et al. 1994). Accordingly, the report endorsed an ecological restoration agenda, one that would utilize adaptive management strategies under the supervision of "biologically trained personnel." Specific recommendations included recovering extirpated predators to reestablish predator-prey relationships, reintroducing fire to park ecosystems, and eliminating nonnative species. Although another thirty years passed before Congress added a scientific mandate to the Park Service's responsibilities and yet another twenty years before education was also added, the agency meanwhile dramatically shifted its resource management policies to recognize the dynamic nature of park ecosystems and to restore such ecological components as predators, wildfire, and even seasonal flooding. As a result, the national parks have become an important workshop for scientific experimentation and education, something akin to "nature's laboratory."

The Organic Act explicitly directs the Park Service to conserve wildlife, and the agency has long been committed to doing so. Its approach to wildlife management, however, has undergone a radical transformation over the years. In the early days, the idea was to put animals on display for park visitors and to distinguish between "good" and "bad" animals (Biel 2006; Pritchard 1999). This resulted in the establishment of a zoo at Yosemite, bear-viewing spectacles at park garbage dumps, and the Buffalo Ranch at Yellowstone—all hardly natural displays. It also resulted in the elimination of wolves, bears, cougars, and other predators to ensure visitors could enjoy elk, bison, and deer meandering peacefully across the landscape. Following the Leopold Report, though, the Park Service shifted direction and adopted a "natural regulation" policy that not only allowed nature to take its course but also sanctioned active restoration efforts (Boyce 1993; Schullery 1997), the classic case being the reintroduction of wolves to Yellowstone (McNamee 1997). Other major ecological restoration efforts have included allowing wildfires to burn in the backcountry, restoring natural water flows in the Everglades, removing dams on the Elwha River in Olympic National Park, and emulating seasonal flood events in the Grand Canyon (Lowry 2009). The basic goal is to maintain and restore ecological processes with minimal human intervention, recognizing that park ecosystems are dynamic—not static—settings subject to ongoing change and adaptation. Of course, this also means acknowledging that park resource management policies can have impacts beyond park boundaries in the form of dispersing wildlife and rampaging wildfires. Conversely, external development activities—such as oil fields, clear-cut logging, and new subdivisions—can adversely affect park resources by fragmenting wildlife habitat and fouling park waters. In short, the national parks are imperfect wildlife or ecological reserves (Keiter 2013).

The realization that national parks cannot be sustained as islands of preservation amid oceans of human activity has prompted the notion that parks represent the vital core of larger ecosystems, which should be managed as an entirety. Building on post-Leopold Report scientific insights, it has become evident that external activities—or external threats—can severely affect national park resources. In 1980, the Park Service itself recognized these dangers in an attention-grabbing report titled *State of the Parks* (National Park Service Office of Science and Technology 1980). Subsequent reports have reconfirmed these concerns (National Parks Conservation Association 2018; US Department of the Interior 1992), drawing upon the emerging sciences of conservation biology and island biogeography to demonstrate that national parks are too small to prevent extirpation of some native wildlife species. One oft-cited study found that all of the major national parks, owing to their limited size, have lost at least one species during the past century (Newmark 1985, 1995). To help address these problems, the Park Service and its supporters have endorsed a notion of ecosystem management that views parks as the heart of an ecosystem and calls for restraint across the nearby landscape to sustain important ecological processes (Keiter 2003, 2013; Skillen 2015). Examples of where this ecosystem approach is being implemented, though with mixed results thus far, include the greater Yellowstone ecosystem, the crown of the continent ecosystem, and the California desert landscape. As climate change further alters existing ecological systems, large-scale management strategies will become even more important to promote resiliency and hence enable ecosystems to adapt to change (White et al. 2010).

This short history of the national park idea vividly illustrates how our notions about these special places have changed over time, responding to new knowledge, values, and concerns. That the management standard set forth in the Organic Act has not been changed suggests it has been flexible enough to accommodate these shifts in the role and purpose of our parks. That Congress has seen fit to give the Park Service explicit new science and education responsibilities while reaffirming its foremost preservationist obligation confirms the importance of the agency's non-impairment mandate and its policies placing nature conservation and restoration before visitor enjoyment to ensure that future generations can continue to appreciate the parks. To be sure, change is not just a matter for the past but is ongoing, inevitably presenting the Park Service with new challenges and the need to adapt to new circumstances and values.

EXPANDING THE NATIONAL PARK SYSTEM

The notion of preserving nature rather than exploiting it for human use represented a sharp departure in federal policy from the privatization and utilitarian perspectives that had long prevailed as white settlers advanced across the frontier continent. No wonder, then, that additions to the National Park System during the past century reflect evolving ideas about what types of places should qualify as potential national parks. Most of the nation's large natural parks have been carved out of the public lands, reflecting a political judgment that these special places should be protected from settlement or development. During the early years, the emphasis was on designating particularly scenic or unique landscapes as parks to promote aesthetic values. Later, Congress was convinced to extend national park status to less scenic settings in order to protect ecological and wilderness values, reflecting a notable shift in the role played by the parks. This section briefly outlines how the National Park System has evolved, observes how this evolution mirrors broader societal changes, and highlights the political dimensions of new park proposals. It is a story of largely haphazard growth and political opportunism, informed by emergent social values and, more recently, scientific insights.

In 1906, confronted with reports of widespread looting of Native American sites across the Southwest, Congress adopted the Antiquities Act. The act gave the president authority to establish national monuments to protect historic and scientific objects, though limited to the smallest area necessary to adequately safeguard these objects.[20] President Theodore Roosevelt promptly employed the act to designate the Grand Canyon as an 820,000-acre national monument, establishing the important precedent, sustained by the courts, that the act could be used by presidents to protect large areas for their scientific or historic value.[21] In 1919, when Congress designated the Grand Canyon a national park,[22] it established the further precedent of converting national monuments into national parks. Since then, Congress has converted more than a dozen presidential national monuments into national parks, including Arches, Bryce Canyon, Carlsbad Caverns, Olympic, and Zion (Harmon et al. 2006; Rothman 1989).

Prior to adoption of the Organic Act in 1916, Congress created several national parks modeled on the seminal 1872 Yellowstone designation. These early parks—which included such iconic venues as Crater Lake, Glacier, Mount Rainier, Rocky Mountain, Sequoia, and Yosemite—were protected to safeguard their unique features and scenic qualities, ensuring that these special places would not fall into private hands for mining, logging, or homesteading. They were viewed as important dimensions of the nation's spectacular natural heritage, not dissimilar to the numerous cultural landmarks—cathedrals, castles, and the like—that were widely treasured, preserved, and visited throughout Europe (Runte 2010). Although placed under the Department of the Interior, the US cavalry actually oversaw the early parks, because the Department of the Interior lacked the financial or human resources to police the lands to prevent poaching, trespassing, and other incursions (Hampton 1971). But after Congress passed the Organic Act, the National Park Service took over, assuming responsibility for protecting the existing parks and attracting visitors to them.

Not surprisingly, the early national parks were established without regard to the Native American tribes that either inhabited or utilized the lands for hunting, fishing, or other purposes. The early "wilderness" national park model envisioned these scenic settings as being without any permanent human settlement, which meant current Indian residents in Glacier, Yosemite, and elsewhere were displaced from their homes and moved outside the new parks (Burnham 2000; Keller and Turek 1998; Spence 1999). This initial approach to national park creation was ironic, given the origins of the national park idea. The idea is generally attributed to the artist and author George Catlin, who in 1832 proposed creating a "Nation's Park, containing man and beast, in all the wildness and freshness of their nature's beauty" (Spence 1999, pp. 9-10) following a westward journey during which he observed the existing Native American cultures being overrun by the rapid advancement of white settlement. Catlin's notion of preserving nature's beauty and beasts eventually took hold in the form of the national park but notably did not include the original native inhabitants.

The result, over time, has strained relations between the Park Service and Native American tribes, as the tribes have gradually asserted treaty and other rights for access to the parks. In several instances, notably at Badlands, Death Valley, and the Grand Canyon, these Indian claims have gained traction, prompting boundary changes and other adjustments to the park-tribe relationship (Keiter 2013). In 2014, increasingly sensitive to Native American concerns, the National Park Service proposed creation of the first "tribal national park" at the south unit of Badlands National Park in South Dakota, but the proposal has yet to gain congressional support (National Park Service and Oglala Sioux Tribe 2012). As the tribes continue to assert claims to their ancestral homelands, social justice concerns will progressively find their way into the national park idea, pressing for recognition and new relationships between the parks and tribes.

Following adoption of the Organic Act, the National Park Service's original leaders endorsed the view that only areas of "national significance"—defined in terms of "scenery of supreme and distinctive quality or some national feature so extraordinary or unique"—merited inclusion in the budding system (Dilsaver 1994). With this focus on scenic splendor, Congress was soon persuaded to add new parks in Alaska, Hawaii, Maine, the Appalachian region, and the Southwest, extending the nascent system across the country. But the "national significance" standard has proven problematic over time. Although 1976 legislation directed the Park Service to employ the "national significance" standard when evaluating potential new park units,[23] Congress has not consistently adhered to the standard when establishing new parks. Further, the standard is inherently difficult to define with precision, given that national values and interests continue to evolve. As different types of new units have been added to the system, critics have complained that a number of them do not meet the system's standards (Foresta 1984; Ridenour 1994).

During the 1930s, both the president and Congress had a hand in enlarging and reshaping the National Park System. In 1933, President Franklin Roosevelt doubled the number of park units when he transferred sixty-four national monuments, military parks, battlefield sites, memorials, and cemeteries to the Park Service, dramatically expanding the scope of the system (Runte 2010, pp. 194-195). These transfers put the Park Service in charge of the nation's cultural heritage, broadening its mission into an entirely new realm. President Roosevelt also employed his Antiquities Act power to enlarge the system, creating eight new national monuments at such locations as Capitol Reef, Channel Islands, Jackson Hole, and Joshua Tree, all of which Congress subsequently converted into national parks (Unrau and Williss 1983).

At the same time, Congress was also involved in reshaping the system. First, Congress designated Florida's Everglades as a new national park, citing the area's wilderness and ecological qualities and thus deviating from the notion that only scenically spectacular areas merited national park status (Runte 2010, pp. 116-123). Congressional recognition that undisturbed wilderness settings merited national park status opened the door for more such additions to the system over the ensuing years. Second, Congress established the first national recreation area at Lake Mead in southern Nevada, creating a new type of designation within the system where recreation took priority over other resource management objectives (Sellars 1997, pp. 37-39). Since then, Congress has employed an array of different designations to establish new park units, which now include national seashores, national lakeshores, national rivers, national preserves, and national trails (see table 8.1). Although these new designations have enabled Congress politically to expand the system and to protect different types of areas or features, they have also sowed confusion and diminished uniformity within the system (National Parks Second Century Commission 2009, p. 43).

Table 8.1. National Park Service Units and Related Areas

National Park Service Units	Number of Units
National battlefields	11
National battlefield parks	4
National battlefield sites	1
National military parks	9
National historic parks	57
National historic sites	76
International historic sites	1
National lakeshores	3
National memorials	30
National monuments	84
National parks	61
National parkways	4
National preserves	19
National reserves	2
National recreation areas	18
National rivers	5
National wild and scenic rivers and riverways	10
National scenic trails	3
National seashores	10
Other designations	11
Related Areas	**Number of Related Areas**
Affiliated areas	25
Authorized areas	9
Commemorative sites	3
National heritage areas	55
National trails system	30
National wild and scenic rivers and trailways	48

Note: The National Park Service currently administers 419 units that encompass twenty different designations, including sixty-one national parks. The Park Service's responsibilities also extend to 170 related areas, most of which are directly administered by other government agencies or nongovernmental organizations.
Source: National Park Service, "About Us," last updated December 23, 2019, https://www.nps.gov/aboutus/national-park-system.htm.

Following World War II, the National Park System experienced enormous growth. Several factors drove this development, including a population boom, widespread prosperity, the new interstate highway system, and burgeoning environmental and wilderness movements. The 1960s and early 1970s—often referred to as the "golden years" for the national parks—saw sixty-eight new park units added to the system, including Canyonlands,

Guadalupe Mountains, North Cascades, Redwood, and Virgin Islands, as well as an assortment of new designations ranging from Cape Cod and Point Reyes National Seashores to Indiana Dunes and Apostle Islands National Lakeshores, while Arches and Capitol Reef National Monuments were converted to national parks (Mackintosh 2005). During the next six years, Congress added yet more units, including Cuyahoga Valley National Recreation Area, Golden Gate National Recreation Area, and Santa Monica Mountains National Recreation Area—all situated near large urban areas—as well as Big Cypress National Preserve and Congaree Swamp National Monument (Mackintosh 2005).

Congress capped this extraordinary growth cycle in 1980 with passage of the Alaska National Interest Lands Conservation Act (ANILCA) (Nelson 2006; Runte 2010),[24] which added 44 million new acres to the system and ten new units, including Gates of the Arctic, Kenai Fjords, Lake Clark, and Wrangell-St. Elias National Parks. In ANILCA, besides doubling the size of the National Park System and greatly expanding the federal acreage dedicated to wilderness, wildlife, and other conservation purposes, Congress consciously sought to "preserve in their natural state extensive unaltered . . . ecosystems." To do so, Congress drew boundary lines for these new Alaskan units to "follow hydrographic divides or embrace other topographic or natural features,"[25] reflecting an emerging sensitivity to ecological conservation. Since then, however, the system has grown more slowly with only occasional large additions, such as Great Basin National Park in Nevada, transformation of Death Valley and Joshua Tree National Monuments into enlarged national parks, and, more recently, Valles Caldera National Preserve in New Mexico as well as Katahdin Woods and Waters National Monument in Maine. In part, this slowdown in growth of the National Park System can be attributed to the fact that the other federal land management agencies—the Forest Service, Bureau of Land Management, and US Fish and Wildlife Service—have assumed wilderness management and other preservation responsibilities, making them resistant to relinquishing their prized scenic lands to the Park Service for a new park designation.

Over the years, National Park System growth has been abetted by private philanthropy as well as state and local support. In several instances, wealthy individuals have provided the funds to acquire private lands that have subsequently been converted into national monuments or parks to be enjoyed the general public. Examples include John D. Rockefeller's land purchases in Jackson Hole, Wyoming, which were incorporated into Grand Teton National Park; Bostonian George Dorr and other wealthy New Englanders who helped purchase lands for Acadia National Park, the Mellon family's purchases on Cape Hatteras and Cumberland Island; and Roxanne Quimby's recent land acquisitions in Maine that have become the Katahdin Woods and Waters National Monument (Butler 2008; Hartzog 1988; Newhall 1957; Winks 1997). Land trust organizations like the Nature Conservancy and the Trust for Public Land have increasingly played important roles in acquiring inholdings and other sensitive lands that either have been incorporated into the park system or are situated adjacent to existing parks (Keiter 2018). During the 1930s, state funds and private donations, including contributions from local schoolchildren, were instrumental in acquiring the private lands that became Great Smoky Mountains and Shenandoah National Parks (Ise 1961). Recent congressional legislation lends support to these types of public-private partnerships to support expansion and maintenance of the National Park System.[26]

Several lessons can be gleaned from the evolution of the National Park System. First, because Congress has reserved for itself the power to designate new national parks, political considerations play a significant role in expansion of the system, and the same can be said about presidential national monument designations. As a result, growth of the system has a haphazard quality to it, linked to national as well as local political sentiments and opportunities. Second, to surmount evident political obstacles, Congress has employed an array of designations, such as national recreation areas or national preserves, to facilitate expansion of the system, but that has also reduced the level of protection for these new units. Hunting, for example, is often permitted in national preserves, while it is generally prohibited in national parks unless specifically authorized by Congress.[27] Third, both Congress and the National Park Service have gradually begun to pay more attention to science and related ecological considerations when identifying and designing new park units to ensure the protected area can accomplish its resource preservation objectives. Finally, because states and local communities have come to recognize the economic impact of a national park designation, politicians have begun to regularly promote new park designations that, in some instances, fall plainly short of encompassing "nationally significant" features or resources (Headwaters Economics 2018; Thomas et al. 2018). In short, driven by politics and opportunism, the National Park System has experienced tremendous albeit haphazard growth that does not always protect the wildlife and other objects that prompted the designation.

CHALLENGES TO THE NATIONAL PARK SYSTEM

As the twenty-first century unfolds, the National Park System confronts multiple challenges, reflecting the natural, social, and other changes occurring across the landscape. The most concerning natural changes facing the parks are global warming and external development pressures, both of which threaten to disrupt park ecosystems and existing resource management strategies. Ongoing social changes of concern include a growing and diversifying population, increasing urbanization that tends to distance people from the natural world, and a related nature deficit disorder malady, particularly among youth. Other imminent challenges revolve around increased park visitation and automobile usage, funding for park staff and maintenance, the role of technology inside and outside parks, and new recreational activities that result in better access to the parks. To address these changes, the Park Service and its advocates are beginning to rethink long-standing resource and visitor management policies.

Climate change, absent dramatic mitigation actions, is predicted to have a substantial impact on national parks, depending on location. Parks in coastal regions, such as Everglades Big Cypress and Hatteras National Seashore, may find themselves submerged owing to rising sea levels, while initial saltwater intrusion will alter native vegetation. Joshua Tree National Park in the California desert is predicted to lose its namesake trees, whose growing range will likely shift northward in response to temperature changes. Drought conditions will affect most of the national parks in the Southwest, changing water cycles in this arid environment and altering wildlife and plant behavior. In the Rocky Mountain parks, including Glacier, Rocky Mountain, and Yellowstone, higher temperatures will lessen snowpack, increase the likelihood of catastrophic wildfires, and prompt wildlife to relocate farther north and up-gradient, perhaps outside park boundaries (Cafferey et al. 2013; Gonzalez et al. 2018; Monahan and Fisichelli 2014).

To address climate change concerns, scientists are urging the Park Service (and other land managers) to prepare risk assessments and to identify adaptation strategies designed to promote ecological resiliency (Baron et al. 2009; Hansen et al. 2014; Hilty et al. 2012). Drawing upon the best available science and employing adaptive management strategies, effective responses to a warming world will probably entail more active or "interventionist" resource management policies and an enlarged, landscape-scale approach to conservation (National Park System Advisory Board Science Committee 2012). These new strategies, which should initially be deployed on an experimental basis subject to careful monitoring, could include more aggressive prescribed burning to reduce the risk of catastrophic wildfires, establishment of secure wildlife movement corridors outside park boundaries, and translocation of species to more hospitable habitat. The ultimate objective is to reduce the risk of devastating change and to maintain ecological integrity while adapting to nature's dynamic processes.

External development pressures are ubiquitous outside national parks. Once regarded as "islands" of nature conservation protected by their remoteness, national parks across the country, including those in the West bordered by public lands, face increasing industrial development and subdivision pressures just outside their boundaries, with accompanying environmental consequences. Theodore Roosevelt National Park in North Dakota is virtually surrounded by oil and gas fields, while national parks in southern Utah confront the prospect of widespread energy exploration and mining projects. With more and more people attracted to scenic locations and outdoor recreation opportunities, subdivision and other development pressures have mounted outside many national parks, including Glacier, Great Smoky Mountains, Rocky Mountain, and Yellowstone, threatening to fragment important wildlife habitat and to create air and water pollution problems. Unsightly overhead power transmission lines now mar scenic vistas at Delaware Water Gap and elsewhere. Air pollution from distant power plants and cities regularly obscures the Grand Canyon, Great Smoky Mountains, and other national parks (Freemuth 1991; National Parks Conservation Association 2018; Schafer 2012).

Park officials, lacking clear jurisdictional authority beyond their borders, are responding to these external pressures by engaging more actively outside park boundaries and promoting collaborative relationships with park neighbors. The agency's *Management Policies*, noting that parks are "integral parts of larger regional environments," endorses the principle of "collaborative conservation" to enable park officials to protect park resources and values (National Park Service 2006). This includes working with neighbors through partnerships and participating in local planning processes to encourage compatible land-use practices. In doing so, given the emergent view of national parks as the vital core of larger ecosystems (Keiter 2013), the Park Service should be in the vanguard promoting landscape-level conservation planning that includes protected wildlife migration corridors, subdivision zoning standards, pollution control requirements, construction design standards, and noise limitations. Additional funding to support strategic land purchases or conservation easement acquisitions can also help to facilitate landscape-scale conservation efforts and to resolve some external threat problems. Moreover, national and local conservation organizations, like the Greater Yellowstone Coalition, National Parks Conservation Association, and Natural Resources Defense Council, must continue to play an assertive advocacy role on behalf of the parks, including pursuing litigation to protect park resources from external threats when necessary (Sax and Keiter 1987).

To address the demographic and other social changes confronting the national parks, the Park Service has already endorsed several interrelated goals. One such goal is to attract a broader diversity of visitors, making parks more hospitable to minority populations that have generally not sought outdoor, nature-based experiences (National Parks Second Century Commission 2009, p. 30). Another goal is to engage tech-focused youth in the natural world of the parks (Louv 2005). Yet another goal is to encourage the expanding urban populace to visit national parks.

To attain these goals, the Park Service, drawing upon its new education mandate, must continue to expand its educational efforts beyond park boundaries, using technology to reach people where they are found, both in their homes and online. Smartphones, social media, and other technologies can be employed inside and outside the parks to introduce visitors to the natural setting and to educate them about park resources and management challenges (Doremus 2018). Since most of our large natural parks are far from urban centers, the Park Service and its constituents should consider establishing new types of parks closer to where people live so they can engage with nature and reap its rewards (National Park System Advisory Board 2012). To attract minority communities to the park experience, we should consider new national monuments, historical sites, and similar designations commemorating important events, individuals, and accomplishments from within these communities to demonstrate that the system is committed to telling the entire American story and to including everyone in that story (National Park System Advisory Board 2012, pp. 9-13). During his tenure, President Obama established several such national monuments under the Park Service's auspices, including Bears Ears, César E. Chávez, Harriet Tubman, and Pullman. Such extended inclusion efforts will not only expose more people to an enriching national park experience, but will also help to spawn a new cadre of national park supporters—an important consideration given that our parks are ultimately a political creation.

At the same time, park officials cannot ignore serious overcrowding and related automobile pressures at some parks or the problems associated with new recreation demands. Although long reluctant to impose limits on visitor numbers or automobiles, park officials have begun to address the latter problem with shuttle bus systems in places like Bryce Canyon, Yosemite, and Zion. If visitation to the parks continues to increase at current rates, it may be necessary to consider an advance reservation system, which is already used to reserve hotel, campground, and backcountry space. Other options include daily or hourly limits at particularly attractive sites, and collaborative education efforts with sister land management agencies designed to funnel visitors to other nearby sites or activities outside affected parks. New recreational activities, such as mountain biking, hang gliding, jet skiing, and slack lining, pose the question of whether a particular activity is compatible with the national park setting and experience. The Park Service's *Management Policies* provides a useful framework for evaluating new types of recreational activities, focusing on the unique values and experiences available in the national park setting; namely, engagement with nature and its inspirational qualities (National Park Service 2006; Sax 1980).

Deferred maintenance and reduced personnel numbers are long-standing Park Service challenges. Because Congress has not appropriated sufficient funds to maintain park roads, buildings, and other infrastructure, park visitors have regularly encountered closed or damaged roads, trails, and campgrounds, while park water and sewerage systems have occasionally been shut down. As the Park Service workforce has shrunk in size, rangers have not been available to lead hikes, or to present interpretive campfire programs, or to patrol the backcountry. These problems can only be addressed with additional funding, either by congressional appropriations or private donations. Congress seems at least open to directing funds derived from onshore oil and gas development revenues toward the park maintenance backlog,[28] and the 2016 centennial legislation makes it easier for the agency to seek private philanthropic support.[29] If these funds do not prove sufficient for the task, then alternate funding sources should be considered—perhaps a federal tax on recreational equipment, increased entrance fees, a park hotel tax, or a personal income tax write-off provision.

National parks, despite having undergone profound changes during the past century, are still governed by the original 1916 Organic Act, with its imperative to conserve park resources in an unimpaired condition while accommodating visitors. Under the Organic Act, Park Service policies have evolved over time, responding to new knowledge and changing social values that have continuously altered our understanding of the national park idea. Although the Park Service originally focused on promoting visitation in a beautiful setting by intervening actively in nature, it has shifted toward allowing natural processes to take their course under a largely hands-off management approach, modified by targeted ecological restoration efforts. Congress has mostly endorsed this shift in policy, adding a science mandate to the Organic Act, supporting large-scale ecological restoration efforts, and demonstrating a degree of ecological sensitivity with additions to the park system. As climate change impacts and growing development pressures become more evident, however, national park policies must be further reoriented toward the larger landscape in order to achieve resiliency and ecological integrity conservation goals. Being the one federal land system dedicated to nature conservation, the National Park Service is uniquely positioned to serve as the anchor—or vital core—for a new national landscape conservation network designed to meet these looming challenges (Keiter 2018).

Just as the original Yellowstone designation was a political act, the future of the National Park System will ultimately be shaped by politics, as reflected in Congress and the presidency. Public opinion dictates the trajectory of American politics, of course, and there continues to be strong support for the national parks, nature conservation, and cultural preservation efforts. But as the nation's populace continues to grow ever more diverse and urban, it will be imperative to extend the national park idea to new constituencies and venues to ensure ongoing political support for the system. That support will be crucial in this ever-changing world to meet the systems' needs, which include high-quality scientific research, well-trained park personnel with new skill sets, sufficient maintenance funding, and innovative public outreach and education efforts. Only then will the Park Service be in a position to continue fulfilling its venerable mission—to conserve unimpaired our natural and cultural heritage for the benefit of present and future generations.

Legal Citations

1 Yellowstone Park Act of 1872, 17 Stat. 32, 33, codified at 16 U.S.C. §§ 21, 22.

2 54 U.S.C. §§ 100101 et seq.

3 54 U.S.C. § 100101(a).

4 54 U.S.C. § 100751(a).

5 54 U.S.C. § 100101(b).

6 54 U.S.C. § 100502.

7 54 U.S.C. § 100751(c).

8 54 U.S.C. § 100702.

9 54 U.S.C. § 100703.

10 54 U.S.C. §§ 100802, 100803. In addition, the National Park Service is authorized to coordinate with organizations and partners to deliver its educational and interpretive programs. See also 54 U.S.C. § 100804.

11 54 U.S.C. § 100507.

12 National Park Service Omnibus Management Act, Pub. L. 105-391 §§ 401-19, 112 Stat. 3497, 3503-19, codified at 16 U.S.C. §§ 5951-66; National Park Service (2006, 10.2 et seq.).

13 16 U.S.C. § 1131(c).

14 16 U.S.C. § 1536(a)(2); see Mausolf v. Babbitt, 125 F.3d 661 (8th Cir. 1997).

15 42 U.S.C. § 4332(2)(C).

16 National Parks Conservation Association v. Babbitt, 241 F.3d 722 (9th Cir. 2001).

17 36 C.F.R. § 2.1 et seq. (2018).

18 Wilderness Society v. Norton, 434 F.3d 584, 596 (D.C. Cir. 2006).

19 River Runners for Wilderness v. Martin, 593 F.3d 1064 (9th Cir. 2010); Organized Fishermen of Florida v. Watt, 775 F.2d 1544 (11th Cir. 1985), cert. denied, 476 U.S. 1169 (1986); National Rifle Association v. Potter, 628 F. Supp. 903 (1986).

20 54 U.S.C. § 320301.

21 Cameron v. United States, 252 U.S. 450 (1920).

22 40 Stat. 1175 (1919), codified at 16 U.S.C. § 221 et seq.

23 Pub. L. 94-458, § 2, 90 Stat. 1940 (1976), codified at 54 U.S.C. § 100507.

24 16 U.S.C. §§ 3111-26.

25 16 U.S.C. § 3101(b) (ecosystems); 16 U.S.C. § 3103(b) (boundary lines).

26 See National Park Service Centennial Act, 54 U.S.C. §§ 100802, 100803.

27 National Park Service (2006, 8.2.2.6); National Rifle Association v. Potter, 628 F. Supp. 903 (D.C. Cir. 1986).

28 National Park Restoration Act, S. 2509 (115th Cong., 2d Sess., 2018); Restore Our Parks and Public Lands Act, H.R. 6510 (115th Cong., 2d Sess., 2018).

29 54 U.S.C. § 101121 (establishing Second Century Endowment Fund for the National Park Service).

References

Baron, Jill S., Lance Gunderson, Craig D. Allen, Erica Fleishman, Donald McKenzie, Laura A. Meyerson, Jill Oropeza, and Nate Stephenson. 2009. "Options for National Parks and Reserves for Adapting to Climate Change." *Environmental Management* 44(6): 1033. https://doi.org/10.1007/s00267-009-9296-6.

Biel, Alice Wondrak. 2006. *Do (Not) Feed the Bears: The Fitful History of Wildlife and Tourists in Yellowstone* Lawrence: University Press of Kansas.

Boyce, Mark S. 1993. "Natural Regulation or the Control of Nature?" In *The Greater Yellowstone Ecosystem: Redefining America's Wilderness Heritage*, edited by Robert B. Keiter and Mark S. Boyce, 183-208. New Haven, CT: Yale University Press.

Burnham, Philip. 2000. *Indian Country, God's Country: Native Americans and the National Parks*. Washington, DC: Island Press.

Butler, Tom. 2008. *Wildlands Philanthropy: The Great American Tradition*. San Rafael, CA: Earth Aware.

Cafferey, Maria A., and Rebecca L. Beavers. 2013. "Planning for Climate Change in Coastal National Parks: Managing for Sea Level Rise and Storms." *Park Science* 30(1): 6-13.

Dilsaver, Larry M., ed. 1994. *America's National Park System: The Critical Documents*. Lanham, MD: Rowman and Littlefield.

Doremus, Holly. 2018. "Foreword." In *Mountains without Handrails: Reflections on the National Parks*. 2nd ed., edited by Joseph L. Sax, xiv-xvi. Ann Arbor: University of Michigan Press.

Foresta, Ronald A. 1984. *America's National Parks and Their Keepers*, 76-80. Washington, DC: Resources for the Future.

Freemuth, John C. 1991. *Islands under Siege: National Parks and Politics of External Threats*. Lawrence: University Press of Kansas.

Gonzalez, Patrick, Fuyao Wang, M. Notaro, D. J. Vimont, and John W. Williams. 2018. "Disproportionate Magnitude of Climate Change in United States National Parks." *Environmental Research Letters* 13(10): 104001.

Hampton, H. Duane. 1971. *How the U.S. Cavalry Saved Our National Parks*. Bloomington: Indiana University Press.

Hansen, Andrew, Nathan Piekielek, Cory Davis, Jessica Hass, David M. Theobald, John E. Gross, William B. Monahan, Tom Olliff, and Steven W. Running. 2014. "Exposure of U.S. National Parks to Land Use and Climate Change, 1900-2100." *Ecological Adaptations* 24(3): 484-502.

Harmon, David, Francis P. McManamon, and Dwight T. Pitcaithley. 2006. *The Antiquities Act: A Century of American Archaeology, Historic Preservation, and Nature Conservation*. Tucson: University of Arizona Press.

Hartzon, George B., Jr. 1988. *Battling for the National Parks*, 197-201. Mt. Kisco, NY: Moyer Bell.

Headwaters Economics. 2018. "Economic Impact of National Parks." Last modified May 2018. https://headwaterseconomics.org/public-lands/protected-lands/economic-impact-of-national-parks/.

Hilty, Jodi A., Charles C. Chester, and Molly S. Cross. 2012. *Climate and Conservation: Landscape and Seascape Science Planning and Action*. Washington, DC: Island Press.

Ise, John. 1961. *Our National Park Policy: A Critical History*. Baltimore: Johns Hopkins University Press.

Keiter, Robert B. 2003. *Keeping Faith with Nature: Ecosystems, Democracy, and America's Public Lands*. New Haven, CT: Yale University Press.

Keiter, Robert B. 2013. *To Conserve Unimpaired: The Evolution of the National Park Idea*. Washington, DC: Island Press.

Keiter, Robert B. 2018. "Toward a National Conservation Network Act: Transforming Landscape Conservation on the Public Lands into Law." *Harvard Environmental Law Review* 42(61): 85-87.

Keller, Robert H., and Michael F. Turek. 1998. *American Indians and National Parks*. Tucson: University of Arizona Press.

Lane, Franklin. 1918. "Letter on National Park Service Management (May 13, 1918)." In *America's National Park System: The Critical Documents*, edited by Larry M. Dilsaver, 48-52. Lanham, MD: Rowman & Littlefield.

Leopold, A. Starker, et al. 1994. "Wildlife Management in the National Parks." In *America's National Park System: The Critical Documents*, edited by Larry M. Dilsaver, 237-251. Lanham, MD: Rowman and Littlefield.

Louv, Richard. 2005. *Last Child in the Woods: Saving Our Children from Nature Deficit Disorder*. Chapel Hill, NC: Algonquin Books.

Lowry, William R. 2009. *Repairing Paradise: The Restoration of Nature in America's National Parks*. Washington, DC: Brookings Institute.

Mackintosh, Barry. 2005. *The National Parks: Shaping the System*. 3rd ed., 64-83. Washington, DC: National Park Service.

McNamee, Thomas. 1997. *The Return of the Wolf to Yellowstone*. New York: Henry Holt.

Miles, John C. 2009. *Wilderness in National Parks: Playground or Preserve*, 139-140. Seattle: University of Washington Press.

Monahan, William B., and Nicholas A. Fisichelli. 2014. "Climate Exposure of US National Parks in a New Era of Change." *PLoS ONE* 9(7): e101302. https://doi.org/10.1371/journal.pone.0101302._

National Parks Conservation Association. 2018. *Out of Balance: National Parks and the Threat of Oil and Gas Development*. Washington, DC: National Parks Conservation Association.

National Park Service. 2006. *Management Policies*. Washington, DC: National Park Service.

National Park Service and Oglala Sioux Tribe. 2012. *South Unit Badlands National Park: Final General Management Plan and Environmental Impact Statement*. Washington, DC: National Park Service.

National Park Service Office of Science and Technology. 1994. *State of the Parks: A Report to Congress*. In *America's National Park System: The Critical Documents*, edited by Larry M. Dilsaver, 405-408. Lanham, MD: Rowman and Littlefield.

National Parks Second Century Commission. 2009. *Advancing the National Parks Idea: National Parks Second Century Commission Report*, 43. Washington, DC: National Parks Second Century Commission. https://www.nps.gov/civic/resources/commission_report.pdf.

National Park System Advisory Board. 2012. *Planning for a Future National Park System: A Foundation for the 21st Century*, 21-23. Washington, DC: National Park Service.

National Park System Advisory Board Science Committee. 2012. *Revisiting Leopold: Resource Stewardship in the National Parks*, 14-15. Washington, DC: National Park Service.

Nelson, Robert H. 2006. "Valuing Nature: Economic Analysis and Public Land Management, 1975-2000." *American Journal of Economics and Sociology* 65(3): 525-557.

Newhall, Nancy Wynne. 1957. *A Contribution to the Heritage of Every American: The Conservation Activities of John D. Rockefeller, Jr*. New York: Alfred A. Knopf.

Newmark, William D. 1985. "Legal and Biotic Boundaries of Western North American National Parks: A Problem of Congruence." *Biological Conservation* 33(197): 198-208.

Newmark, William D. 1995. "Extinction of Mammal Populations in Western North American National Parks." *Conservation Biology* 9(3): 512.

Pritchard, James. 1999. *Preserving Yellowstone's Natural Conditions: Science and the Perception of Nature*. Lincoln: University of Nebraska Press.

Ridenour, James M. 1994. *The National Parks Compromised: Pork Barrel Politics and America's Treasures*. Merrillville, IN: ICS Books.

Rothman, Hal. 1989. *Preserving Different Pasts: The American National Monuments*. Urbana: University of Illinois Press.

Runte, Alfred. 2010. *National Parks: The American Experience*, 1-28. 4th ed. Lanham, MD: Taylor Trade.

Sax, Joseph L. 1980. *Mountains without Handrails: Reflections on the National Parks*. 2nd ed. Ann Arbor: University of Michigan Press.

Sax, Joseph L., and Robert B. Keiter. 1987. "Glacier National Park and Its Neighbors: A Study of Federal Interagency Relations." *Ecology Law Quarterly* 14: 207.

Sax, Joseph L., and Robert B. Keiter. 2006. "The Realities of Regional Resource Management: Glacier National Park and Its Neighbors Revisited." *Ecology Law Quarterly* 33: 233-310.

Schafer, Craig L. 2012. "Chronology of Awareness about U.S. National Parks External Threats." *Environmental Management* 50(6): 1098.

Schullery, Paul. 1997. *Searching for Yellowstone: Ecology and Wonder in the Last Wilderness*, 220-25. Boston: Houghton Mifflin.

Sellars, Richard West. 1997. *Preserving Nature in the National Parks: A History*. New Haven, CT: Yale University Press.

Skillen, James R. 2015. *Federal Ecosystem Management: Its Rise, Fall, and Afterlife*. Lawrence: University Press of Kansas.

Spence, Mark David. 1999. *Dispossessing the Wilderness: Indian Removal and the Making of the National Parks*. New York: Oxford University Press.

Sutter, Paul C. 2002. *Driven Wild: How the Fight against Automobiles Launched the Modern Wilderness Movement*. Seattle: University of Washington Press.

Thomas, Catherine Cullinane, Lynn Koontz, and Egan Cornachione. 2018. *2017 National Park Visitor Spending Effects: Economic Contributions to Local Communities, States, and the Nation*. Fort Collins, CO: National Park Service.

Unrau, Harlan D., and G. Frank Williss. 1983. *Administrative History: Expansion of the National Park Service in the 1930s*. Washington, DC: National Park Service.

US Department of the Interior. 1992. *National Parks for the 21st Century: The Vail Agenda*. In *America's National Park System: The Critical Documents*, edited by Larry M. Dilsaver, ed., 434. Lanham, MD: Rowman and Littlefield.

White, Peter S., Laurie Yung, David N. Cole, and Richard J. Hobbs. 2010. "Conservation at Large Scales: Systems of Protected Areas and Protected Areas in the Matrix." In *Beyond Naturalness: Rethinking Park and Wilderness Stewardship in an Era of Rapid Change*, edited by David N. Cole and Laurie Yung, 197-215. Washington, DC: Island Press.

Wilderness Connect. 2019. "Fast Facts." Accessed November 12, 2019. https://www.wilderness.net/NWPS/chartResults?chartType=acreagebyagency.

Winks, Robin W. 1997. *Laurence S. Rockefeller: Catalyst for Conservation*. Washington, DC: Island Press.

Chapter 9
Introduction to Wildlife Management on Public Lands

LAUREN ANDERSON

Public lands are managed for a variety of resources and therefore have a variety of competing interests. The needs of ranchers must be weighed against the needs of timber harvesters, and those needs in turn must be weighed against the interests of mining and energy companies and, last but not least, wildlife managers and the public. Wildlife are intrinsic to functioning ecosystems and are an incredibly valuable but often overlooked resource. Hunting, fishing, and bird-watching are significant components of the $82 billion outdoor recreation industry, and public lands in the West protect some of the most unique and amazing wildlife in the world (Vincent et al. 2017).

Federally owned lands constitute more than 46% of the eleven coterminous western states and more than 61% of Alaska (Vincent et al. 2017). Managing and protecting this outdoor heritage for future generations have a long and complicated history within the United States, having been undertaken by multiple federal and state agencies. Federal lands are primarily managed by four agencies:

1. Bureau of Land Management (BLM) under the Department of Interior (248.3 million acres),
2. US Fish and Wildlife Service (FWS) under the Department of Interior (89.1 million acres),
3. National Park Service (NPS) under the Department of Interior (79.8 million acres), and
4. US Forest Service (USFS) under the US Department of Agriculture (USDA) (192.9 million acres) (Vincent et al. 2017).

Together, these four agencies manage 90% of all federal lands. The BLM, FWS, and the USFS all have the objective to manage wildlife and habitat on the lands they manage, while the NPS is tasked with conserving land and wildlife.

State fish and wildlife agencies often employ the foremost wildlife managers in the United States. State agencies were responsible for preventing the extinction of species like the Rocky Mountain elk, pronghorn, and bighorn sheep. States have the legal authority to manage federal lands within their borders only to the extent Congress has given them such authority, but one of these authorities most often granted is the management of wildlife. Without explicit federal action, such as listing a species under the Endangered Species Act, states set the population levels of species within their borders. State fish and wildlife agencies are often responsible for managing wildlife populations, while federal agencies are often responsible for managing the wildlife habitat those species depend on (Bureau of Land Management 2020).

While this chapter does not cover wildlife management on private lands, individuals in the West own vast tracts of the landscape, and over the years they have contributed significantly to wildlife conservation efforts and in some cases to the degradation of wildlife habitat. Resentment among private landowners of oversight by federal agencies, as in the case of the Endangered Species Act, rangeland management, and other federal oversight have broken trust on both sides and created barriers to effective communication. Preventing these conflicts, while also ensuring adequate protection of public resources, is an ongoing challenge for wildlife managers.

This chapter provides a brief overview of the responsibilities and authorities of the federal agencies tasked with wildlife management on public lands, summarizes the main environmental laws that guide these efforts, and describes the different governing statutes implemented by agencies to better define this work. This chapter also outlines a few of the key challenges faced by wildlife management on western public lands, including invasive species, wildlife disease, habitat loss, and climate change. The chapter concludes with an overview of a twenty-first-century model for wildlife conservation as intended for managers contending with the evolving challenges of managing public lands.

NATIONAL PARK SERVICE

National parks protect some of America's most beautiful and iconic landscapes. They are home to some of our most vulnerable wildlife and are managed by the NPS under the direction of the secretary of interior. The NPS was established in 1916 to manage a growing number of national parks and monuments. Today, there are many different names for the types of lands the NPS manages, including national parks, national monuments, national preserves, national historic sites, national recreation areas, and national battlefields. All together there are twenty-eight different designations, with more than four hundred managed areas in the United States. The NPS has a dual mission to preserve unique resources and to provide for the enjoyment of the public. Activities that harvest or remove resources from NPS lands are generally prohibited, though there are challenges in conserving resources while also maximizing public access.

BUREAU OF LAND MANAGEMENT

The BLM manages more wildlife habitat than any other federal or state agency (Bureau of Land Management 2020). Created in 1946, the BLM manages more than 245 million acres of public lands primarily located in eleven western states and administers about 700 million acres of federal subsurface mineral estate throughout the nation (Bureau of Land Management 2020). This land includes scrubland, grassland, and forest, as well as vast areas in Alaska's arctic tundra. The BLM coordinates these efforts with federal, state, tribal governments, local agencies, and many other relevant partner organizations. Wildlife conservation efforts by the BLM are funded through partnerships with federal, state, and nongovernmental organizations (Bureau of Land Management 2020). Conservation actions are usually part of an approved conservation plan for special-status species.

US FOREST SERVICE

The US Forest Service, a department housed within the US Department of Agriculture, was established in 1905 and now manages 193 million acres of national forests and grasslands. In addition, the Forest Service is responsible for the stewardship of nearly 500 million acres of nonfederal rural and urban forests, which it manages in collaboration with state and local governments (US Forest Service 2009). Within the Forest Service, the Watershed, Fish, Wildlife, Air and Rare Plants Program (WFWARP) is responsible for working as a crosscutting program that helps to meet the agency's land management and resource stewardship responsibilities. In combination with these responsibilities, the Forest Service must also balance competing needs for the commodities that forest and grassland produce using the sustainable multiple-use management concept. These commodities include clean water, energy, timber, and recreational activities.

Unlike the National Park Service and the US Fish and Wildlife Service, the BLM and Forest Service operate under a multiple-use, sustained-yield mandate, via the National Forest Management Act (NFMA) and the Federal Land Policy and Management Act (FLPMA), respectively. The NFMA requires the National Forest Service to prepare management plans for every forest under its jurisdiction. It also places significant environmental constraints on the Forest Service and gives it a mandate to manage for wildlife diversity. The FLPMA also requires the BLM to prepare resource management plans. These plans are meant to be updated as new data becomes available, and they are meant to be informed by public engagement. Lands managed under these acts are administered for five different purposes: outdoor recreation, range, timber, watershed, and wildlife and fish (Kannan 2009). Combined, the acreage overseen by the two laws amounts to almost 20% of the United States. Two other key management priorities of the Forest Service are the Planning Rule and the Roadless Rule.

Planning Rule

In 2012, the USDA announced a new Planning Rule for the National Forest System. This rule included stronger protections for forests, water, and wildlife and aimed to bolster the economies of rural communities. According to the Forest Service, land management plans under the new rule includes the following components (US Forest Service 2020):

- Restore and maintain forests and grasslands.
- Provide habitat for plant and animal diversity and species conservation. The requirements are intended to protect common native species, contribute to the recovery of threatened and endangered species, conserve proposed and candidate species, and protect species of conservation concern.
- Maintain or restore watersheds, water resources, and water quality, including clean drinking water and the ecological integrity of riparian areas.
- Provide for multiple uses, including outdoor recreation, range, timber, watershed, and wildlife and fish.

- Provide opportunities for sustainable recreation and recognize opportunities to connect people with nature.

Roadless Rule

In 2001, the Forest Service established the Roadless Area Conservation Rule (Roadless Rule). According to US Forest Service (2001), "the 2001 Roadless Rule establishes prohibitions on road construction, road reconstruction, and timber harvesting on 58.5 million acres of inventoried roadless areas on National Forest System lands. The intent of the 2001 Roadless Rule is to provide lasting protection for inventoried roadless areas within the National Forest System in the context of multiple-use management." Roadless areas play a key role in our nation's defense against the impacts of global climate change. They act as an environmental insurance policy, providing the last best hope to keep ecosystems intact. During the coming decades, wildlife will need intact migration corridors in order to survive climate change (US Forest Service 2001).

US FISH AND WILDLIFE SERVICE

President Franklin Roosevelt established the US Fish and Wildlife Service in 1940. Most of this agency's authority stems from the Fish and Wildlife Act of 1956, which requires the agency to protect, conserve, and enhance the country's fish and wildlife resources. Because of its primary use mission, other uses such as recreation and resource extraction are only permitted when they are compatible with the species' needs. When it comes to managing wildlife, the FWS is the lead federal agency tasked with enforcing the laws discussed below.

Migratory Bird Treaty Act of 1917

The Migratory Bird Treaty Act protects more than a thousand bird species from unnecessary death and harm. It is one of the United States' oldest and most important wildlife conservation laws. It allows for the regulated hunting of many bird and waterfowl species, but it also prevents deaths caused by industrial activities, such as open mining pits and oil spills. Specifically, it gives FWS the authority to regulate the take of migratory birds across state boundaries. Administrative actions, taken in 2017 and 2018, have reinterpreted the hundred-year-old law to not apply to incidental take, requiring that the FWS be able to prove intentional harm. This action severely limits the reach of the law and leaves its future influence uncertain. For example, where the government once could regulate a toxic site that was killing birds, the government can now only regulate such a site if it can be proved the company was intentionally killing birds.

Bald and Golden Eagle Protection Act of 1940

This law prohibits anyone, without a permit issued by the secretary of the interior, from "taking bald eagles, including their parts, nests, or eggs." There are limited exceptions for Native Americans' religious purposes, and for scientific purposes. The act defines "take" as "pursue, shoot, shoot at, poison, wound, kill, capture, trap, collect, molest or disturb."

Endangered Species Act of 1973 and Amendments of 1977

The Endangered Species Act (ESA) was a game-changing piece of legislation, shifting responsibility of threatened and endangered species from the states to FWS. The ESA is implemented jointly by FWS and the National Marine Fisheries Service (NMFS), but for the purposes of wildlife management on western public lands, this section will focus on FWS only. The ESA was intended to be the final safety net that prevented species from going extinct, and in that regard, it has been an incredible success. Since it was enacted, the ESA has successfully prevented the extinction of more than 99% of the more than 1,500 domestic species that have been listed through the act.

A major part of the FWS's program for conserving listed species includes designating "critical habitat," which is selected on the basis of what a designated species needs to survive, reproduce, and recover. The FWS must also evaluate the anticipated economic impacts of the designation, with both the designation and economic impact analysis open to public comment. A critical habitat designation does not impose restrictions on private lands; it only triggers the ESA requirement that actions authorized, funded, or carried out by federal agencies must not destroy or adversely modify designated critical habitat. Other federal agencies consult with the FWS to ensure this goal is met. Critics of the ESA point to the long and arduous process of removing species from the ESA, or delisting them, as an argument for rolling back protections under the law. But while the recovery process could be improved, the ESA does have some remarkable success stories, including delisting of the Louisiana black bear, the gray whale, and the brown pelican.

The Endangered Species Act is arguably the strongest wildlife conservation law in the United States, but as wildlife conservation and management has progressed, it is becoming clear that the ESA is not enough to protect America's wildlife. The threats that wildlife face are multiplying and changing in the era of climate change. Emergency measures that are designed to prevent a species from going extinct are becoming insufficient to prevent the chronic background decline that creates the emergency in the first place. It is this cryptic background decline that is creating a true and immediate wildlife crisis in America, and this degradation must be addressed in a twenty-first-century model for wildlife conservation.

There are many examples of the ESA working to protect and recover threatened and endangered species such as gray wolves and bald eagles. The ESA currently attempts to restore grizzles in Washington. Notably, ongoing ESA efforts to protect sage grouse demonstrates how collaborative efforts by stakeholders could hold the key to successful conservation efforts.

The Sage Grouse Rule

As of 2019, the future of the sage grouse rule, which was finalized in 2015, remains uncertain as the Trump administration reevaluates the rule. During the Obama administration, the protection plans established an unprecedented conservation partnership across the western United States. These plans encompassed Northern California, Colorado, Idaho, Nevada, Oregon, Utah, and Wyoming. The initial rule created a model for multistate, multiagency collaboration in order to prevent at-risk species from needing the strict protections of the Endangered Species Act.

This effort was one of the largest conservation undertakings in US history. Sage grouse, which are large and unique-looking birds best known for their "lek" dances, inhabit sagebrush habitat that covers a landscape approximately the size of Texas. This habitat has been severely fragmented by human development and land-use changes, which resulted in the severe decline of sage grouse populations. When the FWS began to evaluate the species to determine whether it warranted protections under the Endangered Species Act, it triggered a unique partnership between scientists, ranchers, industry professionals, and conservationists who all saw the value in preserving the bird and allowing the states to continue with their economic development plans. The result was a first of its kind, landscape-scale management strategy that demonstrated the extent to which a successful collaborative process could enhance wildlife conservation efforts (US Fish and Wildlife Service 2020).

Finally, the FWS also manages the National Wildlife Refuge System. The first of the national wildlife refuges, Pelican Island, was established in 1903, although it was not until 1966 that the various refuges were formed into the National Wildlife Refuge System. Today, there are approximately 560 national wildlife refuges in the United States. This system is managed by the US Fish and Wildlife Service, and it includes wildlife refuges, waterfowl production areas, and wildlife coordination units. The system of refuges protects hundreds of birds, mammals, reptiles, amphibians, and fish, and it also protects almost 380 endangered species, a critical component of the efforts to protect and restore America's endangered wildlife. These same refuges also generate more than $2.4 billion for local economies and create nearly 35,000 jobs annually (National Wildlife Refuge Association 2020).

ENVIRONMENTAL LAWS, RULES, AND PROGRAMS THAT DEFINE WILDLIFE CONSERVATION

Aside from the aforementioned environmental laws, there are many other laws, rules, and programs that have shaped the management of public lands and wildlife conservation in the West. The laws that created public lands in the first place were some of the most influential wildlife conservation laws, as they established protected spaces and gave wildlife room to roam. The 1906 Antiquities Act enabled the president to designate America's special places as national monuments, and the 1964 Wilderness Protection Act created the legal definition of wilderness in the United States and protected 9.1 million acres of federal land. Further, laws establishing the National Park System and the National Wildlife Refuge System protected millions of acres for wildlife. In addition to the laws that established public lands, the following examples highlight other policies that have influenced wildlife conservation.

Clean Water Act of 1948 and Amendments of 1972

Originally called the Federal Water Pollution Control Act, the Clean Water Act was reorganized, expanded, and renamed in 1972. The Clean Water Act made it unlawful to discharge any pollutant from a point source into navigable waters without a permit. Section 404 of the Clean Water Act was established by amendments in 1972. It protects wetlands on private and public lands by regulating the discharge of dredged or fill material into waters of the United States. Wetlands are among the most productive of all ecosystems; the Environmental Protection Agency (EPA) has stated that more than one-third of threatened species and endangered species live only in wetlands, and half use wetlands at some point of their lives. Protecting wetlands likewise protects the species and the other wildlife that depend on wetlands (Kannan 2009). The US Fish and Wildlife Service evaluates impacts to fish and wildlife under Section 404 (Environmental Protection Agency 2020).

National Environmental Policy Act of 1969

The National Environmental Policy Act (NEPA) establishes a broad framework for protecting the environment. NEPA's basic goal is to ensure that all branches of the federal government give proper consideration to environmental impacts before undertaking any major federal action. NEPA allows the FWS to evaluate fish and wildlife impacts that result from federally permitted projects through environmental assessments and environmental impact statements, and allows the agency to require mitigation for unavoidable fish and wildlife losses. It also opens the decision-making process to public comment, allowing people to have a voice on decisions that affect public lands.

Sentinel Landscapes Program

The US Department of Agriculture (USDA), Department of Defense (DOD), and Department of the Interior (DOI) established the Sentinel Landscapes Partnership through a memorandum of understanding in 2013. It covers landscapes that are working lands or natural lands important for the mission of the DoD. The program aims to strengthen the economies of ranches, farms, and forests while also conserving wildlife habitat. These efforts are all made in the context of ensuring that the military installations based on these lands, and the tests and training missions they conduct, are protected. The program aims to encourage coordination of conservation efforts between private landowners and the Sentinel Partnership in order to "reduce, prevent or eliminate restrictions due to incompatible development that inhibit military testing and training" (Texas A&M Natural Resources Institute 2020).

Department of Defense's Integrated Natural Resource Management Plans

The Department of Defense (not including the US Army Corps of Engineers) administers 11.4 million acres in the United States (about 2% of all federal land) (Vincent et al. 2017). These lands consist of military bases and training ranges, but under the Sikes Act, the DOD is also responsible for conserving and protecting biological resources on its lands. According to the DOD and the FWS, Integrated Natural Resource Management Plans "provide for the management of natural resources, including fish, wildlife, and plants; allow multipurpose uses of resources, and provide public access necessary and appropriate for those uses, without any net loss in the capability of an installation to support its military mission" (US Fish and Wildlife Service 2004). These plans guide the use and conservation of natural resources, including wildlife, on lands and waters under Department of Defense control.

Bureau of Land Management's Ecoregional Assessments

The BLM conducted a series of ecoregional assessments in response to climate change and other rapidly changing environmental factors. It is important to understand how climate change and the competing demands for land use will alter the landscape, and the rapid ecological assessments were meant to inform land-use planning and management decisions. The data, maps, and tools will help formulate coordinated, multiagency strategies to respond effectively to climate change, wildfire, and other environmental challenges. Seven of these assessments were conducted on Alaska's Seward Peninsula-Nulato Hills-Kotzebue Lowlands, the Central Basin and Range, the Colorado Plateau, the Middle Rockies, the Mojave Basin and Range, the Northwestern Plains, and the Sonoran Desert.

Clean Water Rule

The Clean Water Rule (also called the Waters of the United States Rule) was published in 2015 regulation by the EPA and the US Army Corps of Engineers. It defines all bodies of water that fall under US federal jurisdiction and the Clean Water Act. This includes streams and wetlands that connect to traditional navigable waters, interstate waters, and territorial seas. These waters offer flood protection, filter pollution, and provide critical fish and wildlife habitat. In 2017, the Trump administration announced its intent to review and rescind the rule. These efforts are ongoing, and the future of this rule remains unclear (Environmental Protection Agency 2019).

CONSERVATION IN THE ANTHROPOCENE: CHALLENGES TO WILDLIFE CONSERVATION ON PUBLIC LANDS

The Anthropocene Epoch is something of a science buzzword, a new definition for the geologic time period we live in today. Technically, we are in the Holocene Epoch, which started after the last ice age, but there have been so many human-caused environmental changes over the last few decades that many scientists and wildlife managers have suggested we are entering a new era—the Anthropocene. Regardless of what we call it, wildlife managers today are facing a host of new challenges, many of which have been caused by the influence people exert on their environment. The below examples highlight some of the challenges wildlife managers must contend with.

Invasive Species

The spread of invasive species on western public lands creates a host of challenges for wildlife managers. Invasive species management costs over $120 billion a year and affects more than 100 million acres. Invasive species have contributed to the decline of 42% of threatened and endangered species (Western Governors' Association 2017). Invasive plants and animals can reduce rangeland productivity, increase the risk of wildfire, and affect outdoor recreation. Species like cheatgrass and salt cedar have been identified on over 79 million acres of BLM-managed lands. Cheatgrass, which is an annual species native to Europe and eastern Asia, thrives in disturbed areas and outcompetes many native species. The grass dries out earlier than other species, lengthening the fire season in sagebrush habitat across the Great Basin (Sage Grouse Initiative 2018). Salt cedar, also called tamarisk, outcompetes other species in riparian ecosystems, creating a monoculture that sucks up large amounts of water. The spread of salt cedar can lower groundwater levels in western ecosystems that are already suffering from the impacts of drought. Invasive animal species include feral hogs, nutria, and the European starling. These are only a few examples of the types of invasive species land managers have to contend with; there are many, many more.

Habitat Loss and Degradation

Habitat loss is one of the greatest threats to wildlife, and public lands offer one of the few remaining safe havens. Wildlife move both daily and seasonally to survive. But the habitats that animals rely on continue to be fragmented by housing, roads, fences, energy facilities, and other man-made barriers. The expanding US population is bringing more people and development into conflict with wildlife and their historic habitats. As a result, animals are increasingly struggling to reach food, water, shelter, and breeding sites. Improving habitat connectivity is one way in which wildlife managers can counter the threat of habitat fragmentation. Habitat connectivity is defined as the degree to which the landscape facilitates or impedes animal movement and other ecological processes, such as seed dispersal. Removing fences and other barriers and building wildlife-friendly infrastructure like wildlife crossings can facilitate wildlife movement in a fragmented landscape.

Climate Change

Climate change is affecting landscapes across the United States, especially public lands in the West. Public lands are already facing a host of threats, including invasive species, wildlife disease, and habitat loss and fragmentation. Climate change is expected to amplify these impacts and add a host of additional threats, including higher temperatures and drought. As the impacts of climate change continue to develop and spread across western public lands, the risk of significant biodiversity loss is growing, leading to a wildlife crisis. Biodiversity includes the diversity within a species, between species, and of ecosystems. A more diverse ecosystem is typically a healthier and more resilient ecosystem, and healthy ecosystems provide a variety of benefits to people and wildlife, including clean water, clean air, and healthy soils. It is important that biodiversity on public lands is protected from worsening climate change. The examples of climate change impacts below illustrate how biodiversity loss is becoming a real problem.

Mega fires. The length of the fire season, and the area burned by mega fires, has increased as a result of climate change and warmer, drier conditions. Invasive species that are spreading as result of climate change, like bark beetles, are also playing a role, as the trees killed by the beetles add new fodder to the fires. New fire regimes are also allowing the spread of invasive species like cheatgrass. These fires and their associated environmental impacts can also lead to hunting restrictions as habitat is lost and degraded, and wildlife populations need more time to recover.

Low snowpack. Reduced snowpack resulting from higher average temperature and changes in weather patterns is also threatening wildlife and public lands. Snowmelt supplies about 60% to 80% of the water in major western river basins, including the Colorado, Columbia, and Missouri Rivers. This snowmelt is also the primary water supply for about 70 million people (Branch 2017). Lower winter snowpack will lead to reduced streamflow during the summer months, which will affect temperature-sensitive aquatic species like trout and amphibians like frogs and newts. Scientists estimate that one-third of the current cold-water fish habitat in the Pacific Northwest will be unsuitable by the end of the century. Fishing on public lands is a favorite American pastime, but this activity may be restricted as a result of low stream-flows and affected fish populations.

Rising temperatures. Public lands support climate-sensitive species, such as American pika. These small rabbit-like creatures live on high-elevation rocky slopes and are suffering from rising temperatures. While some populations seem to be able to adapt to a changing climate, high-elevation populations in the Sierra Nevada Mountains and the Northwestern Great Basin have been less resilient. A population of pika in the Lake Tahoe area of California has been extirpated entirely, a shocking loss to wildlife lovers and one of the first recorded local extinctions of a species resulting directly from climate change (Stewart et al. 2017). Weather data from the area show a 1.9°C rise in average temperatures and a significant reduction in snowpack.

Migration timing. Public lands support one of the largest land-based migrations in North America—that of mule deer in Wyoming. Mule deer time their migration in Wyoming to follow the spring greening as they move from lower winter habitat to higher summer habitat. As seasonal change is altered by a warming climate, these deer are struggling to time their migrations to match the "green wave" of new growth (US Geological Survey 2015).

Drought. Wildlife is also showing signs of stress from drought. Pronghorn populations at the northern end of their range have remained stable, but the populations in the Southwest, which include a geographically and genetically distinct subspecies of pronghorn, have not fared as well. In the Southwest, pronghorn populations have been declining since the 1980s, and scientists believe that climate change is partly to blame. As a result of changing precipitation patterns in the Southwest, 50% of the pronghorn populations examined by researchers could disappear by 2090 (US Geological Survey 2020).

BUILDING A TWENTY-FIRST-CENTURY MODEL FOR WILDLIFE MANAGEMENT

The North American Model of Wildlife Conservation is a set of principles that has guided wildlife management and conservation decisions in the United States and Canada. The models' origins are based largely on advocacy efforts of sportsmen who witness firsthand what overexploitation could do to wilderness and wildlife populations. Examples of this overexploitation include the extinction of the passenger pigeon, the near-extinction of the American bison, and the sharp decline of many migratory bird species in the early 1900s (US

Department of the Interior 2017a). While the model does not have any legal powers, it has still influenced many of the wildlife laws and policies outlined earlier in this chapter. The core principles of the model are elaborated by seven primary tenets (Wildlife Society and the Boone & Crockett Club 2012):

1. *Wildlife as public trust resources.* This means that people cannot own wildlife, though they can own the land on which it resides. Wildlife are held in trust for the public by state and federal governments.
2. *Elimination of markets for game.* There is no commercial hunting or sale of wildlife.
3. *Allocation of wildlife by law.* Wildlife is allocated by law, not other determinations such as market principles.
4. *Wildlife should only be killed for a legitimate purpose.* It is unlawful to kill wildlife unless there is a specific reason, such as a need for food, fur, self-defense, or the protection of property (including livestock).
5. *Wildlife is considered an international resource.* Wildlife do not follow the same boundaries as people do; therefore some resources—for example, migratory birds and aquatic species—must be managed internationally.
6. *Science is the proper tool for discharge of wildlife policy.* Science must be the basis for informed management and decision making. Decisions should not be made based on the goals of different interest groups.
7. *Democracy of hunting.* This tenet is based on the concept that hunting can benefit all of society. It also acknowledges that limiting access to firearms would also limit the average citizen's ability to hunt. This could hamper the goals of the model, as sportsmen were integral to the start of the conservation movement, and their spending on firearms, ammunition, and hunting licenses pays for much of wildlife conservation in the United States.

These seven basic tenets guide much of modern wildlife conservation, though critics have called for strengthening the model to fit the needs of twenty-first-century wildlife management. For example, detractors claim that the scope of the model is too narrow and too specific to game species and the interests of hunters and anglers. Also, critics point to success stories around the privatization and commercialization of wildlife in Europe as examples of the shortcomings of the "elimination of markets for game" tenet, calling instead for more sustainable harvest strategies. While the model is not perfect, it does offer a starting point for building a comprehensive, science-based strategy for twenty-first-century wildlife management. The following areas cover some of the ways in which this model can evolve.

ADEQUATE FUNDING FOR ALL SPECIES

Funding for wildlife conservation on federal lands is an ongoing challenge for wildlife managers. The lack of funds limits maintenance and restoration activities, as well as the acquisition of new lands (such as those needed to improve habitat connectivity). The main funding source for land acquisition is appropriations from the Land and Water Conservation Fund (LWCF). In addition, the Fish and Wildlife Service uses the Migratory Bird Conservation Fund (supported by sales of duck stamps and import taxes on arms and ammunition) as a source of funding. The Department of Defense uses its own appropriations laws to acquire funds for new lands.

While the addition of new lands likely benefits wildlife, there is a critical need for funds to manage wildlife on current public lands. The competing uses of public lands, such as grazing and energy development, can degrade land and result in habitat loss for wildlife. The need for ecological restoration often gets lumped in with other infrastructure needs and falls into the "maintenance backlog," which includes all of the other maintenance needs of public lands that were not performed when scheduled. The four main agencies together had a combined fiscal year 2016 backlog estimated at $18.62 billion (Vincent et al. 2017).

Most funding for wildlife conservation comes from hunters and anglers, and in the West, most public lands are open to hunting and fishing. Money collected from federal excise taxes on certain hunting and fishing equipment under the Pittman-Robertson Act (also called the Federal Aid in Wildlife Restoration Act) goes to states for wildlife restoration and hunter education. Duck stamps are another significant source of funds. Purchase of a duck stamp is required for hunting migratory water fowl such as ducks and geese, and sales have raised more than $950 million, helping to protect or restore nearly six million acres of habitat for birds and other wildlife (US Fish and Wildlife Service 2018).

Because much of the funding for conservation comes from hunters and anglers, game species tend to benefit more than other wildlife. This is a problem, as neglected wildlife populations can decline to the point where they need emergency protections under the Endangered Species Act. Adequate funds must ensure that all wildlife populations are protected, not just those that are hunted and fished (Wildlife Society and the Boone & Crockett Club 2012).

Given the magnitude of the challenges faced by wildlife managers on public lands, it is critical that additional funds be directed toward wildlife conservation needs. While there is no easy answer to this need, there are some options. For example, while sportsmen and -women provide much of the funds for conservation, there are many other people who benefit from wildlife on public lands. Outdoor enthusiasts—including hikers, campers, bird-watchers, kayakers, and many more—all enjoy the wildlife found on western public lands. Ensuring that they become proactive stakeholders and contribute to wildlife conservation funding is a critical first step.

BETTER DEFINE THE ROLES OF LAND MANAGERS AND WILDLIFE MANAGERS

In addition to permanent and adequate funding, there is also a need for role clarity among federal agencies, state agencies, private landowners, and other entities charged with protecting wildlife in the West. While wildlife law in the United States dates back to more than a hundred years ago, there are still issues related to constitutional law, sovereignty, and ownership that create conflict. Further, there are deep-seated tensions between federal and state governments that challenge the interjurisdictional nature of wildlife conservation.

As an example of this type of conflict, in 2015, the National Park Service and US Fish and Wildlife Service overrode the state of Alaska's hunting regulations to prohibit certain practices on national preserves. The National Park Service stated, "to the extent such practices are intended or reasonably likely to manipulate wildlife populations for harvest purposes or alter natural wildlife behaviors, they are not consistent with NPS management policies." In January 2017, Alaska sued the DOI, challenging the right of the federal government to override the state's right to manage wildlife (Schadegg 2017). Now, the National Park Service is proposing to reverse this rule in light of the Trump administration's wildlife conservation goals. Secretarial Order 3347, signed by Interior Secretary Ryan Zinke directs the DOI to increase access to hunting and fishing opportunities and to improve cooperation and communication with state wildlife managers (US Department of the Interior 2017b). The agency also points to Secretarial Order 3356, signed in 2017, that in part directs NPS to "begin the necessary process to modify regulations in order to advance shared wildlife conservation goals/objectives that align predator management programs, seasons and methods of take permitted on all Department-managed lands and waters with corresponding programs, seasons and methods established by state wildlife management agencies" (US Department of the Interior 2017c). This is an example of how shifting politics and new administrative goals can change the dynamics of wildlife conservation on public lands, and highlights the need for more role clarity between state and federal agencies.

STRONGER PARTNERSHIPS WITH PRIVATE LAND OWNERS AND TRIBES

While there is a need to better define roles and clarify the decision-making process among government actors, there is also a need to create a collaborative process that brings more voices to the table and ensures that all Americans are invested in the future of wildlife and public lands. Private landowners have the potential to make significant contributions to wildlife conservation. Wildlife on public lands do not have borders, and they use habitat on private lands as well. Practices like conducting controlled burns, removing invasive species, erecting nest boxes, protecting riparian habitat, reducing erosion, and removing fencing can help wildlife tremendously.

Candidate Conservation Agreements with Assurances (CCAAs) are an example of programs that encourage private landowner participation. These are voluntary conservation agreements between the US Fish and Wildlife Service and one or more public or private parties. Candidate species are species that are at risk and may need to be listed under the Endangered Species Act. The FWS works to identify the threats to these species and partners with private landowners to implement measures to conserve the species. These agreements help address landowner concerns about the potential regulatory implications of having a listed species on their land, as they limit the landowner's future obligations if they comply with the agreement.

The Farm Bill is one of the most significant sources of conservation funding in the United States and focuses on programs for private landowners. Through the Conservation Reserve Program, Wetlands Reserve Program, and Wildlife Habitat Incentive Program, hundreds of millions of dollars are set aside for private landowners to keep wetlands, grasslands, and other fragile lands protected for wildlife habitat. Programs like these, along with CCAAs, build trust between regulators and private landowners and create incentives for them to participate in wildlife conservation efforts.

Native American tribes are another important conservation partner for wildlife managers in protecting wildlife in a changing world. Tribal lands are sovereign lands and are not subject to federal public land laws. But American Indian lands in the Lower 48 comprise more than 45 million acres of reserved lands and an additional 10 million acres in individual allotments. There are another 40 million acres of traditional native lands in Alaska. Partnering with tribes to protect species is important, as many of these lands have remained largely untouched and offer some of the best habitat for at-risk species.

CONCLUSION: CHASE SUCCESS STORIES, NOT SILVER BULLETS

Protecting and recovering wildlife on public lands are challenging tasks. A number of state and federal agencies form a patchwork of authorities across Bureau of Land Management lands, Forest Service lands, national parks, and national wildlife refuges. The laws and regulations that govern this authority are complicated and challenging to navigate. Further, there is no one silver-bullet solution to the many hurdles wildlife managers must overcome. Funding shortfalls, growing and changing threats, and lack of clarity when it comes to decision making on public lands all contribute to the difficulties of this task. Solutions do exist, however, even if there is not a one-size-fits-all model for success. The United States has one of the most advanced and remarkable wildlife conservation legacies in the world, and it is possible to ensure that wildlife populations are protected and thriving in a rapidly evolving and increasingly affected world.

References

Branch, John. 2017. "The Ultimate Pursuit in Hunting Sheep." *New York Times*, February 16, 2017. https://www.nytimes.com/2017/02/16/sports/bighorn-sheep-hunting.html.

Bureau of Land Management. 2020. "Wildlife." Accessed February 7, 2020. https://www.blm.gov/programs/fish-and-wildlife/wildlife/.

Environmental Protection Agency. 2019. "Waters of the United States Rule Making." October 22, 2019. https://www.epa.gov/wotus-rule.

Environmental Protection Agency. 2020. "Section 404 of the Clean Water Act." Accessed February 7, 2020. https://www.epa.gov/cwa-404/section-404-permit-program.

Kannan, Phillip. M. 2009. *Faculty Overview: United States Laws and Policies Protecting Wildlife.* Colorado Springs: Colorado College. https://www.coloradocollege.edu/dotAsset/fc919f40-c24a-4287-ab6c-d649e4dca7a6.pdf.

National Wildlife Refuge Association. 2020. "The Refuge System and FWS." Accessed February 7, 2020. https://www.refugeassociation.org/about/about-the-refuge-system/.

Sage Grouse Initiative. 2018. "Why Is Cheatgrass Bad?" January 30, 2018. https://www.sagegrouseinitiative.com/why-is-cheatgrass-bad/.

Schadegg, Rachel. 2017. "Alaska Challenges Federal Hunting Rules in Court." The Wildlife Society, January 26, 2017. http://wildlife.org/alaska-challenges-federal-hunting-rules-in-court/#prettyPhoto

Stewart, Joseph, David H. Wright, and Katherine A. Heckman. 2017. "Apparent Climate-mediated Loss and Fragmentation of Core Habitat of the American Pika in the Northern Sierra Nevada." *PLoS ONE* 12(8): e0181834. http://journals.plos.org/plosone/article?id=10.1371/journal.pone.0181834.

Texas A&M Natural Resources Institute. 2020. "Sentinel Landscapes." Accessed March 19, 2020. https://nri.tamu.edu/programs/military/sentinel-landscapes/.

US Department of the Interior. 2016. "Invasive Species." April 28, 2016. https://www.doi.gov/ocl/invasive-species-1.

US Department of the Interior. 2017a. "Everything You Need to Know about Hunting on Public Lands." September 1, 2017. https://www.doi.gov/blog/everything-you-need-know-about-hunting-public-lands.

US Department of the Interior. 2017b. "Order No. 3347." March 2, 2017. https://www.doi.gov/sites/doi.gov/files/uploads/revised_so_3447.pdf.

US Department of the Interior. 2017c. "Order No. 3356." September 15, 2017. https://www.doi.gov/sites/doi.gov/files/uploads/signed_so_3356.pdf.

US Fish and Wildlife Service. 2004. *Integrated Natural Resources Management Plans.* Washington, DC: US Department of the Interior. https://www.fws.gov/endangered/esa-library/pdf/INRMP.pdf.

US Fish and Wildlife Service. 2018. "Duck Stamp Dollars at Work." Last updated September 26, 2018. https://www.fws.gov/birds/get-involved/duck-stamp/duck-stamp-dollars-at-work.php.

US Fish and Wildlife Service. 2020. "2015 Endangered Species Act Finding." Accessed February 7, 2020. https://www.fws.gov/greaterSageGrouse/findings.php.

US Forest Service. 2001. "Roadless Rule." January 22, 2001. https://www.fs.usda.gov/roadmain/roadless/2001roadlessrule.

US Forest Service. 2009. *The U.S. Forest Service—An Overview.* Washington, DC: US Department of Agriculture. https://www.fs.fed.us/sites/default/files/media/types/publication/field_pdf/USFS-overview-0106MJS.pdf.

US Forest Service. 2020. "Forest Planning Rule." Accessed February 7, 2020. https://www.fs.fed.us/restoration/planningrule.shtml.

US Geological Survey. 2015. "Linking Mule Deer Migration to Spring Green-Up in Wyoming." December 31, 2015. https://cmerwebmap.cr.usgs.gov/catalog/item/5463ac97e4b0ba83040c6f6d.

US Geological Survey. 2020. "The Effects of Drought on Southwestern Pronghorns." Accessed February 7, 2020, https://www.usgs.gov/centers/casc-sc/science/effects-drought-southwestern-pronghorns?qt-science_center_objects=0#qt-science_center_objects.

Vincent, Carol Hardy, Laura A. Hanson, and Carla N. Argueta. 2017. *Federal Land Ownership: Overview and Data.* CRS Report R42346. Washington, DC: Congressional Research Service. https://fas.org/sgp/crs/misc/R42346.pdf.

Western Governors' Association. 2017. *Top 50 Invasive Species in the West.* Denver, CO: Western Governors' Association. http://westgov.org/images/editor/WGA_Top_50_Invasive_Species.pdf.

Wildlife Society and the Boone & Crockett Club. 2012. *The North American Model of Wildlife Conservation.* Technical Review 12-04. Bethesda, MD: Wildlife Society and the Boone & Crockett Club. http://wildlife.org/wp-content/uploads/2014/05/North-American-model-of-Wildlife-Conservation.pdf.

Chapter 10
Endangered Species, Wildlife Corridors, and Climate Change in the US West

JODI A. HILTY, AERIN L. JACOB, KIM G. TROTTER, MAYA J. HILTY, AND HILARY C. YOUNG

STATUS OF CONSERVATION IN THE WESTERN UNITED STATES

The American West is blessed with an impressive amount of protected and public land. Most of the approximately 127 million hectares (313 million acres) of public protected areas in the United States, totaling 12% of total US lands, are found in the West. Additionally, private land easements and acquisitions conserve another 2 million hectares (5 million acres). Easements sometimes, but not always, enhance biodiversity conservation (Aycrigg et al. 2016a; Jenkins et al. 2018). Continued declining wildlife populations and increasing proposals to list species on the Endangered Species Act are evidence that further conservation is needed. Globally, the United States is lagging behind international standards set by the Convention on Biological Diversity Aichi Biodiversity Targets (the United States is one of a few countries that did not ratify this convention). Among other convention targets, it stipulates that by 2020 the terrestrial and inland water areas under protection in signatory countries should be increased by at least 17% in "effectively and equitably managed, ecologically representative and well-connected systems of protected areas and other effective area-based conservation measures" (Convention on Biological Diversity 2011). The status of protected areas in the West has worsened in recent years with more US "degazetting," or reducing conservation status, of protected areas (Wade 2019).

Representation of ecosystems is a key factor in how effectively protected areas conserve biodiversity, and it contributes to increased resilience of species and systems in the face of climate change. Protected areas in the western

United States have disproportionate representation of high-elevation areas with low-productivity soils compared to other systems such as wetlands, valleys, and prairies with higher productivity (Aycrigg et al. 2013, 2016x; Pimm et al. 2018). Historically, aesthetics and recreation—not biodiversity conservation—tended to be the reason western lands were protected. As we learn more about species' needs and movements, we know that while protected areas are vital, they are often too small to adequately conserve a broad range of species and ecological processes. Large-landscape, multijurisdictional conservation and shifts to ecological networks or connected systems of protected areas are necessary for long-term protection of biodiversity (Damschen et al. 2019).

A changing climate means that species and ecological communities must be able to shift across the landscape; this becomes more challenging given the amount of human development and activities creating barriers to movement and ultimately increasing the risk of extinction. Average temperatures have increased nearly 1.1°C (2°F) since 1895 and are projected to rise another 1.1°C to 2.2°C (2°F to 4°F) over the next few decades (Mattson et al. 1995). In the West, climate changes exacerbate droughts, wildfires, and pest outbreaks; these factors and tree diseases are causing widespread tree die-off in Washington and Oregon (Mattson et al. 1995) and other places across the West. The effects of climate change on biodiversity are being clearly documented—including substantial species' range shifts, community shifts toward more warm-adapted species, phenological changes in populations (e.g., earlier breeding seasons), and changes that disrupt interactions among interdependent species (Mattson et al. 1995). Furthermore, the rate of warming over the next hundred years is predicted to be 2.5-5.8 times greater than the past hundred years (Hansen et al. 2014). Hansen et al. (2014) found that 30% of the area within protected-area-centered ecosystems, such as the Greater Yellowstone Ecosystem, across the United States will experience climates unsuitable for current biomes by 2030. By 2090, 40% of such areas will be affected. Up to 96% of current protected areas in the Rocky Mountains and southwestern regions of the United States will have unsuitable climates for current biomes by 2090.

Exacerbating the problem, climate change increases human demands on natural resources such as land and water; extensive human impacts on either can impair ecosystem function and resilience. Anthropogenic climate change and land-system change are at increasing risk of crossing thresholds that may or may not be reversible. And while freshwater use is still considered safe at global levels (Steffen et al. 2015), reduced water supply across the West is predicted to have far-reaching ecological and socioeconomic consequences (Mattson et al. 1995).

ENDANGERED SPECIES IN THE WEST

The US Endangered Species Act (ESA), arguably the world's strongest wildlife legislation, has significantly influenced western conservation of lands and species. The ESA has a broad scope of influence, primarily enabling protection of species through (1) prohibiting the "taking" of any species or (2) ensuring that no actions are allowed that would jeopardize the listed species or destruction or modification of critical habitat. Relatively few species have gone extinct under the law, and the majority of listed species improve in status over time, which is remarkable considering the severely declining status of most species at their time of listing (Schwartz 2008). Significant problems with the ESA exist, however, including that less than 2% of listed species have recovered to the point of delisting, and at least ten times more species likely qualify for listing than are actually listed (Evans et al. 2016). There are also lengthy delays in listing (Schwartz 2008) and limited data to assess the effectiveness of recovery tools (Gibbs and Currie 2012). In addition, the ESA faces significant political opposition, and in 2019, the United States substantially weakened the law by making it harder to list species and limiting protections to species listed as threatened, including by considering economic impacts in listing (Friedman 2019). Among the concerns about the ESA, two issues have particularly increased frustrations about its implementation in the West.

First is the controversy around whether to delist wolves (*Canis lupus*) and grizzly bears (*Ursus arctos*). Wolves have become emblematic of the ESA after multiple decades of battles among scientists, conservationists, and politicians debating the merits of continued listing (Ellison 2017). The issue became so heated that Montana Democratic Senator Tester and Idaho Republican Congressman Simpson attained a legislative delisting of wolves in the Greater Yellowstone Ecosystem by adding a rider to the budget bill (Byron 2011), effectively undermining the ESA.

Second, the increasing incorporation of climate change into listings, which some see as a one-way listing since wildlife managers have little control over global climate change. Climate change is becoming more of a pivotal factor in species listings, and the ESA provides protection to species likely to become endangered in the "foreseeable future" (Government Publishing

Office 1973), but this language is vague and climate change threats require earlier, more proactive action to prevent the decline of species (Government Publishing Office 1973; Robbins 2015). For instance, a recent proposed listing of wolverine (*Gulo gulo*) found in parts of western mountain ranges was mostly focused on the threat of climate change owing to their dependency on snow cover; this induced considerable debate on the scope and capacity of the act, which is already underfunded (Schwartz 2008). The continued trend of biodiversity loss is further evidence of the need for more comprehensive biodiversity conservation in the West and across the country. The number of species listed as endangered is increasing, and many more species are petitioned for listing. As many as one-third of the best-known groups of US plant and animal species have been found to be vulnerable, with one in five at a high risk of extinction (Stein et al. 2000). The threats to individual species of habitat loss and fragmentation, invasive species, chemical pollution, and climate change continue to compound. For instance, cheatgrass, an invasive species, is estimated to cover more than 40 million hectares (100 million acres) of the Great Basin in the West, leading to total loss of sagebrush in some areas and seriously threatening species like the greater sage grouse (Western Governors' Association 2008). The ESA does not address the large numbers of gradually declining species in the United States and is simply inadequate for conserving species and their habitats.

SPECIES CONSERVATION AT THE STATE LEVEL: FUNDING AND STATE WILDLIFE ACTION PLANS

Conservation measures prior to ESA listings have been inconsistent among states, but most states are moving toward preemptive conservation actions to prevent ESA listings. Aside from ESA-listed species, the states are fully responsible for managing their own wildlife through state fish and wildlife agencies. But concerns exist that while the ESA operates at a federal level, states lack sufficient laws and policies to achieve identified ESA recovery outcomes (Camacho et al. 2017; Goble et al. 1999). For instance, legislation and listing decisions in many states do not apply to plants, have no provisions to designate or protect critical habitat, do not require wildlife management agencies to engage in recovery planning, and may not be based on the best available science. Furthermore, few states require interagency consultation or allow citizens to petition for listing or delisting of species. It is promising that some states have complementary legislation, but they rely on the ESA's more comprehensive structure of statutes and regulations. Although interagency collaboration to protect and recover at-risk species is required, together these limitations mean that devolution of federal authority for ESA species protection ought to be viewed with caution.

One incentive to maintain healthy wildlife populations is that wildlife- and wildland-associated recreation and tourism can bring significant revenue to rural regions; in the contiguous western states, people spent an estimated $33.6 billion on hunting, fishing, or wildlife watching in 2006 (Western Governors' Association 2008).

Traditionally, funding for state wildlife agencies largely has come from three sources: hunting and fishing licenses, the Pittman Robertson Act of 1937, and the Dingell-Johnson Act of 1950. The two acts allocate money to states gathered from taxes on fishing and hunting outdoor gear. The resulting perceived dependency of wildlife agencies on hunters and anglers has led agencies to prioritize conservation of game species over all others (Jacobson et al. 2010; Organ et al. 2012). With such focus, populations of game species have remained generally healthy over the past forty or fifty years—nevertheless, it is increasingly apparent that more focus is needed on the approximately 85% of animal species that are neither game nor listed on the ESA (and thus managed federally). Many populations of nongame species have declined and lack consistently funded efforts to conserve them (Lerner et al. 2006).

As a result of the recognition that states need more financial resources and especially nongame funding, in 2000 Congress created the State Wildlife Grant (SWG) and Tribal Wildlife Grant (TWG) Programs to provide funding to proactively protect at-risk species. Annual appropriations from the SWG, which must be matched by nonfederal funding sources, have fluctuated between $50 and $100 million—averaging $60 to $65 million—which most stakeholders believe is drastically inadequate. It is estimated that the program provides less than 5% of what is necessary to conserve all species identified by the states as being the most in need (Stein et al. 2018).

Nonetheless, an important accomplishment in advancing conservation at the state level was the development of individual state wildlife action plans (SWAPs), which were completed by 2005 under the State Wildlife Grants. SWAPs include information on species distribution and abundance, descriptions of key habitats of species in decline, identification of threats, conservation actions to protect identified species of greatest conservation need and their habitats, monitoring programs for at-risk species, and plans to coordinate use of the SWAPs outside of state wildlife agencies (Association of Fish and Wildlife Agencies 2012). Creating and updating these plans are accomplishments because SWAPs were the first assessment of their type and breadth done by many states, including centralizing available wildlife information within one agency. The most recent plans identified 12,000 species nationwide in need of conservation action (Stein et al. 2018).

Although creating SWAPs was widely heralded as an achievement, many states had insufficient resources to complete the plans thoroughly, so the quality and structure of SWAPs across the West are highly inconsistent. A 2006 review of all SWAPs found that states generally did well in assessing the status of species, their habitats, and the current threats. The majority of western states mapped focal areas (and a few mapped larger priority habitats) to support species of greatest conservation need. Oregon's plan was particularly strong, and both Wyoming and New Mexico developed sophisticated tools for mapping habitat quality. California, though initially lacking maps, created a formal steering committee to ensure that its SWAP was of a high caliber (Lerner et al. 2006).

Moving from assessments to action strategies is where many SWAPs have fallen short. Most states created lists of hundreds of conservation actions instead of prioritizing actions (see, e.g., in relation to threats, Carwardine et al. 2012) and setting reachable goals (Lerner et al. 2006). Further, many states have yet to address funding, resource, and expertise challenges. Other challenges include inadequate incorporation of climate change into conservation planning and inconsistencies among states. When viewed together, western SWAPs do not form a cohesive regional strategy. Additionally, regional cooperation across state boundaries is insufficient to maintain landscape-scale ecological processes and wide-ranging, at-risk species (Meretsky et al. 2012).

Funding for state wildlife agencies across the West is in decline. Despite diverse efforts to increase hunting and fishing, participation is declining in most states; in turn, this contributes to large fluctuations in the annual revenue available for conservation. From 2011 to 2016, the number of hunters across the United States dropped by 2.2 million (US Department of the Interior 2016). In response to the resulting funding gap, bipartisan supporters proposed the new Recovering America's Wildlife Act to Congress. This act would use existing revenue from energy development and would appropriate $1.3 billion annually to implement three-quarters of every state's wildlife action plan (Stein et al. 2018). The Land and Water Conservation Fund, developed with offshore oil and gas royalties, has also provided significant funds to protect biodiversity and habitat in the West via targeted land purchases. While Congress secured permanent reauthorization of the fund in February 2019 (Land and Water Fund Coalition 2019), full funding is not guaranteed. Further, the fund now requires that acquired lands provide public access, which can reduce benefits to biodiversity and habitat protection and discourage landowners from participating. Securing adequate resources will continue to be a challenge for western state agencies.

SPECIES CONSERVATION AT THE REGIONAL LEVEL: THE WESTERN GOVERNORS' ASSOCIATION AND CASE STUDIES

Notable efforts to advance regional species conservation in the western United States have stemmed from the Western Governors' Association (WGA). The WGA is a tool for bipartisan policy development and information exchange, representing the governors of nineteen western states (as well as three territories in the Pacific). The WGA passed policy resolutions in 2015 and 2017 on species conservation that fueled the Species Conservation and Endangered Species Act Initiative. This initiative encourages voluntary conservation (outside the ESA) through identifying sensitive species early and establishing frameworks to incentivize proactive conservation. It promotes landscape-scale conservation efforts to prevent endangered species listings and, importantly, tries to build bipartisan support for its recommendations. Through the initiative, the WGA has hosted workshops and provided a forum to share information about best practices in state species management. In 2018, the WGA also created the Western Working Lands Forum to examine challenges of cross-boundary management of wildlife. The forum produced a comprehensive list of the top invasive species in the West, which together pose some of the most significant threats to the region's biodiversity.

Other conservation efforts have arisen in response to the circumstances of particular regions. A classic example of regional efforts to preserve species in the West was the massive effort to conserve two subspecies of sage grouse (*Centrocercus urophasianus*). In the early 2000s, sage grouse populations were in severe decline, having decreased from historic numbers by an estimated 69% to 99% (Belton and Jackson-Smith 2010) and only occupying just over half of their historical range through the western United States and Canada (Aldridge et al. 2008). Fragmentation of the sagebrush steppe habitat was increasing because of oil and gas development, agriculture, and urban expansion, and invasive cheatgrass was replacing the native sagebrush depended upon by sage grouse. Around 2010, sage grouse were being considered for protection under the ESA, but a strong desire to keep them from being listed by states and businesses resulted in a unique collaboration among diverse groups—including federal and state agencies, private landowners, and energy companies—to devise a conservation approach that would eliminate the need for listing. The Bureau of Land Management (BLM) and the US Forest Service (USFS) increased protection on millions of hectares of land managed for multiple use, while more than sixty local groups across the West were created to implement sage grouse management plans. To avoid further restrictions on economic activities that would occur in the event of an ESA listing, energy companies and local communities supported the effort. The recovery of sage grouse—an indicator of the overall health of sagebrush habitat—is intertwined with the health of many other species. Although sage grouse protections have degenerated under the Trump administration, the effort remains a good example of a multipartner plan advancing to keep a species from being listed. It encompassed principles of conservation on a landscape scale, began to incorporate concerns about climate change threats to the persistence of sage grouse (Schrag et al. 2011), and targeted a single species while ultimately benefitting a range of species.

Another continuing conservation effort in the West for which success has broad implications is the restoration of large carnivores, including gray wolves (*Canis lupus*) and grizzly bears (*Ursus arctos*). Populations of these animals collapsed following European settlement of the West, and both were among the first species listed under the ESA. By the early twentieth century, government control programs had driven gray wolves to extinction throughout the Lower 48. Upon reintroduction in 1995-1996, populations expanded quickly thanks to heightened legal protections in both Yellowstone National Park and central Idaho. Worth noting, the Nez Perce tribe successfully led the reintroduction of wolves in Idaho despite a lack of support from the state because of the tribe's ceded wildlife rights in treaty with the federal government. By 2009, the northern Rocky Mountain gray wolf population exceeded the initial target of three hundred wolves in the recovery area by fivefold (Bergstrom et al. 2009), with individuals traveling into Colorado, Oregon, and Utah (Wayne and Hedrick 2011). Gray wolf recovery succeeded despite strong opposition in many rural communities—although there was also strong public and scientific support for reintroduction—and attitudes toward wolves have generally improved over time (George et al. 2016). Opposition to wolves still exists, but efforts to ensure long-term persistence of wolves continue, and current population sizes are relatively robust.

The conservation story for grizzly bears is similar. Grizzlies were eliminated from 95% of their original range between 1850 and 1920, and they further declined by another 52% until 1970 (Mattson et al. 1995). After the 1975 ESA listing, coordinated federal recovery efforts brought the population of grizzly bears in the US Northern Continental Divide Ecosystem and in the Greater Yellowstone Ecosystem above ESA-stated recovery levels (Mace et al. 2012). Recovery efforts were impressive considering the human-bear conflicts, the major barrier that roads pose to habitat connectivity, and the vulnerability of grizzly bears to human development and activities (Weaver et al. 1996). Grizzly bears have made an enormous recovery in the Greater Yellowstone Ecosystem. The population was estimated at approximately 135 individuals in the 1970s when the species was listed, and it now exceeds 700. The ESA created a recovery zone, the Interagency Grizzly Bear Study Team to lead what has become one of the most intense and long-term carnivore research efforts in the world, and the Interagency Grizzly Bear Committee to maintain strong communication and cooperation among the managers as well as to supervise education, research, and management of trash initiatives (Yellowstone National Park 2019). Three factors greatly contributed to the recovery to date. First, almost all of the designated recovery area for grizzly bears is public land. Second, the strong coordination among the public land managers in proactively facilitating the recovery of the animals has been essential. Finally, the volume of data and sophisticated analyses resulted in strong information to understand the needs of bears, to identify hot spots of mortality, and much more. Although these bears are doing significantly better in number, the population has been listed and delisted in recent decades because of concerns about their vulnerability once delisted, specifically related to the impacts of climate change on future grizzly bear survival and to the need for better connectivity across fragmented populations to enable long-term persistence. The Greater Yellowstone Ecosystem population is still completely isolated from more northern populations, and several populations are fragmented along the US and Canadian border. The population of grizzly bears in the Cabinet Yaak region in Montana was as low as ten in the 1990s. The FWS augmented this isolated population from the nearby Northern Continental Divide Ecosystem population. Complementing this,

Figure 10.1. Grizzly bear family in the Greater Yellowstone Ecosystem. Photo by Jeff Burrell.

a fifteen-year collaboration of nonprofit organizations called the Cabinet Purcell Mountain Corridor Project, facilitated by the Yellowstone to Yukon Conservation Initiative, has secured more than 1295 km² (>500 mi²) of habitat. This was accomplished through road closures, significantly increasing security in three priority corridors, reducing human-wildlife conflict through education, installing more than 170 electric fences to deter bears from attractants, and more. As a result, the grizzly bear population is now more than sixty individuals, grizzly bear-human conflicts have been significantly reduced, and bears have been observed using some of the protected corridors.

The general trend toward recovery for large carnivore species is encouraging because they tend to be umbrella species whose habitat requirements encompass those of many other species (Steenweg 2016), but see Carroll et al. (2001) for discussion about the benefit of using multiple carnivore focal species. In addition, efforts to protect large carnivores lead to the large-scale conservation strategies that include core protected areas, buffer zones, and connectivity between protected areas that are essential to preserving biodiversity.

CONNECTIVITY AND CLIMATE CHANGE IN THE WEST

Conservation is broader than individual species. It is widely recognized that successful long-term conservation of natural resources in the West needs to be planned and implemented at the large-landscape scale, ensuring a portfolio of diverse protected areas that are connected to create functional ecological networks (Bennett and Mulongoy 2006). In the West, various public and private entities engaged in natural resources conservation have already begun to shift toward large-landscape conservation, including connectivity.

The first organization formed to advocate for conserving representative ecosystems was The Nature Conservancy, which was created in 1951. Since then, the idea of a national conservation system has been repeatedly proposed (Aycrigg et al. 2016x). The absence of a cohesive national conservation plan has been problematic given not only continued habitat loss and fragmentation but also climate change (Meretsky et al. 2012). A key element of a system or network is that protected areas are *connected*. The concept of wildlife corridors—a means to achieve connectivity—grew in the 1990s and has continued to expand through research, tools, and policies in the West and around the world. Guidelines to create, implement, and manage connectivity are numerous and are increasingly incorporated into regulations and policy (Hilty et al. 2019). Importantly, connectivity is widely recognized as a tool for helping species adapt to a changing climate. Not only do we need large and well-placed protected areas, but because species need to be able to move through space and time, designated areas for connectivity or corridors are also widely recommended as one way to facilitate species adaptation (Heller and Zavaleta 2009).

Reflecting science-based recommendations, the West has experienced a shift toward large-landscape conservation. Because agencies are generally slower to change practices within larger bureaucracies, some of the initial conceptualization of large-landscape conservation in the West originated with nongovernmental organizations. In 1993, the idea of "protecting and connecting habitat from Yellowstone to Yukon for people and nature to thrive" was one of the first western and international large-landscape plans. This idea has been advancing on-the-ground conservation through the Yellowstone to Yukon Conservation Initiative and more than 450 partner organizations for the past twenty-five years (Yellowstone to Yukon Conservation Initiative 2014). Today, there are hundreds of efforts that self-identify with large-landscape conservation efforts in the West and beyond (see Network for Landscape Conservation 2020).

Federal and state agencies in the West also have shifted increasingly toward large-landscape conservation. Particularly momentous was the announcement of the first federally designated corridor, Path of the

Pronghorn in Wyoming, with commitments from the National Park Service (NPS), the USFS, the US Fish and Wildlife Service (FWS), and the BLM. The corridor helps to maintain a 270-kilometer (167-mile) migration corridor for pronghorn (*Antilocapra americana*) that migrate out of Grand Teton National Park to the Red Desert. The announcement was followed in 2007 by the unanimous approval by the Western Governors' Association (WGA) of a resolution across sixteen western states to protect wildlife corridors and crucial habitat, ultimately approving a report with a series of recommendations and forming the Wildlife Habitat Council (Wildlife Management Institute 2008). The WGA has continued to support this work, including through additional resolutions. Among the substantial impacts of the 2007 resolution is that western states began to map their wildlife corridor and core area priorities (also known as CHATs, or crucial habitat assessment tools). One of the most sophisticated and collaborative efforts occurred in Washington State, when it recognized the importance of thinking beyond its own boundaries and extended its analyses into neighboring jurisdictions (Washington Wildlife Habitat Connectivity Working Group 2010).

Individual federal agencies have begun to fundamentally shift their philosophy to better support connectivity and large-landscape conservation. National Park Service documents such as *Advancing the National Park Idea: Second Century Commission Report, Revisiting Leopold, and the Natural Resources Conservation Framework* demonstrate a shift at the highest levels of the Service toward managing in the context of larger landscapes and incorporating climate change (National Park Service 2001, 2016; National Park System Advisory Board 2012). While it is beyond the scope of this chapter to review the agencies in detail, the other major federal land managers in the West, including BLM, USFS, and FWS, also led departmental efforts to shift planning and institutional cultures to take on large-landscape conservation, incorporating corridors and climate change into forward looking planning and implementation guidelines. The planning and guidance documents across the collective of federal agencies in the West that manage lands represent an enormous shift in practice that affects land-use planning and, in many cases, also provides a mandate to coordinate beyond the boundaries of individual jurisdictions.

One of the more striking overarching US Department of the Interior initiatives was the creation, though ephemeral owing to changing federal administrations, of landscape conservation cooperatives (Landscape Conservation

Cooperative Network 2020). Western cooperatives began to develop and implement—through public and private voluntary partnerships and across large spatial extents—shared conservation priorities such as core area and connectivity conservation in light of climate change. The cooperatives enabled discussions about how to work together across multiple agencies and public and private lands. While federal funding is diminished, many cooperative projects have evolved from these partnerships.

Further demonstration that large-scale multijurisdictional conservation represents the future for the West can be seen in the announcement of the 2018 Secretarial Order No. 3362. Secretary of the Interior Ryan Zinke announced the order—"Improving Habitat Quality in Western Big-Game Winter Range and Migration Corridors"—for eleven western states to enhance and improve big-game winter range and migration corridors on federal lands. The order implies that such efforts may be multijurisdictional and often large scale, given the long-distance movements of pronghorn, deer, elk, and other species that would fall under this order. As such, it is also fostering conversation and cooperation between state and federal agencies.

Western state agencies charged with managing wildlife have also advanced statewide planning, including wildlife corridors through the aforementioned SWAPs and CHATs. Further, the concept of corridors is working its way into global, national, and western state legislation. California has developed and passed wildlife corridor legislation, which among other things requires the Department of Fish and Wildlife to maintain a database identifying those areas across the state that are important for wildlife connectivity.

Critical private-lands work is also advancing in the West. Housing density near protected areas across the United States increased on average by 741% from 1940 to 2000 (Hansen et al. 2014). Projections estimate that urban expansion around protected areas will expand by 67% from 2001 to 2051 (Martinuzzi et al. 2015), which will reduce natural habitats in the areas surrounding those lands by 12% in the period from 1970 to 2030 (Wade and Theobald 2010). As development surrounds and isolates national parks, parks lose species and potential wildlife corridors become less effective. Furthermore, lands within protected areas are at higher risk of alteration—for example, from fire suppression or by invasive species—in addition to the challenges posed by intensification of edge effects, reduction of the functional size of protected areas, and buffers (Swaty et al. 2011). In terms of large-landscape conservation, targeted private land easements and acquisitions have been critical, securing core habitat areas and helping ensure that connectivity areas remain free from activities that could foreclose movement. As but one example, in 2010, the Nature Conservancy through the Montana Legacy Project finalized the single largest land deal in the United States of more than 125,000 hectares (310,000 acres). This project is securing and restoring significant lands, including a part of the Swan Valley that is important at the landscape level for connectivity throughout the Yellowstone to Yukon region and is used by grizzly bears and many other species.

While conservation in the West has begun to move beyond the management of individual parcels and toward large-landscape conservation, these efforts are often disjointed where different entities work within their own vision and scope. There remains significant room for improvement.

FORWARD LOOKING

Conservation in the West is dynamic. We have seen the recovery of a number of endangered species, yet many populations and species are more at risk than ever. The philosophy of conservation has begun to shift from one of fortress conservation, or conservation of isolated protected areas, to multijurisdictional, large-landscape conservation emphasizing connectivity. This shift is necessary and important to conserve species and ecological processes that often have needs beyond the boundaries of any one protected area. Significant and further efforts will be required to achieve a representative connected ecological network, which would be more effective at keeping species from becoming endangered in the first place. Ecological networks are also likely to be more robust as the climate changes. Ultimately, a West-wide conservation strategy that would enable land and wildlife managers to work together on a unified vision would streamline efforts and break down jurisdictional boundaries that can hamper the ability to achieve the necessary scale of conservation.

The West faces significant challenges going forward. Prior to the late twentieth century, the size of protected areas was not as much of an issue in conserving biodiversity because many parks were surrounded by undeveloped land. In 2001, an average of 64% of the land within 10 kilometers (6 miles) of protected areas across the United States was still covered by natural vegetation (Martinuzzi et al. 2015). Over the past two decades, however, the western United States—which has often been characterized by large open spaces—has undergone significant land-use changes and continues to face

Figure 10.2. Natural resource extraction reduces and fragments habitat across the West. Photo taken in Wyoming by Jodi Hilty.

pressures such as energy development and urban expansion (Lawler et al. 2014). Natural gas production in the Rocky Mountain states has increased by 69% since 1996 and continues to grow (Western Governors' Association 2008). Energy development is occurring rapidly across the West, and Department of Energy forecasts suggest the region is poised to expand by upward of 40%. This growth, as well as increasing human populations and expanding development, will challenge conservation as the collection of human activities foreclose opportunities for maintaining a connected and protected network that could secure the conservation of biodiversity now and in the future.

The impact of a changing climate means that the problems of wildfires, flood events, and a lack of available water will likely only grow more acute. How these problems are addressed could have significant impacts on conservation. Because so much of the West is arid, riparian areas adjacent to creeks and rivers are corridors of life and disproportionately important for most species. Decades of fire suppression and other forest management practices have contributed to the increasing expanse, frequency, and intensity of wildfires (a trend expected to continue with further warming; see Schoennagel et al. 2017) and have pushed limited federal and state fire budgets. There are no easy answers. Experts, however, recommend shifting away from fire suppression, widespread forest thinning, and restoring to historical conditions in favor of prescribing fire to begin moving toward future conditions and "firesmart" community planning (Schoennagel et al. 2017).

Because this is a time of change, one thing is certain. We need continued monitoring, evaluation, and applied science to help guide conservation priorities. How do we create protected area networks in the West that are robust in the face of climate and land-use changes? What tools and approaches can help us work across the myriad private lands that may be important for the future of conservation in the West? And if we move toward an ecosystem-based conservation focus, what species may still need special attention if we are to conserve them in the long term? Conducting this research and monitoring, and advancing on-the-ground conservation in the western United States, will take a significant allocation of resources, commitment, and flexibility during this time of rapid and uncertain change.

References

Aldridge, Cameron L., Scott E. Nielsen, Hawthorne L. Beyer, Mark S. Boyce, John W. Connelly, Steven T. Knick, and Michael A. Schroeder. 2008. "Range-Wide Patterns of Greater Sage-Grouse Persistence." *Diversity and Distributions* 14(6): 983-994.

Association of Fish and Wildlife Agencies. 2012. *Best Practices for State Wildlife Action Plans— Voluntary Guidance to States for Revision and Implementation.* Washington, DC: Teaming with Wildlife Committee, State Wildlife Action Plan Best Practices Working Group.

Aycrigg, Jocelyn L., Anne Davidson, Leona K. Svancara, Kevin J. Gergely, Alexa McKerrow, and J. Michael Scott. 2013. "Representation of Ecological Systems within the Protected Areas Network of the Continental United States." *PLoS ONE* 8(1): e54689.

Aycrigg, Jocelyn L., et al. 2016a. "Completing the System: Opportunities and Challenges for a National Habitat Conservation System." *BioScience* 66(9): 774-784.

Aycrigg, Jocelyn L., James Tricker, R. Belote, Matthew Dietz, Lisa Duarte, and Gregory Aplet. 2016b. "The Next 50 Years: Opportunities for Diversifying the Ecological Representation of the National Wilderness Preservation System within the Contiguous United States." *Journal of Forestry* 114(3): 396-404.

Belton, Lorien R., and Douglas Jackson-Smith. 2010. "Factors Influencing Success among Collaborative Sage-Grouse Management Groups in the Western United States." *Environmental Conservation* 37(3): 250-260.

Bennett, Graham, and Kalemani J. Mulongoy. 2006. *Review of Experience with Ecological Networks, Corridors and Buffer Zones.* Technical Series. Montreal: Secretariat of the Convention on Biological Diversity.

Bergstrom, Bradley J., Sacha Vignieri, Steven R. Sheffield, Wes Sechrest, and Anne A. Carlson. 2009. "The Northern Rocky Mountain Gray Wolf Is Not Yet Recovered." *BioScience* 59(11): 991-999.

Byron, Eve. 2011. "Budget Bill Rider Will Delist Wolves." *Helena Independent Record*, April 15, 2011.

Camacho, Alejandro E., Michael Robinson-Dorn, Asena C. Yildiz, and Tara Teegarden. 2017. *Assessing State Laws and Resources for Endangered Species Protection*. Legal Studies Research Paper Series No. 2017-51. Washington, DC: Environmental Law Institute.

Carroll, Carlos, Reed F. Noss, and Paul C. Paquet. 2001. "Carnivores as Focal Species for Conservation Planning in the Rocky Mountain Region." *Ecological Applications* 11(4): 961-980.

Carwardine, Josie, Trudy O'Connor, Sarah Legge, Brendan Mackey, Hugh P. Possingham, and Tara G. Martin. 2012. "Prioritizing Threat Management for Biodiversity Conservation." *Conservation Letters* 5(3): 196-204.

Convention on Biological Diversity. 2011. *Strategic Plan for Biodiversity 2011-2020 and the Aichi Targets*. Montreal: Secretariat of the Convention on Biological Diversity.

Damschen, Ellen I., Lars A. Brudvig, Melissa A. Burt, Robert J. Fletcher Jr., Nick M. Haddad, Douglas J. Levey, John L. Orrock, Julian Resasco, and Joshua J. Tewksbury. 2019. "Ongoing Accumulation of Plant Diversity through Habitat Connectivity in an 18-Year Experiment." *Science* 365(6460): 1478-1480.

Ellison, Garret. 2017. "Wolves Targeted as Congress Moves to De-Fang Endangered Species Act." *Michigan News*, January 18, 2017.

Evans, Daniel M., et al. 2016. "Species Recovery in the United States: Increasing the Effectiveness of the Endangered Species Act." *Issues in Ecology* 20: 1-29.

Friedman, Lisa. 2019. "U.S. Significantly Weakens Endangered Species Act." *New York Times*, August 12, 2019.

George, Kelly A., Kristina M. Slagle, Robyn S. Wilson, Steven J. Moeller, and Jeremy T. Bruskotter. 2016. "Changes in Attitudes toward Animals in the United States from 1978 to 2014." *Biological Conservation* 201: 237-242.

Gibbs, Katherine E., and David J. Currie. 2012. "Protecting Endangered Species: Do the Main Legislative Tools Work?" *PLoS ONE* 7: e35730.

Goble, Dale D., Susan M. George, Kathryn Mazaika, J. Michael Scott, and Jason Karl. 1999. "Local and National Protection of Endangered Species: An Assessment." *Environmental Science and Policy* 2(1): 43-59.

Government Publishing Office. 1973. "Endangered Species Act." Accessed November 12, 2019. https://www.gpo.gov/fdsys/browse/collectionUScode. action?collectionCode=USCODE.

Hansen, Andrew J., Nathan Piekielek, Cory Davis, Jessica Haas, David M. Theobald, John E. Gross, William B. Monahan, Tom Olliff, and Steven W. Running. 2014. "Exposure of U.S. National Parks to Land Use and Climate Change 1900–2100." *Ecological Applications* 24(3): 484-502.

Heller, Nicole H., and Erika S. Zavaleta. 2009. "Biodiversity Management in the Face of Climate Change: A Review of 22 Years of Recommendations." *Biological Conservation* 142(1): 14-32.

Hilty, Jodi A., Annika T. H. Keeley, Adina M. Merenlender, and William Z. Lidicker Jr. 2019. *Corridor Ecology: Linking Landscapes for Biodiversity Conservation and Climate Change Adaptation*. Washington, DC: Island Press.

Jacobson, Cynthia A., D. J. Decker, and John Organ. 2010. "Fish and Wildlife Conservation and Management in the 21st Century: Understanding Challenges for Institutional Transformation." *Transactions of the North American Wildlife and Natural Resources Conference* 75: 107-114.

Jenkins, Clinton N., Kyle S. Van Houtan, Stuart L. Pimm, and Joseph O. Sexton. 2018. "US Protected Lands Mismatch Biodiversity Priorities." *Proceedings of the National Academy of Sciences* 112: 5081-5086.

Land and Water Fund Coalition. 2019. "President Signs Bill Permanently Reauthorizing LWCF." Press release, March 12, 2019. https://static1.squarespace.com/

static/58a60299ff7c508c3c05f2e1/t/5c87fbb04e17b6692133fd7b/1552415664400/
LWCF+Coalition+Statement+-+Reauthorization+Signing+-+Final.pdf.

Landscape Conservation Cooperative Network. 2020. Landscape Conservation Cooperative
Network website. Accessed February 8, 2020. https://lccnetwork.org.

Lawler, J. J., et al. 2014. "Projected Land-Use Change Impacts on Ecosystem Services in the
United States." *Proceedings of the National Academy of Sciences* 111(20): 7492-7497.

Lerner, Jeff, Bobby Cochran, and Julia Michalak. 2006. *Conservation across the Landscape: A
Review of the State Wildlife Action Plans.* Washington, DC: Defenders of Wildlife. https://
defenders.org/sites/default/files/publications/conservation_across_the_landscape_
handout.pdf.

Mace, Richard D., et al. 2012. "Grizzly Bear Population Vital Rates and Trend in the Northern
Continental Divide Ecosystem, Montana." *Journal of Wildlife Management* 76(1): 119-128.

Martinuzzi, Sebastián, Volker C. Radeloff, Lucas N. Joppa, Christopher M. Hamilton, David P.
Helmers, Andrew J. Plantinga, and David J. Lewis. 2015. "Scenarios of Future Land Use
Change around United States' Protected Areas." *Biological Conservation* 184: 446-455.

Mattson, David J., R. Gerald Wright, Katherine C. Kendall, and Clifford J. Martinka. 1995.
"Grizzly Bears." In *Our Living Resources: A Report to the Nation on the Distribution,
Abundance, and Health of US Plants, Animals, and Ecosystems,* edited by E. T. LaRoe et al.,
103-105. Washington, DC: US Department of the Interior, National Biological Service.

Meretsky, Vicky J., et al. 2012. "A State-Based National Network for Effective Wildlife
Conservation." *BioScience* 62(11): 970-976.

National Park Service. 2001. *Advancing the National Park Idea: National Parks Second Century
Report.* Washington, DC: National Parks Service. https://www.nps.gov/civic/resources/
Commission_Report.pdf.

National Park Service. 2016. *National Park Service Natural Resource Stewardship and Science
Framework: Four Pillars to Guide Natural Resource Activities and Investments.* Washington,
DC: National Park Service. https://www.nps.gov/orgs/1778/upload/NRSS_
Framework_Four_Pillars_-WCAG_2-0AA-1.pdf.

National Park Service Advisory Board. 2012. *Revisiting Leopold: Resource Stewardship in the
National Parks.* Washington, DC: National Park Service. https://www.nps.gov/
calltoaction/pdf/leopoldreport_2012.pdf.

National Park Service, Natural Resource Advisory Group. 2016. *Natural Resources
Conservation Framework: Priorities and Focal Areas for natural Resource Stewardship
Activities and Investments of the National Park Service.* Washington, DC: National Park
Service, Natural Resource Stewardship and Science, and Natural Resource Advisory
Group.

Network for Landscape Conservation. 2020. "Knowledge Center." Accessed March 19, 2020.
http://landscapeconservation.org/knowledge-center/resource-library/.

Organ, John F., et al. 2012. *The North American Model of Wildlife Conservation.* Technical
Review 12-04. Bethesda, MD: The Wildlife Society. http://wildlife.org/wp-content/
uploads/2014/05/North-American-model-of-Wildlife-Conservation.pdf.

Pimm, Stuart L., Clinton N. Jenkins, and Binbin Li. 2018. "How to Protect Half of Earth to
Ensure It Protects Sufficient Biodiversity." *Science Advances* 4(8): eaat2616.

Robbins, Kalyani. 2015. "The Biodiversity Paradigm Shift: Adapting the Endangered Species
Act to Climate Change." *Fordham Environmental Law Review* 27(1): 57-105.

Schoennagel, Tania, et al. 2017. "Adapt to More Wildfire in Western North American Forests
as Climate Changes." *Proceedings of the National Academy of Sciences* 114(18): 4582-4590.

Schrag, Anne, Sarah Konrad, Scott Miller, Brett Walker, and Steve Forrest. 2011. "Climate-
Change Impacts on Sagebrush Habitat and West Nile Virus Transmission Risk and
Conservation Implications for Greater Sage-grouse." *Geojournal* 76(5): 561-575.

Schwartz, Mark W. 2008. "The Performance of the Endangered Species Act." *Annual Review of Ecology, Evolution, and Systematics* 39: 279-299.

Steenweg, Robin W. 2016. "Testing and Expanding Umbrella Species—How Large Carnivore Occupancy Correlates with Species Diversity and Food-Web Structure." Chapter 5 in "Large-Scale Camera Trapping and Large-Carnivore Monitoring, Occupancy-Abundance Relationships, and Food-Webs." Doctoral thesis, University of Montana.

Steffen, Will, et al. 2015. "Planetary Boundaries: Guiding Human Development on a Changing Planet." *Science* 347(6223): 1259855.

Stein, Bruce A., Lynn S. Kutner, and Jonathan S. Adams, eds. 2000. *Precious Heritage: The Status of Biodiversity in the United States.* Oxford: Oxford University Press.

Stein, Bruce A., Naomi Edelson, Lauren Anderson, John J. Kanter, and Jodi Stemler. 2018. *Reversing America's Wildlife Crisis: Securing the Future of Our Fish and Wildlife.* Washington, DC: National Wildlife Foundation. https://www.nwf.org/-/media/Documents/PDFs/NWF-Reports/2018/Reversing-Americas-Wildlife-Crisis_2018.ashx.

Swaty, Randy, Kori Blankenship, Sarah Hagen, Joseph Fargione, Jim Smith, and Jeannie Patton 2011. "Accounting for Ecosystem Alteration Doubles Estimates of Conservation Risk in the Conterminous United States." *PLoS ONE* 6(8): E23002.

US Department of the Interior. 2016. *National Survey of Fishing, Hunting, and Wildlife-Associated Recreation.* Washington, DC: US Fish and Wildlife Service, US Department of Commerce, and the US Census Bureau. https://wsfrprograms.fws.gov/subpages/nationalsurvey/nat_survey2016.pdf.

Wade, Alisa A., and David M. Theobald. 2010. "Residential Development Encroachment on U.S. Protected Areas." *Conservation Biology* 24(1): 151-161.

Wade, P. 2019. "U.S. Sees Largest Reduction of Protected Areas in History under Trump." *Rolling Stone.* June 2, 2019. https://www.rollingstone.com/politics/politics-news/largest-reduction-of-protected-lands-under-trump-843457/.

Washington Wildlife Habitat Connectivity Working Group. 2010. *Washington Connected Landscapes Project: Statewide Analysis.* Olympia: Washington Departments of Fish and Wildlife and Transportation. https://waconnected.org/wpcontent/themes/whcwg/docs/statewide-connectivity/2010DEC%2017%20WHCWG%20Statewide%20Analysis%20FINAL.pdf.

Wayne, Robert, and P. W. Hedrick. 2011. "Genetics and Wolf Conservation in the American West: Lessons and Challenges." *Heredity* 107(1): 16-19.

Weaver, John L., Paul C. Paquet, and Leonard F. Ruggiero. 1996. "Resilience and Conservation of Large Carnivores in the Rocky Mountains." *Conservation Biology* 10(4): 964-976.

Western Governors' Association. 2008. *Wildlife Corridors Initiative.* Denver, CO: Western Governors' Association. https://arc-solutions.org/wp-content/uploads/2012/03/Western-Governors-Association-2008-Corridor-Initiative-Report.pdf.

Wildlife Management Institute. 2008. "Western Governors to Focus on Wildlife Corridors." *Outdoor News Bulletin* 62(7).

Yellowstone National Park. 2019. "Grizzly Bears and the Endangered Species Act." Last updated April 8, 2019. https://www.nps.gov/yell/learn/nature/bearesa.htm.

Yellowstone to Yukon Conservation Initiative. 2014. *The Yellowstone to Yukon Vision: Progress and Possibility.* Bozeman, MT: Yellowstone to Yukon Conservation Initiative. https://y2y.net/publications/y2y_vision_20_years_of_progress.pdf.

Part IV

DEVELOPMENT, SOVEREIGNTY, AND CONFLICT IN THE WEST

Chapter 11
Renewable Energy Development in the American West

ANNA KARMAZINA

INTRODUCTION

US energy system configurations are changing at an unprecedented rate. Increasing environmental concerns and energy security worries, as well as falling prices, have contributed to the growth of renewable energy in the United States. Because renewable energy has become more feasible to develop over the past decade, it now competes more successfully against fossil fuels. Given that this trend is likely to continue, more land will be required to site renewable energy projects. Public lands cover large portions of the American West, and therefore the issue of renewable energy siting on western public lands carries great significance.

Davis (2001) identifies three factors that explain the dynamics of fossil energy development on public lands: (1) interest group tensions, (2) political party configurations, and (3) bureaucratic procedures. The first two factors are contested areas. First, the divergence of interests among industry groups and environmentalists results in lobbying battles over preferable policy outcomes. Second, partisanship influences the course of action in the energy policy domain—generally, Republicans tend to adopt pro-business policies that favor the fossil fuel industry, while Democrats tend to be more attentive to environmental consequences.

Compared to fossil fuel policy dynamics, renewable energy policy developments are to some extent less contentious, yet they present some unique challenges. In terms of interest group involvement, both business and environmental coalitions generally support renewable energy development. As illustrated below, however, a unique set of clashes between environmental groups—known as the "green versus green" phenomenon—has been growing recently (Yonk et al. 2013). Furthermore, despite overall public support for renewable energy development, some local communities do not welcome such development proposals (Pierce and Steel 2017). In terms of political party alignments, renewable energy enjoys bipartisan support because it helps achieve environmental goals as well as national energy security and economic development goals. Finally, federal agencies responsible for project permitting processes have been active in improving and expediting procedures pertaining to siting of renewable energy.

This chapter first presents a synopsis of the legislative shift toward renewable energy development is depicted. Second, it provides an overview of regulatory regimes regarding solar, wind, geothermal, and biomass development on public lands. Third comes a snapshot of solar, wind, geothermal, and biomass developments on western public lands. Finally, I outline the controversy regarding renewable energy siting on public lands, including case studies of wind and geothermal energy projects.

MOVEMENT TOWARD RENEWABLE ENERGY DEVELOPMENT

Bernell and Simon (2016) maintain that energy systems in the United States have a major task of ensuring energy security, further specifying the following four goals in that task. The first is to safeguard abundance of energy resources that can guarantee widespread access to energy. The second goal for the energy system actors is to guarantee reliability, which implies that consumers will continue to have undisrupted access to energy sources. The third goal is to ensure affordability of energy sources, that is, that customers have access to energy at reasonable and predicted costs. The fourth goal is to achieve the system's sustainability. Goals can also change over time. In the early twentieth century, the main goal was to provide access to electricity at affordable prices. More recently, concerns over dangers posed by climate change have elevated the importance of energy sustainability.

Advanced energy systems are often associated with societal progress, yet they are also responsible for negative consequences. Burning of fossil fuels (coal, oil, and natural gas) contributes to negative health-related impacts. In addition, climate change due to carbon dioxide emissions associated with the burning of fossil fuels is also an enormous and challenging global issue. The *Fifth Assessment Report* prepared by the Intergovernmental Panel on Climate Change (2014) states that "human influence on the climate system is clear and growing." A decrease in the use of fossil fuels and an increase of renewable energy generation can reduce both negative health-related impacts and carbon dioxide emissions.

External shocks and crises also significantly affect energy policy. According to Grossman (2015, p. 57), "in the United States progress on energy policy requires a crisis." In response to an energy crisis caused by the oil embargo of 1973 declared by the Organization of Arab Petroleum Exporting Countries, the US Congress passed the National Energy Act of 1978. The act aimed to reduce the country's dependence on fossil fuels by supporting the domestic development of alternative fuel sources and promoting energy efficiency and conservation. One of the most important sections of the act was the Public Utility Regulatory Policies Act (PURPA), which brought significant changes to the governing mechanisms of the US electricity sector. Most notably, PURPA created a regulatory framework enabling electricity production from renewable sources by nonutility players. The legislation was resisted by traditional energy players who questioned the legality of PURPA in court. The Supreme Court decision ultimately upheld the rule (Shively and Ferrare 2008).

Given the great importance of having stable and sufficient sources of energy, the Arab oil embargo was a disruptive force for a global economy deeply dependent on energy: "The embargo also sparked a fundamental shift in the definition of energy supply, from a solely technological problem to a bundle of social ones" (Rosa et al. 1988, p. 164). Since the 1970s (following the first oil embargo), the issue of energy diversification became more critical. Concerns over unimpeded access to energy sources and issues pertaining to the finite nature of fossil fuels led to policies aimed to diversify energy production.

The Persian Gulf War of 1990-1991 and several abrupt oil price increases in the late 1980s and early 1990s once again demonstrated the importance of stable access to energy resources. To further enhance resource diversification and domestic renewable energy production, the US Congress passed the Energy Policy Act of 1992. The act created financial assistance for renewable energy development and incentives for the commercialization of renewable energy technologies. Among other provisions, the act introduced a number of significant regulatory changes that set the state for the deregulation of the energy sector. A host of new players emerged in the energy market, including independent power producers procuring renewable energy sources (Shively and Ferrare 2008).

In addition to significant changes in energy policy owing to shocks and crises, substantial modifications can occur without major external disruptions. Mahoney and Thelen (2010, p. 2) underline that incremental endogenous processes can bring about shifts in a policy subsystem. Incremental policy changes cumulatively work toward accomplishing a larger goal (i.e., different institutional changes and policy initiatives increase the prospects for energy sustainability). Governments adopt a broad range of policies that affect energy markets, including financial incentives and regulations affecting energy production and actions limiting or altering consumption patterns (Geri and McNabb 2016).

In the 1970s, environmentalists achieved significant progress in pushing for environmental legislation. A number of major environmental protection acts were adopted during that time, including the Clean Air Act, the Clean Water Act, the Endangered Species Act, the National Environmental Policy Act, and the National Forest Management Act. Several policy provisions have also incrementally increased the utilization of renewable energy sources. First, federal financial incentives—such as the Renewable Electricity Production Tax Credit (PTC) and Business Energy Investment Tax Credit (ITC)—have had a goal to increase the share of renewable energy in the national energy mix. Second, the adoption of regulatory mandates (renewable portfolio standards or renewable portfolio goals) by US states has stimulated the use of renewable energy technologies. Even western states, excluding Idaho and Wyoming, have regulatory policies in place mandating that electric utilities operating in the state procure a certain percentage of electricity using renewable energy sources by a certain year. The most ambitious renewable portfolio standard was adopted by the California State Legislature in 2018, which increased the required level of renewables from 50% to 60% by 2030 and introduced an additional target of 100% of electricity from renewable energy resources and zero-carbon resources by 2045 (California Public Utilities Commission 2020). In some states (e.g., Utah), however, the regulatory provisions are not mandatory and require that utilities procure a certain percentage of renewable energy only if it is "cost-effective" (Database of State Incentives for Renewables and Efficiency 2018).

In addition to federal and state measures, regional agreements have promoted the use of renewable energy. The West Coast Governors' Global Warming Initiative of 2003 and the succeeding Pacific Coast Action Plan on Climate and Energy of 2013 signed by the governors of California, Oregon, and Washington and the premier of British Columbia have demonstrated the regional agreement to coordinate efforts in reducing greenhouse gas emissions and to increase the use of renewable energy sources. The governors from the aforementioned jurisdictions have also actively participated in the Governors' Global Climate Summits held in partnership with the United Nations Environmental Programme (UNEP) (Pierce and Steel 2017).

HISTORY OF REGULATORY CONTEXT

The US Department of the Interior—including the Bureau of Land Management (BLM), the Minerals Management Service (MMS), the US Geological Survey (USGS), and the US Forest Service—is the main manager of public lands that host a majority of renewable energy projects. The BLM authorizes wind and solar energy development; in turn, geothermal energy projects are processed by the BLM, the MMS, and the USGS; and biomass energy development is managed by the US Forest Service. Several federal policy acts comprise the regulatory base for the permitting process of renewable energy projects. Table 11.1 provides a list of major policy acts affecting renewable energy development on public lands.

Table 11.1. List of Major Public and Land Use Policies That Regulate the Development of Renewable Energy on Public Lands

Federal Law	Impact on Renewable Energy Development on Public Lands
National Historic Preservation Act of 1966	Ensures the preservation of historical and cultural foundations; as a result, some portions of public lands may be excluded from a pool of potential sites for renewable energy development
National Environmental Policy Act of 1969, Endangered Species Act of 1973, and National Forest Management Act of 1976	Guarantee environmental protection; as a result, some portions of public lands may be excluded from a pool of potential sites for renewable energy development.
Geothermal Steam Act of 1970	Regulates the authorization process of geothermal energy projects.
Federal Land Policy and Management Act of 1976	Establishes procedures for land-use planning processes on public lands.
Energy Policy Act of 2005	Provides incentives for renewable energy development on public lands.

The federal government has encouraged renewable energy development on public lands in a number of ways. Section 211 of the Energy Policy Act of 2005 signed into law by President George W. Bush mandates that "the Secretary of the Interior should, before the end of the 10-year period beginning on the date of enactment of this Act, seek to have approved non-hydropower renewable energy projects located on the public lands with a generation capacity of at least 10,000 megawatts of electricity."[1] President Obama's Climate Action Plan of 2013 directed the US Department of the Interior to permit 10,000 megawatts of renewables on public lands by 2020 (in addition to previously mandating 10,000 megawatts of renewable energy by 2012, which was achieved by the US Department of the Interior ahead of schedule) (Executive Office of the President 2013).

Wind and Solar

Title V of the Federal Land Policy and Management Act of 1976, as amended, and Title 43 of the Code of Federal Regulations authorize the permitting process of wind and solar energy projects under rights-of-way grants (Bureau of Land Management 2019a). In addition, the National Environmental Policy Act, the Endangered Species Act, the National Historic Preservation Act of 1966, and the Tribal Consultation requirements regulate siting procedures of wind and solar energy projects.

In 2005, the BLM issued the *Wind Energy Development Final Programmatic Environmental Impact Statement*, which provided guidelines for assessing environmental impacts of wind energy development on public lands in the western United States (Bureau of Land Management 2005). In addition, in 2008, the BLM released guidelines on processing wind energy authorizations and summaries of best management practices of wind energy siting, which aimed at mitigating the impact on avian habitat and other potential wildlife threat as well as alleviating any resource conflicts (Bureau of Land Management 2018b).

The West-Wide Wind Mapping Project is an example of the BLM's effort to identify areas with high wind energy generation potential and low resource conflict to make the siting process less complicated. The West-Wide Wind Mapping Project identifies areas across eleven states of the American West that (1) possess high potential for wind energy generation, (2) are located in land-use exclusion zones, and (3) elicit high environmental concerns and generate other potential resource conflicts (West-Wide Wind Mapping

Project 2019). This systematic classification of public lands helps the stakeholders anticipate possible siting complications.

There are restrictions in terms of the type of land that can be utilized for renewable energy development. For example, lands located within the BLM's National Landscape Conservation System face restrictions for solar energy development; likewise, lands located within Areas of Critical Environmental Concern may be unavailable for solar energy development (Bureau of Land Management 2018a). In 2007, the BLM issued an instruction memorandum (IM) for the processing of right-of-way applications for solar energy development projects on public lands, superseding the agency's Solar Energy Development Policy of 2004. The IM explicated in a great detail the authorization process in the hopes of encouraging renewable energy development according to the goals of the National Energy Policy of 2001 and the Energy Policy Act of 2005 as well as ensuring environmentally responsible developments (Bureau of Land Management 2007).

In 2012, the BLM launched the Solar Energy Program (known as the Western Solar Plan) to facilitate utility-scale solar energy development on public lands in six southwestern states (Arizona, California, Colorado, Nevada, New Mexico, and Utah). The program was based on the Final Programmatic Environmental Impact Statement (PEIS) for Solar Energy Development in Six Southwestern States (Solar PEIS) prepared by the BLM and the US Department of Energy (DOE) as well as nineteen cooperating agencies, including various federal-, state-, and county-level entities. More than 200,000 public comments were received on a series of drafts of this document (Bureau of Land Management and US Department of Energy 2012). Solar PEIS established systematic guidelines designed to make the permitting process of utility-scale solar energy projects more efficient and to maximize the mitigation of potential environmental impacts (Bureau of Land Management and US Department of Energy 2012).

In addition, the BLM identified nineteen solar energy zones (SEZs) in six southwestern states as areas "well suited for utility-scale production of solar energy, where the BLM will prioritize solar energy and associated transmission infrastructure development" (Bureau of Land Management 2014). If fully developed, SEZs would provide 27,000 megawatts of solar energy, which is equivalent to the amount of energy necessary to power about eight million homes (US Department of the Interior 2016).

In 2017, the BLM amended existing regulatory guidelines for wind and solar energy development on public lands by enacting the Solar and Wind Rule. The rule expanded the BLM's prerogative to employ a competitive bidding processes on lands for wind and solar development. It also brought the BLM fee structure for new wind and solar energy development in line with existing market conditions (Bureau of Land Management 2019b). In addition, the rule promoted the development of designated leasing areas (DLAs) that would be preferred for solar and wind energy development. These areas would have high energy generation potential, access to transmission lines, and low resource conflict (Bureau of Land Management 2016). In short, this provision aimed to simplify the application process and enhance renewable energy development at sites with fewer resource conflicts (Block 2016).

Geothermal

The Geothermal Steam Act of 1970, as amended, regulates the authorization process of geothermal energy projects on public lands under competitive leasing procedures (Bureau of Land Management 2019a). The Energy Policy Act of 2005 substantially amended the Geothermal Steam Act. Section 225 of the act required the BLM and the Forest Service to issue an interagency memorandum of understanding (MOU) to advance coordination in the leasing and permitting process of geothermal energy applications. The MOU, officially issued in 2006, focused on reducing the lease application backlog by 90% in five years and established a shared database for tracking applications (Bureau of Land Management and US Forest Service 2016).

Section 226 of the Energy Policy Act of 2005 required the USGS to update a geothermal resource assessment first introduced in 1978. The assessment projected the region's total geothermal energy potential and identified areas with the most geothermal energy development promise (Aird 2006).

Biomass

In 2003, an MOU between the US Department of the Interior, the US Department of Agriculture, and the US Department of Energy established the Biomass Research and Development Board with the goal to promote wood biomass development (Aird 2006). Section 210 of the Energy Policy Act of 2005 authorized grants for biomass energy projects (guaranteeing $20 per green ton of biomass delivered). These projects were to be located in preferred communities, including areas near federal lands "at significant risk of catastrophic wildfire, disease, or insect infestation or which suffers from disease or insect infestation."[2] To establish eligibility for the federal grants, Section 210 of the act defined biomass as "nonmerchantable materials or precommercial thinnings that are byproducts of preventive treatments, such as trees, wood, brush, thinnings, chips, and slash, that are removed—(A) to reduce hazardous fuels; (B) to reduce or contain disease or insect infestation; or (C) to restore forest health."[3]

WIND, SOLAR, GEOTHERMAL, AND BIOMASS ENERGY DEVELOPMENTS ON WESTERN PUBLIC LANDS

Wind Energy

Wind energy is the United States' largest source of renewable energy besides hydropower. The first utility-scale wind energy project on public lands was approved by the Bureau of Land Management in 1982—the 40-megawatt Cabazon Wind Energy Facility in Riverside County, California. As of November 2018, the BLM had approved thirty-five wind energy projects located on public lands with a total capacity of 3,249 megawatts, which is sufficient to power about one million homes. Twenty-eight of the approved projects are in California, having a total capacity of 944 megawatts; two projects are in Wyoming with a total capacity of 1,521 megawatts; two projects are in Arizona with a total capacity of 530 megawatts; two projects are in Utah with a total capacity of 100 megawatts; one project is in Nevada with a capacity of 150 megawatts; and one project is in Oregon with a capacity of 4 megawatts. The approved projects range widely in size and capacity—from the 3-megawatt wind energy facilities in California to the 1,500-megawatt Chokecherry and Sierra Madre Wind Energy Project in Carbon County, Wyoming (Bureau of Land Management 2019e).

Solar Energy

The southwestern United States possesses tremendous solar energy potential. The first utility-scale solar energy project on public lands was approved by the BLM in 2010—the 50-megawatt Silver State North thin film photovoltaic system in Clark County, Nevada. As of November 2018, the Bureau of Land Management approved twenty-eight solar energy projects located on public lands with a total capacity of 7,171 megawatts, which is sufficient to power about two million homes. Sixteen of the approved projects are in California, having a total capacity of 5,261 megawatts; nine projects are in Nevada with a total capacity of 1,430 megawatts; two projects are in Arizona with a total capacity of 400 megawatts; and one project is in Wyoming with a capacity of 80 megawatts. The approved projects range widely in size and capacity, from the 20-megawatt Ocotillo Sol photovoltaic system on 100 acres of public lands in Imperial County, California, to the 750-megawatt McCoy Solar Project on 7,700 acres of public lands in Riverside County, California (750 megawatts approved and 250 megawatts in operation), and the 550-megawatt Desert Sunlight Solar Farm on 4,165 acres of public lands in Riverside County, California (all 550 megawatts are in operation) (Bureau of Land Management 2019d).

Geothermal Energy

California possesses the largest amount of geothermal energy potential in the United States because it is located on the Pacific's "ring of fire" and because of tectonic plate conjunctions (California Energy Commission 2020). The first utility-scale geothermal energy project on public lands was approved by the BLM in 1978: the 30-megawat Geysers Units 5&6 and the 30-megawatt Geysers Units 7&8 in Lake County, California. As of March 2018, the Bureau of Land Management approved fifty geothermal energy projects located on public lands with a total capacity of 1,648 megawatts. Out of all approved projects, twenty-five projects are in California with a total capacity of 664 megawatts, twenty-one projects are located in Nevada with a total capacity of 867 megawatts, two projects are located in Utah with a total capacity of 70 megawatts, one project with a capacity of 32 megawatts is located in Idaho, and one project with a capacity of 15 megawatts is located in New Mexico. The approved projects widely range in size and capacity—from the smallest 4-megawatt San Emidio geothermal plant in Washoe County, Nevada, to the largest 120-megawatt Salt Wells Vulcan projects in Churchill County, Nevada (Bureau of Land Management 2019c).

Biomass Energy

The US Energy Information Administration (2019a) reported that about 2% of US energy consumption in 2017 was from wood and wood waste. Shelly (2011) identifies several sources of woody biomass, including (1) nontimber tree removal (dead trees and trees preventing land and urban development); (2) forest management (small-diameter tree removal related to hazard fuel treatment, precommercial thinning related to timber production, and forest health improvement); (3) timber harvesting residues; (4) wood manufacturing residues (sawdust, bark, defective wood pieces); and (5) fast-growing tree plantations. Western states significantly differ in the extent of wood biomass utilization: Pacific coastal states utilize significantly larger amounts of woody biomass compared to the Rocky Mountain region and the four corner states (Arizona, Colorado, New Mexico, and Utah) (Nicholls et al. 2018). Thirty-two electric-generating facilities that use woody biomass feedstocks are located in western states with a total capacity of 847 megawatts, including eighteen facilities in California with a total capacity of 457 megawatts, six facilities in Washington with a total capacity of 193 megawatts, five facilities in Oregon with a total capacity of 156 megawatts, one facility in Arizona with a total capacity of 27 megawatts, one facility in Colorado with a total capacity of 11.5 megawatts, and one facility in Montana with a total capacity of 3 megawatts (Nicholls et al. 2018). In the western United States, issues pertaining to forest have been strongly debated for decades, and environmental opposition has occurred to proposals for biomass energy facilities (Sundstrom et al. 2012).

RENEWABLE ENERGY SITING CONTROVERSY

Despite wide public support for renewable energy development, in some cases the siting of renewable energy facilities proves problematic because of opposition from surrounding communities and environmental organizations. Specifically, the siting of wind energy farms has sparked a significant amount of controversy. This controversy occurs when local ecosystems or the quality of life of the surrounding community are threatened (Pierce and Steel 2017).

Opposition to wind energy projects has been extensively studied by scholars around the world examining Canadian, European, New Zealand, and US contexts. Scholars identified several groups of factors that help explain opposition to proposed projects. First, procedural factors have an effect on how proposed projects are perceived by the surrounding communities. Trust in developers and government agencies is likely to increase the project's acceptance. In addition, community member perceptions on whether decisions are made in an unbiased manner and whether communities are treated fairly determine attitudes toward the project development process (Bidwell 2013). Second, the distribution of positive and negative outcomes of wind energy development on the surrounding community affects the project siting process. Among positive outcomes are the creation of new local jobs and increased tax revenue, while negative outcomes include visual and noise pollution, wildlife threats, public health and safety issues, local infrastructure damage, and decreasing property values (Fischlein et al. 2013; Groth and Vogt 2014; Jones and Eiser 2010). Finally, community-unique contextual factors play a role in the siting process (e.g., past community experiences with energy facility siting and differences in community identity). Devine-Wright (2009) argues that community place attachment and symbolic meanings influence attitudes toward wind energy projects.

Environmental organizations occasionally fight renewable energy developments when they are seen as damaging to local ecosystems (Pierce and Steel 2017). For instance, the Audubon Society has opposed wind and solar energy projects on the basis of potential negative avian impacts—an example of a "green versus green" clash (Yonk et al. 2013). In some cases, however, the biocentric environmental organizations coordinate efforts with developers and regulators in the search of appropriate habitat mitigation solutions.

Giordono et al. (2018) conducted a systematic analysis of fifty-three proposals for wind energy development in California, Idaho, Oregon, and Washington to identify the amount of opposition and understand the processes that affect it. The research concluded that "while some level of local opposition to wind proposals is not rare, it is typically restricted to more benign activities that require few resources and take place in standard institutional settings" (Giordono et al. 2018, p. 119). Specifically, in most cases, opposition was represented by writing letters to the editor and providing comments on drafts of environmental impact assessments, while protests and lawsuits were rare forms of opposition. The following case studies further illustrate this phenomenon.

The Cotterel Mountain Wind Energy Project

In 2001, Boise-based Windland, Inc., in partnership with Shell Wind Energy, filed a right-of-way application to build the 200-megawatt Cotterel Mountain Wind Farm in Cassia County, Idaho. The project site was located mainly on public lands that were managed by the BLM. Residents of Albion, Idaho, a nearby town, became concerned with potential visual impacts, wildlife threats, and negative economic effects associated with the proposed wind energy facility. Twelve residents joined their efforts in opposing the project and created the Committee against Windmills in Albion. The group gathered 224 signatures to sign a petition against the project (Giordono et al. 2018).

In 2005, a draft environmental impact statement was issued and made available to the public. Seventy-two written comments were submitted during the comment period. The comments raised a number of issues related to the proposed project. Several key issues were addressed in detail: sage grouse habitat conservation, protection of tribal treaty rights, mitigation of potential impacts on migratory birds and threatened or endangered species, maintenance of public access to the land, protection of visual resources, and ensuring consistency with the Cassia County Resource Management Plan of 1985. About twenty other issues and concerns were considered, although not as extensively as the key issues. In 2006, the BLM prepared the final environmental impact statement specifying the agency's preferred alternative: the project to be constructed with actions taken to mitigate wildlife issues and concerns (Bureau of Land Management 2006). In 2012, however, the developers decided not to proceed with the project and withdrew their application. In summary, this case is an example of the trade-offs between the needs to produce low-carbon energy sources and the potential negative impacts on a surrounding community and ecosystem. In addition, this is also an example of low-level opposition to wind energy projects.

The Newberry Crater Geothermal Energy Project

Geothermal energy is an important energy source because it emits low levels of air pollution and carbon dioxide. Compared to power plants that use fossil fuels, geothermal power plants emit 97% less sulfur compounds, which contribute to acid rains, and 99% less carbon dioxide, which drives climate change (US Energy Information Administration 2019b). At the same time, geothermal energy provides a consistent energy supply, unlike solar and wind energy sources that are intermittent in their nature. But some geothermal energy projects have sparked controversy owing to their potential local environmental impacts (Pierce and Steel 2017). The case of the Newberry Crater Geothermal Energy Project details how siting processes occur.

The proposed site for the Newberry Crater Geothermal Energy Project is in central Oregon, near the Newberry Volcano, about twenty miles southeast of Bend, Oregon. The project has had a long development history but has not been built to date. The project has been developed by Davenport Power and AltaRock Energy in partnership with a wide range of organizations such as GE Global Research, Lawrence Berkeley National Laboratory, Oregon State University, Pacific Northwest National Laboratory, Statoil, Texas A&M,

Temple University, the University of Oregon, the University of Utah, and the US Geological Survey (Grasso 2016; Petty 2010).

Several governmental bodies have overseen the project's permitting process, including the US Bureau of Land Management, the US Department of Energy, the US Forest Service, the Oregon Department of Energy, and several other Oregon agencies (Petty 2010). A number of policy and regulatory acts have comprised the regulatory base for the permitting process: the National Environmental Policy Act of 1969, the Geothermal Steam Act of 1970, the National Forest Management Act of 1976, the Federal Land Policy and Management Act of 1976, the Energy Policy Act of 2005, and the Programmatic Environmental Impact Statement for Geothermal Leasing in the Western US of 2008. In addition, in 1990, Congress issued an act that established the Newberry National Volcanic Monument. The act restricted geothermal energy development inside the monument and provided guidance for geothermal development in the adjacent areas.[4]

In 2007, Davenport Power obtained a permit from the BLM for an exploratory well-drilling program. The program involved road maintenance and pad preparation (three five-acre well pads), which required clearing trees and compacting the ground. The well pads were situated on federal geothermal leases west of the Newberry National Volcanic Monument (Davenport Power 2008). In 2008, the developer submitted a notice of intent to obtain a site certificate for a geothermal energy facility with a 35- to 45-megawatt capacity and a 12-mile transmission line to a Bonneville Power Administration substation near the town of La Pine, Oregon. The proposed project site was located outside of the Newberry National Volcanic Monument (Oregon Department of Energy 2008). Several public meetings were held by the government agencies to familiarize the public with the proposed project and siting procedures (Davenport Power 2008).

In 2009, Davenport Energy in partnership with AltaRock received a $21 million federal matching grant through the American Recovery and Reinvestment Act for the development of the Newberry Enhanced Geothermal System (EGS) Demonstration Project. The goal of the project was to test the EGS technology with the possibility of applying it later at other sites. The developers submitted to the BLM a notice of intent for developing the Demonstration Project to test the EGS technology. As required by the National Environmental Policy Act, the project was subject to environmental analysis, conducted by the BLM, the US Department of Energy, and the US

Forest Service. A number of public meetings were held at different locations in central Oregon (Bend, La Pine, and Sunriver) (Bureau of Land Management 2011). The BLM issued a draft environmental assessment, which received seven comments from nongovernmental organizations and government entities (Blue Mountain Biodiversity Project, Central Oregon Land Watch, the Klamath Tribe, Leaning Pine Ranch, the Northwest Environmental Defense Center, Oregon Wild, and Region 10 of the Environmental Protection Agency) and four comments from private individuals (Bureau of Land Management 2011). The final environmental assessment identified several "key issues" regarding the project development: (1) safety of the EGS technology; (2) issues related to water quantity and water quality; (3) earthquake risks; (4) impacts to the Newberry National Volcanic Monument; (5) potential visual impact; and (6) threats to wildlife.

As required by the National Environmental Policy Act, the BLM, the Department of Energy, and the Forest Service conducted the environmental assessment to either issue a finding of no significant impact (FONSI) or to prepare an environmental impact statement (EIS). In April 2012, the authorities issued a FONSI concluding that no significant environmental impacts would take place. As a result, the developers were allowed to begin construction of the Newberry Enhanced Geothermal System Demonstration Project (Bureau of Land Management 2012). The Demonstration Project has the goal of providing information on the economic viability of developing a 35-megawatt geothermal energy facility at the Newberry site. Currently, the Newberry Geothermal Energy (NEWGEN) team, a joint partnership of AltaRock Energy, Oregon State University, and Pacific Northwest National Laboratory, continues efforts to make progress on the project, although no final date has been issued for its completion. Obtaining adequate financial resources for the project remains a significant challenge (AltaRock Energy 2019).

CONCLUSION

Renewable energy development is on the rise in the United States. More public lands, especially in the American West, will be identified as possible sites of renewable energy projects. Development of solar, wind, geothermal, and biomass energy is a less contentious area compared to development of fossil fuels. Both business and environmental coalitions are largely in favor of renewable energy development. In addition, renewable energy generally enjoys bipartisan support because it serves several societal goals (i.e., national energy security, economic development, and environmental protection). Furthermore, federal agencies responsible for permitting of renewable energy projects have made significant efforts to create more efficient siting procedures and mitigate potential negative impacts associated with renewable energy developments. Yet siting of renewable energy projects occasionally meets some unique challenges. Specifically, environmental organizations and local communities in some cases oppose proposed projects. Several factors may play a role in increased contentiousness: (1) procedural factors (lack of trust and unfair siting procedures); (2) factors related to uneven distribution of positive and negative outcomes associated with renewable energy developments; and (3) community-unique contextual factors. Thus scholars and policymakers should stay attuned to the challenge of finding a balance between the need to produce low-carbon energy sources and mitigating impacts on local communities and the ecosystem.

Legal Citations

1 Public Law 109-58.
2 Energy Policy Act of 2005, 119 STAT 594, Pub. L. No. 109-58 (2005). To Establish the Newberry National Volcanic Monument in the State of Oregon, and for Other Purposes, 104 STAT 2288, Pub. L. No. 101-522 (1990).
3 Energy Policy Act of 2005, 119 STAT 594, Pub. L. No. 109-58 (2005).
4 Energy Policy Act of 2005, 119 STAT 594, Pub. L. No. 109-58 (2005).

References

Aird, Brenda. 2006. "The Role of Federal Government and Federal Lands in Fueling Renewable and Alternative Energy in America: Hearings before the Subcommittee on Energy and Mineral Resources of the House Resources Committee." Office of Congressional and Legislative Affairs, Department of the Interior, April 6, 2006. https://www.doi.gov/ocl/Renewable-Energy.

AltaRock Energy. 2019. "Newberry Geothermal Energy (NEWGEN), Oregon." Accessed November 12, 2019. http://altarockenergy.com/projects/newberry-geothermal-energy-newgen/.

Bernell, David, and Christopher A. Simon. 2016. The Energy Security Dilemma: US Policy and Practice. New York: Routledge.

Bidwell, David. 2013. "The Role of Values in Public Beliefs and Attitudes towards Commercial Wind Energy." Energy Policy 58: 189-199.

Block, Greg. 2016. "Creating a Path for Renewable Energy on Public Lands." The Hill, November 17, 2016. https://thehill.com/blogs/congress-blog/energy-environment/306509-creating-a-path-for-renewable-energy-on-public-lands.

Bureau of Land Management. 2005. Final Programmatic Environmental Impact Statement on Wind Energy Development on BLM-Administered Lands in the Western United States. Washington, DC: Bureau of Land Management. http://windeis.anl.gov/eis/index.cfm.

Bureau of Land Management. 2006. *Final Environmental Impact Statement for the Proposed Cotterel Wind Power Project*. Washington, DC: Bureau of Land Management. https://archive.org/details/finalenvironment02twin.

Bureau of Land Management. 2007. "Solar Energy Development Policy." April 4, 2007. https://www.blm.gov/policy/im-2007-097.

Bureau of Land Management. 2011. *Wildlife Report: Newberry Volcano Enhanced Geothermal System (EGS) Demonstration Project*. Washington, DC: Bureau of Land Management. http://www.blm.gov/or/districts/prineville/plans/files/Wildlife_Report.pdf.

Bureau of Land Management. 2012. *Decision Record: Newberry Volcano Enhanced Geothermal System (EGS) Demonstration Project*. Washington, DC: Bureau of Land Management. http://www.blm.gov/or/districts/prineville/plans/newberry/files/Newberry_EGS_Demo_Project_Decision_Record.pdf.

Bureau of Land Management. 2014. "Solar Energy Zones." Last updated January 10, 2014. http://blmsolar.anl.gov/sez/.

Bureau of Land Management. 2016. "Competitive Processes, Terms, and Conditions for Leasing Public Lands for Solar and Wind Energy Development and Technical Changes and Corrections." December 19, 2016. https://www.federalregister.gov/documents/2016/12/19/2016-27551/competitive-processes-terms-and-conditions-for-leasing-public-lands-for-solar-and-wind-energy.

Bureau of Land Management. 2018a. "BLM Fact Sheet. Renewable Energy: Solar." Updated March 2018. https://www.blm.gov/sites/blm.gov/files/Solar%20Fact%20Sheet.pdf.

Bureau of Land Management. 2018b. "BLM Fact Sheet. Renewable Energy: Wind." Updated March 2018. https://www.blm.gov/sites/blm.gov/files/Wind%20Fact%20Sheet.pdf

Bureau of Land Management. 2019a. "New Energy for America." Accessed November 20, 2019. https://www.blm.gov/programs/energy-and-minerals/renewable-energy.

Bureau of Land Management. 2019b. "Laws and Regulations." Accessed November 12, 2019. https://www.blm.gov/programs/energy-and-minerals/renewable-energy/laws.

Bureau of Land Management. 2019c. "Geothermal Energy." Accessed November 12, 2019. https://www.blm.gov/programs/energy-and-minerals/renewable-energy/geothermal-energy.

Bureau of Land Management. 2019d. "Solar Energy." Accessed November 12, 2019. https://www.blm.gov/programs/energy-and-minerals/renewable-energy/solar-energy.

Bureau of Land Management. 2019e. "Wind Energy." Accessed November 12, 2019. https://www.blm.gov/programs/energy-and-minerals/renewable-energy/wind-energy.

Bureau of Land Management and US Department of Energy. 2012. *Final Programmatic Environmental Impact Statement (PEIS) for Solar Energy Development in Six Southwestern States*. Washington, DC: Bureau of Land Management and US Department of Energy. http://solareis.anl.gov/documents/fpeis/Solar_FPEIS_ExecutiveSummary.pdf.

Bureau of Land Management and US Forest Service. 2016. *Memorandum of Understanding: Implementation of Section 225 of the Energy Policy Act of 2005 Regarding Geothermal Leasing and Permitting*. Washington, DC: Bureau of Land Management and US Forest Service. https://openei.org/wiki/Memorandum_of_Understanding_between_DOI_and_DOA_-_Implementation_of_Section_225_of_the_Energy_Policy_Act_of_2005_Regarding_Geothermal_Leasing_and_Permitting.

California Energy Commission. 2020. "California Geothermal Energy Statistics and Data." Accessed February 8, 2020. https://www.energy.ca.gov/almanac/renewables_data/geothermal/.

California Public Utilities Commission. 2020. "Renewables Portfolio Standard (RPS) Program." Accessed February 8, 2020. http://www.cpuc.ca.gov/renewables/.

Database of State Incentives for Renewables and Efficiency. 2018. "Renewable Portfolio Goal." Last updated July 3, 2018. http://programs.dsireusa.org/system/program/detail/2901.

Davenport Power. 2008. "Newberry Geothermal Project Update." https://www.wou.edu/las/physci/taylor/newberry/NEWBERRY_GEOTHERMAL_NEWS_2008.pdf.

Davis, David H. 2001. "Energy on Federal Lands." In *Western Public Lands and Environmental Politics*, edited by C. Davis, 141-168. Boulder, CO: Westview Press.

Devine-Wright, Patrick. 2009. "Rethinking NIMBYism: The Role of Place Attachment and Place Identity in Explaining Place-Protective Action. *Journal of Community and Applied Social Psychology* 19(6): 426-441.

Executive Office of the President. 2013. *The President's Climate Action Plan*. Washington, DC: Executive Office of the President. https://obamawhitehouse.archives.gov/sites/default/files/image/president27sclimateactionplan.pdf.

Fischlein, Miriam, Elizabeth J. Wilson, Tarla R. Peterson, and Jennie C. Stephens. 2013. "States of Transmission: Moving towards Large-Scale Wind Power." *Energy Policy* 56: 101-113.

Geri, Laurance R., and David E. McNabb. 2016. *Energy Policy in the US: Politics, Challenges, and Prospects for Change*. Boca Raton, FL: CRC Press.

Giordono, Leanne S., Hilary S. Boudet, Anna Karmazina, Casey L. Taylor, and Brent S. Steel. 2018. "Opposition 'Overblown'? Community Response to Wind Energy Siting in the Western United States." *Energy Research and Social Science* 43: 119-131.

Grasso, Kyla. 2016. *Newberry Geothermal Energy: A Candidate Site for the DOE FORGE*. Salem: Oregon Department of Energy. https://www.oregon.gov/energy/energy-oregon/Documents/2016%20OGWG%20AltaRock%20Presentation.pdf.

Grossman, Peter Z. 2015. "Energy Shocks, Crises and the Policy Process: A Review of Theory and Application." *Energy Policy* 77: 56-69.

Groth, Theresa M., and Christine Vogt. 2014. "Residents' Perceptions of Wind Turbines: An Analysis of Two Townships in Michigan." *Energy Policy* 65: 251-260.

Intergovernmental Panel on Climate Change. 2014. *Climate Change 2014: Synthesis Report. Contribution of Working Groups I, II and III to the Fifth Assessment Report of the Intergovernmental Panel on Climate Change*, edited by R. K. Pachauri and L. A. Meyer. Geneva: Intergovernmental Panel on Climate Change.

Jones, Christopher R., and J. Richard Eiser. 2010. "Understanding 'Local' Opposition to Wind Development in the UK: How Big Is a Backyard?" *Energy Policy* 38(6): 3106-3117.

Mahoney, James, and Kathleen Thelen. 2010. "A Theory of Gradual Institutional Change." In *Explaining Institutional Change: Ambiguity, Agency, and Power*. Cambridge: Cambridge University Press.

Nicholls, David L., Jeffrey Halbrook, Michelle E. Benedum, Han-Sup Han, Eini C. Lowell, Dennis R. Becker, and R. James Barbour. 2018. "Socioeconomic Constraints to Biomass Removal from Forest Lands for Fire Risk Reduction in the Western US." *Forests* 9(5): 264.

Oregon Department of Energy. 2008. "Minutes: Energy Facility Siting Council Meeting." July 25, 2008. http://www.oregon.gov/energy/Siting/docs/Minutes/EFSC_7-25-08.pdf.

Petty, S. 2010. *Geothermal Energy Protecting the Environment—and Our Future*. Seattle: AltaRock Energy. http://altarockenergy.com/projectupdates/WhitePaper.pdf.

Pierce, John C., and Brent S. Steel. 2017. *Prospects for Alternative Energy Development in the US West: Tilting at Windmills?* Vol. 8. New York: Springer.

Rosa, Eugene A., Gary E. Machlis, and Kenneth M. Keating. 1988. "Energy and Society." *Annual Review of Sociology* 14(1): 149-172.

Shelly, John R. 2011. *Woody Biomass Factsheet—WB1*. Berkeley: University of California. http://www.ucanr.org/sites/WoodyBiomass/newsletters/InfoGuides43284.pdf.

Shively, Bob, and John Ferrare. 2008. *Understanding Today's Electricity Business*. Laporte, CO: Enerdynamics Corp. https://www.enerdynamics.com/ProductDetails.aspx?ProductID=4.

Sundstrom, Shiloh, Max Nielsen-Pincus, Cassandra Moseley, and Sarah McCaffery. 2012. "Woody Biomass Use Trends, Barriers, and Strategies: Perspectives of US Forest Service Managers." *Journal of Forestry* 110(1): 16-24.

US Department of the Interior. 2016. "Powering Up Renewable Energy on Public Lands." September 12, 2016. https://www.doi.gov/blog/powering-renewable-energy-public-lands.

US Energy Information Administration. 2019a. "Biomass Explained: Wood and Wood Waste." Last updated May 13, 2019. https://www.eia.gov/energyexplained/index.php?page=biomass_wood.

US Energy Information Administration. 2019b. "Geothermal Explained: Geothermal Energy and the Environment." Last updated December 5, 12, 2019. https://www.eia.gov/energyexplained/geothermal/geothermal-energy-and-the-environment.php.

West-Wide Wind Mapping Project. 2019. "Maps for Wind Energy Siting on Public Lands." Accessed November 12, 2019. http://wwmp.anl.gov/.

Yonk, Ryan M., Randy T. Simmons, and Brian C. Steed. 2013. *Green vs. Green: The Political, Legal, and Administrative Pitfalls Facing Green Energy Production*. New York: Routledge.

Chapter 12
Regulating Oil and Gas on Federal Lands under Presidents Bush, Obama, and Trump

CHARLES DAVIS

INTRODUCTION

This chapter addresses the changing politics of oil and gas regulation by the US Bureau of Land Management (BLM) across the administrations of Presidents George W. Bush, Barack Obama, and Donald J. Trump. The BLM is in charge of managing the federal government's onshore subsurface mineral estate, amounting to about 700 million acres of subsurface rights held by the BLM and other federal agencies. It does so by balancing land uses such as energy development or mining with wildlife conservation, recreation, and watershed protection under its "multiple-use" management philosophy (Bureau of Land Management 2020c).

Operating under the US Interior Department (DOI), the BLM has a long-standing reputation for an agency bias favoring land-use decisions that prioritize commodity production over the conservation of natural resources. Power (2001) and Wood (2006) found that agency decisions from the 1940s through the 1960s tended to align closely with the interests of industry officials engaged in livestock, mineral, energy, and timber harvesting—activities offering employment opportunities for people in rural western states. Policies were developed within a restricted form of policymaking often referred to as subgovernments* that protected pro-development constituencies (Skillen 2009).

---

*A subgovernment is an institutional arrangement that restricts participation in policy decisions to agency administrators, legislators, and interest group representatives with shared programmatic concerns while maintaining a low degree of visibility within the media and the general public (McCool 1998).

But BLM's land-use decisions have also been shaped by larger sociopolitical forces such as the environmental movement of the 1960s and 1970s. The enactment of the Federal Land Policy and Management Act of 1976 (FLPMA) by Congress conferred statutory legitimacy on the agency and assigned new multiple-use management responsibilities akin to those held by the US Forest Service (Clarke and McCool 1996). FLPMA also required BLM to evaluate public concerns linked to the *impacts* of developmental decisions on environmental quality or natural resource conservation (Klyza and Sousa 2013), decisions that eventually led to pushback from traditional land-use constituencies (Skillen 2009).

Since then, BLM has increasingly devoted attention to the expansion of regulatory programs addressing oil and gas operations on federal lands. What accounts for these changes? Perhaps the main source of policy shifts can be attributed to a growing partisan divide between Democratic and Republican presidential administrations over the appropriate balance between economic development and resource conservation policies on federal lands (Rosenbaum 2017). Since differing land-use policy preferences have made it increasingly difficult to make critical decisions within the hallways of Congress thanks to divided control or the lack of a "filibuster-proof" majority in the Senate, a second factor has also emerged—the tendency for presidents to pursue new policy priorities through the exercise of executive authority rather than legislation (Vig 2019).

How does this occur? According to Shafie (2014), executive authority usually begins when the president selects people with similar policy values to head departments or agencies with prior experience or knowledge of natural resource management issues. Other sources of executive authority include the issuance of executive orders (by the president or a department secretary), a moratorium delaying the effective date of rules from the preceding administration, rulemaking, budgetary authority, and coordination with other departments such as the US Department of Energy (DOE) or the US Environmental Protection Agency (EPA). Any of these approaches can be used to advance policy goals largely by identifying budgetary and enforcement priorities.

The main focus of this chapter, however, deals with how BLM and DOI officials have chosen to develop and implement oil and gas regulatory policies on federal lands from the administration of George W. Bush through the Trump administration. Key concerns include the extent to which environmental land uses are given priority in relation to commodity production and whether climate change impacts are considered in agency planning decisions.

How these decisions are made depends on how BLM administrators juggle a mix of procedural approaches such as rulemaking, resource management planning, environmental impact analyses, and enforcement actions in conjunction with the exercise of discretionary judgment. Thus administrators can choose to reinforce the strength of a dominant subgovernment by accelerating energy production to enhance energy independence, or they can decide to place greater emphasis on more sustainable land-use decisions.

Some of these approaches such as rulemaking and the exercise of discretionary authority offer flexibility to administrators to change course policy-wise without the constraints of maneuvering through a legislative gauntlet and are politically neutral in terms of how they might be applied to attain policy goals. But other approaches are more commonly applied to facilitate industry interests, such as restrictions on public participation or greater use of categorical exclusions (CEs) to expedite the issuance of drilling permits by exempting certain types of projects from environmental impact analyses otherwise required under the National Environmental Policy Act (NEPA). Conversely, those favoring a greater emphasis on resource conservation objectives are more inclined to push for increased enforcement of environmental requirements, to expand the size of agency planning areas, and to provide more opportunities for public input.

REGULATORY CONTEXT

The role of the federal government in the regulation of oil and gas drilling operations writ large can best be described as secondary. States have largely assumed regulatory responsibilities since the 1930s with the support of energy interests thanks to the enactment of the Interstate Oil and Gas Compact (IOGC). While a state's membership in this compact represents a contractual relationship among producer states that can bind it to particular policy decisions, it can also be viewed as an organizational arrangement largely designed to avoid federal involvement.

But the division of authority between federal and state government became increasingly difficult to maintain over time because energy and environmental protection policies have become increasingly intertwined. Oil and gas drilling processes are accompanied by the release of contaminants affecting both air and water quality; hence federal agencies like BLM and EPA have gained jurisdiction over some policies restricting production activities. EPA is responsible for regulating air quality under the Clean Air Act, including emissions from fracking operations. In 2005, Congress and allies within the Bush administration decided to limit EPA's authority to regulate the underground injection of wastewater linked to fracking operations (Warner and Shapiro 2013).

Conversely, BLM's mission encompasses more than just environmental protection. It oversees oil and gas production on all 700 million acres of federal and Native American lands and operates under a "multiple-use" mandate requiring agency officials to balance land uses such as economic (including energy) development with environmental policy concerns like wildlife conservation and watershed protection. One of the agency's more challenging responsibilities is managing "split estate" lands where subsurface resources are controlled by the feds and the surface areas are either administered by other federal agencies or are owned by individuals. The BLM's regulatory authority includes activities ranging from reviewing applications to drill (also known as APDs), conducting environmental analyses, issuing leases, and enforcing environmental requirements on the 264 million acres lands under its control (US General Accountability Office 2012). There are approximately 94,000 wells operating on public lands that account for the production of 9% of natural gas supplies and 7% of the oil supplies within the United States (Bureau of Land Management 2020b).

BLM also confers with the US Forest Service and other federal agencies on regulatory decisions dealing with oil and gas production. Agencies that manage surface lands will decide the conditions under which drilling occurs following the development of a surface operations plan, while BLM is responsible for subsequent regulatory decisions involving the oversight and enforcement of oil and gas drilling actions. The legal sources for BLM's managerial role is found in multiple policies, including the Mineral Leasing Act of 1920, the Federal Land Policy and Management Act of 1976, the Federal Onshore Oil and Gas Leasing Reform Act of 1987, and the Energy Policy Act of 2005, as well as federal and state environmental laws (Bureau of Land Management 2020a).

FINDINGS

A basic understanding of energy policy priorities precedes and informs agency use of managerial approaches. President George W. Bush's desire to achieve greater energy independence for the United States as his top domestic policy goal started on day one of his administration with the issuance of Executive Order 13212, which called for federal agencies to expedite the production and transmission of energy.[1] From 2001 through 2008, he worked toward the accelerated development of oil and gas resources on federal lands. To implement these goals, he appointed Gale Norton as interior secretary and Kathleen Clarke as BLM director.

Departmental approaches used to promote increased oil and gas production included using organizational communications and discretionary authority, altering procedures linked to environmental analyses, and rule-making. The first approach was especially important in setting the tone for establishing more flexible working relationships between BLM administrators and industry officials. These new relationships began with White House staff applying pressure by phone to BLM field administrators to cut the amount of time needed to process drilling permits for oil and gas companies, especially in Rocky Mountain states (Miller et al. 2004). This led to a significant increase in the number of permits issued to energy companies between 1999 and 2004 (from 1,803 to 6,399), along with a corresponding rise in the number of acres leased (US General Accountability Office 2005).

Energy companies and trade groups like the Western Energy Alliance were clearly pleased by the expansion of leasing on federal lands. But those with other interests, including sportsmen and environmentalists, had different reactions, seeing the pace of energy production on federal lands to be incompatible with resource conservation goals. The issuance of permits in places like Wyoming's Red Desert or northern New Mexico increasingly generated political resistance from public officials from both political parties because of the perception that other concerns like scenery, recreation, and the preservation of wildlife habitat were receiving short shrift from BLM (Skillen 2009).

In addition, other stakeholders at the state level received some pushback. The split estate regulatory context put BLM officials in the uncomfortable position of siding with energy companies holding permits or subsurface mineral rights against the interests of ranchers owning surface property since the latter are required to grant access. This meant that intrusive actions like the construction of drilling pads or roads on ranch property would legally trump the concerns of surface property owners (Duffy 2008). When state officials in Wyoming passed a law requiring prior notification to surface owners before onsite drilling could take place, BLM raised objections stating that the policy "would impose additional financial requirements that would burden the federal mineral estate" (Associated Press 2005).

The emphasis placed on oil and gas leasing on federal lands was maintained by Secretary Norton and BLM Director Clarke through President Bush's second term. It was reinforced by the enactment of one of Bush's signature achievements, the Energy Policy Act of 2005. The Energy Policy Act was a wide-ranging policy that offered additional incentives for the development of fossil fuels, leading to the issuance of more permits on an expanded acreage of federal lands (Lubell and Segee 2012).

An especially important provision of this law was Section 390, which allowed greater use of categorical exclusions (CEs). A categorical exclusion is a procedure that fast-tracks drilling permits for oil and gas wells by exempting NEPA requirements for environmental impact studies on land parcels smaller than 150 acres on or near drilling sites that have been in operation for five years or more (Heilprin 2005). Its immediate impact between 2006 and 2008 was to contribute to yet another increase in oil- and gas-related activities (US General Accountability Office 2005). Greater CE use was subsequently incorporated into BLM's resource area management plans, thus reducing industry wait times for getting a permit.

Another key regulatory responsibility associated with drilling operations is environmental enforcement to ensure that air and water quality is not jeopardized by drilling operations. Environmental enforcement requires inspections and, if necessary, the imposition of sanctions. While oil and gas production rose significantly during the Bush administration, less emphasis and fewer resources were devoted to enforcement (US General Accountability Office 2012). In terms of workload assignments, the need to encourage permit processing meant that inspectors were sometimes asked to do both.

Barack Obama took office as president in 2009 giving lip service to an "all of the above" energy portfolio that focused more on environmental protection than energy production. He chose former Senator Ken Salazar from Colorado to head DOI and Robert Abbey, a veteran BLM staffer, to head that agency. Upon taking office, Secretary Salazar moved quickly to slow oil and gas leasing decisions made by his predecessor to evaluate environmental impacts, notably in an area of Utah close to national parks and wilderness study areas (US General Accountability Office 2011). This was the beginning of procedural changes in how oil and gas production decisions were made that gave greater weight to environmental concerns, changes that were vigorously opposed by energy company interests. In addition, Salazar devoted considerably more attention to the siting and development of more environmentally friendly renewable energy resources on federal lands such as wind and solar power.

Not surprisingly, Salazar and Abbey had fewer concerns with an expeditious processing of drilling permit requests, a stance that was understandably less popular with industry officials. One analysis indicated that the number of permits issued declined considerably (45%) along with the amount of acreage leased from the Bush administration to the Obama administration. In like fashion, a corresponding decrease occurred in the number of wells actually drilled (Taylor 2014). An important driver for change was reconsidering how and under what circumstances CEs could be used to expedite oil and gas drilling projects.

BLM officials consulted with staff at the White House Council on Environmental Quality to determine factors that would allow the use of CEs in project decisions without doing environmental impact analyses. A guidance was developed that would allow the use of CEs but only after receiving assurances that additional information would be obtained about potential environmental risks. Agency staff subsequently approved a pilot project to determine whether a more narrowly focused CE was feasible (Hurley 2010).

The impact of the new CE guidance on the declining number of energy projects approved was considerable. A comparison of CE use in the final three years of Bush's second term with the number of CEs used under Obama after 2010 revealed a reluctance among agency staff to sign off on projects after reviewing environmental risk factors. This also helps to account for the decrease in the number of drilling permits issued between 2010 and 2014.

Another clear distinction between the Bush and Obama administrations was the emphasis on environmental inspections to ensure that drilling operations were carried out without undue impacts to air and water quality as well as the preservation of wildlife habitat. The number of environmental inspections carried out by BLM administrators on oil and gas facilities increased dramatically between 2009 and 2012 (US General Accountability Office 2012). This increase in inspections was accompanied by an increase in resources, especially full-time inspectors (Herbert and Kendall 2013).

The differences between administrations on drilling activities can largely be attributed to differing land-use preferences linked to partisan orientation. While industry officials and some Republicans in Congress argue that the decline can be linked to a dismissive attitude toward energy production on public lands

(Pearson 2014), other factors can play a part, such as market prices, geology, competing policy goals, and the location of the resources. Geography can be important because many of the most productive shale plays are located on private lands in states like North Dakota, Pennsylvania, and Texas. Government Accountability Office analysts then suggested that greater interest in the development of oil versus gas could be partly attributable to higher oil prices, since the profit margin for producing oil is greater than for natural gas.

An important factor for the decrease in company interest in drilling on federal lands stems from higher costs. Unlike production activities on private lands, BLM has been directed by Congress to consider environmental impacts as well as the logistical challenges of operating in more remote areas. Statutory requirements from the FLPMA task agency administrators to balance land-use goals under multiple-use criteria (Wilson 2014).

Of managerial concern was how changes in public participation and planning could be deployed to further DOI policy goals. A number of leasing reforms undertaken by Secretary Salazar in 2010 included the development of master leasing plans (MLPs). One rationale was to foster an increase in public participation to give stakeholders more opportunity to express land-use concerns. Doing so would in turn reduce delays attributable to land-use conflicts as well as the number of unanticipated environmental impacts from drilling (US Department of the Interior and US Department of Agriculture 2011). After Salazar resigned in 2012, Secretary Sally Jewell continued the push to develop MLPs with pilot projects in Colorado and Utah (Streater 2014).

A key approach to policy change is rulemaking. BLM's attempts to grapple with the environmental challenges posed by the rise of fracking operations on federal lands was complicated by the fact that existing regulatory procedures were more than thirty years old. Since that time, the percentage of federal oil and gas wells using fracking technology rather than conventional drilling exceeded 90%. The goal of crafting a new rule was to come up with an improved balance between accessibility for energy companies and environmental values, especially regarding the need to preserve wildlife habitat. A draft rule was released in May 2012 that focused on a requirement for industry disclosure of fracking fluids used in drilling operations as well as standards for the management of flowback waters and for wellbore integrity (Bureau of Land Management 2012).

Public participation was considerable, with extensive commentary from both supporters and opponents of the proposed rule (Bureau of Land

Management 2013b). Industry trade groups complained that compliance costs were excessive and regulatory requirements were overly duplicative (Streater 2013). Many Republican governors and members of Congress also contended that state regulators should play a larger role since they had the experience and local knowledge to more easily address environmental problems. Supporters like The Wilderness Society supported the rule but wanted stronger water-quality protections, while other groups advocated for including monitoring requirements before and after drilling takes place.

The increased level of controversy led to a revision of the rule to better accommodate industry concerns. The new rule advanced by Secretary Jewell was released in May 2013 after a thirty-day comment period. Because of concerns raised by environmentalists and industry interests, another delay took place (Streater 2013). The final version of the fracking rule was published in March 2015 after four years of deliberations and agency review of more than a million comments. Despite an effort to bridge differences between contending stakeholder groups, the new rule was immediately challenged in the federal courts. A ruling on June 15, 2015, postponed the effective date of the rule's implementation (Gilmer 2015).

The election of President Donald J. Trump in 2016 resulted in another dramatic shift in federal energy policymaking that more closely resembles the policy priorities of President Bush than President Obama. Early on, Trump called for policies designed to promote "energy dominance" and to cut regulations from the Obama administration viewed as "overreach" by incoming public officials (Bomberg 2017; Vig 2019). Consequently, dozens of energy and environmental rules have been overturned or substantially revised to lower industry compliance costs and to provide greater flexibility for regulated parties (Popovich et al. 2018).

Unlike his predecessors, Trump had no prior experience in government and has largely relied upon selected congressional leaders or acquaintances within corporate America for guidance in staffing and policy decisions (Vig 2019). To head DOI, he chose Ryan Zinke, a former member of the US House of Representatives from Montana. Secretary Zinke followed a pro-development path as DOI secretary, pushing for cuts in the acreage of Bears Ears and Grand Staircase–Escalante National Monuments in Utah and for increasing the pace of issuing oil and gas leases on federal lands. Following his resignation in December 2018, Zinke was succeeded by DOI staffer David Bernhardt as acting (now permanent) secretary, pushing an identical set of policy goals.

Turning to oil and gas development, DOI officials have focused on reducing the backlog of applications to drill permits from energy companies. A push for bids to increase oil and gas leasing across larger swaths of federal land has been made, often in areas previously set aside as valuable wildlife habitat under the Obama administration. Bernhardt issued a directive requiring that environmental impact statements (EISs) be limited to no more than 150 pages, or 300 pages for especially complex energy projects, along with a one-year time limit for the completion of the EIS (Dougherty 2018). Trump has facilitated this process with the aid of Congress under the authority of the Congressional Review Act to essentially eliminate energy and environmental regulations enacted by the Obama administration in late 2016 (Konisky and Woods 2018). Two rules aimed at adding greater environmental protection to oil and gas drilling processes on federal lands were successfully eliminated—a rule to encourage more public participation in resource management plans and the fracking rule.

No data are yet available for cross-administration comparisons, but through words and actions it seems plausible to expect a pattern of land-use decisions that closely resemble the policies of DOI and BLM under Secretary Norton and Director Clarke. Zinke has suggested that enforcement decisions may be more appropriate for state officials and that it may also be more useful to emphasize ways to encourage compliance rather than the imposition of punitive measures. A return to a more industry-friendly interpretation of CEs allowing exemption from environmental impact analyses for proposed drilling projects is likely.

How have presidents dealt with climate-related impacts associated with oil and gas production on federal lands? President George W. Bush showed little interest in policies aimed at reducing greenhouse gas emissions during his tenure in office. A high-profile example was the decision to avoid a major US role internationally in the adoption of the Kyoto Protocol, thus ceding to other policy actors the task of pursuing climate change policy goals.

Within the context of domestic policy concerns, Bush placed greater emphasis on the attainment of energy independence through the removal of regulatory barriers to energy production than on environmental protection or on mitigating adverse climate impacts. Bush issued an executive order early on that allowed federal agencies pursuing energy development to take precedence whenever a land-use decision pitted energy against other policy goals such as wildlife conservation or transportation.[2] He pushed for increased power from fossil fuels by working with congressional leaders to enact the

Energy Policy Act of 2005. This law helped to expedite the issuance of drilling permits for energy companies by relaxing procedural requirements for environmental analysis associated with project approval decisions. It also reduced the regulatory role of EPA under the Safe Drinking Water Act to oversee fracking operations, a shift that effectively gave more decision-making authority to state water-quality officials.

The subsequent policy vacuum for addressing adverse climate impacts was filled by federal courts and public officials representing state and local governments between 2001 and 2008. Especially important was a US Supreme Court decision, *Massachusetts v. Environmental Protection Agency* (2007), that paved the way for the EPA to regulate carbon dioxide as a greenhouse gas under the authority of the Clean Air Act. In addition, a number of states passed climate change policies, others joined multistate compacts such as the Regional Greenhouse Gas Initiative in the Northeast, and the US Conference of Mayors adopted greenhouse gas emission reduction goals that were approved by elected officials in more than nine hundred US cities (Betsill and Rabe 2009). The importance of these policy developments lay in establishing a regulatory context for climate policy change that could evolve despite opposition from the Bush administration.

The election of President Barack Obama in 2008 ushered in a new era of support for environmental policymaking, including a major emphasis on climate change. Obama supported a bill in Congress calling for federal restrictions on greenhouse gas emissions that narrowly passed the House of Representatives in 2009. The proposal was subsequently rejected by the US Senate, however, partly because of the emergence of the Tea Party movement in 2010. This new, more conservative Republican majority was skeptical about new regulatory initiatives, including climate change policies. Lacking a base of support in Congress for his environmental policy agenda, Obama turned to exercising executive authority to achieve his policy goals.

Much of Obama's focus on climate was directed toward procedures that affected a wide range of federal policies and projects. For example, the use of NEPA by federal agencies to evaluate environmental impacts of proposed projects added climate as a factor to consider (Council on Environmental Quality 2016). Relatedly, the development of rules by federal departments or agencies incorporated a criterion referred to as the "social cost of carbon" to quantify the economic impact of a proposed rule for projects under consideration (Hulac 2015). Perhaps the most visible and controversial action taken by the Obama administration was EPA's development of the Clean Power Plan, a nationwide rule designed to establish reduction targets for carbon dioxide emissions at power plants (mostly coal) in each state. The Clean Power Plan generated considerable resistance from many state officials, leading to litigation and eventually to efforts by Republicans in Congress to eliminate or replace it (Besco 2018).

A major climate change initiative linked to oil and gas production on federal lands was the Methane and Waste Prevention Rule, advanced by Interior Secretary Sally Jewell in November 2016. This regulation was designed to slow or eliminate the release of methane emissions from "flaring," or leaks associated with oil and gas drilling operations on BLM and tribal lands. Agency officials, state officials (in California and New Mexico), and environmental groups directed attention to environmental benefits, such as limiting the adverse impacts of methane, a greenhouse gas that is considerably more potent than carbon dioxide (Duffy and Cook 2018; Wilderness Society and Taxpayers for Common Sense 2018). Advocates also argued that the rule would reduce waste and preserve revenue for US taxpayers based on royalties earned from drilling operations on federal lands under the Mineral Leasing Act of 1920, including fugitive methane emissions arising from venting, flaring, or leaks originating from gas wells or compressors (Lattanzio 2018).

While this rule enjoyed considerable support from individuals or companies possessing subsurface mineral rights and environmental groups, industry officials considered it to be overly burdensome because BLM drilling sites are often located in remote areas where the costs of capturing methane and delivering the gas for energy users are high. The rule required oil and gas companies to not only restrict and capture methane emissions but to also to upgrade their equipment and to develop plans for minimizing waste when drilling on public lands (Gilmer 2018). The new rule was immediately challenged in the federal courts by energy industry groups.

President Trump took office with little knowledge and experience pertaining to energy policy and climate change. During his presidential campaign, he famously referred to climate change as an "expensive hoax" (Davenport 2016). While key initiatives to resist or overturn Obama's policies, such as decisions committing the United States to withdraw from the Paris Agreement and to redo the Clean Power Plan, were undertaken by EPA, other departments like DOI took action to erase Obama policies aimed at mitigating adverse climate impacts (Davenport 2016).

President Trump quickly discovered that the quickest way to influence policy direction was to make use of executive authority; notably, executive orders and political appointments to head environmental or energy department heads. On March 28, 2017, Trump issued Executive Order 13783, Promoting Energy Independence and Economic Growth.[3] This order called for the BLM to reexamine its 2016 Methane Capture Rule with an eye toward its compatibility with energy independence and to take corrective measures if necessary. He also appointed departmental leaders with some governmental experience, such as former Texas Governor Rick Perry at EPA, former Oklahoma Attorney General Scott Pruitt at EPA, former Montana Congressman Ryan Zinke at DOI, and former Georgia Governor Sonny Perdue at the US Department of Agriculture. All shared Trump's policy priorities, as did appointees with industry ties and former lobbyists, like Andrew Wheeler (Pruitt's successor at EPA), that supported his emphasis on deregulation of environmental and energy programs, including climate change.

Another early indication of a different policy direction was the decision to eliminate agency links to data or information mentioning climate change. Shortly after Trump became president, the official White House website deleted references to the topic. Other federal agencies including DOI did the same, removing links to studies and data pertaining to climate change or global warming (Davenport and Lipton 2017). This resulted in pushback from supporters of climate change research and policy. A number of scientists at US universities subsequently took steps to save and store information to ensure that accessibility to government records could be maintained. Another broad action directly affecting federal natural resource agencies was the withdrawal of the Obama administration guidance requiring the inclusion of greenhouse gas emissions whenever environmental analysis studies were carried out (Popovich et al. 2018). Legal challenges have followed, most recently a decision by a US District Court judge in Washington, DC, on March 20, 2019, that blocked oil and gas drilling in Wyoming after BLM officials failed to consider climate impacts under NEPA (Eilperin 2019).

Perhaps the most direct effort to delete climate impacts from oil and gas production on federal lands occurred when DOI proposed doing away with BLM's 2016 methane rule. It was one among many other energy and environmental regulations adopted by the Obama administration to be targeted for elimination by congressional Republicans under the Congressional Review Act; however, after a vote to disapprove the measure passed in the

House of Representatives, it was narrowly defeated in the Senate (Harvard Environmental Law Program 2018). DOI officials then filed suit to suspend the rule and to rewrite parts of the regulation.

A final BLM rule, Waste Prevention, Production Subject to Royalties, and Resource Conservation; Rescission or Revision of Certain Requirements, was published on September 28, 2018. It eliminated several provisions of the previous regulation, including waste-minimization plans, well drilling and completion actions, and leak detection and repair requirements. In addition, the rule implemented changes in how the measurement and reporting of the volume of gas that is vented or flared are calculated (Bureau of Land Management 2018).

CONCLUSIONS

The regulation of oil and gas production on federal lands has varied dramatically over the past couple of decades. While Congress occasionally offers policy guidance through the enactment of laws like FLPMA of 1976 or the Energy Policy Act of 2005, there is relatively little oversight over what DOI or BLM does to implement them. Unlike detailed legislation such as the Clean Air Act of 1990 that prescribes courses of action for EPA administrators to be taken in response to particular situations, federal land laws are ambiguous, Nie (2008) suggests, which offers more decisional leeway for differing interpretation of statutory meaning. Consequently, policy change often occurs in smaller increments through rulemaking, a useful policy path but one that is less permanent than the enactment of legislation.

In examining changes in the management of oil and gas management practices across the past three presidential administrations, partisan orientation clearly stands out. BLM's policy decisions vary most in terms of following the lead of Republican leaders with a staunchly pro-development goal versus Democratic leaders who prefer greater sensitivity to resource conservation goals. Approaches used most commonly to achieve these goals include organizational communications, the exercise of discretionary authority, and procedural changes in public participation and planning.

The approaches under DOI and BLM leaders vary. In support of Bush's goal to accelerate oil and gas production, Secretary Norton pressured field administrators to more quickly process industry applications for drilling permits, and after the adoption of the Energy Act of 2005, she utilized CEs to exempt environmental impact reviews for proposed drilling projects. These objectives were also advanced by placing less emphasis on inspecting oil and gas drilling operations to safeguard against air- and water-quality violations.

Conversely, DOI Secretaries Salazar and Jewell promoted Obama's pro-environmental agenda by focusing more on the inclusion of environmental policy criteria in public land-use decisions linked to oil and gas production. They achieved this agenda through enacting restrictions on the approval of CEs, adopting a new rule aimed at strengthening environmental quality standards for fracking operations on BLM lands, enlarging the size of resource area planning areas, and increasing the number of environmental inspections on drilling sites.

Although DOI Secretary Zinke and his successor, David Bernhardt, have been on the job for a relatively short period of time, their decisions so far appear to be in sync with Trump's desire to achieve "energy dominance." BLM has set a rapid pace thus far to lease oil and gas federal permits on federal lands with moves to restore access to the use of CEs to expedite the waiver of environmental impact analyses. These efforts have been bolstered by Trump's success in getting Congress to use the Congressional Review Act (CRA) to revoke the Obama rule aimed at expanding BLM resource management planning areas and opportunities for public participation. Greater emphasis has also been placed on incentivizing compliance with environmental laws in drilling operations than with punitive measures to deter future violations.

In terms of addressing the impacts of climate change on federal land management decisions, the decisions made by Secretaries Norton, Salazar/Jewell, and Zinke/Bernhardt have essentially mirrored those made to address energy policy. Climate policies were largely ignored under Secretary Norton in order to accelerate oil and gas production goals. Secretaries Salazar and Jewell actively pursued policies to mitigate adverse climate impacts; notably, the rule designed to prevent flaring and the release of methane in drilling operations. Under the Trump administration, DOI and Secretary Zinke were unable to eliminate the rule via the CRA but succeeded in developing a substantially weaker replacement regulation in September 2018 that offered more flexibility for regulated industries along with reduced compliance costs.

In examining the near-term prospects for achieving a balance between energy production goals, environmental conservation, and the mitigation of climate impacts, the outlook is not bright. Democrats and environmental advocates will continue to utilize litigation strategies to maintain existing regulatory protections. In some cases, policymakers in states like California and Colorado have responded to federal initiatives with policies requiring oil and gas companies to capture and use methane released during fracking operations. Similar efforts may well gain steam because of political momentum from the 2018 midterm elections, which resulted in Democrats regaining control of the US House of Representatives. It is unclear whether ongoing litigation challenging Trump administration policies will succeed. Time will tell.

Legal Citations

1 Exec. Order No. 13,212, 66 Fed. Reg. 28357 (May 18, 2001).
2 Exec. Order No. 13,212, 66 Fed. Reg. 28357 (May 18, 2001).
3 Exec. Order No. 13,783, 82 Fed. Reg. 16093 (Mar. 28, 2017).

References

Associated Press. 2005. "BLM Disputes Wyoming Split Estate Law." *Billings Gazette*, June 21, 2005.

Besco, Laurel. 2018. "Responses to the Clean Power Plan: Factors Influencing State Decision-Making." *Review of Policy Research* 35(5): 670-690.

Betsill, Michele, and Barry G. Rabe. 2009. "Climate Change and Multilevel Governance: The Evolving State and Local Roles." In *Toward Sustainable Communities: Transition and Transformation in Environmental Policy*. 2nd ed., edited by D. Mazmanian and M. Kraft, 201-225. Cambridge: Massachusetts Institute of Technology Press.

Bomberg, Elizabeth. 2017. "Environmental Politics in the Trump Era: An Early Assessment." *Environmental Politics* 26(5): 956-963.

Bureau of Land Management. 2013a. *Budget Justifications and Performance Information, Fiscal Year 2015, 2013*. Washington, DC: Bureau of Land Management. http://www.blm.gov/pgdata/etc/medialib/blm/wo/Communications_Directorate/public_affairs/news_release_attachments.Par.60974.File.dat/FY2015_BLM_Greenbook.pdf.

Bureau of Land Management. 2013b. "Interior Releases Updated Draft Rule for Hydraulic Fracturing on Public and Indian Lands for Public Comment." News release, May 16, 2013.

Bureau of Land Management. 2012. "Interior Releases Draft Rule Requiring Public Disclosure of Chemicals Used in Hydraulic Fracturing on Public and Indian Lands." News release, May 4, 2012.

Bureau of Land Management. 2018. "Waste Prevention, Production Subject to Royalties, and Resource Conservation: Rescission or Revision of Certain Requirements." *Federal Register* 83(189): 49,184-49,214.

Bureau of Land Management. 2020a. "Oil and Gas." Accessed February 9, 2020. https://www.blm.gov/programs/energy-and-minerals/oil-and-gas/about.

Bureau of Land Management. 2020b. "Summary of Onshore Oil and Gas Statistics." Accessed February 9, 2020. https://www.blm.gov/programs/energy-and-minerals/oil-and-gas/oil-and-gas-statistics.

Bureau of Land Management. 2020c. "What We Manage." Accessed February 9, 2020. https://www.blm.gov/about/what-we-manage/national.Clarke, Jeanne N., and Daniel McCool. 1996. *Staking Out the Terrain*. 2nd ed. Albany: State University of New York Press.

Council on Environmental Quality. 2016. "Fact Sheet: White House Council on Environmental Quality Releases Final Guidance on Considering Climate Change in

Environmental Reviews." Press release, August 2, 2016. https://obamawhitehouse.
archives.gov/the-press-office/2016/08/02/fact-sheet-white-house-council-
environmental-quality-releases-final.

Davenport, Coral. 2016. "Climate Policy Faces Reversal by New Leader." *New York Times*,
November 11, 2016.

Davenport, Coral, and Eric Lipton. 2017. "Scott Pruitt Is Carrying Out His E.P.A. Agenda in
Secret, Critics Say." *New York Times*, August 11, 2017.

Dougherty, John. 2018. "Operating under the Radar: Top Zinke Aides Undermine
Protections for Public Lands and Endangered Species." *The Revelator*, April 18, 2018.

Duffy, Robert. 2008. "Conflict Expansion or Conflict Management? Energy Development in
Colorado." Presented at the Western Political Science Association Conference, San Diego,
CA, April 9–11.

Duffy, Robert J., and Jeffrey J. Cook. 2018. "Overcoming Bureaucratic Silos? Environmental
Policy Integration in the Obama Administration." *Environmental Politics* 28(7): 1192-
1213. doi:10.1080/09644016.2018.1511074. http://www.hcn.org/articles/the-
contradictions-at-the-heart-of-the-fight-over-methane-rules.

Eilperin, Juliet. 2019. "Federal Judge Halts Drilling in Wyoming over Climate Concerns."
Washington Post, March 20, 2019. Gilmer, Ellen. 2015. "Federal Judge Postpones BLM
Fracking Rule." *Greenwire*, June 24, 2015.

Gilmer, Ellen. 2018. "Public Lands: The Many Lives of BLM Methane Litigation." *EnergyWire*,
May 3, 2018.

Harvard Environmental Law Program. 2018. "Methane Waste Prevention Rule." Accessed
August 24, 2018. http://environmental.law.harvard.edu/2018/07/methane-waste-
prevention-rule-information/.

Heilprin, John. 2005. "Environmental Studies Waived in Push for Oil, Gas Drilling."
Associated Press. October 19, 2005. https://products.kitsapsun.com/
archive/2005/10-19/73801_environmental_studies_waived_in_.html.

Herbert, Christine, and Sarah Kendall. 2013. *Law and Order in the Oil and Gas Fields: A
Review of the Inspection and Enforcement Programs in Five Western States*. Billings, MT:
Western Organization of Resource Councils.

Hulac, Benjamin. 2015. "The Social Cost of Man's Carbon Dioxide—Measuring the
Unmeasurable?" *EnergyWire*, April 1, 2015.

Hurley, L. 2010. "NEPA: White House Announces Final Guidance on Categorical Exclusions.
Greenwire, November 23, 2010.

Klyza, Christopher, and David Sousa. 2013. *American Environmental Policy: Beyond Gridlock*.
Cambridge: Massachusetts Institute of Technology Press.

Konisky, David M., and Neal D. Woods. 2018. "Environmental Federalism and the Trump
Presidency: A Preliminary Assessment." *Publius: The Journal of Federalism* 48(3): 345-371.

Lattanzio, Richard K. 2018. *Methane and Other Air Pollution Issues in Natural Gas Systems*.
CRS Report R42986. Washington, DC: Congressional Research Service. https://
crsreports.congress.gov/R42986.

Lubell, Mark, and Brian Segee. 2012. "Conflict and Cooperation in Natural Resource
Management." In *Environmental Policy*. 8th ed., edited by Norman Vig and Michael Kraft,
185-205. Washington, DC: CQ Press.

McCool, Daniel. 1998. "The Subsystem Family of Concepts: A Critique and a Proposal."
Political Science Quarterly 51(2): 551-570.

Miller, Alan, Tom Hamburger, and Julie Cart. 2004. "White House Puts the West on Fast
Track for Oil, Gas Drilling." *Los Angeles Times*, August 25, 2004.

Nie, Martin. 2008. *The Governance of Western Public Lands*. Lawrence: University Press of
Kansas.

Pearson, Sam. 2014. "Industry Slams BLM for Barriers to Oil Drilling." *E&E Daily*, February 6, 2014.

Popovich, Nadja, Livia Albeck-Ripka, and Kendra Pierre-Louis. 2018. "67 Rules on the Way Out under Trump." *New York Times*, January 31, 2018.

Power, Thomas. 2001. *Post-Cowboy Economics*. Washington, DC: Island Press.

Rosenbaum, Walter A. 2017. *Environmental Politics and Policy*. 10th ed. Thousand Oaks, CA: CQ Press.

Shafie, David. 2014. *Presidential Administration and the Environment*. New York: Routledge.

Skillen, James. 2009. *The Nation's Largest Landlord: The Bureau of Land Management in the American West*. Lawrence: University Press of Kansas.

Streater, Scott. 2013. "Industry, Conservationists Split on BLM Rule Proposal at Comment Deadline." *E&E News PM*, August 22, 2013.

Streater, Scott. 2014. "New BLM Policy Defers Leasing on Millions of Acres in Colorado, Worrying Industry." *E&E News PM*, April 14, 2014.

Taylor, Phil. 2014. "Oil Production on Public Lands Grows as Gas Continues Slide." *Greenwire*, March 14, 2014. US Department of Agriculture. 2016. *Trends in U.S. Agriculture's Consumption and Production of Energy: Renewable Power, Shale Energy, and Cellulosic Biomass*. Washington, DC: US Department of Agriculture.

US Department of the Interior and US Department of Agriculture 2011. *New Energy Frontier Balancing Energy Development on Federal Lands: A Joint Report to Congress on Siting Energy Development Projects on Federal Lands*, 84-85. Washington, DC: US Department of the Interior and US Department of Agriculture. https://www.doi.gov/sites/doi.gov/files/migrated/whatwedo/energy/upload/NewEnergyFrontier050511.pdf.

US Government Accountability Office. 2005. *Oil and Gas Development: Increased Permitting Activity Has Lessened BLM's Ability to Meet Its Environmental Protection Responsibilities*. Report No. 05-418. Washington, DC: US Government Accountability Office.

US Government Accountability Office. 2011. *Energy Policy Act of 2005: BLM's Use of Section 390 Categorical Exclusions for Oil and Gas Development*. Report No. 11-941T. Washington, DC: US Government Accountability Office.

US Government Accountability Office. 2012. *Unconventional Oil and Gas Development: Key Environmental and Public Health Requirements*. Report No. 12-874. Washington, DC: US Government Accountability Office.

Vig, Norman. 2019. "Presidential Powers and Environmental Policy." In *Environmental Policy*. 10th ed., edited by Norman Vig and Michael Kraft, 88-116. Washington, DC: CQ Press.

Warner, Barbara, and Jennifer Shapiro. 2013. "Fractured, Fragmented Federalism: A Study in Fracking Regulatory Policy." *Publius* 43(3): 474–496.

Wilderness Society and Taxpayers for Common Sense. 2018. *The State of Methane*. Washington, DC: Wilderness Society and the Taxpayers for Common Sense. https://www.wilderness.org/sites/default/files/media/file/methane_report_web_0.pdf.

Wilson, Randall. 2014. *America's Public Lands*. Lanham, MD: Rowman & Littlefield.

Wood, Robert. 2006. "The Dynamics of Incrementalism: Subsystems, Politics, and Public Lands." *Policy Studies Journal* 34(1): 1-16.

Chapter 13
Mining on Federal Land
Policy and Costs of Doing Business

P. CASEY GIORDANO

As the summer of 2018 began, several media outlets reported that Canadian mining company Glacier Lake Resources, Inc., was set to conduct exploratory mining in Utah for several different metals on Colt Mesa, land that was once part of Grand Staircase–Escalante National Monument. This developing story suggests that in the early years of the Donald Trump presidency, the priority pendulum of the federal government concerning public lands is seemingly swinging away from preservation and conservation toward land use, specifically extraction of natural resources. Unsurprisingly, several organizations have spoken out publicly about the plan to mine (Cramer 2018; Greenberg 2018; Sybert et al. 2018) in what was until recently officially considered by the federal government to have significant ecologic, geologic, paleontologic, archaeologic, and cultural value.[1] The debate regarding federal land-use policy is a spirited one. Stakeholders on all sides of the mining debate (the federal government and the mining industry and miners on one side and "environmentalists" of every stripe on the other) believe that precedent and law support their cases. These opening salvos regarding land use in what was formally federally protected land is only the latest in the long and complicated history that the government of the United States has had with mining, especially in the West. Historically, policy and political issues regarding mining can be grouped into two broad categories: (1) under what terms public land be used for mining and (2) identification of threats to the environment caused by mining and subsequent development of legislation that mitigates those threats. In addition to these two historic issues, global climate change presents some unique challenges to the mining industry. In order to better understand what the future holds for mining on Colt Mesa and other sites, it is important to review these three factors.

WHOSE LAND IS IT ANYWAY?

Industrial mining has been part of land use in the West for as long as there have been Europeans and Americans on the continent. Starting in the late 1500s, the Spanish were extracting metals from mines in Mexico (Studnicki-Gizbert 2017). Americans were not far behind, as thousands made their way west in the name of manifest destiny, chasing rumors of gold and silver strikes in the mountains and deserts. As the number of mining claims being staked in the West increased, the federal government felt it necessary to codify the claims process on federally owned land. This effort culminated in the Mining Law of 1872, signed into law by President Ulysses Grant. While there are other federal, state, and local laws and statutes that apply to mining claims, the Mining Law of 1872 is arguably the most contentious because, with the exception of a minor revision in 1993, its terms have remained virtually unchanged since 1872.[2]

While the full text of the Mining Law of 1872 can be easily accessed, it is still worthwhile to review the important points therein. With that in mind, a bit of historical perspective is useful when reviewing the terms of the law. Postbellum America was an industrial powerhouse on the verge of entering the Gilded Age. The first transcontinental railroad had been completed in 1869, and because of that and other technological innovations, Americans were able to head west (and were encouraged to do so with the Homestead Acts and other enticements) with relative ease. Corporate interests were also heading west in search of raw materials for industry. Many of the federal agencies in charge of managing public lands (such as the US Geological Survey, National Park Service, and National Forest Service) were born out of this era. While the West might have still been metaphorically "wild," the literal wildness of the West was becoming tamer by the year. Wallace Stegner (1992, p. 117) describes the situation nicely in *Beyond the Hundredth Meridian*:

> Postwar Washington permitted and encouraged the development of professionals and put them in charge of operations of incalculable potential. Less than twenty years after the war, Washington was one of the great scientific centers of the world. It was so for a multitude of causes, but partly because America had the virgin West for Science to open, and Washington forged keys to open it with.

In short, federal government was becoming serious about cataloging and organizing the west, and the Mining Law of 1872 was one of the blunt instruments used to accomplish the task of regulating land use.

As currently constructed, the Mining Law of 1872 applies only to the mining of hard-rock minerals (the original law specifies quartz, gold, silver, cinnabar, lead, tin, copper, or "other valuable deposits"[3]); however, it originally also covered coal claims. Coal, oil, natural gas, and "common variety minerals" like sand and gravel were removed from the Mining Law after the implementation of the Mineral Leasing Act of 1920 and the Materials Act of 1947, respectively (Morriss et al. 2004). Although there are coal mines in the western states (US Energy Information Administration 2019), most mining activity involves hard-rock mining (National Mining Association 2018), the relationship between hard-rock mining and the Mining Law of 1872 is the focus of this chapter.

The leading section of the law gives a sense of its broad scope:

> All valuable mineral deposits in lands belonging to the United States, both surveyed and not surveyed, are hereby declared to be free and open to exploration and purchase, and the lands in which they are found to occupation and purchase, by citizens of the United States and those who have declared their intention to become such, under regulations prescribed by law, and according to the local customs or rules of miners in the several mining-districts, so far as the same are applicable and not inconsistent with the laws of the United States.[4]

While there may be several points of contention in that initial section of the law (such as the definition of "valuable"), things become much more interesting when the economics of the law are considered. Filing the paperwork to work a claim may cost nothing but time, but obtaining title to the claim incurs a fee to be paid to the federal government. As the law was originally written, "not less than one hundred dollars' worth of labor shall be performed or improvements made during each year" on any claim that has been staked on federally owned land since May 10, 1872. The labor requirement was then changed to an annual holding fee of $100 in 1993. Additionally, obtaining title (or what is more technically referred to as "patent") will cost the applicant $2.50 per acre for placer claims and $5.00 per acre for lode claims.[5] (Placer deposits are those deposits that have been transported downstream from the main deposit and must be separated from the typically lighter material, like sand, that it is deposited in by processes such as panning. Lode deposits are typically found emplaced in weak points in host rock and are sometimes known as vein deposits. Lode deposits are extracted in situ; see Bureau of Land Management 2019.) While the law includes restrictions on total acreage of claims, the claims are subject to 1872 prices, which is at first glance a clear example of fleecing the federal government. Or is it?

STILL THE LAW OF THE LAND

While the provisions of the Mining Law of 1872 invite plenty of criticism, it is important to consider the scope of the land to which the law applies. In eleven western states, five federal agencies (Bureau of Land Management, Department of Defense, US Forest Service, Fish and Wildlife Service, and National Park Service) administer approximately 350 million acres of public land (Vincent et al. 2017). Even if one were to subtract the lands that are protected from development (Department of Defense, Fish and Wildlife Service, and National Park Service), there are still approximately 314 million acres of public land up for grabs, so to speak (Vincent et al. 2017) (see table 13.1). Not all of this land is governed by the Mining Law of 1872, however. The law only applies to land that has always been federally owned. There are other

Table 13.1. Public Lands Available for Mining in the Western States

State	Total Acres of Bureau of Land Management and US Forest Service Land in the State	Active Mining Claims on Public Land in the State
Arizona	23,408,358	49,022
California	36,126,989	23,378
Colorado	22,796,560	10,408
Idaho	32,058,928	22,048
Montana	25,171,172	14,504
Nevada	52,737,568	203,231
New Mexico	23,319,130	10,285
Oregon	32,244,257	6,893
Utah	33,267,621	25,596
Washington	9,757,667	2,272
Wyoming	27,765,470	30,291

Source: Vincent et al. (2017).

laws that apply to acquired federal land (by gift, purchase, or condemnation), Native American lands, and most state-owned lands (Gerard 1997). With that said, on the eligible federal lands, there are approximately 400,000 active mining claims (The Diggings 2019).

Critics of the Mining Law of 1872 argue that reform is needed in the form of more federal control. Proponents argue that the law is having (and has had) its desired effect and that no reform is needed. The National Mining Association (2016) lists ten federal laws and a dozen categories of state laws that currently apply to minerals mining. David Gerard of Lawrence University discusses three central issues regarding the reform debate. First is that the private sector can make land-use decisions relatively unsupervised, and therefore there should be more "administrative control by government agencies" (Gerard 1997). Second is that there are no provisions within the Mining Law of 1872 that address environmental protection. Finally, there is the economic concern. Not only is the cost for staking and maintaining claims low (as discussed above), but also critics are quick to point out that the Mining Law of 1872 has no royalty provisions, and the federal government is losing out on potentially billions of dollars in revenue (Gerard 1997).

The Mining Law of 1872 has been referred to as "one of the most reviled federal land laws" (Morriss et al. 2004, p. 765), "one of the last remaining American dinosaurs of the old public resources giveaways" (Earthworks n.d.), and "the undisputed surviving king of nineteenth century congressional underpinnings of the westward expansion" (Leshy 1988) Yet is it still the law of the land. Why? A Cato policy analysis offered two practical reasons in 1998 that arguably still hold true today: "First, the media and many mineral analysts poorly understand the distribution of wealth under the current system. Second in their moral quest to prevent giveaways and generate revenue for the federal government, reformers have proposed policies that will make the extraction of minerals less efficient and may even increase the burdens on taxpayers" (Gordon and VanDoren 1998). A similar perspective is offered by Morriss et al. (2004, p. 763): "[first] the Mining Law is the relic of a bygone era, persisting through a combination of inertia and special interest lobbying. In the second, the Mining Law is an institutional response to the incentive problems of public ownership of resources and an effective, evolved mechanism for solving the problem of determining how to use those resources."

Failure to change oversight of mining via the Mining Law of 1872 could be attributed to political and economic geography. Since most federal land lies in western states, "states without mining interests form a majority coalition in favor of converting those resources into a form which potentially benefits their citizens at the expense of mining state citizens" (Morriss et al. 2004, p. 753). Expressed more simply, easterners want revenue and westerners want free access to land (Morriss et al. 2004). The bicameral structure of the federal legislature has to this point prevented eastern interests from prevailing in spite of their superior representative numbers in the House. Proponents of the law argue to keep it in place but to add more federal oversight. Earthworks (2019), a nonprofit organization that supports sustainable solutions in the mining industry, has argued for federal authority to deny mining permits and greater citizen involvement in all levels of mining regulation (Earthworks n.d.). Permit/lease systems have also been advocated because they are more in line with other federal land management practices (Gerard 1997). The problem with greater federal oversight may be obvious: more bureaucracy means more red tape, which means more time and money for miners to expend. The problem of an expanded bureaucratic role is argued well by Gerard (1997): "Mineral development would be in the hands of an agency that has little interest in whether the land is developed. They [miners] argue that it would lead to *de facto* administrative withdrawals of the land, as well as delays in issuing and renewing permits."

The perceived problem of the Mining Law of 1872 that garners the most research (and is potentially one of the most contentious issues), however, is the question of fair return. It is fairly easy to understand why. A miner or a mining company can stake a claim for $2.50 to $5.00 per acre; pay their $100 annual fee, and owe no other money to the federal treasury regardless of the actual value of the minerals extracted at the claim. Critics argue that the federal government is giving away billions of dollars of taxpayer money in what amounts to a massive subsidy for mining. But closer examination of the law and the mining industry may prove otherwise. While it is difficult to assess empirically the efficacy of more or less regulation on mining claims, analyzing the economic implications of the law is easier. Three primary criticisms of the law regard the lack of royalties, the low price of federal land, and "returns from speculation" (Gerard 1997; Leshy 1988; Morriss et al. 2004).

In the years since 1872, it has been suggested that a royalty be placed on production revenue from mining to compensate for the low cost of taking title for a claim. For example, in 1993, President Bill Clinton suggested a "12.5% royalty on the gross value of the hardrock minerals extracted from mining claims on public lands" (Clinton 1993). In the autumn of 2017, the Hardrock Mining and Reclamation Act was introduced in the Senate.[6] Part of that bill includes the imposition of a more modest 2% to 5% royalty on the gross income of new production (Tom Udall, Senator for New Mexico 2017). That bill has not left the introduction phase,[7] arguably mostly because of the groundwork laid by retired senator Harry Reid. As the son of a miner, Senator Reid was particularly attentive to the calls for reform of the Mining Law of 1872 and spent years organizing mining interests to bring their case against reform to the Senate (Simon 2018). More recently, Rep. Raúl Grijalva of Arizona introduced H.R. 2579, and as of publication of this chapter, the bill is making its way through Congress. One of the provisions of this bill is an implementation of a 12.5% royalty on new mining operations and an 8% royalty on existing operations (exempting miners with less than $50,000 in mining income) (Natural Resources Committee 2019).

So, what is it about the royalty, a seemingly logical measure for the federal government to take, that has not allowed any reform to occur? There are several factors. Gerard (1997) argues that it would create a "high-grading" effect that would incentivize mining companies to mine only high-grade ores. Additionally, "hardrock mining is characterized by uncertainty, long time horizons, and only rare success" and is dependent on a significant investment of capital on infrastructure and machinery (Gerard 1997). Being subject to a royalty whose rate could change on a political whim may be deal breaker for a miner who would otherwise be willing to take a financial chance on exploration. The reasonable rate for a claim and the absence of a royalty "offers a means for the government to credibly reduce the possibility of later expropriation" (Morriss et al. 2004, p. 763). Morriss et al. (2004, p. 767) also make the case that "governments have a problem making credible commitments for the future through contracts." The economic benefit of a royalty does not play out either. According to Gordon and VanDoren (1998, p. 3), "If the 1872 law has created any 'giveaways,' they range from $2.5 million to $16 billion (with the true number probably closer to the lower figure)," and "Each recipient of that 'giveaway' pocketed at most $8,000 that was rightfully the taxpayers.' Although subsidies are objectionable, that amount pales in comparison with the exaggerated figures ($231 billion is a number that is frequently cited by opponents of the law) that have been widely cited in news reports and in the halls of Congress." An imposition of a royalty, unless it was at an extraordinarily high percentage, would be largely symbolic.

Another interesting by-product of the low cost and limited bureaucracy in the Mining Law of 1872 is that it may limit government corruption. Although many different systems of government regulations on mining exist in other countries, it may be useful to examine some foreign cases as examples of what could occur with expanded government involvement in the United States. In a 2017 report, Transparency International concluded "that vulnerabilities to corruption exist in mining approvals regimes across the world, irrespective of their stage of economic development, political context, geographic region, or the size and maturity of their mining sectors" (Caripis 2017). In countries where the government owns key infrastructure needed for mining; is responsible for analyzing social and environmental impact; is involved with development, health, and safety standards; and invests and distributes revenue from mining, opportunities for corruption are many (Ernst and Young n.d.). Government officials are involved at several different layers of the mining process and can block or delay projects while soliciting bribes to allow the mining to proceed (Ernst and Young n.d.). In 2017, the Organized Crime and Corruption Reporting Project reported on a mining corruption scandal in the Democratic Republic of the Congo (DRC) that resulted in payments of between $750 million and $1.3 billion to various entities tied to the president of the DRC (Mackie 2017). In a 2018 study of state-owned enterprises involving natural resource extraction, the Brookings Institute remarked that in countries where "state-owned enterprises play an oversized role in the fiscal health of the state," "damaging shocks across the economy and political system" could result (Gillies et al. 2018). They point to bribery in Algeria, Brazil, Colombia, Iraq, and Venezuela; awarding contracts to politically favored companies in the Democratic Republic of Congo, Nigeria, and Russia; and movement of funds to illicit organizations in South Sudan (Gillies et al. 2018). That is not to say that state-owned enterprises cannot work well: Ectopetrol in Colombia and Statoil in Norway are two successful examples (Gillies et al. 2018).

Limiting corruption may be where the Mining Act of 1872 is most successful. Although there is a low price paid to the government on the front end of a mining project, "the government does not forego all revenue from the mineral resources, only the revenue from their sale. Revenue from the exploitation of the resource may be taxed via income taxes on the mineral rights owners' profits or on their employees" (Morriss et al. 2004, p. 745). Additionally, it can be argued that governments with state-owned enterprises spend significant money on corruption avoidance. If the layers of bureaucracy are removed with limited government involvement, however, "foregoing revenue from mining claim sales means a loss of one source of revenue, but it also entails a compensating savings and increased tax revenues from other sources" (Morriss et al. 2004, p. 745). While there is certainly room for improvement of the economic factors in the Mining Law of 1872, it would appear that for the most part it has had its intended effect of promoting exploration and limiting government corruption.

ENVIRONMENTAL PROTECTION UNDER THE LAW

As the American West began to open up to hard-rock and other types of mining, it was soon realized that, in the quest to extract as much valuable material from the ground as quickly and profitably as possible, mining was taking a toll on the environment as well as on miners and their communities. While this realization did not immediately result in legislation that addressed the problems, at least it provided evidence that the nascent American mining industry was aware that pulling natural resources from the earth was not going to be a simple process. Several pieces of environmental protection legislation, at all levels of government and across multiple agencies have been enacted, especially in approximately the past forty years, that apply to mining. At the time of the writing of this chapter, however, environmental protection legislation, especially at the federal level, is fluid. *The New York Times* keeps a running count of "Environmental Rules on the Way Out under Trump" that as of August 2018 is sitting at seventy-six (Popovich et al. 2018). Forty-six of those rules have been overturned, and thirty are on their way out. One of the most recent rollbacks is addressed in a July 2018 memorandum from the Bureau of Land Management that drops the mandatory "compensatory mitigation" standard from public land use and makes it voluntary (Bureau of Land Management 2018). Several of these rollbacks have been challenged in courts, and more lawsuits are sure to follow (Milan 2018). While the future of environmental policy regarding mining is in flux, it is still worthwhile to discuss environmental policy as it has historically applied to mining.

A notable criticism of the 1872 Mining Law is that it contains no provisions for environmental protection. From Earthworks (n.d.), "because the Mining Law contains no environmental provisions, hardrock mining wreaks havoc on the environment and taxpayers are all too often left to clean up the mess that companies leave behind." From the Sierra Club, "For well over a century, companies have been able to mine a site until they didn't think they could profit from in any longer, then declare bankruptcy and walk away, leaving taxpayers holding the bag for cleaning up toxic metals, polluted water supplies, and anything else they happened to leave behind" (Grijalva 2018). From the Pew Charitable Trust, "[the Mining Law of 1872] fails to protect water quality, wildlife habitat, and other natural resources. Nearly 40% of western headwaters have been contaminated by hardrock mining, and a 2004 government analysis found that nearly 60% of mine contamination cases studied will require water treatment for 40 years to perpetuity" (Pew Environment Group 2009). While all of these criticisms are valid, they are arguably missing the point. Although the Mining Law of 1872 contains no specific environmental protections, there are plenty of environmental protection laws across many levels of government that apply to mining. In addition to state and local laws, mining is regulated on the federal level by the National Environmental Policy Act; the Clean Air Act; the Resources Conservation and Recovery Act; the Clean Water Act; the Toxic Substances Control Act; and the Comprehensive Environmental Response, Compensation, and Liability Act (American Geosciences Institute 2018). Additionally, "the Environmental Protection Agency, for the time being, also helps protect the communities surrounding mines and mining operations around the United States, ensuring that all generations have access to clean water and air" (Micromine 2017). Proponents of adding environmental protection language to the Mining Law of 1872 may cite the approximately fifty abandoned mine sites on the EPA's National Priorities List (US Environmental Protection Agency 2020). But many of these sites were abandoned long before reclamation and environmental protection laws were enacted. If the current hierarchy of environmental protection laws and enforcement agencies remains the same for the foreseeable future as it is now, Gerard (1997) argues that changing the environmental laws is where reform is needed, not in the addition of environmental stipulations to the Mining Law of 1872. In a time of environmental regulatory flux, it would be wise for both proponents and opponents of environmental protection measures in mining to pay careful attention to the goings on in Washington, DC.

EFFECTS OF GLOBAL CLIMATE CHANGE ON MINING

In the coming years and decades, global climate change is going to affect mining just as it will many other land-use concerns. Although climate change has become part of the global zeitgeist with most private citizens and industry, the mining industry has been late to the table on this issue. For example, between the publication of its first issue in 2014 and January 2018, the journal *Extractive Industries and Society* has published zero articles with "climate change" in the title (Odell et al. 2018). In 2014, Jason Phillips (2016) reported, "Within the literature, there has been no generic review or synthesis of the fundamental interactions between climate change and surface mining." Additionally, possibly because of the federal government's wavering stance on the validity of global climate change, specific literature on the effects of climate change on hard-rock mining in the United States is sparse or instead addresses the impact that mining (especially coal mining) has on global climate.

There are some themes presented in global literature on the subject that can be applied to hard-rock mining in the western United States, however. The advocacy organization Climate Diplomacy lists four impacts that climate change can have globally on the industry (Ruttinger and Sharma 2016). There is no reason to think that these factors will not affect mining in the western states. First, because the mining sector is one of the major emitters of greenhouse gases, the industry will have to find a way to deal with increased pressure to reduce emissions, even as the industry need for fossil fuels increases. Second, climate change may have a direct effect on operations or an indirect effect on supply chain and or rising energy costs. Third, climate change may exacerbate changes in ecosystems, agriculture, and raising livestock. While this factor may affect developing nations disproportionately because they are not well equipped to respond to large-scale changes, it can certainly affect the United States. As mining already affects ecosystems, agriculture, and raising livestock (usually indirectly with factors such as toxic runoff of mining products or windblown heavy metal particulates), the industry will have to be aware of its effects on an unnaturally stressed environment. Finally, since a "large and increasing number of extractive resources come from developing nations which already lack resources for climate adaptation," developed nations like the United States must become more involved in ensuring supply chains are protected from the impacts of climate change (Ruttinger and Sharma 2016, p. 1). While this final factor does not directly affect mining in the West, threats to foreign supply chains may cause the mining industry in the United States to increase extraction and production rates, which could in turn put more stress on an environment that is experiencing the effects of climate change. Although he also comments on the lack of available literature, Phillips (2016) conducted as comprehensive of a review as possible of available data on the impacts of climate change on the global surface mining industry and identified several factors that can potentially be affected by global climate change. The results are summarized in table 13.2 (Torres et al. 2017).

Table 13.2. Effects of Climate Change on Mining

Themes	Impacts of Climate Change
Acid Mine Drainage	• Increasing temperature leads to increased oxidation rates. • Increasing precipitation could lead to contaminated surface water and shallow groundwater. • Prolonged drought could lead to higher evaporation rates and could thin overlying water or cause it to dry out completely. • Increased severity of wet/dry seasons could cause capping layers in mine spoils or water facilities to crack or degrade increasing oxidation rates. • Waste stockpiles may be exposed to rapid oxidation and acid production because of increased temperature and precipitation.
Atmospheric Transport	• Atmospheric transport of heavy metals such as mercury, arsenic, and cadmium could become more hazardous owing to extreme weather events and changing climate patterns.
Hydrospheric Impacts	• Increased dry/drought seasons may concentrate heavy metals and allow atmospheric transport by dust or vapor. • Increased wet seasons could cause transport of heavy metals at levels above those typically expected.
Soil Contamination	• Increased precipitation can cause heavy metals to be transported and deposited in soils far from mining sites. • Contaminated soils can inhibit plant growth, which may lead to increased rates of soil erosion. • Increased soil erosion can prevent new soils from forming.
Impacts on Hydrological Processes and Resources	• Increased precipitation can lead to increased contamination of surface and groundwater with minerals and mining wastes. • Mining activity can affect groundwater recharge rates because it can increase surface evaporation rates. Increasing temperature can further decrease recharge rates in both active and inactive mine sites. • Mining activity often involves deforestation (and all of the ecological changes that go along with it). Climate change could slow the rate of reforestation with unknown consequences. • Mining activity often changes the dynamics of local flooding. Increased precipitation could exacerbate this flooding.
Coastal and Fluvial Processes	• Global sea level rise will affect surface mining near or at coastal zones. (This may have a disproportionate effect on sand and gravel mining.)* • Precipitation changes coupled with mining activities can change sediment loads that are transported by fluvial systems.
Water Resources	• Mining will exacerbate water resource issues in areas where climate change causes precipitation rates to decrease.

Ecological Succession and Disruption	• Changes in weather and climate can cause mining areas to release larger quantities of environmental hazards or pollution, which can retard ecosystem development in areas being reclaimed. • Increased disruptions to ecosystems caused by mining will likely increase. • Climate change will likely increase deforestation. Because deforestation to some degree is frequently involved with mining, the situation is likely to deteriorate.
Impacts from Pollution	• Rates and effects of eutrophication caused by mining activities will likely increase. • Mining-related pollution in lakes may remain in place longer and at more concentrated levels.
Air Pollution	• Global changes in wind patterns and weather can lead to changes in dispersal of dust and particulate matter as well as ground-level ozone.
Mass Movement	• Climate change makes long-term mass movements like solifluction and soil creep less predictable.

* Global sand supplies may already be at risk (Torres et al. 2017).

In addition to the environmental impacts listed in table 13.2, Phillips (2016) also discusses some issues that climate change may have on the mining industry ranging from extraction practices to impacts on employees. Although Phillips (2016) and others speculate on the impacts climate change will have on the mining industry, the lack of available data and research limits the scope of the conclusions.

While the general concerns about mining in the era of climate change mentioned above can certainly apply to mining in the United States, one specific climate change-related issue that is a concern for mining in the western United States, and more specifically in the southwestern United States, is the issue of water usage. In hard-rock mining, water is typically used for drilling, crushing, wet screening, semi-autogenous grinding, and ball/rod milling (Mavis 2003). Much effort is also put into controlling water flow at mine sites by using "diversion systems, containment ponds, groundwater pumping systems, subsurface drainage systems and subsurface barriers" (National Mining Association 2016, p. 54). The US Geological Survey (USGS) conducts a quinquennial survey of water use across all aspects of mining. The most recent survey shows three of eleven western states falling into the highest category of water withdrawals (California, Nevada, and Utah in the range of 201–1,140 million gallons per day) and two falling into the second-highest category (New Mexico and Wyoming in the range of 101–200 million gallons per day) (US Geological Survey 2019). Although total water withdrawals dropped significantly between the 1990 and 1995 USGS surveys, they have been on a slow and steady rise in the years since (US Geological Survey 2019). Problematically, as water usage has increased, precipitation trends have almost without exception either decreased or remained unchanged in the western states (especially in southwestern states) in the interval between 1895 and 2016 (National Oceanic and Atmospheric Association 2019b). Additionally, the average mean temperature in the western states south of the 42nd parallel has increased anywhere from 1 to 4 degrees Fahrenheit between 1988 and 2017, and all of the western states have seen an increase in average mean temperature in the 1895-2017 interval (National Oceanic and Atmospheric Association 2019a). If these trends continue, water use for the mining industry is on an unsustainable track. Although most mining operations reuse water when possible, water needs to be present in order to be used (Mavis 2003).

CONCLUSIONS

Conflicts over the use of public lands have existed as long as there have been public lands. While many of the so-called land grab laws of the nineteenth and twentieth centuries have been repealed or altered, the Mining Law of 1872 still governs hard-rock mining claims on federal public lands. Some argue for repealing the law altogether, and others argue that it is effective as is. However, there is certainly room for reevaluating the terms of the law that would better reflect economic and technological advances in mining that have occurred over the course of the past 150 years. The Mining Law of 1872 covers Washington, DC's thoughts on mining, but there are also layers of state and local mining laws that at times are at odds with federal law. This can lead to confusion at best and outright conflict at worst. Although past efforts to pass new federal mining laws that replace the Mining Law of 1872 have been blocked in Congress, the terms of the law are in serious need of a fact-based, data-driven debate of their efficacy.

The second part of this chapter discussed the impact of climate change on the mining industry. This is an area that is in desperate need of further research. Most of the available information regarding climate change and mining has to do with discussing how the industry affects climate change, not the other way around. Most of the available data come from studies in developing nations. There are limited data available for the effects of climate change on mining in the United States as a whole, much less the western United States. Climate change is occurring, and it would serve the mining industry well to seriously study the potential impacts of climate change on their industry. Currently, it seems as if the industry as a whole is taking a wait-and-see approach. This is a bad strategy for an industry that is reliant upon long-term (years to decades) development to turn a profit.

Legal Citations

1 Proclamation No. 6920, 61 Fed. Reg. 50223 (Sept. 18, 1996).
2 Mining Law of 1872, R.S. § 2319 et seq.; 30 U.S.C. § 22 et seq. (1872).
3 Mining Law of 1872, R.S. § 2319 et seq.; 30 U.S.C. § 22 et seq. (1872).
4 Mining Law of 1872, R.S. § 2319 et seq.; 30 U.S.C. § 22 et seq. (1872).
5 Mining Law of 1872, R.S. § 2319 et seq.; 30 U.S.C. § 22 et seq. (1872).
6 Hardrock Mining and Reclamation Act of 2017, S. 1833, 115th Cong. (2017).
7 Hardrock Mining and Reclamation Act of 2017, S. 1833, 115th Cong. (2017).

References

American Geosciences Institute. 2019. "What Are Environmental Regulations on Mining Activities?" Last modified 2019. https://www.americangeosciences.org/critical-issues/faq/what-are-regulations-mining-activities.

Bureau of Land Management. 2018. "Compensatory Mitigation." Accessed July 24, 2018. https://www.blm.gov/policy/im-2018-093.

Bureau of Land Management. 2019. "Explanation of Location." Accessed September 19, 2019. https://www.blm.gov/programs/energy-and-minerals/mining-and-minerals/locatable-materials/explanation-of-location.

Caripis, Lisa. 2017. *Combating Corruption in Mining Approvals: Assessing the Risks in 18 Resource-Rich Countries.* Melbourne, VIC: Transparency International. https://www.transparency.org/whatwedo/publication/combatting_corruption_in_mining_approvals.

Clinton, William J. 1993. *A Vision of Change for America.* Washington, DC: Office of Management and Budget. https://files.eric.ed.gov/fulltext/ED351810.pdf.

Cramer, Virginia. 2018. "ICYMI: Canadian Firm Stakes Claims in Grand Staircase-Escalante National Monument." Last modified June 21, 2018. https://www.sierraclub.org/press-releases/2018/06/icymi-canadian-firm-stakes-claims-grand-staircase-escalante-national-monument.

Earthworks. n.d. *The Last American Dinosaur . . . The 1872 Mining Law.* Washington, DC: Earthworks. https://earthworks.org/cms/assets/uploads/archive/files/publications/MPCfs_LastAmericanDinosaur.pdf.

Earthworks. 2019. "Our Mission." Accessed April 12, 2019. https://earthworks.org/about/ourmission/.

Ernst and Young. n.d. "Fraud and Corruption in Mining and Metals: 1. High Levels of Government Regulation." Accessed November 12, 2019. https://www.ey.com/gl/en/industries/mining---metals/fraud-and-corruption-in-mining-and-metals---common-areas-of-fraud-and-corruption-risk---high-levels-of-government-regulation.

Gerard, David. 1997. "The Mining Law of 1872: Digging a Little Deeper." PERC Policy Series PS-11. Bozeman, MT: Property and Environment Research Center. https://www.perc.org/wp-content/uploads/2018/02/ps11.pdf

Gillies, Alexandra, Patrick Heller, and Daniel Kauffmann. 2018. "What Makes an Accountable State-Owned Enterprise?" Last modified March 26, 2018. https://www.brookings.edu/blog/future-development/2018/03/26/what-makes-an-accountable-state-owned-enterprise/.

Gordon, Richard, and Peter VanDoren. 1998. *Two Cheers for the 1872 Mining Law*. Cato Policy Analysis 300. Washington, DC: Cato Institute. https://www.cato.org/publications/policy-analysis/two-cheers-1872-mining-law.

Greenberg, Max. 2018. "Update: Mining Interests Stake Claims in Grand Staircase-Escalante and Bears Ears National Monuments." Wilderness Society, last modified June 27, 2018. https://wilderness.org/blog/mining-company-now-staking-claim-invade-grand-staircase-escalante-national-monument.

Grijalva, Raul M. 2018. "Our Mining Laws Are More Than a Century Old—Time to Update Them." Sierra Club, last modified May 15, 2018. https://www.sierraclub.org/sierra/our-mining-laws-are-more-century-old-time-update-them. Leshy, John D. 1988. "Reforming the Mining Law: Problems and Prospects." *Public Land Law Review* 9(1): 1-29. http://repository.uchastings.edu/faculty_scholarship/391.

Mackie, Kyle. 2017. " 'Legalized Corruption' Siphoned One-Fifth of Mining Revenues from Congo's State Budget." Organized Crime and Corruption Reporting Project, July 24, 2017. https://www.occrp.org/en/27-ccwatch/cc-watch-briefs/6762-legalized-corruption-siphoned-one-fifth-of-mining-revenues-from-congo-s-state-budget.

Mavis, Jim. 2003. *Water Use in Industries of the Future: Mining Industry*. Washington, DC: Center for Waste Reduction Technologies. http://citeseerx.ist.psu.edu/viewdoc/download?doi=10.1.1.593.3544&rep=rep1&type=pdf.

Micromine. 2017. "Environmental Regulations on Mining in the United States." July 17, 2017. https://www.micromine.com/environmental-regulations-mining-united-states/.

Milan, Oliver. 2018. " 'Sloppy and Careless': Courts Call Out Trump Blitzkrieg on Environmental Rules." *The Guardian*, February 20, 2018. https://www.theguardian.com/environment/2018/feb/20/donald-trump-epa-environmental-rollbacks-court-challenges.

Morriss, Andrew P., Roger E. Meiners, and Andrew Dorchak. 2004. "Homesteading Rock: A Defense of Free Access under the General Mining Law of 1872." *Environmental Law* 34: 745. https://scholarship.law.tamu.edu/facscholar/71.

National Mining Association. 2016. "Facts, Stats and Data." Accessed November 12, 2019. https://nma.org/wpcontent/uploads/2016/11/factbook20163.pdf.

National Mining Association. 2018. "Major Metals Operations in the United States." Last modified 2018. https://nma.org/wp-content/uploads/2016/09/metal-mines-map-2018.pdf.

National Oceanic and Atmospheric Association. 2019a. "National Trends in Average Mean Temperature." Accessed April 13, 2019. https://www.ncdc.noaa.gov/temp-and-precip/us-trends/tavg/ann#us-trends-select.

National Oceanic and Atmospheric Association. 2019b. "National Trends in Precipitation." Accessed April 13, 2019. https://www.ncdc.noaa.gov/temp-and-precip/us-trends/prcp/ann#us-trends-select.

Natural Resources Committee. 2019. "Mining Reform Legislation." Accessed October 27, 2019. https://naturalresources.house.gov/imo/media/doc/HR%202579%20Mining%20Reform%20Fact%20Sheet.pdf.

Odell, Scott D., Anthony Bebbington, and Karen E. Frey. 2018. "Mining and Climate Change: A Review and Framework for Analysis." *Extractive Industries and Society* 5(1): 201-214. https://doi.org/10.1016/j.exis.2017.12.004.

Pew Environment Group. 2009. *The 1872 Mining Law: Time for Reform*. Washington, DC: Pew Charitable Trusts. http://www.pewtrusts.org/~/media/assets/2009/01/24/mining-law-time-for-reform.pdf.

Phillips, Jason. 2016. "Climate Change and Surface Mining: A Review of Environment-Human Interactions and Their Spatial Dynamics." *Applied Geography* 74: 95-108. https://doi.org/10.1016/j.apgeog.2016.07.001.

Popovich, Nadja, Livia Albeck-Ripka, and Kendra Pierre-Louis. 2018. "76 Environmental Rules on the Way Out under Trump." *New York Times*, July 6, 2018. https://www.nytimes.com/interactive/2017/10/05/climate/trump-environment-rules-reversed.html?_r=0.

Ruttinger, Lukas, and Vigya Sharma. 2016. *Climate Change and Mining: A Foreign Policy Perspective*. Berlin: Adelphi. https://www.climate-diplomacy.org/publications/climate-change-and-mining-foreign-policy-perspective.

Simon, Julia. 2018. "The Mining Act of 1872 Digs Up a Lot of Issues." March 30, 2018. https://www.npr.org/2018/03/30/598192105/the-mining-act-of-1872-digs-up-a-lot-of-issues.

Stegner, Wallace. 1992. *Beyond the Hundredth Meridian: John Wesley Powell and the Second Opening of the West*. New York: Penguin.

Studnicki-Gizbert, Daviken. 2017. "Exhausting the Sierra Madre: Mining Ecologies in Mexico over the Longue Durée." In *Mining North America: An Environmental History since 1522*, edited by J. R. McNeill and George Vrtis, 19-20. Oakland: University of California Press.

Sybert, Brian, Nicole Croft, and David Polly. 2018. "Local Groups Evaluating Options against Mining in Sensitive Area within Utah's Grand Staircase-Escalante National Monument." Grand Staircase Escalante Partners, June 20, 2018. http://gsenm.org/wp-content/uploads/2018/06/Final-Press-Release-Colt-Mesa.pdf.

The Diggings. 2019. "Gold, Silver, and Other Mining Claims in the United States by State." Accessed April 12, 2019. https://thediggings.com/usa/states.

Tom Udall Senator for New Mexico. 2017. "Senators Introduce Bill to Reform Antiquated Hardrock Mining Laws." Last modified September 19, 2017. https://www.tomudall.senate.gov/news/press-releases/senators-introduce-bill-to-reform-antiquated-hardrock-mining-laws.

Torres, Aurora, Jianguo "Jack" Liu, Jodi Brandt, and Kristen Lear. 2017. "The World Is Facing a Global Sand Crisis." Last modified September 7, 2017. https://theconversation.com/the-world-is-facing-a-global-sand-crisis-83557.

US Energy Information Administration. 2019. "Major U.S. Coal Mines, 2018." Accessed November 12, 2019. https://www.eia.gov/coal/annual/pdf/table9.pdf.

US Environmental Protection Agency. 2020. "Abandoned Mine Lands: Site Information." Last updated January 27, 2020. https://www.epa.gov/superfund/abandoned-mine-lands-site-information.

US Geological Survey. 2019. "Mining Water Use." Accessed April 13, 2019. https://water.usgs.gov/watuse/wumi.html.

Vincent, Carol Hardy, Laura A. Hanson, and Carla N. Argueta. 2017. *Federal Land Ownership: Overview and Data*. CRS Report R42346. Washington, DC: Congressional Research Service. https://fas.org/sgp/crs/misc/R42346.pdf.

Chapter 14

Implications of Tribal Sovereignty, Federal Trust Responsibility, and Congressional Plenary Authority for Native American Lands Management

SHANE DAY

INTRODUCTION

Many Americans express surprise when they discover that Native American reservation lands are not technically owned by the tribes themselves but are instead owned by the federal government and held in trust for the benefit of the tribes. Furthermore, specific tracts of lands within reservation boundaries have been converted to individual ownership, such that most reservations exhibit a complex matrix of property rights distributed among the federal government, tribal governments, individual Native Americans, and nontribal individuals. While some general patterns can be identified, for the most part, each of the 573 federally recognized tribal governments in the United States has had a unique historical relationship with the US federal government, with land ownership and land management responsibilities varying considerably from tribe to tribe owing to the vicissitudes of official government policies toward individual tribes (fig. 14.1). In order to grasp the multitude of contemporary Native American land management policy issues, one must understand the history of US federal policy toward tribes, the structural characteristics that explain why policy has been so inconsistent and ad hoc in implementation, and how individual tribes have been affected differentially by various federal policies on land management issues.

This chapter briefly outlines federal Indian policy with a focus on major developments that affect land ownership and management in the contiguous

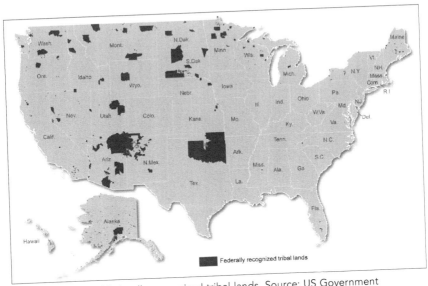

Figure 14.1. Map of federally recognized tribal lands. Source: US Government Accountability Office (2018).

United States. The chapter highlights various political conditions and policy developments, including the condition of inherent tribal sovereignty, the federal trust responsibility toward tribes, reserved treaty rights, congressional plenary authority, different pathways to federal recognition, and the rise of self-governance authority, each of which has shaped the specific kinds of land management activities undertaken by tribal governments. Several emergent issue areas are then highlighted as a means of illustrating the diverse range of land management issues facing tribes, including devolved tribal land management of reservation resources, comanagement authority of off-reservation federal lands, consultative authority regarding land-use planning on private lands, and relocation initiatives as an adaptation strategy for negative impacts of climate change. It concludes with the assertion that while many Native American tribes have dramatically expanded the scope of their land management responsibilities, others have not, as a result of either being unwilling to do so or not enjoying the same set of opportunities as enjoyed by other tribes, owing to their specific relationship with the federal government. It is thus impossible to generalize about tribal land management activity across all tribal governments. Regardless, the tenuous position of Native Americans vis-à-vis the federal government always casts a shadow over the specific range of governance activities carried out by tribal governments, with the status quo involving any particular tribe being potentially overturned at any moment by a fundamental change in federal policy.

HISTORY OF TRIBAL-FEDERAL RELATIONS

The relationship between Native Americans and European settlers during the colonial era can best be characterized as a "nation-to-nation relationship" in which the English negotiated treaties with tribes as co-sovereign entities, even as the English disparaged their "savage" cultural practices and "primitive" forms of political organization (Wilkins and Stark 2011, pp. 52-53). These treaties largely served to attain land cessions in areas that were attractive to English settlers, in exchange for reserved areas that were fully under the control of the tribes themselves. These treaties were often negotiated to end periods of open hostilities between colonists and tribes, and thus frequently reflected asymmetrical bargaining positions between the vanquishers and the vanquished, although some treaties were struck against a backdrop of peaceful relations that the signatories hoped to codify and perpetuate into the future. Upon independence, the US government continued this practice, implicitly recognizing the inherent sovereignty of indigenous nations. But the substance of the treaties negotiated by the US government increasingly began to shift toward land cession in exchange for monetary concessions and direct provision of services by the federal government over such things as health care and education, which opened the door for subsequent interventions in tribal affairs.

As the balance of power between Native Americans and colonial settlers began to tilt toward the latter, treaties were increasingly used by tribes to get what concessions they could get while avoiding the perceived inevitability of armed conflict. For instance, tribes in the Pacific Northwest for the most part avoided armed conflict at the cost of land cessions, but while preserving treaty-codified rights to culturally significant resources and practices such as whaling, shellfish harvesting, and fishing (Bernholz and Weiner 2008; Richards 2005). The tilt in the balance of power also led to the federal government's chipping away at principles of tribal sovereignty and, ultimately, to the ending of the practice of treaty-making altogether by 1871 (Pevar 2012, p. 94). After 1871, several reservations were established through the use of executive orders, but Congress ended this practice in 1919, such that today, only Congress can create a reservation (Pevar 2012, p. 95).

Several Supreme Court cases set the stage for this diminishment of tribal sovereignty. The question of land title was addressed in *Johnson v. M'Intosh*,[1] which established that the US government acquired ownership of all lands by virtue of discovery and conquest, but Indians retained possessory title, although not outright ownership, to the land (Pevar 2012, pp. 24-25). Among other things, this forbids the sale of Indian lands without the authorization of the secretary of the interior, who serves as the primary federal agent in carrying out congressional policy toward tribes. The so-called Cherokee Cases, especially *Cherokee Nation v. Georgia* and *Worcester v. Georgia*,[2] furthermore established that while tribes were sovereign entities, and thus not subject to the jurisdiction of state governments, they were nonetheless "dependent nations" whose relationship with the United States was akin to that "of a ward to his guardian." This judgment was foundational to the emergence of the doctrine of trust responsibility, in which the federal government has both power over Indians and responsibility toward them, particularly in carrying out the specific promises enshrined in treaties. Trust responsibility furthermore implies that a treaty holds the same weight as a federal law; that is, it is the "highest law of the land" (Duthu 2008). In the case of *Lone Wolf v. Hitchcock*, however, the court held that Congress possesses "plenary," or complete and unshared, authority over tribes under the logic of the Commerce Clause of the Constitution.[3] Thus, while treaties and federal laws are theoretically equal, Congress has the right to unilaterally abrogate the terms of a treaty, albeit subject to the provisions of the Due Process and Just Compensation Clauses (Duthu 2008; Pevar 2012). As a result, tribes have a vulnerable relationship with the federal government. While the government has a set of recognized obligations toward tribes, it can effectively terminate the relationship with any given tribe, along with all of its obligations toward it, with a simple act of Congress. Arguably, the only thing that impedes Congress from completely doing away with tribes is the pressure of public opinion.

The inconsistent pattern of federal policy toward tribes can be seen as reflecting the changing tides of public opinion. Subsequent outrage in the state of Georgia in the wake of the Cherokee Cases, and President Andrew Jackson's refusal to uphold the Supreme Court's judgement in *Worcester v. Georgia*, led to the policy of "Indian removal," in which several tribes were forcibly removed to present-day Oklahoma, which was originally designated as a self-governing "Indian Territory." Outside of Indian Territory, reservations were used to distribute promised goods and services, while maintaining a "safe" degree of separation between tribal and settler communities. Implementation, however, was heavily concentrated in the hands of a respective Indian Agent, which, owing to the relative lack of oversight and control on the frontier, could often run reservations as personal fiefdoms (Wilkins and Stark 2011). After the Civil War, the government followed a general policy of "assimilation," in which individual Indians were either encouraged or forced to adopt western customs. Perhaps the most disruptive policy of this area was established by the General Allotment Act of 1887, which sought to break up the reservation system, assimilate Indians into the private property rights system, and encourage economic development by making individual Indians commercial farmers (Royster 1995). Toward this end, allotment typically entailed dividing up communally held reservation lands into 160-acre parcels that were then given to each tribal member, who after a twenty-five-year period could sell the deed to the property (Royster 1995). Furthermore, once all 160-acre properties were distributed, any "surplus land" was sold off to non-Indians. Individual allotments that were not sold off were frequently subdivided as a result of inheritance, such that the promise of economic development through agriculture rarely materialized, as each subsequent generation had less and less land with which to farm (Royster 1995).

In response to publicized abuses by Indian agents, controversy over the condition of boarding schools, and the failure of allotment, the Progressive movement picked up the cause of Indian rights and initiated a dramatic shift in federal Indian policy. In 1934, the federal government repealed allotment and encouraged the development of tribal governments through the Indian Reorganization Act (IRA). Although the IRA period maintained certain assimilationist policies, paternalistically restricted the range of government types and functions available to tribes, and perpetuated the power and high degree of delegated discretion of the secretary of interior, it nevertheless represented the most favorable political position of tribes since US independence (Pevar 2012). In terms of land issues, while the damage from allotment had already been done, such that by 1834 less than one-third of tribal lands that had existed pre-allotment remained in tribal hands, by 1953, tribes in aggregate increased their landholdings by more than two million acres (Pevar 2012, p. 11).

This more positive orientation toward tribes ended in 1953, however, as new fiscal priorities in the wake of World War II led the federal government to roll back its fiduciary responsibilities to tribes. During these "Barren Years"— also known as the "Termination Era"—the federal government, acting under congressional plenary authority, terminated the recognition of more than a hundred tribal governments, devolved federal criminal and civil jurisdiction to certain state governments under Public Law 280, and officially encouraged the migration of individual Indians to urban areas to obtain better employment opportunities (Deloria and Lytle 1984). An unforeseen consequence of the latter was the emergence of a pan-Indian ethnic identity and social movement that reacted against these new attacks on tribal sovereignty. The resulting Indian rights movement was largely coterminous with the broader civil rights movement of the 1960s and helped to usher in a sea change in popular opinion toward Native American causes.

As a result of Indian activism, the official policy of Congress since the late 1960s has been the promotion of tribal sovereignty and self-determination. While the specific definition of self-determination is somewhat ambiguous and contested among indigenous peoples, at a minimum it refers to "the right to participate in the democratic process of governance and to influence one's future—politically, socially and culturally" (Wessendorf 2011). To this end, tribes have been granted greater discretion to develop their own government forms with less fear of intervention by the secretary of interior through the use of their de facto veto authority, attained the power to operate gaming operations, won court cases upholding various treaty provisions that had been under attack by state and federal governments, gained jurisdiction over child custody cases, and have seen a general expansion in the range of governmental services they provide (see generally Harvard Project on American Indian Economic Development 2008; Pevar 2012; Wilkins and Stark 2011). Additionally, many formerly terminated tribes have reattained federal recognition, albeit without a full restoration of their former land bases, and many tribes have gained formal recognition for the first time. From the end of the treaty-making era in 1871, the process of formal recognition has essentially come through three different pathways: an act of Congress, an administrative process through the Department of the Interior for petitioning tribes that meet seven different criteria, or a federal court order (Pevar 2012, pp. 271-274). The primary pathway is via administrative recognition; however, the process has been criticized as burdensome, cost-prohibitive, and time-consuming, leading many tribes to seek, with mixed success, congressional or judicial recognition (Pevar 2012, pp. 271-274). These latter two pathways, however, potentially expose tribes to a greater degree of restrictions on tribal government powers and access to particular federal programs. For instance, the Lumbee Act of 1956 merely recognized the existence of the Lumbee of

North Carolina as "Indians" but denied them all of the benefits of full federal recognition (Harvard Project on American Indian Economic Development 2008, p. 61), and almost half of the recognition bills introduced in Congress since 1975 have contained some form of restriction of tribal authority, most commonly in the form of granting criminal or civil jurisdiction over tribal lands to state governments, restricting gaming rights, or restricting tribal hunting and fishing (Carlson 2016). Furthermore, the political status of Alaskan Natives is distinct from tribes in the Lower 48, because the process of their federal recognition under the Alaska Native Claims Settlement Act, which conveyed full rights of land ownership to more than two hundred Native Village Corporations, are further agglomerated into thirteen Regional Corporations that collectively hold subsurface mineral rights (Pevar 2012, pp. 261-264). As a result, tribal authority and jurisdiction over their own lands vary considerably between tribes and are dependent upon whether a tribe has been recognized by treaty, administrative action, court order, or a specific act of Congress.

Perhaps the most significant modern development in tribal governance has been the gradual expansion of self-governance authority (for an overview of the history of self-governance policy, see Strommer and Osborne 2014). In 1975, Congress passed the Indian Self-Determination and Education Assistance Act (ISDEAA), which provides a framework for tribes to negotiate contract agreements with federal agencies to take over implementation responsibility for programs that otherwise would be provided by the federal government, principally the Bureau of Indian Affairs and the Indian Health Service, with funding coming from the federal government. In 1988, Congress approved the Indian Self-Governance Demonstration Project, in which participating tribes could essentially receive block grants covering multiple programs and services. This allowed tribes to redesign programs and allocate funding across program areas as they saw fit. In response to the success of this program, in 1994 and 2000, Congress amended the ISDEAA to effectively make self-governance authority permanent and available to any interested tribe. Although participation is optional, and more than half of all tribes choose to participate, many do not owing to a political perspective that the federal government has never lived up to its treaty obligations, that levels of available funding under the program are insufficient, and that by participating in self-governance, tribes are effectively releasing the federal government from its trust responsibilities (Harvard Project on American Indian Economic

Development 2008). These tribes essentially continue to rely upon the federal government for direct service provision, jurisdiction, and management authority. Tribes that do choose to contract and compact for direct implementation of government services have an enhanced position that can make them significant players in a variety of land management activities.

THE SCOPE OF INDIAN LANDS AND JURISDICTION

The term "Indian country" is used to designate all lands that have been set aside and designated primarily for use by Indians. Technically, it refers to all lands within a reservation, but the designation also extends to some lands outside of a reservation that are either owned by a tribe, owned by the federal government and used primarily for the benefit of Indians (such as housing projects, schools, health clinics, etc.), or restricted individual allotments of land owned by Indians that are no longer part of reservations that have been terminated by acts of Congress, as is the case for most federally recognized tribes in Oklahoma (Pevar 2012, pp. 20-23). The term is also used by many to refer to off-reservation areas where tribes enjoy special rights of way or usufruct rights, such as treaty fishing access sites along the Columbia River in Washington and Oregon (Columbia River Inter-Tribal Fisheries Commission 2020), or public lands such as various national parks or monuments to which they hold concurrent jurisdiction or comanagement authority, such as Kasha Katuwe Tent Rocks National Monument in New Mexico (Pinel and Pecos 2012). As a matter of law, claims that these latter areas are Indian country are contestable, but while tribes' primary land-use activities and jurisdiction lie within areas that conform to the legal definition of Indian country, their activities and policymaking authority frequently extend beyond that definition.

A further complication in delineating the scope of tribal land management authority is that even within reservation boundaries tribal jurisdiction is often fragmented. As a result of the various changes in federal Indian policy as outlined above, patterns of land ownership within a particular reservation are highly varied and often entail a complex patchwork of ownership and property rights. Most reservations consist of significant portions of "Indian trust land," which is land that is technically owned and held in trust by the federal government with the explicit requirement that it be held for the collective and exclusive benefit of the tribe (Pevar 2012, pp. 94-95). As a result of this trust relationship, tribes cannot unilaterally dispense of or use these lands without approval by the federal government, thus representing a significant check on tribal authority. But those tribes that participate in self-governance authority often hold a de facto higher level of management authority over these lands, as such authority has effectively been devolved to them by the federal government as a function of self-governance (Clow and Sutton 2001). As a result of the policy of allotment, on many reservations, significant portions of formerly trust reservation lands were converted into fee-simple ownership held by individual tribal citizens. Over the years, many of these fee-simple tracts held by Indians were sold off to nontribal members, adding to the holdings that were sold off as "surplus" lands. As a result, any given reservation may consist of a complex mix of federal trust lands, fee-simple lands held by tribal members, and fee-simple lands held by nonmembers.

This situation entails significant jurisdictional issues. For trust lands, the federal government either manages these lands or devolves authority to the tribes themselves under the logic of self-governance policy. Federal decisions regarding land use and dispensation are theoretically constrained by the Due Process Clause, which stipulates that any decision made by Congress must be reasonable and nondiscriminatory; the Just Compensation Clause, which requires Congress to provide fair and adequate compensation for any taken property, including the value of all resources on it; and the doctrine of trust responsibility, which forces the government to manage lands in the best interests of and in government-to-government consultation with the tribes themselves (Pevar 2012, p. 76). Tribes have broad powers to regulate land-use activities occurring on fee-simple lands held by tribal members but significantly constrained authority over fee-simple holdings of non-Indians. In this latter instance, state governments have primary jurisdiction, although tribes have relatively broad zoning authority and may petition for regulatory jurisdiction when a nonmember's action threatens the political integrity, economic security, or health or welfare of the tribe, although current precedent significantly limits this scope to "cases in which the tribe's survival is threatened by non-member conduct" (Ford and Giles 2015, p. 538; Smith 2013).

In addition, certain land areas can be subject to a claim of "Indian title land." Land that a tribe can claim to be a part of its ancestral homelands may potentially entail a right of continued occupancy if the federal government has never taken any formal action to terminate it (Pevar 2012, p. 25). Thus federal or even private lands outside of an established reservation, which have not been formally subjected to formal extinguishment by congressional action, may be subject to a possessory claim. This policy has generated a number of claims where federal lands have been abandoned and declared as surplus, such as in the occupation of Alcatraz from 1969 to 1971 (Fortunate Eagle 1992). For land that has passed into private ownership, however, tribes have faced significant obstacles in establishing title. Current precedent set in the Supreme Court case *City of Sherrill v. Oneida Indian Nation of New York*,[4] for instance, establishes a time limit on tribes in staking their possessory claims (Pevar 2012, p. 25).

Owing to the legacy of allotment and the overall complexity of land ownership and rights, tribes have an obvious interest in obtaining additional land or consolidating ownership of lands within reservation boundaries, and there are several ways that tribes have been successful in expanding their landholdings. Tribes often purchase fee-simple lands, and they may do so both off and on reservation. Such landholdings are subject to state taxation, however, whereas trust land is not (Pevar 2012, pp. 74-75). Therefore tribes have a financial incentive to hold most of their lands in trust. Most tribes can request that the secretary of interior convert, or "take into trust," lands that have been purchased by the tribe, although there is ambiguity over which tribes are eligible to do so, as historically this has been interpreted to be limited to tribes that had been federally recognized by 1934, when the Indian Reorganization Act was enacted (Pevar 2012, pp. 74-75). Tribes that have gained federal recognition in the modern era are relatively more constrained in their ability to expand their land bases and are often forced to hold fee-simple lands that are subject to state taxation. Additionally, the federal government has established a process for the secretary of interior to purchase lands to be taken into trust on behalf of tribes, although Congress often does not appropriate sufficient funds for such purposes (Pevar 2012, pp. 74-75). The primary use of such programs has been to regain territory within reservations that was lost as a result of allotment, and off-reservation purchases are relatively rare. Furthermore, off-reservation purchases can be politically controversial, particularly in situations where such purchases are for the purpose of establishing gaming enterprises, and the Department of Interior is currently considering sweeping changes that will make future trust land acquisitions more difficult (Cummings 2017).

TRIBAL LAND MANAGEMENT ACTIVITIES

The particular mix of a particular tribe's land management authority and activities is thus dependent upon several factors. Arguably the most important pertains to the specific process by which a tribe attained federal recognition. Those tribes that were recognized by treaty hold a relatively advantaged position owing to the status of treaties that are the "supreme law of the land" under Article VI of the Constitution, have been established for longer, and generally have larger reservation territories. "Treaty tribes" furthermore may hold unique reserved treaty rights that explicitly grant or otherwise imply greater authority over land management practices, even on nontribal lands off reservation. Tribes that have been recognized by executive order or via the Bureau of Indian Affairs administrative process essentially have a status similar to that of treaty tribes, although typically without any of the special reserved rights enjoyed by treaty tribes. Congressionally recognized tribes meanwhile typically enjoy all of the rights and responsibilities of federal recognition, except for any specifically restricted rights embodied in the recognition statute, such as hunting, fishing, and gaming rights. In addition, congressional recognition does not always come with a grant of reservation or trust territory (Carlson 2016). Also, regardless of the specific process behind a tribe's recognition, all tribes remain vulnerable to congressional plenary power up to and including full termination of recognition and liquidation of land assets.

The specific matrix of land ownership on a particular reservation can have significant impacts on the de facto authority of tribes to effectively regulate various land-use activities. In instances where a reservation is predominately trust land in large contiguous parcels, land-use regulation is relatively straightforward, whether it is undertaken by the federal government under its trust responsibility or by the tribe itself under their self-governance authority. More commonly, tribes confront the checkerboard legacy of allotment, termination, and other policies. In these instances, land within a reservation is often an interspersed mix of communally held trust lands, individual Indian-held allotments, and non-Indian-held fee-simple land. Planning, coordination, and regulation of reservation territories in these situations are frequently a jurisdictional mess, as trust land management and Indian-held fee-simple lands are managed either by the federal government or the tribes themselves, whereas non-Indian-held land falls under the jurisdiction of state and county governments. Finally, for non-reservation tribes with no trust territory and heavily dispersed individual allotments, land management activity is severely diminished, for there is not much land to manage directly.

Self-governance status is another key factor in determining the range of land-use activities carried out by tribes. In the case of tribes that do not have or want self-governance authority, land-use decision making continues to be dominated by the federal government, although frequently decisions are made in direct consultation with tribes as a function of various collaborative governance mechanisms (Fischman 2005). For those tribes that are certified self-governance tribes, they may choose to seek direct delegated management authority over trust lands within their reservation. Yet self-governance authority is derived from a negotiated compact that covers a variety of programmatic areas of the tribe's choosing, and a tribe may decline authority in certain areas, in which case implementation authority is retained by the federal government. That is to say, the status of a tribe as being a self-governance entity does not automatically imply that a tribe holds self-governance authority over all land management decisions within the reservation—just the operations that they choose to contract for.

Certain tribes hold significant land management roles and responsibilities that extend beyond tribally owned land and reservation boundaries. Tribal comanagement of natural resources, or "management in which government shares power with resource users, with each given specific rights and responsibilities relating to information and decision-making" (Organisation for Economic Co-operation and Development 2007), is a major area of activity for some tribes. There are at least three broad areas in which tribes participate as institutionalized comanagement partners: management of federal protected lands, management of migratory resources such as fish and game, and management of state and private lands upon which tribal resources depend. In the first category, a growing number of federal protected lands such as national parks, national monuments, wilderness areas, and other specialized units have established formal comanagement roles for certain Native American tribal governments. Making generalizations across these cases is difficult, however, as each formal grant of comanagement authority entails different specific comanagement responsibilities to be undertaken by tribes, and reflects different processes. Furthermore, there is no singular path toward the establishment of such comanagement roles. Some have argued that such "place-based collaboration" and the formalized collaborative decision-making institutions that are developed to facilitate comanagement must be approved by congressional statute (Fischman 2005, p. 199). A prime example of this process is the enabling legislation that created Canyon de Chelly National Monument, in which the Navajo retained ownership and most day-to-day management responsibilities of the monument, or that which created trust lands for the

NATIVE AMERICAN LANDS MANAGEMENT

Timbisha Shoshone Tribe within Death Valley National Park, seventeen years after the tribe's formal federal recognition (Fowler et al. 2003; King 2007). In other instances, comanagement derives from unique treaty rights that grant privileged access to areas adjacent to reservation lands (Nie 2008).

But there have been instances in which de facto comanagement has been developed as a function of agency discretion and negotiation with tribes in the absence of congressional approval, as in the Ti Bar Demonstration Project in California (Diver 2016). In other cases, comanagement has evolved from a similar bottom-up approach of initial negotiation and collaboration between the relevant administrative agency and tribe before formal codification via congressional statute, as in the case between the Bureau of Land Management and Cochiti Pueblo over management of Kasha Katuwe Tent Rocks National Monument (Pinel and Pecos 2012), or between the US Fish and Wildlife Service and the Confederated Salish and Kootenai Tribe for a wide range of management activities in the National Bison Range (Fischman 2005; King 2007). Furthermore, opportunities for comanagement can be an outgrowth of self-governance contracting, as occurred in Grand Portage National Monument between the National Park Service and the Grand Portage Band of Minnesota Chippewa, although this avenue appears to have occurred only once and reflected a unique set of circumstances (King 2007). Below the federal level, tribes have also been engaged in comanagement in various watershed management bodies convened by state governments (Cronin and Ostergren 2007). In instances where tribal advocacy has been instrumental in pushing for new national monument designations under the Antiquities Act, tribes have agitated for formalized comanagement roles, such as with Bears Ears National Monument (Ruple et al. 2016), a comanagement role that has been supported by the Trump administration despite its recent and unpopular (within Indian country) reduction in size (Eilperin 2017). That Secretary of Interior Zinke additionally suggested to the president that he seek congressional approval for tribal comanagement within other national monuments, including the proposed national monument designation of Badger-Two Medicine in Montana (Hegyi 2017), is perhaps a sign that the practice of tribal comanagement of federally protected lands is here to stay, even if it is judged by some to be merely a ploy for co-opting tribal interests (Spaeder and Feit 2005). There are no automatic opportunities for coman-agement by tribes, however, and the openness to embracing comanagement is context-specific and likely dependent upon issue salience, political clout by tribes, effective tribal leadership, sufficient resources, the legacy of past relations between settlers and tribes, and the general milieu of support by elites and society in general for tribal sovereignty and self-governance, along with other factors (Cronin and Ostergren 2007; Day 2014).

Another class of comanagement arrangements involves tribes with specific reserved treaty rights and entails formalized comanagement between tribes and state fish and wildlife management agencies in situations that would otherwise normally represent unshared areas of state authority. For instance, several tribes in the Pacific Northwest have specific treaty provisions to fish "in usual and accustomed places" and "in common with the citizens" of the state (Singleton 1998). This rather innocuous-sounding treaty language has had far-reaching implications, as the courts, in response to conflicts largely surrounding the salmon fishery, soundly reaffirmed these rights and held that, as a shared fishery, tribes are entitled to a roughly 50% share of the resource along with regulatory comanagement authority with the states of Idaho, Oregon, and Washington (Singleton 1998). Similarly, eleven Ojibwa tribes in Michigan, Minnesota, and Wisconsin have had off-reservation treaty rights to hunting, fishing, and wild rice-gathering activities upheld by court order, and actively participate in data sharing, developing management plans, setting harvest goals, and conducting other activities with state departments of natural resources (Great Lakes Indian Fish and Wildlife Commission 2019; McClurken 2000). Furthermore, such rights have provided a gateway for tribes to participate in comanagement authority even at the international level, as in the case of the twenty-four treaty tribes of the Pacific Northwest who collectively hold commissioner and other high-level positions in the Pacific Salmon Commission (Day 2012).

Third, such reserved treaty rights *may* entail a significant land-use planning role for tribes involving activities occurring on private lands. For instance, in Washington State, the aforementioned fishing "treaty tribes" have long argued that the right is meaningless if the resource is severely depleted, and therefore tribes must have a prominent role in the protection of habitat that is necessary for the propagation of salmon. Such arguments were instrumental in the inclusion of the treaty tribes during the development of the Washington State Timber, Fish, and Wildlife Plan, which developed new rules governing logging practices on private forestlands that were designed to protect riparian zones and thereby improve salmon-rearing habitat (Flynn and Gunton 1996). The right to habitat protection has recently been codified in the courts by the so-called Martinez Decision, in which tribes successfully sued the state of Washington to mandate remediation of faulty road culverts that impede salmonid fish passage (Blumm 2017). An implication of this and other judicial decisions is that consultation with tribes will be mandated in advance of regulatory rulemaking for any land use or other activity that negatively affects salmon (and there are many) and thus the treaty right, although this will likely play out on a case-by-case basis (Blumm 2017).

Finally, an emergent land issue in response to climate change impacts is the wholesale relocation of Native American groups in response to catastrophic localized ecological changes. Because of the particular vulnerability of many Native American groups to climate change impacts, and the constrained range of adaptation options available to them, relocation of Native American groups in response to catastrophic localized ecological changes has recently become a specific class of adaptation response that has garnered much publicity. Recent land swaps involving the Quileute and Hoh Native American Tribes in Washington State, a proposed resettlement for the Biloxi-Chitimacha-Choctaw Tribe in Louisiana, various village resettlement initiatives for Alaska Native Village Corporations, and other cases have been trumpeted by the press and Native American activists as models for climate change adaptation strategies involving Native American tribes (see, e.g., Campbell and de Melker 2012; Davenport and Robertson 2016; Jackson 2016; Maldonado et al. 2013; Marshall 2016; Murphy 2009; Spanne 2016). These relocation efforts raise a variety of challenges regarding land-use planning and decision making on both tribal lands and in adjacent jurisdictions that are being proposed as potential relocation sites. The mere suggestion of a proposed relocation is a politically sensitive matter owing to the legacy of the Indian Removal period (Bronen 2011; Ford and Giles 2015). If such relocation is amenable to a tribe, planning is further hampered by enormous costs associated with securing an alternative land base and actual moving costs, such that most plans do not satisfy established cost-benefit guidelines (Bronen 2011). As a result, current efforts are focused on mitigation efforts such as sea wall construction that may only delay the inevitable need to relocate and that may not be cost-effective over the long run (Martin 2018). However, simply allowing entire communities to disappear would be a clear violation of the federal trust responsibility, such that relocation as an adaptation strategy is likely to be necessary and more commonplace in the future. In the interim, however, the list of implemented and in-progress relocation efforts suggests that the current prospects for relocation may be limited to situations in which an affected tribe has a small and remote existing land base adjacent to federally held tracts that provide for culturally appropriate land-use activities and that could be swapped if public opposition is low, political support for the tribe is high, and the interests of the administrative agency with oversight of the proposed tract are not significantly disrupted (Day 2019).

CONCLUSION

No two tribes have the same range of land management responsibilities. The means by which a tribe has attained federal recognition, the degree to which a tribe holds special reserve treaty rights, whether it engages in self-governance authority over federal trust lands, and the extent to which it has been significantly affected by allotment policies all condition the range of opportunities available to a tribal government to engage in particular land management activities. Furthermore, congressional plenary authority renders a tribe's political status and authority tenuous and subject to the whims of Congress. Past federal policy has resulted in more entanglements with state governments than most tribal governments would prefer, and certain periods have entailed such low amounts of funding as to represent a failure of the federal government's trust responsibility toward tribes and to diminish the capacity of tribes to carry out their authority and responsibilities. Despite the shadow of plenary authority, however, the modern era is marked by a more consistent policy orientation toward tribes, upholding the government-to-government relationship and generally supporting the expansion of tribal government responsibilities in areas that the tribes themselves wish to take on. As a result, the scope of tribal land management activities has expanded greatly in the last forty or so years and continues to evolve into new areas that have increased the complexity of intergovernmental relations between tribes, the federal government, and certain state governments. Understanding the specific land management responsibilities of a particular tribe necessitates an examination of its particular historical relationship with federal and state governments and the specific policies that have affected land tenure patterns and the distinctive land management issues facing a given tribe.

Legal Citations

1 Johnson v. M'Intosh (21 U.S. (8 Wheat.) 543 (1823).
2 Cherokee Nation v. Georgia (30 U.S. (5 Pet.) 1 (1831)); Worcester v. Georgia (31 U.S. (6 Pet.) 515 (1832)).
3 Lone Wolf v. Hitchcock (187 U.S. 553 (1903)).
4 City of Sherrill v. Oneida Indian Nation of New York (544 U.S. 197 (2005)).

References

Bernholz, Charles D., and Robert J. Weiner Jr. 2008. "The Palmer and Stevens 'Usual and Accustomed Places' Treaties in the Opinions of the Courts." *Government Information Quarterly* 25: 778-795.

Blumm, Michael C. 2017. "Indian Treaty Fishing Rights and the Environment: Affirming the Right to Habitat Protection and Restoration." *Washington Law Review* 92(1): 1-38.

Bronen, Robin. 2011. "Climate-Induced Community Relocations: Creating an Adaptive Governance Framework Based in Human Rights Doctrine." *NYU Review of Law and Social Change* 35(2): 356-406.

Campbell, K., and S. de Melker. 2012. "Climate Change Threatens the Tribe from 'Twilight.'" *PBS Newshour*, July 16, 2012. https://www.pbs.org/newshour/science/science-july-dec12-quileute_07-05.

Carlson, Kristen M. 2016. "Congress, Tribal Recognition, and Legislative-Administrative Multiplicity." *Indiana Law Journal* 91(3): 955-1021.

Clow, Richmond L., and Imre Sutton. 2001. "Prologue: Tribes, Trusteeship, and Resource Management." In *Trusteeship in Change: Toward Tribal Autonomy in Resource Management*, edited by Richmond L. Clow and Imre Sutton, xxix–liii. Boulder: University Press of Colorado.

Columbia River Inter-Tribal Fisheries Commission. 2020. "Fisheries Timeline." Accessed February 11, 2020. https://www.critfc.org/about-us/fisheries-timeline/.

Cronin, Amanda E., and David M. Ostergren. 2007. "Democracy, Participation, and Native American Tribes in Collaborative Watershed Management." *Society and Natural Resources* 20(6): 527-542.

Cummings, Jody A. 2017. "Proposed Changes to Off-Reservation Trust Application Criteria and Acquisition Process." *Steptoe*, October 30, 2017. https://www.steptoe.com/en/news-publications/proposed-changes-to-off-reservation-trust-application-criteria-and-acquisition-process.html.

Davenport, Coral, and Campbell Robertson. 2016. "Resettling the First American 'Climate Refugees.'" *New York Times*, May 2, 2016. https://www.nytimes.com/2016/05/03/us/resettling-the-first-american-climate-refugees.html.

Day, Shane. 2012. "Indigenous Group Sovereignty and Participatory Authority in International Natural Resource Management Regimes." Doctoral thesis, Indiana University.

Day, Shane. 2014. "The Evolution of Elite and Societal Norms Pertaining to the Emergence of Federal-Tribal Co-Management of Natural Resources." *Journal of Natural Resources Policy Research* 6(4): 291-296.

Day, Shane. 2019. "Relocation of Native American Communities in Response to Climate Change: Current Initiatives and Future Challenges." Paper Presented at the Western Political Science Association Annual Meeting, April 18-21, 2019, San Diego, California.

Deloria, Vine, Jr., and Clifford M. Lytle. 1984. *The Nations Within: The Past and Future of American Indian Sovereignty.* Austin: University of Texas Press.

Diver, Sibyl. 2016. "Co-Management as a Catalyst: Pathways to Post-Colonial Forestry in the Klamath Basin, California." *Human Ecology* 44(5): 533-546.

Duthu, N. Bruce. 2008. *American Indians and the Law.* New York: Penguin.

Eilperin, Juliet. 2017. "Shrink at Least 4 National Monuments and Modify a Half-Dozen Others, Zinke Tells Trump." *Washington Post*, September 17, 2017.

Fischman, Robert L. 2005. "Cooperative Federalism and Natural Resources Law." *NYU Environmental Law Journal* 14(1): 179-231.

Flynn, Sarah, and Thomas I. Gunton. 1996. "Resolving Natural Resource Conflicts through Alternative Dispute Resolution: A Case Study of the Timber Fish Wildlife Agreement in Washington State." *Environment* 23(2): 101-112.

Ford, Jamie K., and Erick Giles. 2015. "Climate Change Adaptation in Indian Country: Tribal Regulation of Reservation Lands and Natural Resources." *William Mitchell Law Review* 41(2): 519-551.

Fortunate Eagle, Adam. 1992. *Alcatraz! Alcatraz! The Indian Occupation of 1969–1971.* Berkeley: Heyday Books.

Fowler, Catherine S., Pauline Esteves, Grace Goad, Bill Helmer, and Ken Watterson. 2003. "Caring for the Trees: Restoring Timbisha Shoshone Land Management Practices in Death Valley National Park." *Ecological Restoration* 21(4): 302-306.

Great Lakes Indian Fish and Wildlife Commission. 2019. "Treaty Rights Recognition and Affirmation." Accessed November 12, 2019. https://www.glifwc.org/Recognition_Affirmation/.

Harvard Project on American Indian Economic Development. 2008. *The State of the Native Nations: Conditions under U.S. Policies of Self-Determination.* New York: Oxford University Press.

Hegyi, Nate. 2017. "Blackfeet Hesitant about Proposed National Monument at Badger-Two Medicine." *Montana Public Radio*, October 19, 2017. https://www.mtpr.org/post/blackfeet-hesitant-about-proposed-national-monument-badger-two-medicine.

Jackson, Ted. 2016. "Stay or Go? Isle de Jean Charles Families Wrestle with the Sea. *Times Picayune*, September 13, 2016. http://www.nola.com/weather/index.ssf/2016/09/stay_or_go_isle_de_jean_charles_families_wrestle_with_the_sea.html.

King, Mary Ann. 2007. "Co-Management or Contracting? Agreements between Native American Tribes and the U.S. National Park Service Pursuant to the 1994 Tribal Self-Governance Act." *Harvard Environmental Law Review* 31(2): 475-530.

Maldonado, Julie K., Christine Shearer, Robin Bronen, Kristina Peterson, and Heather Lazrus. 2013. "The Impact of Climate Change on Tribal Communities in the US: Displacement, Relocation, and Human Rights." *Climatic Change* 120(3): 601-614.

Marshall, Bob. 2016. "The People of Isle de Jean Charles Aren't the Country's First Climate Refugees." *The Lens*, December 6, 2016. http://thelensnola.org/2016/12/06/the-people-of-isle-de-jean-charles-arent-the-countrys-first-climate-refugees.

Martin, Amy. 2018. "An Alaskan Village Is Falling into the Sea. Washington Is Looking the Other Way." *Public Radio International*, October 22, 2018. https://www.pri.org/stories/2018-10-22/alaskan-village-falling-sea-washington-looking-other-way.

McClurken, James M. 2000. *Fish in the Lakes, Wild Rice, and Game in Abundance: Testimony on Behalf of Mille Lacs Ojibwe Hunting and Fishing Rights.* East Lansing: Michigan State Press.

Murphy, Kim. 2009. "An Indian Reservation on the Move." *Los Angeles Times*, February 1, 2009. http://articles.latimes.com/2009/feb/01/nation/na-hoh-reservation1.

Nie, Martin. 2008. "The Use of Co-Management and Protected Land-Use Designations to Protect Tribal Cultural Resources and Reserved Treaty Rights on Federal Lands." *Natural Resources Journal* 48(3): 1-63.

Organisation for Economic Co-operation and Development. 2007. *OECD Glossary of Statistical Terms.* Paris: Organisation for Economic Co-operation and Development.

Pevar, Stephen L. 2012. *The Rights of Indians and Tribes.* 4th ed. New York: Oxford University Press.

Pinel, Sandra L., and Jacob Pecos. 2012. "Generating Co-Management at Kasha Katuwe Tent Rocks National Monument, New Mexico." *Environmental Management* 49(3): 593-604.

Richards, Kent. 2005. "The Stevens Treaties of 1854-1855." *Oregon Historical Quarterly* 106(3): 342-350.

Royster, Judith V. 1995. "The Legacy of Allotment." *Arizona State Law Journal* 27(1): 1-78.

Ruple, John C., Robert B. Keiter, and Andrew Ognibene. 2016. *National Monuments and National Conservation Areas: A Comparison in Light of the Bears Ears Proposal.* White Paper No. 2016-02. Salt Lake City: Wallace Stegner Center.

Singleton, Sara. 1998. *Constructing Cooperation: The Evolution of Institutions of Comanagement.* Ann Arbor: University of Michigan Press.

Smith, Jane M. 2013. *Tribal Jurisdiction over Nonmembers: A Legal Overview.* Washington, DC: Congressional Research Service.

Spaeder, Harvey A., and Joseph J. Feit. 2005. "Co-Management and Indigenous Communities: Barriers and Bridges to Decentralized Resource Management— Introduction." *Anthropologica* 47(2): 147-154.

Spanne, Autumn. 2016. "The Lucky Ones: Native American Tribe Receives $48m to Flee Climate Change." *The Guardian*, March 23, 2016. https://www.theguardian.com/ environment/2016/mar/23/native-american-tribes-first-nations-climate-change- environment-indican-removal-act.

Strommer, Geoffrey D., and Stephen D. Osborne. 2014. "The History, Status, and Future of Tribal Self-Governance under the Indian Self-Determination and Education Assistance Act." *American Indian Law Review* 39(1): 1-75.

US Government Accountability Office. 2018. *Broadband Internet: FCC's Data Overstate Access on Tribal Lands.* GAO-18-630. Washington, DC: US Government Accountability Office.

Wessendorf, Kathrin. 2011. *The Indigenous World 2011.* Copenhagen: International Work Group for Indigenous Affairs. https://www.iwgia.org/images/publications/0454_THE_ INDIGENOUS_ORLD-2011_eb.pdf.

Wilkins, David E., and Heidi Kiiwetinepinesiik Stark. 2011. *American Indian Politics and the American Political System.* 3rd ed. Lanham, MD: Rowman & Littlefield.

Chapter 15
Western Rebellion
Who Owns the West?

CHRISTOPHER A. SIMON, ERIKA ALLEN WOLTERS,
AND BRENT S. STEEL

INTRODUCTION

Many rural western groups have been active in promoting county and local control over federal public lands. The movement has been called "county supremacy," and it is considered to be a foundation of the wise use movement. The beginnings of this movement can be found during the early 1900s, when the federal government began reserving public lands and developing water supplies for settlements (High Country News 2016). The movement ramped up during the Sagebrush Rebellion of the 1970s, when Congress passed the Endangered Species Act, the Clean Water Act, the Clean Air Act, and other environmental legislation that affected how public lands are managed in the West. At the basis of this movement is the notion that management of federal public lands should emphasize "a preference for extractive (e.g., mining, oil drilling) or utilitarian (e.g., grazing) uses over ecological, scenic, wildlife, or aesthetic values" (Pollution Issues 2019). This chapter discusses the law and policy context of western rebellion and then provides some case studies to illustrate the dynamics of the conflict.

LAW AND POLICY CONTEXT

The evolution of laws and policy governing public land management has been shaped by the values of policy actors, contextual considerations and circumstances, and the dynamics of policymaking. Land management has played a prominent role in the United States since its colonial period. The vast tracts of wilderness that greeted the early European colonists, who either bartered, often in bad faith, for land ownership or confiscated land from Native American tribes through force of arms, were then organized into privately owned parcels and lands reserved for public purposes, such as government lands for public schools. The Land Ordinance of 1785 and the Northwest Ordinance of 1787 are two early examples of land policy in the United States. Many individuals known through historical accounts as the founders—white European American men such as Thomas Jefferson and James Madison— played a prominent role in shaping the new laws governing land policy as it related to US territorial expansion.

The founders and those white European American men who followed were driven by a vision to expand the United States through territorial expansion into western lands controlled or influenced by European powers, such as France and Spain, and inhabited by indigenous native peoples. Through the Louisiana Purchase in 1803, the United States acquired from France approximately 827,000 square miles of land, and the US victory in the Mexican War of 1846-1848 resulted in the expansion of US lands by approximately 529,000 square miles. Enormous pressure was left to bear on land policy enactments governing the organization and parceling out of public lands to private individuals and states. In the case of lands ceded after the Mexican War and lands purchased from Mexico, the passage of the Homestead Act of 1862, the General Mining Law of 1872, and the Taylor Grazing Act of 1934 played prominent roles in the governing of the vast amount of acquired territory.

The values of political actors during this period were largely shaped by a desire to significantly increase the size and influence of the United States. Circumstances of the time period were largely shaped by the needs of a rapidly growing nation with a high demand for agricultural resources for domestic civilian use, to feed and clothe an increasingly powerful military, and for export to overseas markets. Resources extracted through mining were also in high demand—metals for building materials or for use in coinage for economic exchange or demanded purely for numismatic value, and extracted subsurface or surface fuel resources used as energy sources for heating or for powering equipment. Land management law was therefore largely intent on creating those mechanisms necessary to meet social and economic demands through distribution policy.

HOMESTEAD ACT OF 1862

The Homestead Act of 1862 distributed free, publicly held land to settlers who agreed to build a home on it and farm the land for a minimum of five years. Each settler was offered 160 acres of land. After the five-year period elapsed, the settler could purchase the land for $1.25 per acre. In the century that followed passage of the act, nearly four million individuals lay claim to more than a quarter billion acres of public land that would eventually become private land under the terms of the Homestead Act.

Not all of the available lands were claimed under the Homestead Act. Some lands were not farmable owing to poor soil quality and lack of readily available sources of water, thus making it nearly impossible to raise sufficient food to support a family or for commercial purposes. Other lands were not available for claim staking because they had been designated as public lands, national parks, or national forests, or they were reserved for military reservations or designated as Native American reservation land. Military reservations were often sited on lands of strategic importance with access to needed resources. Conversely, Native American reservations were often sited on less valuable land with more limited resource availability (see Simon 2015).

GENERAL MINING LAW OF 1872

In the nearly eight years following the discovery of gold in California, there were no federal laws or regulations governing mining on public lands. The gold miners in California were, for the most part, operating on US-occupied land following the Mexican War, yet without federal laws in place, it was impossible to regulate gold mining claims, and without a well-ordered regulatory bureaucracy, royalties were not paid to the federal treasury for the extraction of a valuable public resource used for private commercial purposes. Two other landmark federal statutes—the Lode Mining Act of 1866 and the Placer Mining Act of 1870—preceded the General Mining Law of 1872, which still governs mining on public lands in the West.

The 1872 law established the process and costs associated with staking a claim. Mining claims involve surface rights to mining development and subsurface rights to mineral exploration. As per the 1872 law, mining claims involve annual payment of between $2.50 and $5.00 per acre. While Congress has attempted to impose royalty charges on hard-rock minerals extracted by miners, the bills have failed to gain passage. As a result, miners and mining corporations do not pay royalties on the precious minerals extracted from beneath public lands (US Department of the Interior 2019). Depending on the nature of ownership—in other words, if the mining concern holds title to lands being mined—miners or mining corporations may be subject to state and local property taxes. While royalties are not paid, hard-rock miners and mining corporations are subject to income taxes on the goods they produce and sell. In the case of fossil fuel exploration, however, extractive resource firms do pay a nominal royalty (Bowlin 2019).

As a policy designed to distribute public goods to private concerns, the General Mining Law has been effectively reformed or curtailed through the passage of other landmark legislation. The Mineral Leasing Act of 1920, for example, more clearly defined mineral development by separating claim staking of previously unknown mineral deposits from the development of known mineral deposits. The 1920 law established that the latter would be subject to a competitive leasing process. Additionally, the 1920 law developed rules governing the management of petroleum and gas, which would be subject to royalty payment based on their gross value (see Bernell and Simon 2016). Subsequent to the law's passage, presidential directives and the Department of Interior, which governs public lands, have established rules to protect lands and promote conservation of resources. While there were laws governing the extraction of hard-rock minerals and petroleum and gas resources, the Minerals Materials Act of 1947 allowed for the extraction of sand and gravel resources. These resources became particularly important in the postwar period. Sand and gravel are important components for the development of roads and the manufacture of building materials such as concrete. Despite the passage of landmark legislation, such as the Federal Land Policy and Management Act of 1976, which sought to restrict environmentally harmful mining practices, critics would argue that the evolution from near-pure distributive policy to one that focuses on the social and environmental costs of extractive industries has been far too slow and offers much in the way of recompense via royalty to the general public.

TAYLOR GRAZING ACT OF 1934

The Taylor Grazing Act of 1934 is a distributive policy that provided for the grazing of privately owned livestock on public lands. Under the Homestead Act, not all available lands were able to support a family of homesteaders owing to the quality of the land and the lack of a readily available source of water and timber needed to construct homes, outbuildings, and other structures for farm development, fuel, and sustainability. Some of these lands, however, were suitable for rangeland for livestock grazing with sufficient sources of water, and federal policy was created to provide for a grazing permit system. With access to these grazing lands, ranchers and farmers were able to provide additional feed to their livestock so as to make homesteading in semiarid or arid regions more feasible.

Through a permitting process, grazing rights were based on available feed and restrictions on the number of animal units allowed to graze on various grazing tracts. In the case of cattle grazing, for instance, an "animal unit" is considered to be one cow and her calf. The intent was to limit the possibility of overgrazing and land and vegetation degradation. The permitting process did not grant a property right to the permit holder—it simply provided access to a resource under strict terms. The permits are "non-transferable and revocable . . . granted for a period of 10 years, and may be renewed" (US Department of the Interior 1959, p. 204).

The Taylor Grazing Act, which is administered by the Bureau of Land Management, was intended to provide access to grazing lands, but it was also believed that the quality of the land would be improved through the permit process. Permit holders were required to maintain fencing and water availability through wells and reservoirs, and they would be reimbursed for these improvements by subsequent permit holders. The improvement of a grazing tract through good grazing management would likely lead to increased animal units permitted to graze on a grazing tract, which meant more money in the pockets of a livestock rancher (Donahue 2000).

Policies such as the Homestead Act, the General Mining Law, and the Taylor Grazing Act established new policy constituencies who benefitted from federal policy governing the public lands of the western United States. Farmers, miners, and ranchers owed their livelihood to these largely distributive policies. Federal agencies tasked with managing the distribution of these public goods imposed limited restrictions on their clientele, in large part because there were limited statutory powers granted to the agencies to do so. Additionally, the public lands of the West, while mostly governed by the federal government although there are state lands as well, were overlaid by maps of political representation—local, state, and federal politicians represented the constituent interests of farmers, miners, and ranchers in local, state, and federal government. In 1934, the year the Taylor Grazing Act gained passage, forty of the then ninety-six senators represented states that contained the grazing lands. While the population-based representation in the US House of Representatives was certainly not in their favor, the nature of politics and political compromise meant that western states were able to protect the increasingly powerful interests who had a stake in maintaining the status quo in the land management arena. State legislatures, too, were constructed to protect the interests of ranchers, miners, and ranchers. Until the 1970s, state senate representation was often based on geography rather than population, thus overrepresenting the rural interests of agricultural and extraction-based industries and effectively shielding them from the often progressive-minded reformers in the cities.

PUBLIC LAND MANAGEMENT IN THE 1970S AND BEYOND: A SHIFT TOWARD GREATER ENVIRONMENTAL REGULATION

The 1970s witnessed a growing concern about environmental quality. Rachel Carson's landmark book *Silent Spring* (1962) detailed the horrors of environmental degradation in the United States and reflected the values of the post-World War II generation. The National Environmental Policy Act of 1969 (NEPA) established federal standards governing the impacts of human activity on the environment. NEPA encompasses a wide range of environmental issues to include both natural and human-made environments in urban as well as rural areas in relation to air, land, and waterways. In the case of public lands, NEPA served as the starting point of a broad policy dialogue about the nature of public lands and their use. Whereas nearly a century of policy had focused on the distribution of public lands for private use, the policy dialogue now shifted toward issues of marginal social and environmental costs associated with private activities on public lands. This shift, as rapid as it was, was undoubtedly enhanced by a shift in public values reflected through the entrance of often young and enthusiastic progressively minded institutional actors into elected office, and the rise of powerful environmental interest groups.

Within a dozen years of the passage of NEPA, several other environmental laws were passed that had a direct impact on the use of public lands for private purposes. Included among those landmark federal laws were the Clean Air Act of 1970, the Endangered Species Act of 1973, and the Clean Water Act of 1977. Other landmark laws of the period, although not always directly related to public lands policy, include the Occupational Safety and Health Act of 1970 and the Comprehensive Environmental Response, Compensation, and Liability Act of 1980 (known as CERCLA or Superfund). Late to the move toward increased environmental regulation was the Pollution Prevention Act of 1990. All of these laws can count NEPA as their parent law in moving public land management policy from purely distributive toward a greater focus on regulation of use (see Simon 2017).

One of the purposes of regulation is to impose on the private sector the true cost of accessing a public good. In other words, regulation was intended to recover for human society, nonhuman species, and the environment the marginal social and environmental costs imposed by the private sector when it uses public goods in the pursuit of profit. Coincidentally or not, the first moves toward a "wise use" reaction by farmers, ranchers, and miners occurred following the passage and implementation of 1970s environmental regulations. The wise use movement intended to reverse progressive public land management policies of the 1970s and 1990s, effectively returning the US public land management to its nineteenth-century laissez faire distributive policy roots.

The passage of landmark environmental legislation took a brief hiatus during the Reagan administration. Reagan was a strong supporter of free market economics and distributive policy approaches in the use of public lands and natural resources. With a Republican-controlled Senate from 1981 to 1987, progressive public land management advances were stymied. Reagan appointed conservatives to head the Department of Interior—James Watt, followed by William Clark and Donald Hodel. Reagan's first appointee to head the Environmental Protection Agency (established in 1970) was Buford, who sought to reduce federal regulation of environmental quality.

The 1990s, however, led to a major shift back to the priorities established in the 1970s, albeit constrained by the Republican resurgence in the 1994 congressional elections. A baby boomer-era progressive governor, William J. Clinton, was elected to the presidency in 1992. President Clinton appointed Bruce Babbitt to serve as US Secretary of the Interior. Babbitt, an ardent environmentalist, focused a great deal of attention on reforming the Mining Law of 1872 and Taylor Grazing Act of 1934. In terms of mining reform, Babbitt sought an increase in the royalties and fees paid by mining companies to the US government, as the royalty and fee schedule had not changed in nearly 120 years. Babbitt expressed similar concerns about grazing fees. Babbitt argued that neither miners nor ranchers were covering the marginal social and environmental costs associated with their activities. Particularly in the case of mining, Babbitt's policy reforms focused on nonrenewable high-value resources practically being given away to private profit-driven firms. A pro-business Republican-controlled Congress in the late 1990s meant that Babbitt's efforts to reform mining law and grazing policy fell on deaf ears in the national legislature (CNN 1998).

Clinton and Babbitt's efforts to catalogue biodiversity in the United States were also constrained. In 1993, Secretary Babbitt created the National Biological Survey (NBS). An idea first conceived in the late 1970s, NBS was to be a new agency headed by personnel from existing federal agencies such as the FWS, BLM, NPS, and USGS (Krahe, 2011). The primary mission of the NBS was of "collecting, analyzing, and disseminating scientific data without any entanglement in the regulatory and managerial responsibilities of its sister agencies" (Krahe, 2011). In reality, the agency suffered from not being managed by seasoned administrative leadership, budget constraints, and a lack of administrative cover provided by more established administrative agencies. The agency survived the Republican 104th Congress and actually grew in terms of budget following its relocation to the National Park Service, which provided experienced administrative leadership (Wagner 1999). Now called the Biological Resources Discipline (formerly known as the Biological Resources Division), the agency focuses on wildlife conservation through "consultation, technical assistance, and policy guidance to manage native and exotic wildlife species in parks," as well as provides animal health services and manages national park landscapes (Biological Resources Division 2019).

While Congress has failed to act on mining and grazing reforms, in part because of well-organized business interests in the mining, oil and gas, and livestock industries, the president has discretionary policy tools to be used for the protection of public lands. The Antiquities Act of 1906, which was signed into law by President Theodore Roosevelt, authorizes the president "to declare by public proclamation historic landmarks, historic and prehistoric structures, and other objects of historic or scientific interest that are situated upon the lands that are owned or controlled by the Government of the United States to be national monuments."[1] Since the passage of the act, "16 presidents have designated 157 national monuments under this authority" (National Parks Conservation Authority 2019). In 2017, in a highly controversial move, President Trump used the power of executive order to reduce the size of Bears Ears and Grand Staircase–Escalante National Monuments, a move that was supported by extraction industries (Lipton and Friedman 2018). In response to Trump's actions, New Mexico Senator Tom Udall and

Representative Debra Haaland introduced legislation to prevent presidential action to reduce the size of national monuments (Udall 2019).

In the 1980s and 1990s, the management of publicly owned forest witnessed one of the most successful efforts to reduce the impact of extractive industries on public lands and to direct policy to reduce marginal social and environmental costs. In 1987, a citizen petitioned the US Fish and Wildlife Service (FWS) to list the northern spotted owl as an endangered species. In that same year, FWS determined that such a listing was not needed because the owl was not threatened with extinction. The decision led to the 1988 case *Northern Spotted Owl v. Hodel*,[2] in which a US district court judge determined that the FWS did not conduct a proper study in arriving at its conclusions about the owl and its status as a threatened or endangered species. The court ordered that further and proper scientific study was needed prior to any conclusive decision.

After further study, the federal agency found that the northern spotted owl was threatened. As was found in further court decisions at the district court level and at the Ninth Circuit Court of Appeals, however, the agency response to this finding did not follow proper administrative procedure and was unlawful and inadequate. In making their determination that the owl was threatened, federal land and wildlife management agencies had failed to define the owl's habitat, a critical aspect of protecting the owl from extinction. Furthermore, the guidelines for timber sales that might threaten owl habitat (the owl nests in old-growth forests in California, the Pacific Northwest, and parts of Arizona, Colorado, New Mexico, and Utah). In further court action, *Northern Spotted Owl v. Lujan*,[3] a US district court in Washington State found that in order to adequately protect the owl, further sales of timber on public lands within its habitat region would be halted. Through judicial action, a major shift in public land management was accomplished (Sher 1993; Verner et al. 1992).

FROM SAGEBRUSH REBELLION TO MILITIA: CONFLICT IN THE WEST

The evolution of land management in western states from one of distributive to regulatory policy (Simon 2015) has instilled deep divisions among some in the West whose livelihoods depend on unfettered resource use. The Endangered Species Act (ESA), access to federal lands for grazing, water rights, and other challenges have come to a head in the last two decades with a new iteration of Sagebrush Rebels taking up the call to push back against a government they feel is overstepping its reach. The first Sagebrush Rebellions largely took place in the '70s and '80s as a reaction to the regulatory restrictions of laws like the Federal Land Policy and Management Act of 1976 (FLPMA) and the ESA of 1973, but rebellions in the '90s and that continue today have become decidedly more confrontational and violent. The Sagebrush Rebellions of the '70s and '80s worked within the political process (even getting tacit support from President Reagan), and the rebellions of today work against the authority of the federal government by challenging the political process and even the constitutional authority in which laws were formed.

The following sections provide a brief review of recent, arguably more memorable, Sagebrush Rebellions. These cases illustrate the mounting frustration of resource-dependent individuals and communities over government regulation and oversight. They also demonstrate that there is a strong constituency (including local governments and law enforcement) that is sympathetic or supportive of these rebellions, casting a new light on the legal implications and consequences of the rebellions.

Klamath Water War

In 1988, the endangered species listing of the Lost River sucker and shortnose suckerfish went unopposed (and with minimal attention) by the California Department of Fish and Game, the City of Klamath Falls, and the Oregon Department of Fish and Wildlife (Doremus and Tarlock 2008). Almost a decade later (in 1997), Coho salmon were listed as threatened in the Klamath Basin. In 2001, after a particularly harsh drought season, water scarcity in the Klamath Basin forced a state of emergency in the region. The species previously listed under the ESA suddenly took on new significance for the Bureau of Reclamation (as well as for local farmers, ranchers, commercial fishers, and tribes), which had a legal requirement under Section 7 of the ESA that prohibited "any federal actions that further jeopardize a listed species" (Gosnell and Kelly 2010, p. 369). In the spring of 2001, the Bureau of Reclamation (BOR) in the Klamath Basin submitted a biological assessment of projected water management in the region for consultation (under Section 7 of the ESA) with the FWS and the National Marine Fisheries Service (NMFS). Both the FWS and NMFS "issued biological opinions that required the BOR to take a number of controversial actions, including the maintenance of higher water levels in Upper Klamath Lake (for the suckers) and higher in-stream flow levels in the Klamath River below the Iron Gate Dam (for the Coho)" (Gosnell and Kelly 2010, p. 369). In response, the BOR essentially cut off irrigation water to the 1,400 farms in the region, thus signaling the beginning of a water war in the Klamath Basin.

The decision to cut off the irrigation headgates in Klamath Falls, Oregon, in order to maintain water in the Upper Klamath Lake to protect the endangered suckerfish became the foundation of the modern Sagebrush Rebellion movement (Wentz 2001). Irrigators saw the move by the BOR as an effort to put fish over people and to reallocate water that many irrigators believed they had a legal right to (although four tribes in the region had senior water rights that allow them to maintain water levels to support fish populations for their use under existing treaty rights). The decision affected more than a thousand farmers with projected financial losses of "hundreds of millions of dollars" (Southern Poverty Law Center 2001). The farmers, incensed by the water cutoff and having failed to convince the courts that they would suffer substantial economic harm for a disputable biological solution to protect suckerfish, took matters into their own hands.

Protest began almost immediately after the water shutoff, with nationwide coverage of the event bringing supporters to the region to help the embattled farmers. In May, a symbolic "bucket brigade" was convened with thousands (estimates range from 10,000 to 13,000) of supporters drawing water from a nearby lake to distribute to the dry irrigation canals. Tensions continued to rise when in July "hundreds of farmers and their supporters used torches and crowbars to open the head gates of an irrigation canal four times in one week" (Clarren 2001). The presence of federal agents, who were guarding the headgates, set in motion other ways to illegally obtain water; namely, laying a pipeline to transport water from Upper Klamath Lake to irrigators (Clarren 2001).

Protests continued throughout the summer of 2001, as did legal challenges, but after the September 11th attacks, the focus on the Klamath water crisis began to wane (Southern Poverty Law Center 2001). With nonlocal antigovernment protesters gone from the region, the local farmers and ranchers agreed to a suspension of protests in order to try to negotiate an agreement with the government to resolve the water crisis. While efforts have been made (and even agreements reached) to find a manageable, equitable solution for all interests in the Klamath Basin (farmers, ranchers, commercial fisheries, tribes, and environmentalists), to date there is no water management agreement in place that could help avoid another economic, ecological, and cultural loss to the region.

It is estimated that farmers lost more than $35 million as a result of the irrigation water shutoff in 2001 (Jaeger 2004). While other stakeholders (tribes, commercial fisheries, etc.) certainly sustained losses, ranchers and farmers believed that the actions by the BOR were particularly misguided. The impacts to the broader community were also felt with dwindling supplies at food banks, shuttered businesses, and declining school enrollments (Clarren 2001). The hostility between stakeholders further affected the community with a breakdown of civility and fears over personal safety (Clarren 2001).

The protests that occurred in the Klamath Basin were in response to an event that affected the main industries and communities in the region. Illegal actions were taken by ranchers and farmers (and their supporters) in a desperate effort to provide relief from both the drought and withheld water. And the shutdown did little to reduce the antigovernment sentiment in the region that Sagebrush Rebellions are founded on. It is unsurprising, then, that one of the most notorious Sagebrush Rebellions, the Malheur Wildlife Refuge occupation, happened a few hundred miles away from Klamath Falls. But the differences between the rebellions are stark.

Fire Starters to Occupiers

In 2012, Oregon ranchers Dwight and Steven Hammond (father and son) were convicted on multiple counts of arson on federal land. The first incident occurred in 2001 in what became known as the Hardie-Hammond Fire in the Steens Mountain Cooperative Management and Protection Area in Oregon (land managed by the Bureau of Land Management, or BLM). The Hammonds intentionally started a fire in the area in an effort to cover up an illegal deer hunt (which several witnesses corroborated). The Hammonds claimed that the fire, which burned more than 139 acres of federal land, was done to control invasive species. In reality, the fire "destroyed all evidence of the game violations" (US Department of Justice 2015), which was the intent of the fire.

The second fire, the Krumbo Butte Fire in the Malheur National Wildlife Refuge, occurred in 2006. Although a burn ban was in effect (and firefighters were busy putting out wildfires in other parts of the refuge due to lightning strikes), Steven Hammond started multiple backfires to save the ranch's winter feed (US Department of Justice 2015). The illegal backfires, which spread onto nearby public land, were conducted without consultation or notification of the BLM and presented an additional concern (and a safety threat) to firefighters already combating fires in the refuge.

Under the law, the Hammonds were to receive a five-year minimum mandatory sentence for their convictions. But the federal district judge presiding over the case found the mandatory sentencing "grossly disproportionate to the crimes" (Freda 2016), instead sentencing Dwight Hammond to three months and Steven Hammond to a year (Freda 2016). A federal appeals court, however, determined that the Hammonds were to be resentenced based on the ill-founded leniency the lower court applied when it did not uphold the minimum mandatory sentence. The Hammonds were then sentenced to the mandatory five years (with time served).

The convictions for these two fires represented the tip of the iceberg with regard to the Hammonds' illegal actions. Court records show that the Hammonds set many fires, threatened federal officers and employees, and impeded efforts of BLM firefighters. In short, the Hammonds consistently and regularly engaged in illegal activities to fulfill their own goals or to coerce federal officials into backing down with threat of violence. Even so, the Hammonds became the government "victims" that antigovernment groups could rally around.

The resentencing of the Hammonds in 2015 was the spark that ignited one of the most notorious Sagebrush Rebellions in the West, the occupation of the Malheur Wildlife Refuge in Oregon. For roughly five weeks beginning in January 2016, militants, led by Ammon Bundy, took over the Malheur Wildlife Refuge in protest of the Hammonds' sentencing and more broadly to challenge federal land management in the West. The protestors believed that the federal government did not have constitutional authority to maintain the land. Instead, they demanded the land be turned over to the states so the local governments could determine how to manage it. What started out as a protest in the town of Burns, Oregon, took an unexpected turn when organizers encouraged supporters to occupy the refuge.

The occupation of Malheur continued for a total of forty-one days, into early February 2016. During this time, militant occupiers (later known as Citizens for Constitutional Freedom) demanded the release of the Hammonds and that the federal government turn the Malheur National Forest over to residents so they could extract and utilize the natural resources of the forest for the local economy. Interestingly, neither the Hammonds nor even many people in the local community supported the militants in their occupation.

The lack of planning left the occupiers in a difficult position. But the government, wanting to avoid another Waco or Ruby Ridge, was hesitant to respond. The occupiers of the refuge sought to conflate their support by stating that 150 armed militia were on-site (Odinson 2016), but an on-site reporter counted between 20 and 25 (Zaitz 2016). Attempts at negotiations failed, and efforts by the occupiers to incite a reaction by the government (by purportedly removing fences, utilizing refuge vehicles, and vandalizing property) did little to garner sympathy for their cause. Opposition to the occupation from locals, other anti-government groups, as well as opponents in Oregon and Idaho who held rallies calling for an end to the occupation made clear the lack of broad support that the militants claimed to have.

During the occupation, militants were generally given the freedom to travel to and from the refuge. On January 26, however, several of the leaders of the occupation, including Ammon Bundy, were intercepted on their way to a public talk in John Day, Oregon. While Ammon Bundy and others were taken into custody without incident, another leader, LaVoy Finicum, was shot and killed as he was reaching for a weapon in his jacket. With most of the momentum taken out of the occupation, the remaining occupiers were cut off from supplies and from use of electronics, leading to their eventual surrender on February 11, 2016.

In total, twenty-six people were indicted for the occupation of the Malheur National Wildlife Refuge. Of those, there were a handful of convictions, but many were acquitted or had their case dismissed. Ammon Bundy was among those acquitted, leaving many to feel that justice was not served and, perhaps more concerning, setting a precedent for (and emboldening) anti-government groups who disagree with federal land ownership in the West.

With the election of President Trump, antigovernment Sagebrush Rebels found an ally. President Trump has worked to deregulate federal land, reduce federal land holdings (such as Bears Ears and Grand Staircase–Escalante National Monuments), and appoint industry allies to top resource positions (such as Ryan Zinke as head of the Department of the Interior). With the appointment of Karen Budd-Falen, a private property rights advocate whose concept of property includes public lands adjacent to privately owned land (Thompson 2018), to deputy interior solicitor for wildlife and parks in July 2018, Trump in essence appointed an opponent of public land to oversee the protection of public land. (Notably, Budd-Falen also once defended Cliven Bundy in a case against the federal government; see Thompson 2018). Similarly, William Perry Pendley, who once advocated for the sale of federal lands, is the most recent acting director of the BLM.) Further, President Trump pardoned both Dwight and Steven

Hammond, with White House Press Secretary Sarah Huckabee Sanders stating the resentencing of the Hammonds was "unjust" and "overzealous" (Sullivan and Turkewitz 2018). The end result of the occupation of the Malheur Refuge (which began over the imprisonment of the Hammonds) was minimal convictions and little, if any, deterrent from engaging in similar actions in the future. In early 2019, as Zinke was leaving office, he reinstated the original 26,000 acres of federal land in grazing rights to Steven and Dwight Hammond (Wilson). However, after an appeal by environmentalists, a federal judge revoked the grazing rights later that year.

Where to From Here?

The contrasts between the Klamath water war and the Malheur standoff are stark. In the Klamath, some farmers and ranchers took illegal action only after they had been denied water for their farms. Some would argue that these actions were taken out of necessity, as there was an impending financial loss to farmers and ranchers because of the shutoff. Protests to resume delivery of water to the farmers and ranchers focused on the inequitable favoritism for endangered fish versus the livelihood of the farmers and ranchers (recognizing, of course, that other stakeholders were affected; namely, the tribes and commercial fisheries).

In contrast, the Malheur occupation stemmed from illegal actions by the Hammonds on federal land. The Hammonds held grazing permits, which are essentially temporary access rights for a specific duration and under set guidelines; the Hammonds did not have ownership or the unrestricted use of federal land. The Hammonds' use of federal land as their own (starting fires, illegal hunting operations, etc.) inherently challenged the authority of the federal government to manage public lands in the West (although the matter of who should manage these lands is a sticking point for those arguing for local control considering the amount of money required to fight wildfires, manage the lands, etc.). It was not a reactive response to resource distribution for competing interest. Rather, it is a proactive move to establish a consistent pattern of undermining federal authority for the grander purpose of getting the federal government to relinquish control and ownership of western public lands.

Each of these cases drew the interest of anti-government militants who came to the regions to join and in some cases escalate the already tense situation. What is potentially concerning is the lack of accountability for these illegal actions. The pardoning of the Hammonds, the few (and minimal) convictions from the Malheur occupation, and a presidential administration that overtly supports the actions of anti-government groups could potentially set the stage for more violent and disruptive actions.

CONCLUSION

As climate change continues to alter the landscape of the western United States, access to resources has the potential to become far more combative. Extended and intense periods of drought, combined with more frequent and powerful wildfires, will further exacerbate conflict over available resources. Some groups, particularly anti-government groups, are busy trying to dismantle federal land ownership in the West, while other stakeholder groups (ranchers, farmers, tribes, environmentalists, etc.) are desperately trying to create an environment of sustainability for current and future use. The current presidential administration is only adding fuel to the already simmering fire by overtly supporting actions that undermine environmental protections or access to resources for tribes, suggesting that things could get much, much worse in the future.

Legal Citations

1 Antiquities Act of 1906, 16 U.S.C. §§ 431-433.
2 Northern Spotted Owl v. Hodel, 716 F. Supp. 479 (W.D. Wash. 1988), November 17, 1988.
3 Northern Spotted Owl v. Lujan, 758 F. Supp. 621 (W.D. Wash. 1991), February 26, 1991.

References

Bernell, David, and Christopher Simon. 2016. *The Energy Security Dilemma: US Policy and Practice.* New York: Routledge.

Biological Resources Division. 2019. "What We Do." Accessed May 24, 2019. https://www.nps.gov/orgs/1103/whatwedo.htm.

Bowlin, N. 2019. "Judge Orders Industries to Pay Royalties for Public Land Extraction." *High Country News,* April 25, 2019. https://www.hcn.org/articles/energy-and-industry-judge-orders-industries-to-pay-for-public-land-extraction.

Carson, Rachel. 1962. *Silent Spring.* Boston: Mariner Press.

Clarren, Rebecca. 2001. "No Refuge in the Klamath Basin." *High Country News,* August 13, 2001. https://www.hcn.org/issues/208/10647.

CNN. 1998. "Babbitt Pushes for Mining Law Reform." May 1, 1998. http://www.cnn.com/EARTH/9805/01/babbitt.mining/.

Donahue, Debra L. 2000. *The Western Range Revisited: Removing Livestock from Public Lands to Conserve Native Biodiversity.* Norman: University of Oklahoma Press.

Doremus, Holly, and A. Dan Tarlock. 2008. *Water War in the Klamath Basin: Macho Law, Combat Biology, and Dirty Politics.* Washington, DC: Island Press.

Freda, Kimberley. 2016. "Court Papers: Hammonds Entered Plea Deals Knowing Mandated Sentences Loomed." Oregon Public Broadcasting, January 19, 2016. https://www.opb.org/news/series/burns-oregon-standoff-bundy-militia-news-updates/hammonds-entered-plea-knowing-sentences-loomed/.

Gosnell, Hannah, and Erin Clover Kelly. 2010. "Peace on the River? Social-Ecological Restoration and Large Dam Removal in the Klamath Basin, USA." *Water Alternatives* 3(2): 361-383.

High Country News. 2016. "Forty Years of Sage Brush Rebellion." January 4, 2016. https://www.hcn.org/articles/sagebrush-rebellion.

Jaeger, William K. 2004. "Conflicts over Water in the Upper Klamath Basin and the Potential Role for Market-Based Allocations." *Journal of Agricultural and Resource Economics* 29(2): 167-184.

Krahe, Diane. 2011. "The Ill-Fated NBS: A Historical Analysis of Bruce Babbitt's Vision to Overhaul Interior Science." In *Rethinking Protected Areas in a Changing World: Proceedings of the 2011 George Wright Society Conference on Parks, Protected Areas, and Cultural Sites.* Retrieved June 22, 2020 from http://www.georgewright.org/1130krahe.pdf

Lipton, Eric, and Lisa Friedman. 2018. "Oil Was Central to Decision to Shrink Bears Ears Monument, Emails Show." *New York Times*, March 2, 2018. https://www.nytimes.com/2018/03/02/climate/bears-ears-national-monument.html.

National Parks Conservation Authority. 2017. "Monuments Protected under the Antiquities Act." January 13, 2017. https://www.npca.org/resources/2658-monuments-protected-under-the-antiquities-act.

Odinson, Baldr. 2016. "The Oregon Occupiers Are Simply Domestic Terrorists." *Newsweek*, January 4, 2016. https://www.newsweek.com/oregon-occupiers-are-simply-domestic-terrorists-411539.

Pollution Issues. 2019. "Wise-Use Movement." Accessed November 19, 2019. http://www.pollutionissues.com/Ve-Z/Wise-Use-Movement.html.

Sher, Victor M. 1993. "Travels with *Strix*: The Spotted Owl's Journey through the Federal Courts." *Public Land and Resources Law Review* 14: 41-79.

Simon, Christopher A. 2015. "A Crucible for Populist Resistance: Tracing the Roots of the Sagebrush Rebellion." In *Cities, Sagebrush, and Solitude: Urbanization and Cultural Conflict in the Great Basin*, edited by Dennis R. Judd and Stephanie L. Witt. Reno: University of Nevada Press.

Simon, Christopher A. 2017. *Public Policy: Preferences and Outcomes.* 3rd ed. New York: Routledge.

Southern Poverty Law Center. 2001. "Conflict in the Klamath: A Battle over Irrigation Rights in Oregon Becomes, for a Time, the Latest Flash Point for Antigovernment Activists." *Intelligence Report*, November 29, 2001. https://www.splcenter.org/fighting-hate/intelligence-report/2001/conflict-klamath.

Sullivan, Eileen, and Julie Turkewitz. 2018. "Trump Pardons Oregon Ranchers Whose Case Inspired Wildlife Refuge Takeover." *New York Times*, July 10, 2018. https://www.nytimes.com/2018/07/10/us/politics/trump-pardon-hammond-oregon.html.

Thompson, Jonathan. 2018. "Sagebrush Rebel Appointed to Interior Department." *High Country News*, October 15, 2018. https://www.hcn.org/issues/50.20/sagebrush-rebellion-sagebrush-rebel-karen-budd-falen-appointed-to-interior-department.

Udall, Tom. 2019. "Udall, Haaland Introduce Antiquities Act to Protect America's National Monuments from Unlawful Attacks." Accessed November 11, 2019. https://www.tomudall.senate.gov/news/press-releases/udall-haaland-introduce-antiquities-act-toprotect-americas-national-monuments-from-unlawful-attacks.

US Department of the Interior. 1959. *Department of the Interior Grazing Decisions, 1936-1958.* Washington, DC: US Government Printing Office.

US Department of the Interior. 2019. "Nonenergy Minerals." Accessed November 11, 2019. https://revenuedata.doi.gov/how-it-works/minerals/.

US Department of Justice. 2015. "Eastern Oregon Ranchers Convicted of Arson Resentenced to Five Years in Prison." October 7, 2015. https://www.justice.gov/usao-or/pr/eastern-oregon-ranchers-convicted-arson-resentenced-five-years-prison.

Verner, Jared, Kevin S. McKelvey, Barry R. Noon, R. J. Gutierrez, Gordon I. Gould Jr., and Thomas W. Beck. 1992. *The California Spotted Owl: A Technical Assessment of Its Current Status*. PSW-GTR-133. Albany, CA: Pacific Southwest Research Station, US Forest Service.

Wagner, Frederic H. 1999. "Whatever Happened to the National Biological Survey?" *BioScience* 49(3): 219-222.

Wentz, Patty. 2001. "The Good Americans: Is Klamath Falls the Wellspring of a New Sagebrush Rebellion?" *Willamette Week*, August 14, 2001. https://www.wweek.com/portland/article-261-the-good-americans.html.

Wilson, Conrad. 2019. "Oregon Ranchers Who Led to Wildlife Refuge Takeover Can Graze on Public Lands Again." Oregon Public Broadcasting, January 29, 2019. https://www.opb.org/news/article/oregon-ranchers-hammonds-grazing-rights-restored/.

Zaitz, Les. 2016. "Oregon Militant Leader Ammon Bundy Exudes Calm as He Presides over Occupation." *Oregonian*, January 3, 2016. https://www.oregonlive.com/pacific-northwest news/2016/01/ammon_bundy_exudes_calm_as_he.html.

Chapter 16
Conclusion
The Old West, the New West, and the Next West?

BRENT S. STEEL, ERIKA ALLEN WOLTERS,
AND REBECCA L. WARNER

INTRODUCTION

With the election of Donald Trump in 2016, many commentators have argued that the key to his success was the mobilization of rural and Rust Belt constituencies that felt disenfranchised, disconnected, and threatened from the current socioeconomic and political system (Cramer 2016a; Kurtzleben 2016). Rural communities arguably felt threatened by their perception of an establishment of political and media elites in urban areas dominating the national policy agenda that ignore their more traditional and conservative values and beliefs. Cramer's *The Politics of Resentment: Rural Consciousness in Wisconsin and the Rise of Scott Walker* (2016b) and Hochschild's *Strangers in Their Own Land: Anger and Morning on the American Right* (2016) both document the resentment and anger of many on the right and within rural communities with governmental and media elites. As Cramer (2016a) comments after some follow-up research for her book,

> since 2007, I have been inviting myself into conversations in rural Wisconsin to try to understand how people in such communities are making sense of politics. I have been listening in during early morning coffee klatches in gas stations that serve coffee, in diners, and in churches. The resentment I uncovered predates Trump, but it set the stage for his ascendance . . .What I found was resentment of an intensity and specificity that surprised me. The pervasiveness of resentment toward the cities and urban elites, as well as urban

institutions like government and the media, was inescapable after several visits to these groups.

Cramer found that the politics of resentment in rural communities is "fueled by political strategy . . . more casually called notions of 'us' and 'them'" (2016a, p. 8). This rural consciousness can lead to resentment toward the urban "liberal elite" (them), who they believe make policy decisions that disadvantage and exclude rural voices (us). Cramer (2016b) argues that place-based identity is a strong driving force, with three major perceptions coming together to form rural consciousness: (1) that policymakers ignore rural areas, (2) that rural areas do not get their fair share of resources, and (3) that rural folks have fundamentally distinct values and lifestyles that are misunderstood and disrespected by urbanites. As discussed in many of the chapters in this book, rural consciousness takes on an especially anti-government perspective in the western United States, where the rural-urban divide over the management of public lands has led to timber, water, ranching, and salmon "wars" the last several decades, often with government agency scientists and managers at the center of the conflict (Clucas et al. 2011; Johnson and Swanson 2009; Wolters and Steel 2015). The anti-science themes evident in Trump's presidential campaign along with his pro-resource extraction cabinet appointments have resonated well in many western rural communities that feel as though they are under siege by environmental laws and policies (Volcovici 2017).

Two competing natural resource management paradigms resonate throughout most of the chapters in this collection and reflect the rural-urban divide concerning the management of western public lands (or what Lybecker calls the "Old West" versus the "New West" in chap. 1). These conflicting management paradigms have been labeled by Brown and Harris (1992) as the "Dominant Resource Management Paradigm" and the "New Resource Management Paradigm" (see table 16.1). The Dominant Resource Management Paradigm—often found in western rural communities—advocates the anthropocentric belief that the management of public lands ought to be directed toward the production of services beneficial to humans. The New Resource Management Paradigm has emerged more recently and grown in popularity since the 1970s. It has a more biocentric view toward public lands management that emphasizes maintaining intact all the elements of forest and rangeland ecosystems.

Table 15.1. Conflicting Natural Resource Management Paradigms

New Resource Management Paradigm [Biocentric]	Dominant Resource Management Paradigm [Anthropocentric]
Nature for its own sake.	Nature to produce goods and services primarily for human use.
Emphasizes environmental protection over commodity outputs.	Emphasizes commodity outputs over environmental protection.
General compassion for future generations (long-term perspective).	General compassion for this generation (short-term perspective).
Less intensive rangeland management; stream protection, less grazing, etc.	Intensive rangeland management; maintain traditional grazing practices.
Less intensive forest management; selective cutting, prescribed fire, watershed protection, etc.	Intensive forest management; clear-cuts, herbicides, slash burning, road building, fire suppression, etc.
Limits to resource use and growth; earth has a limited carrying capacity.	No resource shortages; science and technology will solve production problems.
New politics, consultative and participative.	Old politics, determination by the experts.
Decentralization and devolved decision making (e.g., collaborative governance).	Centralized and hierarchical decision making.

Source: Revised from Brown and Harris (1992).

As the New West becomes increasingly urbanized, urban populations are inclined to develop sympathy for wildlife, wilderness, old-growth forests, deserts, and other amenities found on public lands (Wolters and Steel 2015). Too often, however, we forget about the families and communities of the western rural periphery, about the value they attach to the rangeland, forests, and fish habitats that have provided for their livelihood. For their part, the residents of the rural periphery too often refuse to believe that the inexorable forces of societal change will require a fundamental change in how they will have to relate to the public lands and waters around them. Both sides in urban and rural spheres have much to learn and think through with respect to the management of public lands; there is ample room for better understanding in this relationship as well.

The editors of this book hope these essays will promote an informed and productive dialogue on the trade-offs associated with the rural-urban divide. Change has come rapidly to the West, showing little mercy for those caught in its grip. When we think of the state of Nevada being the most rural state about fifty years ago and now being one of the most highly urbanized, we begin to get a good sense of the scale and scope of change affecting our lives as citizens of the American West. Under the pressure of this type of change, we need to encourage and support efforts to promote public deliberation and dialogue.

THE NEXT WEST: COLLABORATIVE PROCESSES?

The New Resource Management Paradigm suggests that decentralization and devolved decision making are essential today given the complexity of natural resource management issues. One such approach is collaborative governance. Collaborative processes have had some success in mediating western US natural resource disputes between rural and urban interests concerning forest and rangeland management, public lands management, endangered species, and renewable energy siting (Weber et al. 2017). Collaborative approaches that involve significant public engagement with scientists, managers, and other stakeholders have been effective in helping to resolve conflict and integrating science into management decisions (Ansell and Gash 2008; Leach and Pelkey 2001; Weber 2003).

More specifically, Ansell and Gash (2007), Ostrom (2007,) and Weber et al. (2017) have identified antecedent conditions necessary for robust collaborative processes to develop as well as a list of principles that lead to effective collaborative network approaches to problem solving. Collaborative governance, as outlined by Ansell and Gash (2007, p. 543), is a governing system reliant upon "consensus-oriented decision making" while bringing together a variety of stakeholders—both private and public. Implicit in this definition is that networks of stakeholders instead of a singular entity make decisions for the public good (Ansell and Gash 2007, p. 3).

The frameworks created by Ostrom (2007), Ansell and Gash (2007), and Weber et al. (2017) each identify antecedent conditions for the collaborative process, respectively, including (1) sense of community, (2) historical context, and (3) a level playing field. Ostrom (2007, p. 28) identifies the first step in analyzing a situation is to identify the "action arena," which "refers to the social space where individuals interact, exchange goods and services, solve problems, dominate one another, or fight." Once the action arena is defined, such as a collaborative, Ostrom emphasizes the importance of understanding the physical and material conditions that affect the action arena. The physical world may dictate the possibility of certain actions and the probability of certain outcomes. Additionally, the physical world may also influence how actors (or stakeholders) act in certain situations (Ostrom 2007, p. 39). Finally, Ansell and Gash (2007), Ostrom (2007), and Weber et al. (2017) state that a level playing field is necessary for stakeholder networks to be functional. Inequality between stakeholders on the basis of capacity, organization, status, or resources can often lead to control by and bias toward the powerful. It is of utmost importance that stakeholders have the foundation and ability to be fully represented in a collaborative setting. Resource asymmetries are seen when stakeholders are unable to address highly technical problems owing to poor communication skills.

Credible commitment to the collaborative network, as defined by Weber et al. (2017), is necessary for successful collaborations because stakeholders are voluntarily cooperating with one another to reach a certain goal. One aspect of credible commitment is that participants are dedicated to facilitating meaningful action while considering and including existing livelihoods into planning. Additionally, Weber et al. (2017) identify eleven factors that contribute to effective collaborative networks: (1) inclusiveness, (2) technical expertise and beyond—integrating and applying a broad knowledge base, (3) formal binding of collective choice rules, (4) ongoing or repeat games, (5) credible commitment to collaboration, (6) a commonsense strategic approach to early problem-solving choices, (7) appropriate participant norms, (8) collaborative capacity-building leadership/champions, (9) shared expenses / cost sharing, (10) a focus on real-world results, and (11) sufficient autonomy of action.

Collaborative governance and partnerships may not be appropriate for all disputes over public lands given the large scale of issues and regulatory frameworks in place. In addition, academics, practitioners, and potential participants alike have harshly criticized collaboratives (Blumberg and Knuffke 1998; Britell 2019; Duane 1997; McCloskey 1996). For example, some environmental groups have been skeptical of collaboratives because of power and economic imbalances between themselves and industry as well as skepticism about local control over federal lands and the optimal use of science for sound management decisions (Britell 2019; Moldavi 1996). There is also a concern of becoming "co-opted" by other interests, thus leading to suboptimal management plans (Moldavi 1996). Further, with policies favoring mobility and lack of permanence of many agency staff, long-term collaborative work and community relationship building can become challenging. Finally, Bodin (2017, p. 1) states that "no single blueprint exists for how to succeed by using collaborative approaches to solve environmental problems," making each situation unique and requiring buy-in, trust building, and a development of a collaborative roadmap to facilitate a collaborative process to address public lands debates.

With the onslaught of climate change, however, the possibility of increased conflict over public lands as a result of drought, wildfire, insect outbreaks, higher temperatures, habitat loss, and other associated disturbances may require new ways of thinking and problem solving. As Beschta et al. (2013, p. 474) have warned:

> Climate change affects public land ecosystems and services throughout the American West and these effects are projected to intensify. Even if greenhouse gas emissions are reduced, adaptation strategies for public lands are needed to reduce anthropogenic stressors of terrestrial and aquatic ecosystems and to help native species and ecosystems survive in an altered environment.

Many commentators argue that collaboration involving a wide variety of stakeholders has the potential to produce more innovative and creative approaches to natural resources management than standard top-down approaches (Wondolleck 1991; Yaffee 1998). As Keiter (2004, p. 25) has observed, "central authority has also exacerbated federal, state and local tensions over public land policy. While such conflicts are not surprising . . . they can create unnecessary management inefficiencies, frustrate legitimate local interests, and promote jurisdictional fragmentation."

The potential trust building that collaboratives can produce will also be essential to adapting to climate change effects, as they create what Yaffee and Wondolleck (1995) call "knowledge pools and relationsheds." An example of such an effort is located in Harney County, Oregon, home of the infamous Malheur National Wildlife Refuge occupation discussed in chapter 15. The US Fish and Wildlife Service, local ranchers, environmental groups, and other stakeholders formed the Harney County Candidate Conservation Agreement with Assurances (CCAA) to develop a program and management plan "that would implement sage grouse conservation measures while providing assurances of regulatory protection to local landowners" (Taylor 2016, p. 39). The impetus for the Harney County CCAA was a possible listing of sage grouse under the Endangered Species Act on Bureau of Land Management lands. While there were many disagreements between stakeholders, the efforts were ultimately successful as the group adopted a science-based management plan developed by the Eastern Oregon Agricultural Research Center, which is a cooperative effort between Oregon State University and US Department of Agriculture. These efforts were so successful that the Harney County CCAA became the model adopted by all other Oregon counties with sage grouse populations (Taylor 2016). In fact, while some Harney County residents sympathized with some of the messages by the occupiers of the Malheur National Wildlife Refuge, the collaborative survived the occupation and continues to operate successfully today.

After examining several successful and unsuccessful sage grouse management efforts in three western states, Taylor (2016) concludes that collaborative approaches were much more effective than the traditional top-down "expert" approach. Taylor (2016, pp. 186-187) also has the following advice for collaborative processes:

> Building trusting relationships takes time and effort. It requires effective communications and agencies that are able and willing to engage with stakeholders in an open and flexible manner about the nature of the problem, the constraints involved in addressing the problem, possible actions that could be taken, and the potential consequences of those actions. It requires taking the experiences and perspectives of diverse stakeholders seriously, and giving them fair consideration. That does not mean that decisions must be universally supported by all stakeholders, which is not feasible in cases with competing values and policy priorities. However, although some stakeholders may not be happy with a particular decision, most should be satisfied that their needs and interests were taken into account.

Although collaboration is not a panacea for all of the conflict surrounding western public lands and other approaches may be more effective, listening to each other and trying to find common ground will be essential as the climate changes and the potential for heightened conflict increases. Further, as it is in everyone's best interest to protect the West's valuable environment to ensure that all needs including ecosystem health, cultural values, and economic values are met, westerners will need to push back against divisive politics and work together to protect a landscape that all westerners value.

References

Ansell, Christopher, and Alison Gash. 2008. "Collaborative Governance in Theory and Practice." *Journal of Public Administration Research and Theory* 18(4): 543-571.

Beschta, Robert, Debra L. Donahue, Dominick A. DellaSala, Jonathan J. Rhodes, James R. Karr, Mary H. O'Brien, Thomas L. Fleischner, and Cindy Deacon Williams. 2013. "Adapting to Climate Change on Western Public Lands: Addressing the Ecological Effects of Domestic, Wild, and Feral Ungulates." *Environmental Management* 51(2): 474-491.

Blumberg, Louis, and Darrell Knuffke. 1998. "Count Us Out." *Chronicle of Community* 2: 41-44.

Bodin, Orjan. 2017. "Collaborative Environmental Governance: Achieving Collective Action in Social-Ecological Systems." *Science* 357(6352): 1-10.

Britell, Jim. 2019. "Criticism of Partnerships and Roundtables." In *Organize to Win*, 10-15. Pearland, TX: Bookfunnel. https://dl.bookfunnel.com/23is0w4g7z.

Brown, George, and Charles Harris. 1992. "The U.S. Forest Service: Toward the New Resource Management Paradigm?" *Society and Natural Resources* 5: 231-245.

Clucas, Richard, Mark Henkels, and Brent S. Steel. 2011. "The Politics of One Oregon: Causes and Consequences of the Rural-Urban Divide and Prospects for Overcoming It." In *Toward One Oregon: Rural-Urban Interdependence and Evolution of the State*, edited by Michael Hibbard et al., 11-16. Corvallis: Oregon State University Press.

Cramer, Katherine J. 2016a. "For Years, I've Been Watching Anti-Elite Fury Build in Wisconsin. Then Came Trump." Vox, November 16, 2016. https://www.vox.com/the-big-idea/2016/11/16/13645116/rural-resentment-elites-trump.

Cramer, Katherine J. 2016b. *The Politics of Resentment: Rural Consciousness in Wisconsin and the Rise of Scott Walker.* Chicago: University of Chicago Press.

Duane, Timothy P. 1997. "Community Participation in Ecosystem Management." *Ecology Law Quarterly* 24: 796.

Hochschild, Arlie Russell. 2016. *Strangers in Their Own Land: Anger and Mourning on the American Right.* New York: New Press.

Johnson, K. Norm, and Fred J. Swanson. 2009. "Historical Context of Old-Growth Forests in the Pacific Northwest—Policy, Practices, and Competing Worldviews." In *Old Growth in a New World: A Pacific Northwest Icon Reexamined*, edited by Tom A. Spies and Sally L. Duncan, 12-28. Washington, DC: Island Press.

Keiter, Robert. 2004. *Keeping the Faith: Ecosystems, Democracy, and America's Public Lands.* New Haven, CT: Yale University Press.

Kurtzleben, Danielle. 2016. "Rural Voters Played a Big Part in Helping Trump Defeat Clinton." NPR, November 14, 2016. https://www.npr.org/2016/11/14/501737150/rural-voters-played-a-big-part-in-helping-trump-defeat-clinton.

Leach, William, and Neil W. Pelkey. 2001. "Making Watershed Partnersheds Work: A Review of the Empirical Literature." *Journal of Water Resources Planning and Management* 127(6): 378-385.

McCloskey, Mike. 1996. "The Skeptic: Collaboration Has Its Limits." *High Country News* 28: 7.

Modavi, Neghin. 1996. "Mediation of Environmental Conflicts in Hawaii: Win-Win or Co-optation." *Sociological Perspectives* 39: 301-316.

Ostrom, Elinor. 2007. "Institutional Rational Choice—An Assessment of the Institutional Analysis and Development Framework." In *Theories of the Policy Process*, edited by Paul A. Sabatier, 21-54. Boulder, CO: Westview Press, 2007.

Taylor, Casey. 2016. "The Challenges and Opportunities of a Proactive Endangered Species Act: A Case Study of the Greater Sage Grouse." Doctoral thesis, Oregon State University.

https://ir.library.oregonstate.edu/concern/graduate_thesis_or_dissertations/h415pc939?locale=en.

Volcovici, Valerie. 2017. "EPA Head's Top Regret: Failing to Connect with Rural America." *Reuters*, January 6, 2017. https://www.reuters.com/article/us-usa-epa/epa-heads-top-regret-failing-to-connect-with-rural-america-idUSKBN14Q2GH.

Weber, Edward P. 2003. *Bringing Society Back In: Grassroots Ecosystem Management, Accountability, and Sustainable Development*. Cambridge: Massachusetts Institute of Technology Press.

Weber, Edward P., Denise Lach, and Brent S. Steel, eds. 2017. *New Strategies for Wicked Problems*. Corvallis: Oregon State University Press.

Wolters, Erika Allen, and Brent S. Steel. 2015. "Cheatgrass Empire: Public Lands as a Contested Resource." In *Cities, Sagebrush, and Solitude: Urbanization and Cultural Conflict in the Great Basin*, edited by Dennis R. Judd and Stephanie L. Witt, 129-145. Reno: University of Nevada Press.

Wondolleck, Julia M. 1991. *Public Lands Conflict and Resolution: Managing National Forest Disputes*. New York: Plenum Press.

Yaffee, Steven. 1998. "Cooperation: A Strategy for Achieving Stewardship Boundaries." In *Stewardship across Boundaries*, edited by Richard Knight and Peter Landres, 299-324. Washington, DC: Island Press.

Yaffee, Steven, and Julia Wondolleck. 1995. "Building Knowledge Pools and Relationsheds." *Journal of Forestry* 93: 60.

Contributors

LAUREN ANDERSON works for the National Wildlife Federation, covering climate, energy, and wildlife conservation policy. She received a master of public policy from Oregon State University, where she worked on climate and renewable energy issues. Prior to obtaining her degree, she worked for the San Diego Zoo Institute for Conservation Research and the Great Basin Institute after receiving a bachelor of biology from California Polytechnic State University in San Luis Obispo.

MARK W. BRUNSON is a professor of environment and society at Utah State University. His work applies concepts and methods from the social and ecological sciences to understand the complex dynamics of human-environment interactions, focusing on the causes and consequences of human behaviors in deserts and rangelands.

CHARLES DAVIS is a professor of political science at Colorado State University. His teaching interests lie within the areas of energy and environmental policy, and his recent research activities include papers on the politics of fracking and renewable energy policymaking.

SHANE DAY is an assistant professor in the Mark O. Hatfield School of Government at Portland State University and an affiliated faculty member in the Ostrom Workshop at Indiana University Bloomington. His research focuses on the intersections of environmental policy, indigenous group self-governance, economic development, and intergovernmental relations. He is particularly interested in fisheries, forestry, and protected lands management; indigenous comanagement of natural resources; agricultural policy; and multiscale and multilevel governance.

P. CASEY GIORDANO received his bachelor of science in geology from the University of North Carolina Wilmington and his master of science in secondary education from Molloy College. He is currently a graduate student at Oregon State University. Casey lives on Long Island, New York, where he works as a science teacher and is a part-time park ranger for the National Park Service.

JODI A. HILTY is an expert on wildlife corridors and is the president and chief scientist of the Yellowstone to Yukon Conservation Initiative. For more than twenty years, she has worked to advance conservation by leading science- and community-based and collaborative conservation to advance policy and management. Jodi has been the coeditor or lead author on three books. She currently serves on the board of the Smith Fellowship and as deputy chair of the International Union for the Conservation of Nature Connectivity Committee.

MAYA J. HILTY, hailing from Grand Junction, Colorado, is an undergraduate student studying biology at Carleton College in Minnesota. Maya interned with the Yellowstone to Yukon Conservation Initiative (Y2Y) in 2019, researching endangered species, corridor connectivity, and climate change policy on public lands in the western United States. She is eager to spend more time with Y2Y during the summer of 2020 compiling information about indigenous peoples throughout the Y2Y region. An avid wildlife and nature enthusiast, Maya loves hiking, cross-country running, and camping. At school, she enjoys volunteering on the student farm and playing piano in her free time, and she is looking forward to studying abroad in Patagonia during the fall of 2020 with Round River Conservation Studies.

AERIN L. JACOB, is the conservation scientist at the Yellowstone to Yukon Conservation Initiative. She previously held a Liber Ero and Wilberforce Fellowship. Aerin earned her bachelor of science at the University of British Columbia and her doctorate at McGill University, and she conducted post-doctoral research at the University of Victoria.

CHRISTEAN JENKINS holds a bachelor's degree in environmental studies from University of Washington Tacoma, where she served as staff reporter for the *Tacoma Ledger* newspaper. Christean is passionate about educating youth to create a sustainable impact. She is committed to ensuring that all communities, including those of low-income and people of color, are educated and represented in environmental issues.

ANNA KARMAZINA is a PhD candidate in the School of Public Policy at Oregon State University. The focus of her research is on energy politics and policy, with accent on transitions to sustainable energy systems. Her research has been published in *Energy Research and Social Sciences*.

ROBERT B. KEITER is the Wallace Stegner Professor of Law and a university distinguished professor at the University of Utah S.J. Quinney College of Law. His books include *To Conserve Unimpaired: The Evolution of the National Park Idea* and *Keeping Faith with Nature: Ecosystems, Democracy, and America's Public Lands*.

DOUG KENNEY is director of the Western Water Policy Program at the University of Colorado. He has written extensively on several water-related issues, including law and policy reform, watershed-scale planning, and climate change adaptation, and he has made presentations in twenty-one states, eight nations, and five continents.

TOM M. KOONTZ is a professor of environmental policy at the University of Washington Tacoma. For more than twenty years, his research has examined collaborative watershed governance, institutions, citizen participation, and natural resource management. He has authored more than fifty peer-reviewed journal articles, two books, and numerous policy reports and book chapters. He has served as associate editor of the *Journal of Forestry* and *Society and Natural Resources*, and he currently serves on the editorial board of the *Policy Studies Journal* and the *Journal of Public Administration Research and Theory*.

DONNA L. LYBECKER is a professor in and chair of the Department of Political Science at Idaho State University. Her research and teaching focus on environmental politics and international relations, with emphasis on water policy, political narrative, and border studies. Publications include articles in *Environmental Politics*, *Policy Sciences*, and *Politics and Policy*.

KATHLEEN DEAN MOORE is a writer, moral philosopher, and environmental thought leader whose work addresses the moral urgency of action on the climate and extinction emergencies. She is author or coeditor of thirteen books, most recently *Moral Ground, Great Tide Rising,* and *Piano Tide,* winner of the Willa Award for Contemporary Fiction. *Witness: The Human Rights Impacts of Fracking* and *The Terrible Silence of the Sky* are forthcoming in 2020. Distinguished professor emerita at Oregon State University, she writes from Oregon and Alaska.

JOHN RUPLE is an associate professor of law and fellow with the Wallace Stegner Center for Land Resources and the Environment at the University of Utah's S.J. Quinney College of Law. He is a faculty affiliate with the university's Global Change and Sustainability Center and its Institute for Clean and Secure Energy.

CHRISTOPHER A. SIMON is a professor of political science at University of Utah. He conducts research in alternative energy policy, land-use policy, public administration, and military sociology. He is coauthor (with David Bernell) of *The Energy Security Dilemma: US Policy and Practice,* coauthor (with Brent Steel and Nicholas Lovrich) of *State and Local Government: Sustainability in the 21st Century,* and sole author of *Alternative Energy: Political, Economic, and Social Feasibility* and the third edition of *Public Policy: Preferences and Outcomes.* His articles have appeared in *American Politics Research, Armed Forces and Society, Comparative Technology Transfer and Society, Energy Research and Social Science, Land Use Policy Journal, Policy Studies Journal, Public Administration Review,* and *Social Science Quarterly.*

BRENT S. STEEL is a professor and director of the Public Policy Graduate Program in the School of Public Policy at Oregon State University. He teaches courses in comparative public policy, politics, and administration. Steel is coeditor of *New Strategies for Wicked Problems: Science and Solutions in the 21st Century* and editor of *Science and Politics: An A-to-Z Guide to Issues and Controversies.*

ERIC TOMAN is an associate professor in the School of Environment and Natural Resources at the Ohio State University. His research examines environmental management decisions in the context of environmental and social change. Born and raised in the Intermountain West, Eric earned his doctoral and master's degrees in forest resources from Oregon State University and his bachelor's degree in environmental studies from Utah State University.

KIM G. TROTTER is the US program director of the Yellowstone to Yukon Conservation Initiative (Y2Y). Before joining Y2Y, she served as executive director at the Community Foundation of Teton Valley, and was previously the director of Trout Unlimited's Idaho Water Project. She received a master of environmental management from Duke University's Nicholas School of the Environment.

REBECCA L. WARNER is a professor of sociology in the School of Public Policy at Oregon State University, where she teaches courses in research methods. She is the principal investigator of Oregon State Advance, a five-year program funded by the National Science Foundation to broaden the implementation of evidence-based systemic change strategies that promote equity for science, technology, engineering, and mathematics faculty in academic workplaces and the academic profession. Professor Warner has published on environmental policy, science policy, and renewable energy policy in journals such as the *Journal of Rural Community and Development, Environmental Management, Science, Technology, and Human Values,* and *Comparative Technology Transfer and Society.*

ERIKA ALLEN WOLTERS is an assistant professor in the School of Public Policy at Oregon State University. She is the former director of Oregon State University's Policy Analysis Laboratory. Her research and teaching interests include science and policy, environmental politics and policy, and the politics of climate change. She is coauthor of *When Ideology Trumps Science: Why We Question the Experts on Everything from Climate Change to Vaccinations.*

HILARY C. YOUNG is the Alberta program manager for the Yellowstone to Yukon Conservation Initiative. The connectivity of habitats at different scales was a key component of her PhD work, which focused on how animals in Alberta's Kananaskis Country move in and around forest cut blocks.

Index